SAG HARBOR

SAG HARBOR

The Story of an American Beauty

Dorothy Ingersoll Zaykowski

Foreword by Wilfrid Sheed

SAG HARBOR, NEW YORK

Copyright © 1991 by Dorothy Zaykowski

All rights reserved.

Third Printing.

Printed in the United States of America.

No part of this book may be used or reproduced
in any manner whatsoever without written permission
except in the case of brief quotations
embodied in articles and reviews.

Published by the Sag Harbor Historical Society

Box 1709

Sag Harbor, N.Y. 11963

to whom all queries concerning this publication should be addressed.

Portions of this book have appeared previously in
the *Sag Harbor Express*. Detailed information can be found
in the Bibliography and References section.

Grateful acknowledgment is made to ARCHITECTURAL DIGEST
for permission to use Mr. Sheed's article "Sag Harbor—An American Beauty."
Text by Wilfrid Sheed, Courtesy of ARCHITECTURAL DIGEST.
© 1990 Architectural Digest Publishing Corp. All rights reserved.

Library of Congress Catalog Card Number: 91-62524

Book Design by Loring Eutemey

ISBN: 0-8488-0899-1

Foreword

by
Wilfrid Sheed

SAG HARBOR: AN AMERICAN BEAUTY

"The un-Hampton" is what it calls itself, and that's one way of looking at it. If ever a place could be opulently defined by what it isn't, the place is Sag Harbor. When its famous neighbors, East, South and Bridge Hamptons, were still a God-fearing paradise of farms and fish, Sag Harbor proposed itself as sin city, the libido of the South Fork, full of foreigners and mischief and whale oil, the fool's gold of the 1820s and 1830s; but when the neighbors began to take in rich boarders, and acquire the sheen of a vast real estate ad, Sag Harbor resurfaced as the industrial north or blue-collar Hampton, triumphantly the wrong side of the tracks.

And even today, when all the Hamptons, both real and un-, are obliged to depend on outside visitors rather more than they care to, the local styles remain as different as Laurel and Hardy, yin and yang: bearing out the historical principle that no area is too small (we're talking here of four miles at the nearest, ten at the farthest) to generate total opposites.

That, as I say, is one way to look at it. But Sag Harbor has always had more important fish to fry than worrying about the damn Hamptons. Thanks to a relatively peaceful history, America is blessed with an unusual number of historical sites in which nothing much happened (one civil war is barely enough to go round, by European standards), and day-trippers to the South Fork sometimes seem politely puzzled as to just what it is they're supposed to look at around here. Our greatest hero in the revolutionary war, one David Hand, is mostly famous for having been captured by the British five different times, only to escape each time (Sag Harbor distrusts conventional heroics), while in the War of 1812, the town garrisoned itself to the teeth, but nobody came—just one measly incursion, easily repelled. And these were just our high points. Sag Harbor simply doesn't go in for that kind of history, God bless it—the official textbook history of death and destruction—but for the kind of history you simply pick up going from house to house, or, in our case, from whaling cottage to entrepreneur's mansion, and on to church for both of them: the history of a peaceful life lived so colorfully it would make your eyes pop. To wit and as follows.

Picture, if you will, a whaleboat sailing right up to the foot of Main Street—and this could be any day of the week or month of the year—loaded with several fortunes and God knows how many great stories, while at the next dock another hopeful is being outfitted with ten tons of bully beef for the captain alone, and all the hardtack they can eat for whatever rogues and dreamers, slaves and novelists (Melville was here), Queequegs and Ishmaels, the company has managed to con or dragoon into serving under him.

It's a small town, twenty-five hundred tops, but the number is forever being augmented by passing Fijians, Sandwich Islanders, and whatever else the wind has blown in—a far cry from today's summer people with their designer clothes and hurry-up suntans. Along the shore, shipwrights and sailmakers and other boat-minded people work, it's fair to suppose, with the special zest one gets from being part of a great enterprise: Unlike most twentieth-century workers, they have only to look out the door to see the flourishing fruit of their labors. It is, in short, a town with a purpose in life, and it always has something to look forward to. And make me a better offer than that.

All this is the patrimony of the Sag Harborite every time he looks out the door, and the reason he has it is that this is still recognizably the same town it always was, with all the inevitable changes somehow working in the right direction. A politician might call this effect the Miracle of Sag Harbor and he might be right; but it had nothing to do with politicians or with any human intention whatever. But at this point, we have to start over—and forget for a moment you ever heard of the Hamptons.

It takes a bunch of luck and good management for a pretty town to survive in America, with its architectural and landscaping virtue intact. Charleston has been blessed with perhaps the perfect history—neglect at just the right time, so the houses remained just so, but then attention from a powerful historical association. Williamsburg, countrariwise, is what happens when you try to do it on management alone: Life gets choked off too thoroughly, and you wind up with a professional virgin among cities, too pure to be real.

Until recently Sag Harbor has made it almost entirely on luck. The town came into money at a very good time—the first half of the nineteenth century— and ran out (and stayed out) of it at a good time too: ever since. In the 1830s and 1840s, when Sag Harbor was a booming whale town, you didn't need good taste to build well—it took genius not to. And by the time ugliness had entered America, Sag Harbor couldn't afford it.

In between, and before and since, Sag Harbor has been visited by a host of withering fires that would have gutted the charm out of a less favored community, but have only served to prune it, while sparing, to our eyes at least, just the right amount, like a biblical plague that knows precisely what it's doing. (The fires also left us with undoubtedly the world's finest volunteer fire department and what might be called a fire department culture: The firemen and the houses they operate from are simply the cream and quintessence of Sag Harbor, as I learned with joy the night my chimney almost burned down.)

Sag Harbor's Golden Age of whaling was over in a blink: a gaudy, vivid dream of no more than thirty years or so that stamped the town forever. Up until the end of the eighteenth century, whales had frisked along the coast and just about come on shore, so hunting them was no big deal: Indians and white men practically took turns at it—the whites for cash, and the Indians for worship (and what could be better to worship than whales?). But by 1817, when Sag Harbor's first deep-sea expedition was launched, the whales had gotten the hint, and there ensued one of the great cat-and-mouse hunts in history, ennobled perhaps by our greatest novel: Sag Harbor thinks so anyway, and every summer, residents combine to read *Moby Dick* out loud and right through at Canio's rare-book store.

The game reached a fever peak in 1847, Sag Harbor's greatest year; and then the fever broke and the whole thing was over, just two years later. Unlike New Bedford, Sag Harbor had no hinterland to speak of; it was a great port attached to nothing much. So when the first batch of adventurers sailed for California to track down the Great Gold Whale, there was no one left to replace them. Local capital was still tied up paying for the latest fire—the 1845 edition was a beaut—and besides, petroleum was moving up fast on sperm oil in the market, and the rest you know.

Ever since, Sag Harbor has been playing catch-up history. The American landscape is strewn with towns that have been seduced, and abandoned like trash cans in the wake of our latest whale, but Sag Harbor might be described as a ghost town that wouldn't lie down. From the Civil War onward, successive enterprises have started up with a high heart, only to burn down or otherwise fail, until God's greatest gift to mankind, the humble watchcase, arrived to stay in 1881.

Joseph Fahys's watchcase factory, which was later purchased and run by the Bulova Company, is the symbolic building of Sag Harbor's never-ending effort to get back on its feet. A gorgeous specimen of Gradgrind architecture, the factory now stands out from its gentle neighbors as stately as the Eiffel Tower in Paris, or Keble College, Oxford, one of those epic anomalies that help to define a landscape by clashing with it.

The Bulova building also represents a prickly, permanent-outsider strain in the local psyche that also clashes slightly with the landscape and saves us from any temptation to prettify or sentimentalize our surroundings. Like a WPA mural in the 1930s, the factory reminds one that, no matter how charming or instructive other people may happen to find it at the moment, Sag Harbor always goes on about its business as if bad times were just around the corner. Unlike other famous beauties, it has neither the time nor the inclination to preen or rest on its laurels—if anything, quite the contrary. "I'm fed up with being quaint," said a candidate for trustee not so long ago, meaning, I presume, "I'm fed up with being stared at." And the chip on her shoulder goes back a long way and is very much part of our living history.

When Mr. Fahys opened his factory, and later when Grumman Aircraft opened another one, which is now utterly deceased, the Poles and Germans and Italians who showed up for work there had no reason to be interested in whaling history, or in the great houses and great families that celebrated it: The families sure as hell weren't interested in *them*. If a visitor today gets the feeling that some old-timers are not totally glad to see him, he can rest assured his welcome is warmer than theirs or their grandparents' ever was. In fact, he is part of a great tradition. Sag Harbor has been going to the dogs for a long time now, and the visitor is just the latest evidence of it.

The Sag Harbor response to this ever-miserable state of affairs is creative grumbling, our secret language: You can fit in anywhere if you know how to grumble wittily enough. But in truth, all those infusions of new, unwanted blood seem to have given Sag Harbor a jump and an edge that the other towns out here lack. Driving home from Southampton on a winter evening last year when all the stores there had closed, I found Sag Harbor still humming and brimming with life, and I thought, "This is the live one"; the others will have to wait till spring.

Contributing to—or at least, not detracting from—this full-calendar vitality is a growing corps of "year-round summer people," as they're called, who

FOREWORD

weekend out here and actually use the village as opposed to just hiding in their houses and sending out for food. When a newcomer approaches a Hampton with his wallet out, local beauty lovers tremble and zoning boards brace themselves until they know exactly what the fellow has in mind. But most of the new settlers to Sag Harbor get the point right away: They came here because they like it exactly as it is, and will fight anyone, even the locals themselves to keep it that way.

This, of course, reverses the classic picture of marauding Manhattanites and bestial developers riding roughshod over local sensibilities. If anything the tensions ran the other way. To a no-nonsense Sag Harborite, the late arrivals must have seemed no better than a pack of precious, independently wealthy antiquarians bent on keeping them from expanding their businesses and creating jobs and living like the rest of America: hence the "quaintness" charge.

But quaintness is good for business too, and in a Ralph Lauren and L.L. Bean world, even the Merchants Association, or MASH (or Main Street Mafia, as it's playfully called—the title is only an insult if you mean it to be), has come to value the old Sag Harbor as much as anyone. And, in a curious way, the year-rounders value the merchants too, because that is part of what "getting the point" means. One doesn't settle here just for the sake of the whales or even for the sake of old houses, but for the whole package: the business as usual, unself-conscious tradition that puts out fires and votes against everything and still uses fans instead of air-conditioning in some of the stores—*not* because it's quaint, it's just the way we do it. The twentieth century never quite seems to take in Sag Harbor, although we have nothing against it.

Writers have proved particularly partial to this style, but only such writers as share some of it already. Our first big name, if one excepts the transient Fenimore Cooper, was John Steinbeck, the chronicler of Okies and paisans and the roustabouts of Cannery Row: Sag Harbor suited him to a T. (When Steinbeck won the Nobel Prize for literature, legend has it that local residents polled about it knew him mostly for his boat, which he kept admirably clean and shipshape. First things first in Sag Harbor, and water is both our history and our esthetic.)

Our current writers in residence include Lanford Wilson, E.L. Doctorow and Thomas Harris, and I'll say no more about them: No writer ever came to Sag Harbor in search of more attention. But it might be taken as a general principle that if you see someone in particularly shabby work clothes—and I don't mean designer work clothes, either—it just might be a writer, and not necessarily a famous one. Sag Harbor actually contains some writers who haven't made it yet, as well as a number of no-name or some-name journalists who probably enjoy the intricacies of small-town gossip as much as anything.

"Did you see what they've done to the old Bagbalm house?" "I hear the lady who just moved in was the mistress of Calvin Coolidge." The houses are like characters in a long-running play that the whole town is invited to watch, and tell stories about forever—a hard offer for a writer to refuse.

Sag Harbor had to wait a lot longer than Charleston for its historical society: In fact, a preservationist might have despaired of its ever getting here at all. But it got here all right, and it's not just a Manhattan Project either, but a properly homegrown association of new and old Sag Harborites who love the town to about equal distraction. Largely thanks to its good work, the robust heart of Sag Harbor is now safe, both from outsiders and from itself.

If one compares it with some of the museum-towns one has known, a case can be made that this vibrant, idiosyncratic little town is all the better for the wait.

Preface

Although I grew up in Sag Harbor, like my mother and my grandfather before me, I had little interest in Sag Harbor's past until I was asked to write a local history column for the *Sag Harbor Express*. That was about twelve years ago and the experience left me consumed with learning more about the fascinating history of the village I had grown up in. But, as I discovered early on, finding the relevant facts was no easy task. Though many sources were available to me in the Library, in the town records, or in nearby communities, there was little in the way of complete information and certainly not in a single volume. The more fascinated I became with my self-appointed task of research, the more I realized the need for a detailed, comprehensive reference book; one that would cover more thoroughly the various stages of Sag Harbor's remarkable growth. Working at the John Jermain Memorial Library, I had at my disposal early newspapers, letters, maps, manuscripts, and previously printed matter. It became obvious that I could put my desire into action; thus began the lengthy job of compiling and writing this history of Sag Harbor.

Sag Harbor's history is truly unique. Throughout the years it has undergone an evolution of events, ever changing, ever growing. Considering what had taken place during the early years, its very existence is something of a wonder. Having survived what seemed at times to be insurmountable obstacles, the village refused to succumb to its frequent misfortunes. The early citizens of Sag Harbor were a hardy group of individuals; strong-willed and determined; failure an unknown word in their vocabulary. Although their business district was thrice consumed by fire and although they struggled through an enormous economic slump following the demise of the golden years of whaling, they persevered. With courage and fortitude they started over and over again and finally met with success. The establishment of new industries, an improvement in fire-fighting methods, and a brisk summer tourist trade, all contributed to strengthening the economy.

PREFACE

Sag Harbor: The Story of an American Beauty traces the progression of Sag Harbor's remarkable history from its settlement in the early 1700s through the year 1940. It is the story of wartime and peace, whaling and industry, people and places, failures and successes. Its all-inclusive text covers obscure little-known facts as well as major accomplishments and familiar happenings, thereby creating a vital tool for reference and research. Every effort has been made to keep errors at a minimum. Youngsters as well as adults will find the book informative, interesting, and easy to comprehend.

Sag Harbor: The Story of an American Beauty came to be not only as the result of extensive research, but also due to the encouragement and assistance of many people in the community. I would like to extend my sincere thanks and appreciation in particular to the following:
Foremost, to the Sag Harbor Historical Society and its president, Joan B. Tripp, for recognizing my manuscript as an important and valuable source of information with the potential of becoming a book on Sag Harbor history, and for taking on the monumental job of arranging for its publication. To the editors, Pace Barnes and Alison Bond, for their expertise, guidance, and hours spent attending to the many details involved. To Mary Ann Gauger who did such a conscientious and thorough job editing and proof-reading. To Joan Whitman for her professional handling of the index. To all those members of the Sag Harbor Historical Society who volunteered their time and their energies to the publication of this book; to those responsible for its promotion, for fund-raising, and of course to the party-planners; my thanks to all of you.

To Architectural Digest for allowing Wilfrid Sheed's delightful article, *Sag Harbor—An American Beauty*, that appeared in their May 1990 issue, to be used as the foreword. To Alexandra Eames for her skill and perseverance in finding such wonderful old photographs to use in the book, and to Richard Hornell for his professional work with the photographs, portraits, and maps. To Loring Eutemey for his clear-sighted sense of design which transformed a pile of papers into a real book, thank you.

My sincere thanks also go to the *Sag Harbor Express*; Gardner Cowles III and Bryan Boyhan, for permission to include in the book, articles previously written by me and published in the newspaper between 1979 and 1984, some in their entirety and others in a revised form. To the John Jermain Memorial Library, James C. Ashe, Director, for allowing some of the early photographs from their extensive collection to be copied, and for making available the treasure trove of material from the local history room, which provided me with my major source of information. To the East Hampton Library,

PREFACE

Dorothy King, Curator, for her assistance throughout the years as I researched early church records, census records, early families, and other vital statistics.

Thanks also to Jeanne Vielbig of the First Presbyterian Church Historical Committee, who made sure my facts on the Presbyterian churches were correct. And to Ethel Ruehl for providing me with a list of the Methodist ministers. Also to Kathleen Tucker for verifying my information on St. David A.M.E. Zion Church. Thanks to my son, Joseph Zaykowski, Jr., for information on the Hog Neck windmills, to Barbara G. Elliott for the list of Court Martial Records.

I would also like to thank the First Presbyterian Church Historical Committee for providing information on the Sag Harbor Lawn Tennis Club, and Patricia Donovan for sharing her knowledge of Captain John B. Phillips with me. And Jane Kiernan for proof-reading (after our proof-reading) and still finding typographical errors.

My gratitude also goes to the following people and organizations for sharing their precious photographs of early Sag Harbor, and whose contributions really make the book special:
The John Jermain Memorial Library, James C. Ashe, Director; The Friends of the John Jermain Memorial Library; The Society for the Preservation of Long Island Antiquities, Carol Traynor; The Sag Harbor Whaling and Historical Museum, Inc., George Finckenor, Curator; the Eastville Community Historical Society, Kathleen Tucker; Temple Adas Israel, Charles Egosi; the First Presbyterian Church Historical Committee, David Cory; Christ Episcopal Church, Reverend Eliot G. Frederic; East Hampton Library, Dorothy King; East Hampton Historical Society; Sotheby's Inc., New York; The Oysterponds Historical Society, Orient, New York, Barbara Fertig.

And to the following individuals for generously allowing me to use photographs from their private collections: First and foremost to Otto Fenn for lending so many of his marvelous photographs of early Sag Harbor. Also to Patricia Donovan, Eugene Hodenpyl, and Richard Hornell for sharing their special pictures, and to Martin Cohen of Watermill, for permission to use the oil painting of the young Ephraim Niles Byram.

And finally, to all those individuals and organizations who enabled us to realize the publication of this book by their active sponsorship, my warm thanks. Your generosity and interest made this book possible.

Dorothy Ingersoll Zaykowski

Sag Harbor, N.Y.
August 1991

ACKNOWLEDGMENTS

Many photographs were loaned by individuals and organizations to whom we are very grateful. The credit lines which appear on the same page as the photographs are brief because of space limitations. They refer to those individuals whose names follow:

Coll. Otto Fenn	Private collection of Otto Fenn, Sag Harbor
Whaling Museum	From the collection of the Sag Harbor Whaling and Historical Museum, Inc., Sag Harbor.
JJML	From the collection of the John Jermain Memorial Library
SPLIA	From the collection of the Society for the Preservation of Long Island Antiquities
ECHS	Used by courtesy of Kathleen Tucker and the Eastville Community Historical Society

The painting of *Henry P. Dering*, ca. 1794, is by William Vestille, used by courtesy of SPLIA

The portrait of *Charles Watson Payne III*, ca. 1865, is taken from William S. Pelletreau, *A History of Long Island*, Vol. III. Lewis Publishing Co., New York, 1903

The photo of the *First Presbyterian Church*, taken in April 1938, is used by courtesy of Dorothy Zaykowski and of the Historical Committee of the First Presbyterian Church

Some maps and line drawings by the author and Annie Cooper Boyd; additional line drawings throughout are used courtesy of the John Jermain Memorial Library, the Society for the Preservation of Long Island Antiquities, and the East Hampton Historical Society. The lithograph of the Barque Oscar, ca. 1846, is used courtesy of SPLIA, photo ©Sotheby's Inc., New York.

Endpaper maps: From *Atlas of Long Island, New York*, Beers, Comstock & Cline, New York, 1873. Courtesy of Lorraine Dusky and Anthony Brandt.

CONTENTS

Foreword — Wilfrid Sheed v

Preface xi

Acknowledgments xiv

PART I. SETTLEMENT AND EARLY GROWTH OF THE PORT
1707–1820

1. The Founding of Sag Harbor. 3
   The Settlement
   Early Roads and Village Streets
   Traveling by Stagecoach
   The Toll Roads

2. Along the Waterfront. 18
   The Wharves in the Early days
   Mankesack Island
   The Bridges
   The Windmills
   Building the First Windmill
   A Description of the Village in 1804

3. Law and Order in the Growing Port. 33
   Regulations for Keeping the Law
   Braddock Corey
   The Custom House and Its Collectors
   Henry Packer Dering
   Mail Delivery and the Early Post Office
   A Description of the Village in 1819

4. Social Life in the Early Days. 42
   Childhood Days
   Early Education
   Early Private Schools
   Building Churches
   Organizations and Societies

CONTENTS

5. Sag Harbor in the Wars. 57
    The Revolutionary War
    Early Military Companies
    Remembering the Suffolk Guard
    The Embargo and Fortification
    The Arsenal
    The War of 1812
    Court Martial Trials at the Sag Harbor Garrison

6. The Great Fires of Sag Harbor. 75
    The Fire of 1817
    The Establishment of a Fire Department

PART II. THE GOLDEN ERA OF THE WHALE FISHERY
1820–1850

1. The Golden Years of Whaling. 81
    The Business of Whaling
    How Sag Harbor Looked in 1834
    The Whaleship Thames
    James Fenimore Cooper
    The Whaleship Konohassett
    The Whaleship Cadmus
    Outfitting the Bark Pacific
    Edward Cooper, the Cooper
    Making Needed Repairs

2. Whaling Before the Decline. 93
    Mutiny on the Whaleship Oscar
    Captain Royce and His Bomb Lance
    The Bark Highland Mary
    A Voyage on the Henry Lee
    Polly Sweet, Pioneer
    Whaleships Sold for the Slave Trade
    The Fate of the Whaling Fleet

3. The Great Fires of Sag Harbor. 109
    The Fire of 1845

PART III. INDUSTRIAL GROWTH AND BUSINESS OPPORTUNITIES
1850–1880

1. Early Industries and Craftsmen. 113
    The Industries at Peter's Green
    Samuel L'Hommedieu
    The Oakland Works
    Other Early Industries

CONTENTS   xvii

    The Clockmakers: Ephraim Niles Byram and Benjamin Franklin Hope
    The Old Stationery Shop of Russell Wickham
    Nathan Tinker, Cabinetmaker
    John Hildreth, Shoemaker
    The Old Department Store
    The Blacksmiths: John Fordham and Thomas Overton
    The Mills at Trout Pond
    Ice Harvesting at Round Pond
    The Sag Harbor Savings Bank
    Mail Delivery and the Growth of the Post Office

2. Health Care in the Early Days. 132
    The Early Drugstores and Pharmacists
    Strange Illnesses; Stranger Remedies
    The Cholera Scare

3. The Lights Go On. 138
    The Era of Gas Lights
    Sag Harbor Gets Electricity

4. The Great Fires of Sag Harbor. 141
    The Fire of 1877
    Recollections of a Fire Fighter
    Other Serious Fires
    The Growth of the Fire Department

        PART IV. EXPLORING THE SOCIAL SCENE
                      1820–1880

1. The Newspapers in Sag Harbor. 151

2. The Schools in the Nineteenth Century. 161
    The Schooldays of Oliver Wade
    The Sag Harbor Academy and Institute
    The Union School District
    Segregation in the Schools
    The Union School
    St. Andrew's Roman Catholic School
    The Academy of the Sacred Heart of Mary

3. Organized Religion in Sag Harbor. 169
    The First Presbyterian Church (Old Whaler's)
    The Bethel Baptist Church
    The Methodist Church
    Remininiscences of the Methodist Sunday School
    St. Andrew's Roman Catholic Church
    St. David A.M.E. Zion Church

CONTENTS

    David Hempstead
    Christ Episcopal Church
    Temple Adas Israel
    The People's Pentecostal Church of the Nazarene
    Nearby Chapels:
        North Haven Union, Noyac Chapel, St. James Episcopal
    The Temperance Societies
    The Burying Grounds

4. Inns, Hotels, and Boarding Houses. 196

5. Interesting People and Places. 201
    Prentice Mulford, Philosopher
    Huntting's Spectacular Music Hall
    Hubbard Latham Fordham, Artist
    The Atheneum
    The Sag Harbor Brass Band
    Fannie Tunison, Extraordinary Lady

6. Sag Harbor in the Wars. 210
    The Civil War
    Slavery in the Sag Harbor Area

PART V. INDUSTRY, INNOVATION AND EXPANSION
1870–1900

1. Travel on Long Island Sound. 221
    Steamboats Dock at the Long Wharf
    A Description of the Village in 1875
    The W.W. Coit
    Captain John B. Phillips
    The Shelter Island
    The Wreck of the Sloop David Porter
    The Long Island
    The Shinnecock
    Other Local Steamboats

2. New Industry in the Age of Decline. 235
    The Steam Cotton Mill
    The Maidstone Steam Flouring Mills
    The Hampton Flour Mill Company

3. The Coming of the Railroad. 241
    Extending the Tracks
    The Brick Depot
    The Pottery Works
    The Years of Brickmaking

CONTENTS

    Charles Watson Payne III, Merchant
    Fahys Watch Case Factory and Alvin Silver Works
    William Wallace Tooker, Algonquinist and Pharmacist
    Paving the Village Streets

4. The End of the Era. 253
    The Bottling Works
    Bailey's Cut Tool Company
    The Montauk Steam Laundry
    The Sag Harbor Water Works

5. Sag Harbor in the Spanish-American War. 257

PART VI. AN AMERICAN BEAUTY IN THE TWENTIETH CENTURY 1900–1940

1. Along the Waterfront. 263
    The Breakwater
    The Frank Havens Mansion (Cor Maria)
    The E.W. Bliss Torpedo Company
    Saloons, Prohibition, and Rumrunning
    Rum Running During Prohibition

2. New Buildings for New Beginnings. 272
    The Otter Pond
    The Parks
    Mrs. Russell Sage
    Pierson High School
    The John Jermain Memorial Library and Earlier Libraries

3. The Social Scene and the Arts. 287
    The Era of the Movies
    The Public Golf Course
    The Yacht Club
    The Village Beach
    The Sag Harbor Historical Society and Other Organizations
    The Ku Klux Klan Meeting

4. New Business Enterprises. 301
    Eaton's Engravers and Printers Machinery Company
    C. Weidlog's Manufacturing Company
    The Suffolk County Building Block Company
    The Bloch Hat Pin Factory
    The Kiss Art Pottery Company
    The Cloak Factory
    The C.W. Butts, Inc. Factory

CONTENTS

    B. Aptheken & Son Rayon Factory
    The Bulova Watch Company

5. Sag Harbor in the Wars. 308
    World War I
    The World War I Monument
    Other War Monuments and Memorials

6. The Great Fires of Sag Harbor. 312
    The Alvin Silver Works Fire of 1925

Epilogue. 314

Maps and Diagrams. 317

Appendix. Sag Harbor Names. 333

Bibliography and References. 377

Index. 387

Sponsors. 393

Illustrations follow page 96.

Part One

THE SETTLEMENT AND EARLY GROWTH OF THE PORT

1707–1820

1

THE FOUNDING OF SAG HARBOR

The earliest inhabitants of what is now Sag Harbor were Indians of the Algonquin tribe and they called the place Weg-wag-onuch, derived from the Algonquin word "We-quae-adn-auke," meaning "the land or place at the end of the hill." As an aboriginal site the location was ideal, with an abundance of fish, clams, and fresh water ponds nearby.

During the latter part of the 1600s, white men came to the area. In those early years water flowed over much of the land at the time of the high tide, and people from neighboring villages called the place Great Meadows. Hog Neck, or North Haven, was purchased from the Indians of Shelter Island in 1665 by some early citizens of Southampton who laid out the lots. The Great Meadows was included in the Hog Neck Division and took in all of what is now the northern part of Sag Harbor west of Division Street. It was a valuable piece of property with its bountiful supply of seaweed and salt hay.

The little village of Sagaponack, south of Sag Harbor, benefited greatly from the convenient location of the Great Meadows, with the harbor providing an excellent port from which they could ship their goods. They called the place Sagaponack Harbor or the Harbor of Sagg.

SETTLEMENT AND GROWTH OF THE PORT

The Settlement

The Southampton Town Records first mention Sag Harbor by name in 1707, when William S. Pelletreau was charged "for going to Sag Harbor to evidence for ye town 3^s 6^d." The East Hampton Town Records, although not calling the place Sag Harbor, recorded that Joseph Stretton was left, by his father, "a share of the piece of meadow that lies nearest Hog Neck in this (East Hampton) town's bounds." That was in 1698. The property described stood east of Division Street, which still separates the East Hampton and Southampton townships.

As far as can be determined, no permanent homes existed in Sag Harbor at that time, and before it was to become a village, a major job of reconstruction was necessary. Swamps and marshland had to be filled in to make the land passable. Henry P. Hedges, in his 1896 "Address Before the Historical Society of Sag Harbor," explained that originally the meadow swept across what is now Main Street at the junction of Madison, and northerly to the cliff at the foot of the village. From that 50-foot-high cliff, Turkey Hill, located behind the present American Hotel, rose and gradually fell, until it was lost in the swamp behind it and Meeting House Hill at Church and Sage Streets. Eventually, Turkey Hill was pushed into the north and west sides of Main Street, filling it in to a depth of 4 to 6 feet to make the land passable. Meeting House Hill was moved into Main, Madison, Division, Washington and Hampton Streets, which before that time had been marshland. A large swamp was also located to the south and east of the Old Burying Ground, Meeting House Hill, and Turkey Hill, and water flowed down what is now Burke Street and into the harbor. In those days, with no equipment other than man and beast, the task of moving the many tons of earth was an overwhelming job and an incredibly lengthy operation.

Ephraim Fordham of Sag Harbor, in his advanced years, stated that he could remember when there was but one house at Sag Harbor landing, that there was no permanent settlement prior to 1730, and at that time only a few fishermen who sailed their small craft to Connecticut and Rhode Island. Three hut-like dwellings were said to have been built into the side of Turkey Hill about 1730 and occupied by John Foster, Joseph Conkling, and Nathan Fordham. The Town Records state that in 1737 Samuel Russell bought four poles of land (which is roughly 22 yards square) at Sag Harbor on which to build a house, becoming one of the original settlers.

In November 1738 a large portion of the Town of Southampton was allotted, and included in this allotment was Sag Harbor, which was laid out into the Great North Division and the Great South Division. The North Division

THE FOUNDING OF SAG HARBOR

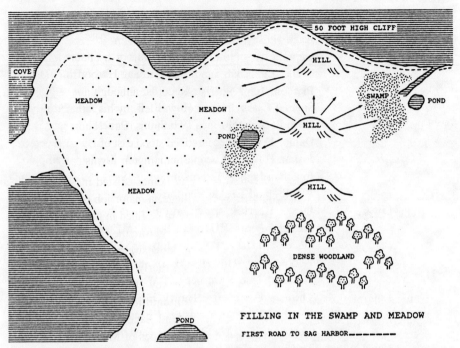

extended to the boundary of Union Street, which ran from East Hampton Road to Main Street. The allotment of the Great Meadows as drawn went to 23 people who lived in or near Southampton, and they became the first owners of the meadowland and property along the waterfront. They were: James White, Arthur Howell, Joseph More, Thomas and Isaac Halsey, Widow Cooper, Christopher Cooper, William Russell, Joseph Fordham, Benjamin Davis, Thomas Reeves, Cornelius Vonk, John Foster, Richard Post, John Cook, Justice John Topping, John Laughton, John Jennings, George Harris, Thomas Cooper Jr., Jonathan Raynor, Obediah Rogers, and Thomas Topping.

On November 18, 1745 a division of 17 lots and 17 amendments, from 24 to 40 feet wide, were laid out in the lower part of Sag Harbor, running from the cliff along the shore to the point where Main and Madison meet, and from Division to Main Street. The first lot was at the cliff. Washington Street was between the fifth and sixth lot. A stone wall marked the south line.

The following names were drawn in the 1745 division of lands.
Lot 1   John Cook, James Haines, Jeckamiah Scott, Ephraim White, Joseph Hildreth (deceased) and Elias Cook.
Lot 2   Abraham Howell Jr. (deceased), Thomas Cooper, David

6   SETTLEMENT AND GROWTH OF THE PORT

	Cooper, Eliphalet Clark and brothers, John Mitchell, Isaac Halsey Jr. and Samuel Ludlam.
Lot 3	Captain Theophilus Howell, John Morehouse, Daniel Wick, Zachariah Sandford, Nathaniel Woodruff, David Pierson, John Norris and Josiah Hand.
Lot 4	Samuel Clark, Henry Howell, Daniel More, Abraham Howell, Samuel Jones, Job Sayre, Obediah Rogers, and Daniel Foster (deceased).
Lot 5	Joshua Howell, Theophilus Howell, Stephen Kempton, Jonathan Jagger, Jeremiah Jagger, Samuel Jagger, John Wooley and Ezekiel Sanford.
Lot 6	James Herrick, Benjamin Foster, heirs of Richard Halsey, Peter Hildreth, Stephen Foster, John Post (deceased), Isaac Post, Widow Hannah Halsey and son, Widow Mary Howell and son, Jeremiah Howell, John Mackey, Joseph Burnet and Widow Mehitable Burnet.
Lot 7	Thomas Foster Jr., Henry Halsey (deceased), John Foster, Christopher Foster, Hezakiah Howell, Thomas Stephens, Thomas Cooper Jr. and John Reeves.
Lot 8	Thomas Sanford.
Lot 9	Jonathan Pierce, Benjamin Woodruff, heirs of Jeremiah Halsey, Abram Halsey, Nathaniel Halsey, Thomas Lupton, heirs of Christopher Lupton, Jonah Rogers and sons, Abram Howell Jr. (deceased), Hugh Raynor and Adonijah Raynor.
Lot 10	Job Pierson, Daniel Hedges and brothers, Edward Johnes, Joseph Ausbond, Daniel Ausbond, Josiah Pierson, Abram Pierson and Elnathan White.
Lot 11	Stephen Herrick, Nathan Herrick, Justice Chatfield, Hugh Gelston, Samuel Jennings, Aaron Burnett Jr., Silas Cook, Elias Pelletreau, Jonathan Smith, heirs of Richard Wood and John Clark, heirs of Abram Sayre (deceased), Theophilus William (deceased), heirs of Joseph Taylor (deceased), heirs of John Willman (deceased), John Reeves and Mr. Wood (deceased), Abram Halsey, Theophilus Willman (deceased), David Raynor and Abram Cooper.
Lot 12	Thomas Sandford.
Lot 13	Captain Burnett, Stephen Topping, Hezekiah Topping,

THE FOUNDING OF SAG HARBOR

Theophilus Pierson (deceased), Henry Wick, Samuel Haines, Benjamin Howell, Josiah Topping and Jonathan Cook.

Lot 14　Jeremiah Halsey, Nathan Halsey, William Jennings Jr., David Rose Jr., Thomas Foster, David Haines, Nathaniel Rusco, Joseph Howell, Josiah Howell, Jonathan Smith, Elisha Halsey, assigns of James Cooper and assigns of Ichabod Cooper.

Lot 15　Silas and Charles Howell, Samuel Howell, Thomas Jessup, John Sayre, Job Wick, Josiah Halsey, David Fithian and John Howell.

Lot 16　Elias Cook, Widow Martha Halsey, Ephraim Hildreth, Nathan Hildreth, Samuel Bishop, James Hand Jr., Richard Howell or son, Elisha Aubrid, David Leek, Daniel Scellinks, Nathan Fordham, John Flint, Moses Culver, Hackaliah Foster, James Hand, and John Bishop.

Lot 17　Elisha Howell, Thomas Halsey, and Daniel Sayre.

William S. Pelletreau described the origin of land titles in Sag Harbor as follows:

> In 1745 all the land in Sag Harbor between the Great Meadow or the present line of Main Street and the East Hampton Town line was included in what the Town Records justly call, "an highway of uncommon width." When it was seen that the place was likely to be, in time, a port of some importance, the propriety of narrowing the road and laying out the vacant lands into lots became apparent, and the Town Trustees, acting for the proprietors of the undivided lands, made what is known as the Sag Harbor Little Division.
>
> The whole number of shares of Proprietor Rights was fifty-one, and in all the Great Divisions, the land was divided into that number of lots. At that time there were only two men who owned a whole share of a £150 right; the rest of the rights were owned by men who had only fractions of a right. This new division at Sag Harbor consisted of so small a tract of land that it was impractical to divide it into fifty-one lots, and so the trustees made seventeen lots, and the same number of amendments which were to be added to the lots to make them of equal value. The east line of the highway was laid out as the street line now exists, and the lots fronted on this, the rear being the East Hampton line.
>
> The manner in which the Trustees divided the lands among the Propri-

etors was not only perfectly fair but very plain and simple. As stated before, as there were only seventeen lots in the division, each lot would have to contain three £150 rights, or nine £50 rights. The Trustees selected at random from among the list of Proprietors and names of men whose shares or fractions of a share would amount to 9£50's. The names of the men with the amount of their rights were plainly written on slips of paper and the seventeen slips folded were placed in one receptacle. Seventeen smaller slips were prepared and on them were written the numbers from one to seventeen. These were folded and placed in another receptacle. The slips in both were mixed and from one box a slip was drawn, and from the other box another slip. This one would contain the names of the men who drew the lot, and the other would be the number of the lot which they drew. The two slips were then pinned together, or sewed together, both means were used. A careful list was made and recorded in the Town Book of Records and the work was complete. In the Sag Harbor Division the slips were fastened together with thread. The following illustration is a facsimile of the slips for lot 2 which included the land where the Nassau House stood.

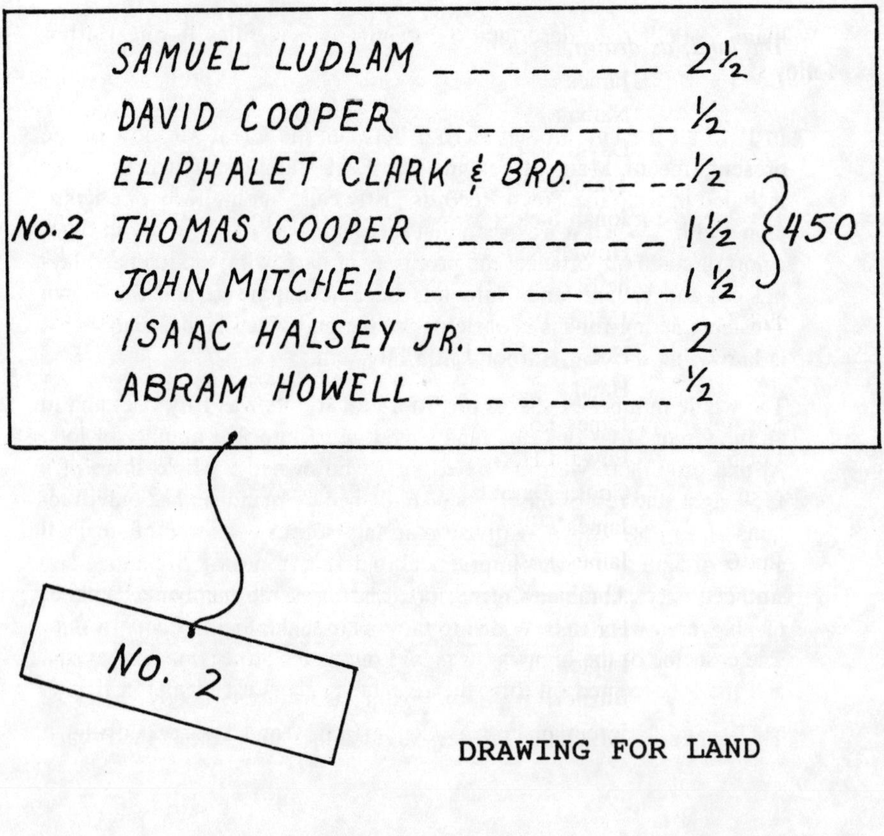

```
                SAMUEL LUDLAM _____ 2½
                DAVID COOPER _____ ½
                ELIPHALET CLARK & BRO. ___ ½  ⎫
        No. 2   THOMAS COOPER _____ 1½  ⎬ 450
                JOHN MITCHELL _____ 1½  ⎭
                ISAAC HALSEY JR. _____ 2
                ABRAM HOWELL _____ ½

           ┌─────────────────┐
           │    NO. 2        │
           └─────────────────┘
```

DRAWING FOR LAND

The slip shows that in this lot Samuel Ludlam owned two and a half 50's. David Cooper owned half a fifty. Eliphalet Clark and his brother also owned a half a 50. Thomas Cooper owned a 50 and a half, as did John Mitchell Jr., Isaac Halsey Jr. owned two 50's and Abram Howell (deceased) had half a 50. The whole being nine 50's or a £450 lot. The lots were held in undivided shares till the time of the Revolution. John Mitchell sold his share to Daniel Fordham in 1775. The lots were very narrow, number 2 being just twenty-eight feet in front and twenty-four feet in the rear.

These seventeen lots and seventeen amendments were bounded on the south by a tract of land called the Twelve Acre Division. On November 30, 1761 it was surveyed and lots drawn. Lot number one was at the junction of Main and Madison, and all the lots were bounded on the south by Union Street. The Trustees of Southampton Town ordered James Foster to impower Josiah Pierson and Thomas Sandford to lay out the Twelve Acres into as many lots as they thought convenient, and Pierson, Sandford, and David Howell were to regulate the "fifties" in drawings of the lots.

The land, as drawn, went to the following.

Lot 1	James Foster, heirs of Jonah Rogers, Thomas Topping, Nathan Norris, heirs of Samuel Jennings, Silas Halsey, David Woodruff, heirs of Samuel Woodruff and heirs of Timothy Woodruff.
Lot 2	Jonah Sandford, Silas Sandford, Jesse Howell, Lemuel Howell, Elisha Howell, Henry Pierson, John Cook and heirs of John Topping.
Lot 3	Josiah Pierson, Theophilus Howell, heirs of Abram Halsey, Thomas Sandford, Burnet Miller, and David Hand.
Lot 4	James Foster.
Lot 5	Edward Howell, John Morehouse, Henry Howell, Elias Cook, Daniel More, Joel Sandford, David Topping, James Hildreth and Samuel Howell.
Lot 6	James Foster.
Lot 7	Abraham Cooper, Elisha Howell, Joshua Howell, James Haines, Widow Mehitable Mackie, heirs of Thomas Lupton, heirs of Daniel Halsey, Jeremiah Howell, Joseph Burnet, William Foster, Cornelius Halsey, heirs of Jeremiah Jagger, Elisha Halsey and Henry Ludlam.

SETTLEMENT AND GROWTH OF THE PORT

Lot 8	Thomas Cooper, John Russell, Captain Thomas Stephens, Samuel Ludlam, Zebediah Osborn, Captain Silas Cook, Jonathan Hedges, Matthew Jagger, Ichabod Sayre and Samuel Bishop.
Lot 9	James Foster.
Lot 10	Heirs of Justice Josiah Howell, Samuel Jagger, Hugh Raynor, John Haines, Captain John Post and brother, Captain Post, John Jagger, Elias Foster, heirs of Stephen Kempton and William Jones.
Lot 11	James Foster.
Lot 12	Heirs of Samuel Russell.
Lot 13	James Foster.
Lot 14	Jeremiah Halsey, Zebulon Halsey, heirs of Henry Halsey, Obediah Jones, Samuel Howell III, Abraham Rose, heirs of Jonathan Cook, Jeckomiah Scott, John Chatfield, heirs of John Hildreth, and heirs of John Flint.
Lot 15	Silas Howell, David Howell, David Rose, Thomas Jessup, Nehemiah Sayre, Joseph Sayre, Daniel Hildreth, Thomas Scott, Elias Pelletreau and Captain John Howell.
Lot 16	John Sandford, Edward Topping, heirs of Christopher Lupton, David Carwithy, heirs of Caleb Carwithy, David Cook, Jeremy Halsey, heirs of Nancy Halsey, Eli Halsey, heirs of Jonathan Smith, Hackaliah Foster, heirs of Ephraim White and Thomas Jennings.
Lot 17	Heirs of Samuel Russell, heirs of Jonathan Raynor, assigns of Samuel Ludlam, Joseph Burnet, Elisha Howell, Judge Gelston, Joseph Post, Isaac Post, and the rest unknown.

These men and women became the first owners of the Twelve Acre Division at Sag Harbor in 1761. James Foster was the largest single investor, acquiring lots four, six, nine, eleven, fourteen, and a portion of lot one. The Howells, 15 in all, bought fifties in the division, as did 13 members of the Halsey family. Many of these individuals were merely speculators and never actually lived in Sag Harbor.

The 1775 census lists a number of families, among them the Howells, Fordhams, and Halseys, whose descendants still live in the area, who, with others, played a vital role in the establishment of Sag Harbor. The 1775 census of Sag Harbor, North Haven, and Noyac can be found in the Appendix.

THE FOUNDING OF SAG HARBOR

Others, living in the area and not listed in the census records, were the Wentworths, Vails, and Russells, residing in Sag Harbor in 1750. Members of the Russell and Vail families were united in marriage at Sag Harbor in 1750, and as early as 1740 the Reverend Huntting of East Hampton came to Sag Harbor to baptize five children of John Vail. The Sandfords, Ripleys, and Rysams, also unlisted, lived in the village as well. The Howells, Fosters, Hedges, and Sayres came from Southampton. Silas Norris was from Sagaponack, John Hulbert from Bridgehampton, the Duvalls and Havens from Shelter Island, the Coreys from Southold, the Gildersleeves from Huntington, the Ripleys from Massachusetts, Benjamin Coleman from Nantucket, Rysam from Norfolk, Virginia. With these families establishing homes and businesses in Sag Harbor, the place began its slow but steady growth.

Early Roads and Village Streets

Before it was possible to use the waterfront at Sag Harbor as a port, it was necessary to cut roads through the woods between it and the nearby settlements. Sagaponack would benefit most from the founding of the new port. East Hampton already had a landing at Northwest, and Southampton had one at North Sea, but Sagaponack was close to neither.

The earliest road from Sagaponack followed a course much different from the present one. In April 1726 the northerly part of Sagg Road led down to the Harbor, beginning at Theodore Pierson's to the Great Meadow or common landing at the Harbor, six poles wide all the way. The road crossed the "big ditch," as it was called, and came upon the turnpike near the northern part of Samuel T. Hildreth's orchard. From that point it crossed the land between Otter Pond and the Cove and followed the waterfront of the Cove to Zachary's Point near the docks and cooperages of C.D. Dering, and then along the beach to the old wharf. This indirect course was necessary to avoid the meadow and marshland that covered much of the land.

The roads from Wainscott and Sagaponack came together at the north end of Long Pond, and Scuttle Hole and Brickkiln Roads united with them where they came together on the turnpike at what was then Captain Jesse Halsey's corner. This was before Sag Harbor as a village was settled, and the present road that leads to Bridgehampton had not yet been cut through. It isn't known what year the 6-rod highway to the landing was discontinued and the present Main Street opened, but it was probably about the year 1775.

From East Hampton a road had been cut through the Great Pine Swamp north of Northwest Creek. After passing the bluffs of Ninevah Beach, it ran

12 SETTLEMENT AND GROWTH OF THE PORT

along the shore of the bay to the landing. Tradition tells us that the path ran so close to the water that at high tide one wagon wheel would tilt against the cliff while the other was in the water. Until the settlement of Sag Harbor, these roads were the only ones necessary, for the sole reason to come to the port was for shipping or to gather seaweed and salt hay.

Sources date the settlement of the village at about 1730, at which time three dwellings stood, built into the north side of Turkey Hill. In all probability they were nothing more than hovels, built as temporary shelters against the elements. Soon after, a few small shacks were built by fishermen who came to the harbor to make their living. After the allotment of the land in 1745, the property owners sold and traded land and built the first permanent homes at Sag Harbor.

According to W.W. Munsell's *History of Suffolk County, New York*, the highway originally included everything between the meadow and East Hampton Town line. In 1745 the highway was narrowed to the present size, and the land east of it laid out into lots. This later became the street Sag Harbor's business district was built upon. After the meadowland and swamps were filled in, roads were laid out at the north end of the village. As Main Street ran south, it followed a more circuitous course than at present, to avoid areas that were still marshy.

West Water Street was laid out in 1795, a 3-rod-wide highway from the northeast corner of Captain John N. Fordham's heading west. Originally, it had been part of the ancient road that first led to the landing. East of the Long Wharf, the street continued as Shore Road, with the most westerly section part of the original road from East Hampton. In 1841 the name of the street was changed to East Water Street, and changed again to Bay Street thirty years later.

Washington Street separated lots five and six in the Sag Harbor Division when it was laid out in 1787. Henry P. Dering donated land between Union and Sage Streets and opened Church Street in 1792. This property adjoined his home and land on Union Street.

Another early road, long since gone, was Cooper Street. In 1789 the Southampton Town Trustees recommended the Commissioner of Highways go to Sag Harbor, with Caleb Cooper and Jonathan Rogers, to lay out a road from Main Street to the old wharf. It is most likely that Caleb Cooper gave this street its name.

Following the closing of the ancient road that ran between Sag Harbor and East Hampton, a new one was laid out, which entered the village in the Eastville section of town. Nearer the business section it was known as Exchange Highway in 1809. In later years it became Division Street. In 1838 at the southern part of the village, South Street connected Main Street and Sagg Street

(Madison). We know it today as Jermain Avenue, having been renamed in memory of John Jermain. Before Suffolk Street was cut through the dense woodland in 1830, a narrow path led to Jason Beebee's mill and was simply called "the path to the mill."

The following letter to the editor of *The Sag Harbor Express* appeared in the September 30, 1869 issue. It was a request to the trustees to consider placing name signs at the street corners in the village, a custom that had long since disappeared.

> Long years ago, although not quite back to the time when Adam was a little boy, the streets of Sag Harbor used to be named, and boards used to be nailed upon the corners with the names there on; or so we are told by our ancient citizens; and we have some faint recollections of seeing a few of the old split boards nailed to the old engine house, denoting Madison Street, in the rear of Benjamin Babcock's house, another which formerly stood at the corner of Madison and Sage Street at the residence of the late Captain Thomas Smith, and another on Jefferson Street, which stood in the corner of the yard of Deacon James Nickerson, deceased; all of which signs were then not only time worn and weather beaten, but were badly damaged by stones hurled at them by unruly boys.
>
> But these old sign boards, like our ancestors who put them there, have long since passed away, leaving our streets without any visible names and making it a very awkward task for strangers to hunt up their friends while visiting our pleasant little village, and even still more awkward for one to attempt to direct a person to any particular house or street.

A number of the streets in Sag Harbor were named after the individuals who gave the property on which they were built, or from families who lived on the land nearby. Burke Street, although given by the Sleights, was named for Michael Burke, who lived there and is remembered as the founder of Catholicism in Sag Harbor. Rose Street, opened sometime before 1859, received its name in memory of Colonel Abraham Rose. Rysam Street, named for Captain William J. Rysam, ran from Hampton Street to the bay, where Rysam had both a boatyard and a ropewalk. Meadow Street, given by John Fordham, had not been named until after 1859, although the road existed prior to that time. Oakland Avenue, cut through in 1882, got its name from the fact that it ran through an oak forest which led to Oakland Cemetery. Nearby Palmer Terrace, earlier known as Huntting's Hill, opened in 1895 on land given by F.H. Palmer.

SETTLEMENT AND GROWTH OF THE PORT

Traveling by Stagecoach

Long ago at the end of the route
The stage pulled up, the folks stepped out.
They all passed under the tavern door,
The youth and his bride and the gray three-score.
Their eyes so weary with dust and gleam,
Three days gone by like an empty dream.
Soft may they slumber and trouble no more
For their dusty journey, its jolt and roar
Has come to an end at Fordham's door.
Author Unknown

In 1704 the legislature passed a law by which three commissioners were appointed in each county on Long Island to lay out a highway from Brooklyn to East Hampton. It was known as the King's Highway and followed the lines of existing farm roads and early lanes. By 1733 three roads stretched the length of the island, one on the south shore, one on the north, and the third through the center of the island. Stagecoaches made the 100-mile journey from Brooklyn to the East End in three long days.

In 1772 Samuel Nichols, Benjamin Havens, and Nathan Fordham established a "stage wagon" run between Sag Harbor and Brooklyn, once a week in the summer months and once a month in the winter. Starting at the Brooklyn Ferry at 10 A.M. on a Monday morning, the stage traveled to Samuel Nichols' on the "Hempstead Plains," where they were put up over night. On Tuesday morning they set out for Benjamin Havens' at St. George's Manor or Epinetus Smith's at Smithtown, where they made another overnight stop, and Wednesday morning they continued on to their destination, Sag Harbor. In those years the last part of the trip, from Southampton on, was torturous. An Indian guide, familiar with the trail, walked ahead of the stage with the aid of a lantern, leading the way through the darkness of a 3-mile forest. It took eight hours to complete this part of the trip. The road widened as they entered the village before the final stop at Fordham's Inn, where all passengers disembarked. For those wishing to continue on to Connecticut, passage could be arranged by packet boat across the Sound.

The Connecticut Gazette of May 1784 advertised another stage that ran between Sag Harbor and New York. From New London arrangements could be made to sail to Sag Harbor and from there take the stage to New York. Henry

THE FOUNDING OF SAG HARBOR

Moore's stagecoach left Sag Harbor at 5 A.M.; the cost for each passenger, four dollars. Baggage in excess of 20 pounds would have an additional charge. No more than six ladies and gentlemen per trip were permitted.

In May 1791 Josiah W. Wentworth, one of Sag Harbor's early residents, opened his stage run from Sag Harbor to New York. With comfort in mind, his advertisement stated that his complete light coach was hung on springs and finished off in a neat and most fashionable manner. It carried five or six passengers with comfort, and the charge was threepence per mile. Anyone interested in making the trip was asked to sign their names in the "stage book" at Captain Daniel Fordham's.

A much needed improvement was made in 1825 when one whole day was cut off the traveling time. Silas Payne's stage left from the Union Hotel in Sag Harbor at 6 A.M. bound for Brooklyn. The stage made a stop for breakfast at S. Griffing's in Westhampton, after which they proceeded to Patchogue for an overnight stop at J. Rowe's. The next morning they continued on to E. Dodd's in Babylon for their breakfast stop and then off to their destination, Brooklyn. Payne's two-day trip cost five dollars.

In 1842 the steamboat *Williamsburgh* and the stagecoach brought mail and passengers on the old mail line every Wednesday and Saturday. As late as 1870 a mail and passenger stage ran between Southampton and Greenport via Sag Harbor. Although the railroad had recently been extended on the south fork of the island, it wasn't until 1874 that it started to carry the mail. The stage connected with the mail train arriving and leaving from Greenport on the north fork. Soon after the branch line of the railroad was extended to Sag Harbor, the mail and passenger stage was no longer used and so ended more than a century and a half of stagecoach travel in the area.

The Toll Roads

Most of the roads on Long Island in the early 1800s were in a deplorable condition, although those on the East End were said to have been somewhat better than the rest. Horses and buggies, the stagecoach, and teams of animals that were driven across those early roads caused deep mud-filled ruts in the rainy season, and dusty, dirty conditions during the dry summer months. Up until 1813 the State had not yet assumed the duty of building and maintaining the roads, and the toll system was devised to raise funds for that purpose.

Entering Sag Harbor from East Hampton a stop at the toll house on the East Hampton Turnpike was required. From Bridgehampton, tolls were collected at the Bull's Head toll house. At the inception of the toll roads, opposition was strong. To see the roads fenced and a fee charged for their use proved unpopular, but after road conditions were improved, the opposition lessened.

In 1840 the Bull's Head Turnpike Company charter sold shares at $25 each, with a small return paid to the stockholders. The toll house stood on the west side of the turnpike about two miles from the Sag Harbor business district. Daniel McCullin and his family occupied the house and collected toll for every horse, carriage, and team of animals that passed through. The following rates were posted on the toll house sign.

> For every wagon or cart drawn by two horses, mules or oxen — eight cents. And for every additional horse, mule or oxen — two cents.
>
> For every wagon or cart drawn by one horse or mule — four cents.
>
> For every coach, coachee, barouche, phaeton or other four wheeled pleasure carriage drawn by two horses — sixteen cents. And for every additional horse — three cents.
>
> For every chair, or other two wheeled pleasure carriage drawn by one horse — six cents. And for every additional horse — three cents.
>
> For every horse and rider — three cents.
>
> For every horse led, or drove without being attached to a carriage — one cent.
>
> For every sled or sleigh drawn by one horse, mule or ox — four cents. For every additional horse, mule or ox — two cents.
>
> For every score of cattle or mules — ten cents.
>
> For every score of hogs or sheep — four cents.
>
> And in the same proportion for a greater or less number of cattle, mules, hogs or sheep.

After the railroad was built and extended to this area in 1870, the turnpike road deteriorated to such an extent it no longer paid the company to maintain it. On August 19, 1905 the toll gate was opened by the court on a complaint of the highway commissioner. As a result, the owners disposed of the charter and the gate was removed. The following year the road was taken over by Southampton Town.

On November 11, 1909 the toll house burned to the ground. Mrs. McCullin, who still lived there, was not home at the time. Although the place was completely destroyed, the toll board was saved and can be seen at the Whaling Museum.

THE FOUNDING OF SAG HARBOR

The incorporation of the East Hampton Turnpike Company took place in 1844, with a charter secured under the laws of New York State Chapter 190. A turnpike road was built connecting Sag Harbor and East Hampton, and in the mid 1840s it was straightened and improved. Rates were comparable to the Bull's Head toll house.

After 60 years of charging tolls at the little toll house that stood opposite the Jewish Cemetery, the road became so bad that people refused to pay to use it. On September 23, 1905 the franchise was released. To accomplish this, it was necessary for owners of two-thirds of the company's stock-certificate holders to signify their willingness to end the company. The East Hampton Town Records stated the following:

> We the undersigned being stockholders in the East Hampton Turnpike Company Road, a corporation created and existing under the laws of the State of New York of 1844 Chapter 190, representing two thirds of the stock of said corporation as follows: Alden S. Douglas—fifty eight shares, Brinley D. Sleight—twelve shares, William R. Reimann—fifty seven shares, Edward Dayton—five shares, William H. Youngs—two shares (total one hundred thirty-four shares). Now this instrument witnesseth our consent that the directors of said Turnpike Road Company, surrender and abandon the whole of said Turnpike Road and that the same shall revert and belong to the Town of East Hampton through which it was originally and since maintained.

Reimann had purchased the stock of A.H. Rogers, and Reimann and Rogers circulated a subscription to raise funds to throw open the gate. By that time the road was in such a deplorable condition that tolls hadn't been collected for several months. The toll house on the East Hampton road burned to the ground on June 20, 1905, with Mr. Douglas, the owner, having vacated the place just ten days before. Sag Harbor's toll gates were the last two to be removed in the State of New York.

2

ALONG THE WATERFRONT

The Southampton Town Records tell us that the first two attempts to establish wharves at Sag Harbor were in the years 1742 and 1753. On May 5, 1742 the Trustees appointed a committee to "go down to Sagg Harbor and make a choice of a suitable place to build a wharfe, but not to charge the town." Eleven years later (1753) the Commissioner of Highways was sent to Sag Harbor to stake out a piece of land where John Russell could "build a wharf, to be paid for by himself."

The Wharves in the Early Days

In the year 1761 Nathan Fordham Jr. and James Foster received permission from the Town of Southampton to build what was the first sturdy wharf and try works at Sag Harbor. (Try works consist of a furnace in which the iron "try" or whale pots boil down whale blubber to oil.) The wharf was "to extend sixty feet in width, east and west, and not infringe upon or hinder the public highway that goeth along the beach, and the town reserves the privilege of landing their whale upon said wharf at all times and receive it into their try house and try said whale on reasonable terms." The wharf was constructed east of the old Payne Bridge that connected Sag Harbor and Hog Neck. It served the shipping needs of Sag Harbor until 1770, when it became apparent that a larger and more substantial wharf was needed. The remains of this early wharf were said to have been visible still in 1830. From 1830 to 1855 the site was improved by filling it in with earth and stone and making a suitable place to store and retain large quantities of casks of oil after they were removed from returning whale ships.

On February 12, 1770 an association consisting of men from both East Hampton and Southampton Townships hired Attorney William Nicoll and, through his efforts, acquired land from property owners of both townships on which to build a new wharf. This property at the north end of the village, and the land beneath the water, was issued to them with a provision that the wharf be completed within three years. Its dimensions were: 30 rods long, 35 feet wide, and have 60 feet of land under the water on either side. Provisions were made to give the townsmen "liberty to pass and repass on said wharf with their carts and other carriages." The wharf was finished in the course of one year.

The first grant from East Hampton Town to the Wharf Company found in Volume 4, pages 220 and 221 of the East Hampton Town Records reads:

> To all people to whom these presents shall come know ye that whereas Trade and Commerce in general, a benefit to mankind and in particular to the inhabitants of this town we, the subscribers, trustees for the proprietors of the Town of East Hampton, etc., have, and by these presents do upon the petition and special request of John Foster, William Jones, Nathan Fordham Jr., James Foster, David Corwithe, David Gelston, John Sandford, Uriah Rogers, William Smith, Zebulon Cooper, John Hulbert, Robert Hudson, Leir Howell, Henry Howell, Daniel Fordham, Ephraim Howell, Edward Topping, Samuel L'Hommedieu, Thomas Foster, John Russell, Elias Pelletreau, George Mackey, James Haines, William Hallock, Joseph Marshall, Matthew Jagger, of Southampton, and Abraham Gardiner, Stephen Hedges, John Davis, Thomas Wickham, William Hedges and Isaac Barnes of East Hampton, and William Nicoll of said county, desiring the liberty to build a wharf at the place called and known by the name of Sagg Harbor, for the more convenient carrying on of trade and navigation, do fully, freely and absolutely give, grant, convey, and unto the above names John Foster, William Jones, etc., and their heirs and assigns full and free liberty to build and maintain a wharf at Sagg Harbor, thirty-five feet wide, beginning at Southampton east patent line where Southampton grant for said wharf ends (and to run north-easterly thirty rods) and to have sixty feet of water on each side of the wharf, on these conditions only, that said wharf be completely built and finished at or before the end of three

years from the date hereof and that all persons shall have liberty to pass and repass on said wharf, with carts or other carriages, they not unnecessarily or obstructing the above grantees in the free and sole use and benefit of said wharf, always providing said wharf be kept under the following regulations, (viz) That for this present year the committee, Burnett Miller, Thomas Sandford, Nathan Fordham Jr., and Silas Howell shall have the sole ordering thereof and the proprietors of said wharf annually to choose a committee of the most suitable persons of said propriety grantees, to manage the whole affair of said wharf, and that the fare, custom to other places be charged, and said wharf to contain forty rights, reckoned at twenty pounds a right, and no person to be allowed as a voter, but what is entitled to a whole share, and that the profit arising from said wharf shall be divided to each proprietor according to their right, annually or once a year, by the person that takes the fare, except what is wanting to repair said wharf, to have and to hold all the above granted premises with all the privileges and appurtenances thereunto belonging under the above conditions and restrictions as above expressed, in witness and confirmation whereof we, the subscribers in the name and behalf of the proprietors of the Town of East Hampton and as Trustees have hereunto set our hands and fixed our seals this 12th day of February 1770.

Signed, David Mulford, Jeremiah Miller, Elisha Conkling, Ezekiel Mulford, Henry Conkling, Jeremiah Miller Jr., Timothy Mulford, John Parsons.

In presence of: David Baker and Edward Conkling, Entered and Compared March 2, 1771 by Burnett Miller, Town Clerk.

This was the original Long Wharf, for, according to Henry P. Hedges, an ancient deed stated that on April 25, 1771 Thomas Foster conveyed to Daniel Fordham one-half share in the new Long Wharf at Sag Harbor. A Wharf Company was formed with the capital dividend into 40 shares of 20 pounds each, with one whole share entitled to one vote. Annual meetings were held and dividends as high as 30 percent were paid by the company, making it one of the best investments on Long Island. The company remained in existence until January 1896 and was one of the oldest incorporations in the State of New York.

During the Revolutionary War many families fled to Connecticut to escape the oppression of the British, and Onderdonk's *Revolutionary Incidents* states that on September 15, 1776 "the wharves at Sag Harbor were crowded with immigrants awaiting passage across the Sound." At that time the wharf became in need of repair, and at a town meeting in April 1783, it was agreed that any person who worked repairing the wharf at Sag Harbor would be exempt from mending the highway.

In 1791 at the annual meeting of the proprietors it was voted that the following rates for usage of the wharf would be charged:

Every vessel of 100 ton upward	020 per day
80 ton upward	019 per day
60 ton upward	016 per day
40 ton upward	013 per day
20 ton upward	010 per day

For coasting vessels:

40 ton and under 50	350 per day
30 ton and under 40	200 per day
20 ton and under 30	200 per day
10 ton and under 20	140 per day

Boats and other craft at the discretion of the wharfinger.
For every 1000 feet boards and lumber not otherwise mentioned, landed on the wharf—006.
If not removed within 48 hours, for every 24 hours after—006.
Every horse taken off or landed—003.
100 nails estimated equal to 1000 lumber—006.
Every load of stone under above regulations—003.
Every 1000 short shingles—001.
Every cord of wood—006.
The wharfinger is empowered to remove any vessel when necessary or conveniency requires and to regulate all matters and disputes which may arise.

John Gelston, Clerk
William Davall, Wharfinger

On September 5, 1808 the East Hampton Town conveyed to the people of the State of New York a piece of land covered with water, from the end of the existing wharf, extending northward 300 feet. This was the grant for what was known as the State Pier, constructed by the authority and at the expense of the State. This was the second section of the Long Wharf. In 1821, with a growing fleet and an expanding whale fishery, a third section was added, making the wharf 1000 feet long. On August 27th of that year, the Trustees met pursuant to adjournment and agreed to sell to the State of New York a water lot at the end of the wharf at Sag Harbor for the cost of $125.

From the Town Records of East Hampton, Volume Four, the second grant from East Hampton to the wharf is recorded.

> This indenture made the fifth day of September in the year of our Lord, 1808, between Abraham Miller, David Hedges, Isaac Barnes, Mulford Hand, Joseph Mulford, David Talmage Jr., John Strong Jr., and John Miller Jr., trustees of the freeholders and commonalty of the Town of East Hampton, in the county of Suffolk, and the State of New York, of the first part, and the people of the State of New York of the second part, witnesseth that the said party of the first part for, and in consideration of the sum of one hundred dollars, lawful money, of the United States, to them in hand paid by the party of the second part, the receipt whereof is hereby acknowledged, have granted, bargained, sold, released and confirmed, and by these presents do grant, bargain, sell, release and confirm unto the said party of the second part, a certain tract or parcel of land covered with water at a place called Sag Harbor, in the Township of East Hampton, and bound as follows: Southwardly, upon the end or head of said wharf, three hundred feet parallel with said wharf and extending in breadth sixty feet on the east side and sixty feet on the west side of the above described tract of land covered with water, which said tract of land and water is conveyed to the people aforesaid, for the purpose of making piers, wharves, or other accommodations for shipping at the port of Sag Harbor, aforesaid, in pursuance of the act entitled, and act for making further provisions for improving the navigation between the villages of Troy and Waterford, and for other purposes, passed on March 19, 1803, to have and to hold the said granted and bargained premises, with the appurtenances, to the said part of the second part, with all the rights, title, claim or demand whatsoever, of the said party of the first part, of, in, and to the same for so long a time as the said piers, wharves or other accommodations shall be preserved for the uses aforesaid...
>
> Signed, Abraham Miller, David Hedges, Joseph Barnes, Miller Dayton, Huntting Miller, Josiah Mulford, David Talmage Jr., John Strong Jr., Isaac Barnes.
>
> Signed, sealed and delivered in presence of us: Henry Conkling Jr. and Jonathan H. Straton.

Mankesack Island

Mankesack Island, an ancient two-acre piece of land in the waters off Sag Harbor, no longer exists. Tidal currents and northeast storms swept it away years ago, and the only trace of the island left today is a cluster of rocks visible when the tide is at its lowest.

According to the Southampton Town Records, Sacataco Indian of "Montocket" sold to Robert Cody of East Hampton "all that island lying and being in the sound or harbor, between Hog Neck and Sag Harbor or there abouts, called by the name of Mankesack or Stony Island, and all that can be found unpatented in the bounds of East Hampton from ye north side of Alwife Brook Neck to ye line between East Hampton and Southampton." This transaction took place October 3, 1712, and the price paid for the island was five pounds sterling. A year later Cody sold the island to Ezekiel Sandford of Southampton Colony for ten pounds.

In those early years Conklin's Point reached out toward Mankesack, and the sandy point of the island stretched back toward Conklin's Point, indicating that, at some remote time in the past, the two were connected. The grassy meadow on the island provided fine pasture land, and tradition tells us that Penny Conklin of North Haven and, later, Pop Wentworth of Sag Harbor often took their cattle there to graze. Along the shore of Mankesack gulls and terns built their nests and raised their young during the summer months.

Henry P. Hedges, in his 1896 address to the Sag Harbor Historical Society, spoke of Mankesack by saying:

> An amusing tradition has survived the wrecks of time; in substance that Mankesack Island, reported anciently as much larger, cultivated and used as a pasture field, has dwindled into insignificance. The meadow, anciently more extensive, has diminished and is disappearing (1886). Wentworth was the last person who attempted to pasture on the island. Taking them by boat, he left a couple of donkeys to pasture there. Whether the pasture was poor or the tides high, the donkeys left the island and it is said reached home before their owner.

By the start of the 20th century little was left to the island, and, today, the remaining rocks are a menace to navigation as they are often submerged and unseen by boaters.

The Bridges

Before a bridge to Hog Neck (North Haven) was built, it was necessary to make the short trip by boat, unless the road to Noyac and across the beach was taken. As the community grew it became apparent that the construction of a bridge connecting the two places would make more sense.

The first mention of a bridge was recorded in the Southampton Town Trustee Records when, in 1799, the Trustees granted James Mitchell the right to build a bridge to North Haven so he could construct a mill on that shore, for the consideration of ten pounds. It is not known how long the bridge stood, or even if it was for public use, but in all probability it was a narrow rickety one that merely served the purpose for which it was intended.

By 1831 it became apparent that a more substantial bridge be constructed, and at that time the Payne Bridge Company was formed. It was incorporated with a capital stock of $2000 with stocks selling at 25¢ each. Named to receive subscriptions were Luther D. Cook, Charles Watson Payne, and Marcus Osborn. The contract for material was given to Sag Harbor lumber dealers Gorham & Osborne. The wooden bridge was built by John Monks, and it spanned the water from the foot of Bridge Street to the sandy point on the North Haven shore. It was a drawbridge, constructed to open so that vessels built at the shipyards along the upper cove could pass through and out into the bay. A two-cent toll was charged to foot passengers and eight cents for each team crossing, with tolls collected on the Sag Harbor side by a tollkeeper, Mr. Fields, and later his successor H.T. Williamson. An interesting item appeared in the May 23, 1844 newspaper which stated that Charles Watson Payne had lots for sale, and by paying an extra five dollars, the buyer would be entitled to free bridge crossing.

After little more than a decade the bridge began to deteriorate and settle due to damage by the sea terado, the destructive sea worm which eats away at the underwater piles supporting it. A gale in 1847 added further to its weakening condition and made it sorely in need of renovation. It was rebuilt and continued in use until 1891. When the toll company dissolved in 1868, the bridge was taken over by Suffolk County through an act of legislature. Lewis J. Corwin, boss carpenter, and his gang of men made the repairs, putting up new rails, floor timbers, and logs.

In 1891 Joseph Fahys was granted permission to build a new iron drawbridge at a cost of $23,000, to replace the old wooden structure which again was in a poor state of disrepair. A land easement was needed in order to do away with an approach across the railroad tracks. On July 23, 1891 the Town Trustees granted him a perpetual easement privilege and right of way over the lands under water belonging to the Town of Southampton, from the slip at the north end of Main Street to a point at North Haven, according to the description in a certain proposed deed submitted to the Board by Fahys, to a width of 30 feet for the purpose of erecting a free bridge. "The grant to be subject to the condition that the grantees will, within two years, construct such a bridge, and if the said Joseph Fahys shall fail to construct the bridge aforesaid or it the same shall at any time hereafter cease to be maintained and used as a public bridge, than the grant hereby made shall cease, and be absolutely void and it be further enacted that the president and clerk sign and seal the agreement. Albert J. Post, clerk."Although the bridge was constructed of iron, the wooden piles that supported it were again attacked by the terado, and the bridge collapsed just nine years after it was built. Following the collapse of the bridge, a ferry service run by George Page was put into operation.

In September 1900 another bridge was built. The Board of Supervisors decided that a steel bridge would be the answer. Supervisor Edwin Bailey, Jr., of the Committee on Bridges, was appointed with full power to act in its construction. He was fortunate in securing, from the Wrought Iron Bridge Company of New York City, one of the finest bridges of its kind in New York State. It cost $13,000 and was transported to Sag Harbor in December 1900. The Secretary of War formally approved the plans and work got underway to remove the old bridge.

The length of the new bridge was 370 feet, and 8 feet above the water. At each end were piers with a steel casing, each 30 inches in diameter and one-quarter inch thick, with one steel pile in each. The ends of the draw had large piers, each with a diameter of 42 inches, one-quarter-inch thick, with two steel piles in their center. The center pier on which rested the 85-foot draw, was 18 feet in diameter, one-quarter-inch thick, with eight steel piles in the center. Two other supporting piers of the bridge were 30 inches in diameter with one regular steel pile in the center of each. All the casings were filled with concrete. From the land pier to the first draw pier it was 70 feet with a 40-foot clearing of the draw on each side. From the end of the second draw pier to the first supporting pier, it was 63 feet 4 inches, and from the second supporting pier to the next to last land pier, 63 feet 4 inches. The roadway was 18 feet wide; and the sidewalk, 4 feet wide.

In 1911, with the bridge only 11 years old, repairs were necessary. The York Bridge Company of York, Pennsylvania submitted a bid of $2965 to repair the draw, which failed to open, and was awarded the contract. This steel bridge solved the problem of the sea terado, and it remained in use for 25 more years.

In 1936, after negotiating for five years and getting the Suffolk County Board of Supervisors' approval, work began on a new concrete bridge to replace the old span. The first operation consisted of driving and testing eight piles, the larger ones tested under a load of 144 tons, which was double the maximum weight the bridge supports would have to bear. Twenty-five men employed to cast the piles did so in forms set up on the Long Wharf. The Hampton

Dredging Company of Westhampton Beach arrived in the village with a hydraulic dredge and dug a channel at the site of the proposed bridge. Construction of the $200,000 390-foot span began June 1, 1936, with Frank A. O'Hare, Inc. of Madison Avenue, New York City, contractor, and Francis J. Weber, supervisor.

The reinforced concrete bridge was made up of two causeways and rested on nine rows of piers. A week before it opened, the 36-year-old steel drawbridge was demolished, cut into sections, and floated away on a barge, having been sold for junk. The new concrete bridge opened to vehicular traffic December 26, 1936 and is still in use today.

The Windmills

For many centuries windmills had been used in Europe, utilizing the motion of the wind to power the great mills which ground their grain. With Sag Harbor's increasing population, a more modern means of making flour and meal was needed. Pounding corn and grain with mortar and pestle was no longer practical, and the time had come when windmills were constructed in and near Sag Harbor.

An article in *The Sag Harbor Express* stated that the first mill stood on the beach near the south end of Payne's Bridge.

> The first and second mills were pulled down or blown down or removed to the country. The third, belonging to Hubbard Latham was removed upon the hill (now Howard Street) and later known as Ryder's Mill are now gone. One also stood near the last mentioned site belonging to Stephen Howell. It is now in Bridgehampton. The old water mill formerly standing at Otter Pond was taken down and put up as a store on the wharf. It was burned during the fire of 1817. About 1820 Lester Beebee built his.

Most of this information is probably what the author remembered, as he gives no sources to verify his statements. The Southampton Town Records tells us the following facts.

In 1760 Mordaci Homan decided to build a mill in Sag Harbor. On June 24th of that year a meeting was held by the Southampton Town Trustees, and it was voted that William Rogers and Israel Halsey go down to the Harbor to inspect the place where Homan wished to build his mill. Permission was granted, and the first recorded mill in Sag Harbor was constructed on a site east of the old wharf.

The second mill built in the village was the Jermain Mill. In 1782 Ebenezer White, Nathan Fordham, and Deacon David Hedges were granted the right to cut an inlet from the cove to Otter Pond to make a fish pond. In 1793 the grant was transferred to John Jermain, with the additional privilege of building a mill on the stream. Jermain built a fulling mill to make cloth and grind grain for Sag Harbor and vicinity, and the Trustees gave him and his heirs the privilege of operating it. Jermain was also given the right to dig a brook that would connect the waters of Long Pond and Crooked Pond with Otter Pond, provided that he should build a bridge across the brook so that carriages could pass over it. The mill, however, never lived up to Jermain's expectations because of a sluggish flow of water from the ponds, and after ten years he gave up his milling business. The artificial brook was later diverted to outside the village limits and connected to the cove.

In February 1799 on nearby Hog Neck (North Haven) James Mitchell petitioned the Town Trustees for a grant to construct a bridge across the water between Sag Harbor and Hog Neck for the purpose of erecting a mill there. On May 14th of that year permission was granted for the consideration of nine pounds, seventeen shillings, and Mitchell built his mill.

A second mill was erected on Hog Neck in 1800. Although it is not certain who built this mill, it was said to have been framed with lumber cut from the local forests and built by local mechanics. An inscription carved on the staircase string states, "began to grinde August 1, 1800." It was probably operated by a man named Ludlam, a miller of that time. Fourteen years later James Corwith purchased the mill and moved it to Water Mill, Long Island, using twelve yoke of oxen to transport it. It is believed that Corwith acquired it from Joshua Howell for $750. The Corwith Mill was still grinding grain as late as 1887, when it was owned and operated by James Corwith's son Samuel.

On Peter's Green, off Glover Street on the cove, stood a mill of a different style. It was known as a "spider-legged" mill, built in the early 1800's and tended by Peter Hildreth. There were only eight mills of this type on all of Long Island. The body of the mill was set and turned on a huge center post or pivot supported by heavy braces footed into large timbers. Two strong beams were attached to the lower frame of the mill and extended down and out to the ground level, where they were fastened to a large cart wheel for turning the mill about. The millhouse, built 30 feet above ground, was mounted on a pedestal of 3-foot square timbers. The pedestal, topped with a brass collar and a shaft and axle, made it possible to turn the whole building, enabling the large sails to face the wind. Heavy bags of flour and grain were raised and lowered by a block and fall. The mill had but one set or run of stones.

28 SETTLEMENT AND GROWTH OF THE PORT

In 1820 the Beebee Mill, the last operating windmill in Sag Harbor, was erected. Built by Amagansett millwright Samuel Schellinger and his apprentice, Pardon Tabor, for Captain Lester Beebee, it was started on September 5, 1820 and completed 119 days later. The Beebee Mill was built at a time when the whaling industry was in full swing and is probably the one that the greatest number of people are familiar with. From this mill, which stood on Sherry's Hill on Suffolk Street, a flag would be flown from a pole on its roof indicating that a ship had been sighted in the bay. It was also known as the "Flag on the Mill, Ship in the Bay" windmill. The Beebee Mill is a fine example of a smock mill with stone foundation, four story tower, cast iron gears, and iron cogwork and shafting. When it went up for sale in 1835, *The Republican Watchman* ran the following advertisement:

Mill for Sale
The subscriber offers for sale this valuable WINDMILL, situated in the village of Sag Harbor. The Mill is built of the best materials, has two runs of Burr Stones, a fly, etc., and is in good repair. The property tax can be examined at any time previous to the sale. If the above described mill is not sold at private sale by Saturday the 16th day of May next, it will at two o'clock in the afternoon of that day, be sold at public auction at the house of Mrs. Mary Fordham in Sag Harbor. For further particulars, inquire of the subscriber.
JASON BEEBEE

Judge Abraham Rose, of Bridgehampton, and Richard Gelston, owner of the Bull's Head Tavern, bought the mill and moved it to Bridgehampton. They placed it on Mill Hill, the site of two previous mills. Subsequently, the mill was sold 12 times before John E. Berwind bought it in 1915 and moved it to his property on Ocean Road, Bridgehampton. Early owners of the Beebee Mill were: Charles K. Norris, Roger Francis in 1851, a company made up of E. Jones Ludlow, Charles Henry Topping and Hedges Miller, then William Hand, Albert Topping, Lafayette Seabury, and Topping and Hildreth in 1880. Later James S. Sandford moved it from Windmill Hill to a site near the railroad station, where he converted it to steam. Commissioner Kennedy was interested in purchasing it for the Prospect Park in Brooklyn, but the contract was later cancelled because of moving problems. In 1894 Oliver Osborn moved it across the tracks and set in on a brick foundation. In 1895 it was owned by the Bridgehampton Milling Company, with William Schellinger, the miller. Reverend Robert Davis owned the mill in 1915, and he, in turn, sold it to Mr. Berwind.

Today none of the old mills of early Sag Harbor remains on their original sites, the two surviving ones having been moved to their present locations in Bridgehampton and Water Mill.

Building the First Windmill

Taken from "Chronicle le First, of ye towne and Wonderfulle Historie of ye Harbore called Sagge," by John Wallace Burke of Sag Harbor, and printed in *The Corrector*.

> About the year 1762 our wise progenitors bethought themselves of building a windmill wherein the grists of the colony could be ground and the corn made into meal by a more expeditious process than the mortar afforded. General public meetings were held at which the measure was fully discussed at length, and a great deal of windy argument advanced to prove the necessity of this great enterprise. Of course as soon as any measure of public utility was proposed, there immediately arose a party who violently opposed it. Not that they could possibly hope to gain anything by the opposition, but simply for the pleasure of being contrary. The leaders of the opposition were mighty men in our midst, and carried their pretensions with a high hand; their chief weapon, the tongue.
>
> The windmill was an epoch in our history. On the one hand it was contended that windmills were a triumph of art over nature; that they were highly necessary and eminently useful and ornamental, that one of them would do the work of a hundred samp mortars in a quarter of the time; that pounding corn in mortars was a heathen and barbarous custom derived from the savages, unworthy to be used by a Christian people, a moreover tedious and laborious process, calculated to wear out the clothes, muscle, and patience of the operator; that the old rude, cumberous wooden mortars were behind the age, played out; a heathen rarity, a vexation of spirit, of business, of flesh, and a tearer of trowsers; and they should be done away with, and windmills, those mighty evidences of the industry, thrift, and genius of man, used in their stead.
>
> On the other hand, it was maintained with great bitterness and pertinacity, that they were noisy abominations, inventions of the arch enemy; uncouth, unsightly and unnecessary, fit only to frighten children, stray cattle, and nervous old ladies; instead of being evidences of thrift and industry, they were glaring proof of upstart arrogance, pride and laziness; that the miller was a lazy and useless official who would plunder the public crib, always have the finest hogs, and nobody would know whose corn they were fattened with; that he would live off the labors

of others, feast on the fat of the land, and give himself airs in consequence; that the much abused method of pounding corn was an ancient, convenient and conservative way; true it was borrowed from the Indians; so was the corn, but by use in Christian hands, it had become naturalized and orthodox; that the exercise of operating the mortars was pleasant and healthful, and tended to promote digestion and habits of industry; that boys and idle youth when set at work at them were kept out of mischief and that therefore they were great moral agents in the preservation of the physical and moral well-being of the community, and they ought not to be done away with, but by all means retained.

...The controversy while it lasted, was exceedingly bitter and personal, and several fat men on each side wasted much breath that on going up stairs of uphill, they were short-winded ever afterward. This is a curious fact in natural philosophy, and I mention it in this place for the benefit of philosophers, and also as a caution to fat people not to engage too heartily in windy discussions.

At length, after wind enough had been wasted sufficient to keep it in operation several years, the mill was erected, amid great rejoicing, at a point near what is now called Mitchell's Wharf. The first man who had charge of the mill was named Anak Smith, but by common consent he was called the Miller, and from him descended that numerous and prolific family resident hereabout who bear that cognomen to this present day.

After the mill was erected and in successful operation, corn meal became plenty and cheap. Every family had its johnny cake, corn dodgers and Indian dumplings to eat with clams and eel chowder, and wheat flour was no longer a luxury in the village. Rye grits soon became a quite common article of consumption.

Those who had at first opposed it began to perceive its beneficial workings, and would patronize it instead of the slow old-fashioned mortars, but the party in possession determined to punish them for their unwarrantable opposition. Therefore when one of them brought a grist to mill he was obliged to wait till all others were served. This of course produced much jealousy and the opposition, after several years of fresh discussion, built another mill near the present site of Huntting's cooperage. This was built as much unlike the former one as possible, and the villagers took sides with each as it pleased them, and the feuds that did ensue between the adherents of the "wheel-mill" and those of the "peg-mill" were as bitter and violent and provocative of as much "biting of thumbs," as ancient ones in Verona, between the houses of Capulet and Montague.

The samp-mortars, meanwhile, fell into disuse, and at last were totally neglected except by a few highly conservative villagers who still adhere to and use them, and maintain that they are venerable relics of a genius of a former age. The antiquary, curious in such matters, can still find finely preserved specimens of them in the back yards of some of the older houses. The believers in poetical justice may be glad that both Cowper and I agree in praising the great Lo! and unite in giving honor to whom honor is due.

Soon after the "Chronicles of Sag Harbor" appeared in *The Corrector*, John Wallace Burke "dropped the pen and took up the sword" for the Union's cause. The Civil War was in progress and Burke joined the New York 81st Regiment. He served in that outfit until his death June 2, 1864. At the age of 31, John Wallace Burke was killed in battle at Gaines Ferry near Cold Harbor, Virginia. "While at the head of his company, gallantly cheering on his men, he was struck by a musket ball in the forehead and fell to the ground dead."

A Description of the Village in 1804

Dr. Dwight of Yale University visited Sag Harbor in 1804 and described the place as it appeared then.

> Sag Harbor is a very pretty village, situated on a mere mass of sand. The harbor, which is excellent, and the only good one for a great distance on the eastern part of the Island, allured the inhabitants to this unpleasant ground. Not unpleasant from want of prospect, but because it furnishes unpleasant streets and walks, and is unfriendly to every kind of vegetation. The village contains, at this time, about one hundred twenty houses; the principal part of which are on a winding street terminating at the shore. The rest on some other streets of less consequence. Many of the houses, outhouses and fences are new and neat, and an appearance of thrift, elsewhere unknown in this part of the Island is spread over the whole village.
> The topography of Sag Harbor, both in East Hampton Town and in Southampton Town, has changed enormously since first settled. The meadow originally extended across Main Street. At the east side was Turkey Hill or Cliff Hill. Between this eminence and Meeting House Hill was a swamp, and a stream of water ran from the east part of the latter hill, following a course where is now the factory yard of Joseph Fahys & Company, across the dividing line of the town and thence to ponds at the extension of Burke Street (since filled in), and a drain con-

nected with the waters of the bay. Turkey Hill was dragged down and dumped to a depth of four or five feet on what is now the Main Street of Sag Harbor. Before that time, the ground was almost impassable. Less than thirty years ago the Sleights extended Burke Street to Bay Street, and Mott's Pond was filled in. The road bed passes over where once was the pond.

The relevant business directories for the years 1700s and 1804-1810 can be found in the Appendix.

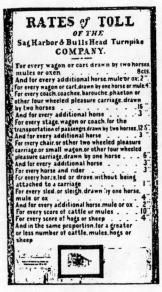

3

LAW AND ORDER IN THE GROWING PORT

As the village population grew, some means of law enforcement had to be implemented. Rules and regulations were enacted to keep things running smoothly, and punishment for offenses carried out with harshness and severity.

Regulations for Keeping The Law

A whipping post stood at the north end of Main Street in front of Huntting's building and was used without discrimination. Man or woman, black or white, fell victim to the sting of the whip if found guilty of some infraction of the law. The Southampton Town Records tell us that as early as 1773 a woman identified only as Mary N. was sentenced to twenty lashes on her bare back for theft and breaking the King's peace by disorderly and violent conduct. In 1788 it was also recorded that a negro man was sentenced to "be stript and receive thirty lashes on his bare back for stealing a sheep, and that Braddock Corey execute the punishment."

BRADDOCK COREY

The Corey name goes back to the earliest days in Sag Harbor's history. Braddock Corey and his wife, Charity, along with 30 others, made up a group of people who were the first permanent residents of the new settlement. Corey, born in 1735 at nearby North Haven, came to Sag Harbor some years before the American Revolution and became a property owner when land was allotted in the Great North and Great South Divisions. He took an active role in village affairs and became a man of influence and position. Braddock Corey was a craftsman by trade, but a butcher by necessity, and, typical of the rural craftsmen, found he had to pursue more than one occupation. He combined carpentry and joinery with butchering, which seemed to be a far more profitable vocation than woodworking.

In all probability, Braddock Corey became involved in keeping law and order in the growing village, for the records tell us that in 1788 he inflicted thirty lashes to the bare back of a man caught stealing.

In 1795 Corey donated property on the corner of Madison and Jefferson Streets in order that the schoolhouse on the next lot could be enlarged. He is also credited with giving the land on which Union Street is now located. Corey built at least two houses in Sag Harbor as well as making chairs, cupboards and window sashes, which he sold to the local residents. At the time of his death on February 1, 1809 his estate comprised of butcher's tools, 15 joiner planes, four screw augers, 13 chisels and gouges, four old saws, and a basket of nails. What happened to the influential Mr. Corey? We can only speculate, but it appears that he died a poor man. Braddock Corey and his wife are buried in Oakland Cemetery.

Another means of discipline was the village stocks, where one was forced to endure the humiliation of being locked in the contraption in full view of neighbors and friends. The first pound and stocks were built in Sag Harbor in 1792 when the Town Trustees voted that John Fordham should erect a "public pound and stocks at a convenient place at Sag Harbor at the expense of the town." They were erected on Meeting House Hill, near the northwest corner of Church and Sage Streets, and stood only six weeks before someone tore them down and threw them into a nearby pond. In 1795, with a new location selected, other stocks were built. Perhaps the village officials felt that Madison Square would be within view of more people and less likely to be tampered with. Captain Stephen Howell was paid by the Trustees to construct them next to the Hay Scale opposite Tiffany and Roger's store. However, it wasn't long after that they met with the same fate as the first, as they were broken up and thrown into the meadow behind the village. On another occasion stocks were built at the foot of the village near the liberty pole. It isn't known how long they remained at that location.

LAW AND ORDER

By the mid 1800s an assortment of by-laws and ordinances were adopted, and physical punishment was reduced to a minimum. Fines became a more acceptable means of dealing with those who failed to obey the law. Some of the more interesting ordinances follow.

> No person shall leave any horse or mule untied in the streets or public grounds; and if any horse or mule shall run away for the want of being properly tied or secured, the person having such animal under his charge shall forfeit and pay the sum of five dollars.

> No person shall play ball, fly kites, pitch quoits or play at marbles in or upon any part of Main Street, between Spring Street and West Street, under a penalty not exceeding three dollars.

> No person shall lead, ride or drive any horse or team, nor lead or drive any cow upon any of the sidewalks of said village, under penalty of five dollars for every such offense.

> No person shall indecently expose his or her person, nor swim or bathe during the daytime in the Otter Pond or Cove, or in that part of the bay adjoining the village limits between Conklin's Point and the North Haven bridge, under penalty not exceeding five dollars.

> No person shall keep or assist in keeping a brothel or a house of assignation, nor entertain or assist in entertaining lewd women for the purpose of prostitution, nor procure or aid in procuring lewd women for that purpose, under the penalty of twenty-five dollars for each offense.

> No person shall injure or mutilate any of the tombstones, fences, or inclosures upon or surrounding the Old Burying Ground, nor wantingly trample and run over the graves therein, under penalty not exceeding ten dollars.

> No person shall keep in any building more than twenty pounds of gunpowder at any one time, which shall be secured in tin canisters with proper covers, and any person violating either or both of the provisions of this by-law shall forfeit and pay the sum of ten dollars.

> No person shall fire or assist in firing any gun, squib, cracker, or other preparation of gun powder or other combustible material in any street or public ground, nor within one hundred feet of any building, except on the day celebrated as the anniversary of our National Independence, under a penalty not exceeding fifteen dollars in the discretion of the court before conviction shall be had.

As time went on, a jail was constructed in the village. It stood at the rear of the Hook and Ladder Fire Company, which at that time stood on Washington Street. It was an iron building with three cells 6 by 6 feet and 7 feet high. It had an iron grating door, iron ventilators, iron beds, and was encased in a wooden building "sufficiently large enough to have anti-rooms and other modern improvements." John Fordham did all of the iron work at his blacksmith shop in Sag Harbor.

During the 1800s the officials of the Village consisted of three trustees, a clerk, a collector of the port, two police constables, and a pound master.

The Custom House and Its Collectors

Custom houses in America were first established during the colonial period, and after the Revolution broke out, they were set up in the parts freed from British control. Under the control of the Confederation, the lack of national custom houses contributed to the inability to raise revenue and control shipping. As a consequence, Article 1, Section 8 of the Constitution gave Congress the power to lay and collect taxes, duties, imports and excises, and to regulate commerce with foreign nations.

The first tariff act was passed July 4, 1789, and custom districts, as well as the machinery to carry on their duties, were established later the same month. Custom houses were placed under the jurisdiction of the Treasury Department by a September 2, 1789 act.

The collector was the central figure and operating agent, and no custom house could exist without him. He was the earliest of the officials to be appointed and the one upon whom fell the weightiest obligations. One of his most important duties was to act as informer before the Vice Admiralty Court.

Sag Harbor was made a port of entry by an Act of Congress passed July 31, 1789 at the second session of the First Congress of the United States held at New York City. The law is Chapter XXXV.

> An act to provide more effectively for the collection of duties imposed by law on goods, wares and merchandise imported into the United States, and on the tonnage of ships and vessels. In the State of New York shall be two districts; to wit, Sag Harbor on Nassau or Long Island, and the city of New York, each of which shall be a Port of Entry. The district of Sag Harbor shall include all bays, harbors, rivers and shores within the two points of land which are called Oyster Pond Point and Montauk Point. Signed: Frederick Augustus Muhlenberg, Speaker

of the House of Representatives; John Adams, Vice-President of the United States; and approved by George Washington, President of the United States.

By the time the Revolutionary War was in full swing, the Port of Sag Harbor had built up a thriving coastal and foreign trade. This came to an abrupt end when interrupted by the war. When Washington approved the creation of Sag Harbor as a Port of Entry, the village had more tons of square-rigged vessels engaged in commerce than even New York City.

John Gelston of Bridgehampton, named first collector, held the position for one year. He was succeeded by Henry Packer Dering, who held the position from 1790 to 1822. When he died he was succeeded by his son Henry Thomas Dering, who held the office from 1822 to 1829, 1842 to 1845, and again in 1848. The custom office was located in the Dering residence on the corner of Union and Church Streets and then, for a time, in the Arsenal across the street.

HENRY PACKER DERING

As collector of the Port of Sag Harbor and its first Postmaster, Henry Packer Dering held positions of great influence not only in Sag Harbor but in all of eastern Long Island as well. Born at Shelter Island July 3, 1763 Henry Packer Dering grew up with a strong sense of patriotism and love for his town and his country. From the year 1790 up to the time of his death in 1822, he devoted his life to public service.

Henry Packer Dering became Collector of the Port in 1790, a position he held for 32 years. In 1794 he also became Sag Harbor's first Postmaster under the Federal Government of the United States, having been appointed by Thomas Pickering, first Postmaster General, as his deputy. At that time the Custom House and Post Office were located in the Dering residence on the north-east corner of Union and Church Streets. In his role as Collector and Postmaster, Henry Packer Dering proudly flew the stars and stripes from his office and home. This flag was flown when he went aboard a United States vessel or a chartered boat to transact official business. When the Custom Office and Post Office moved across the street into the Arsenal Building, the flag went along.

In addition to these prestigious positions, Dering served as Deputy County Clerk in Riverhead, Commissioner of Highways, and other influential committees. He often acted as an arbitrator. Henry Packer Dering was one of the commissioners named to attend to the survey of the grant at Hog Neck Beach and to mark the limits and boundaries of the beach and meadows which were granted to the Parish of Sag Harbor.

During the War of 1812 Henry Packer Dering was placed in charge of government property at Sag Harbor, subject to the orders of General Abraham Rose of Bridgehampton. Dering wrote, with dismay, in one of his letters, "The officers and crews of their (British) vessels are daily feasting on the rich produce of American soil at a liberal price. They are permitted to come ashore and get whatever they choose." Dering wrote that the British left pay for what they took, an act that he considered "a bad thing, as it has a tendency to cool our patriotism."

When the sea wall was built at Little Gull Island in 1817, Henry Packer Dering represented the United States government as agent, going to and from the island by boat to inspect its progress. His son, Henry Thomas Dering, (next Collector of the Port), took an active part in the wall's construction, being employed to measure and calculate its dimensions. Henry Thomas wrote a daily journal while at Little Gull Island and noted with pride the meeting he had with President James Monroe while working there. He wrote in his June 28, 1817 entry that the President arrived at Little Gull Island from New London on a sloop of war, accompanied by four cutters, after intending to sail into Gardiner's Bay. The wind failed and they came ashore at Little Gull, and Dering went on to say he had the pleasure of shaking the President's hand during their brief 15-minute stop.

Along with his governmental duties, Henry Packer Dering was a member and a Trustee of the Presbyterian Church, a member of the Public School Committee, and often served as administrator of estates. In later years Dering appointed his son Henry Thomas as his deputy, and upon his father's death on April 30, 1822, Henry Thomas Dering succeeded him as the next Collector of the Port of Sag Harbor.

Henry Thomas Dering was succeeded by Jonathan P. Osborn of East Hampton in 1829, but continued as Deputy Collector. In 1842 Dering was re-appointed Collector and held the position until 1845. At that time Abel Huntington of East Hampton assumed the position, with Dering again as Deputy. He was again appointed Collector in 1849 for another year. For more than half a century, the Derings were involved in the operation of the Custom House.

Those serving after the Derings were: Edwin Rose of Bridgehampton, 1849-52; Samuel L. Gardiner, 1852-57; Jason M. Terbell of East Hampton, 1857-61; John Sherry, Sr., 1861-65; Captain Wickham S. Havens, 1865-80; Captain William Lowen, 1880-85; Clothier H. Vaughn, 1885-90; John Sherry, Jr., 1890-92; Cornelius Sleight, 1892-96; Peter Dippel, 1896-1909; Frank

Harris, 1909-12; and Frank W. Corwin, as Deputy, 1912-13.

In later years, as business in the port of entry declined, the Custom House continued mostly out of respect to sentiment. On June 30, 1913 Deputy Corwin received the announcement that the Custom House at Sag Harbor would be abolished. John Farrell of the New York office came to Sag Harbor along with William W. Griffin, Deputy Collector of the Surveyor District of Greenport, and packed up the archives of the custom office to take to Greenport where a branch of the New York office was to be maintained. All ships were then required to register at the Greenport office.

In 1948, through the efforts of the Old Sagg Harbour Committee, New Jersey's ex-Governor Charles Edison and the parish of St. Andrew's Roman Catholic Church, who at that time owned the building, the old Custom House was saved from destruction and moved to its present site on Garden Street. Following restoration, the historic landmark opened to the public during the summer months.

Mail Delivery and the Early Post Office

In early times, prior to the Revolution, a pony express rider delivered mail, traveling the 239-mile route between New York and the East End. Before reaching Sag Harbor, stops were made in Brooklyn, Jamaica, Smithtown, Riverhead, Southold, Shelter Island and North Haven. After leaving Sag Harbor, he rode on to East Hampton, Southampton, and other villages on the south shore before returning to New York. In the 1770s the mail was carried by stagecoach, traveling the length of Long Island in three days and transporting passengers as well.

Sag Harbor's first post office was established in October 1794 in a small lean-to attached to the home of the first Postmaster, Henry Packer Dering. Both East Hampton and Southampton relied on the Sag Harbor Post Office, as neither had post offices of their own. Upon completion of the Arsenal, diagonally across from Dering's home, his son, Henry Thomas Dering, became Sag Harbor's second Postmaster.

In January 1833 a mail route was established between Sag Harbor and New London, Connecticut, by boat across Long Island Sound. Once a week a delivery and pickup was made. The service lasted for only one year because of a difference of opinion regarding the postal rates. The Postmaster General announced that the mail would be rated with postage according to distance of the route the mail was actually sent, and it would be sent on the "most expeditious and frequent route, although the longest, unless the parties in any particular case required a transmission on the short route, in which case postage would be charged according to the distance of said route." It was evident that this met with disapproval, and in December of the same year, the New London-Sag Harbor route was discontinued.

Samuel Phillips, editor of the local newspaper, *The Republican Watchman*, became the third Postmaster and in 1829 moved the post office into his printing establishment on Main Street, opposite the present Municipal Building. Of the 50 post offices on Long Island at that time, Sag Harbor ranked third in importance; Brooklyn being first, and Flushing, second. An Act of Congress in 1836 determined the postage rates and declared that a connection of mail routes throughout the United States would be made. Each letter carried less than 50 miles would cost five cents; 50 to 100 miles, 10 cents; 100 to 200 miles, 15 cents; 200 to 400 miles, 20 cents; 400 to 800 miles, 25 cents; and over 800 miles, 30 cents.

Of all the many men and women who served as Postmasters in the early years, none expressed their patriotism to the degree that Thomas S. Crowell did. Crowell, whose term of office spanned between 1853 and 1861, painted all the call boxes in the post office red, white and blue!

A list of the men and women who served as Postmasters throughout the years is found in the Appendix.

A Description of the Village in 1819

The Reverend Fitch Reed, who was a Methodist minister at Sag Harbor, wrote in an interesting letter of 1819:

> The houses principally stand upon two or three streets, which run back from the water. The streets are not paved, but very sandy, which in dry weather renders them very unpleasant to travel. But in wet weather they are far superior and preferable to even New York. (The New York streets were paved with rough cobblestones, many of which were obtained at Montauk and taken by vessel to the city.)
>
> Sag Harbor has one hundred and fifty houses and seven hundred and fifty inhabitants, two churches, Presbyterian and Methodist, and an Arsenal belonging to the United States, in which are situated the Post Office and the Police Office, this being a port of entry.
>
> The inhabitants have lately obtained from the legislature an act of incorporation with a view of extending the convenience and privileges of the streets. And this when accomplished will render the place far more pleasant. The people are generally better informed than most of the

county. They have a circulating library and a printing office has been established for a number of years, since 1791, from which is issued a weekly paper called the *American Eagle*.

Considering there is but little back country, this place is a place of considerable business. It finds employment for a number of coasting vessels which run to New York, various ports of Connecticut, Boston, and to Southern states. The exports are wood, wheat, leather, rye, corn, oats, flaxseed, fish, etc.. The imports are lumber, stone, brick lime and merchandise of all kinds. There is a convenient harbor for sloops and a little distance from town, for ships and other larger vessels. There is considerable whale fishery carried on from Sag Harbor. Six or eight ships are employed in the service which brings into port from eight hundred to two thousand barrels of oil each year. The oil sells from $15 to $20 a barrel. Each ship, according to size, is manned with eighteen, twenty-four, or thirty hands and employ three, four or five boats, six men to each boat. Provisions are laid in for twelve or eighteen months according to the length of the voyage intended. A great many Indians are employed as hands on board, and it is found necessary to use the utmost caution lest they abscond after they have received many and necessary and convenient articles as part of their pay. In order to prevent this they are taken on board, the ships anchored some distance from shore, and they are not suffered to set their feet on land again. The ships depart in August or September and return the next June or July, but those that go around the Cape Horn into the Pacific Ocean are commonly gone two years.

4

SOCIAL LIFE IN THE EARLY DAYS

Childhood days in early Sag Harbor were times filled with adventure and joy — uncomplicated, carefree, unpretentious. Growing up in a place abounding in ponds for fishing and skating, and woods for hiking and hunting, provided all that any child could possibly desire. After school was over and the daily chores done, the magical time of exploring, pretending, and just "being a child" began.

Childhood Days

Collecting eggs was a favorite pastime, and in those days it was considered acceptable to take a set of bird eggs to add to one's growing collection. Some boys had the eggs of over 200 varieties, from the huge egg of the wild goose to the tiny one of the hummingbird, whose nests could be found in Sleight's Woods.

Ah, Sleight's Woods! What a marvelous spot, overgrown with huge chestnuts and oaks, whose lofty branches provided a shady retreat in the summer for whittling toy whistles or just plain daydreaming. In winter months the snow-covered hills in Sleight's Woods made for some of the best coasting around, and it wasn't essential to have a store-bought sled to enjoy the sport. Wooden crates filled with straw and placed on runners gave the same thrill as they flew down the icy surface of the freshly packed snow. Old farm sleighs pulling groups of children were a common sight, and tradition tells us that Oliver Sleight had a green sleigh with a high back to which any boy could hitch his sled. It wasn't unusual to see eight or ten sleds trailing behind him as he drove his horse and sleigh along the snow-covered streets. And skating. Just about everyone had a pair of skates. Round Pond, Otter Pond, and Mott's Pond (near Rysam Street and since filled in) were always filled to capacity, with the local boys showing off their skills on their steel blades.

When springtime came and the last snow of the season had finally melted, thoughts of other outdoor sports filled the minds of Sag Harbor's youth. Shooting marbles, catching "peepers" in the neighborhood swamp, and of course, baseball were activities of great interest. In the empty lot at High and Bay Streets, the Silver Skates and the Mohawks met in friendly rivalry, each trying to out-hit and out-run the other as their friends and fans cheered them on.

Every summer the circus came to town, usually setting up in a lot at the end of Main Street or at the Old Orchard at Atlantic, Jermain, Division, and Elizabeth Streets. Acrobats, wild animal acts, trained horses and dogs, and clowns, provided thrills and entertainment for old and young alike, and every boy made it a point not to miss watching the tents being raised. Fourth of July brought a day of excitement unequalled. Fireworks held at Sleight's Hill and the firing of the old cannon were events that no child would miss. The fences on both sides of the street on top of the hill were lined with children watching the loading, firing, and swabbing of the old nine-pounder. Parades, picnics and often a Punch and Judy show filled the day from dawn to dusk.

The Suffolk Guard, Sag Harbor's classy military company, marched in all of the parades, and the practice drills held a fascination to every youngster. Dressed in blue swallow-tail coats with shiny brass buttons, crisp white pantaloons and hats that resembled upside-down buckets, they were an inspiring sight to see. To march along beside them, with a trusty stick over his shoulder, a youngster dreamed of someday becoming part of that patriotic group.

Another place that had an almost magical quality was the local shipyard. A child could spend hours watching a vessel being built; the carpenters busily working with axe and adz, shaping the ribs and beams, which in a matter of weeks, grew from a skeleton into a newly fashioned ship. Launching day was a time of great excitement, as with accompanying cheers the vessel would slide into the water with a cloud of spray and then proudly float out into the cove with its flags unfurled.

By the time a boy reached his mid-teens, life took a serious turn. Many signed up for voyages on whaleships, leaving the port as boys and returning two to four years later as men. Adventure beyond belief beckoned and they answered the call. Childhood things were left behind; danger and hardship lay ahead. And if a boy didn't go to sea, cabinetmakers, blacksmiths, shopkeepers and other onshore related industries were always looking for apprentices to learn the trade. Childhood was over; days of play in Sleight's Woods, a thing of the past. But the memories of childhood days in Sag Harbor would remain forever in the hearts of those fortunate enough to have grown up in the area.

Early Education

Attending school in the early days was not required by law, and many children grew up without a formal education. Daughters learned the skills of homemaking from their mothers, and fathers taught their sons a useful trade that would provide them with a means of making a living when they grew to manhood. When they were fortunate enough to attend school, prayers, catechism and hymns were as much a part of their education as reading and writing. It was evident that the schoolmaster was a highly respected individual and certainly of good moral character, for he was entrusted to instill in his students the need for a good moral upbringing. In fact, the schoolmaster stood next to the minister in importance in the community.

THE FIRST SCHOOL

The first building in Sag Harbor constructed for the sole purpose of being a school house was erected in 1786-87. It stood on the corner of Madison and Jefferson Streets on a lot given by Braddock Corey. Several individuals from the area furnished the material for the building, fashioning the clapboard siding, timbers and shingles with their own hands. The structure took two years to complete. Many children had to walk through the woods to reach the place, as it was located on what was then the outskirts of the village.

The old school faced south, with a door at each front end and five or six windows in both the front and rear. The place was neatly papered, for the times, and the wooden floors were scrubbed and sanded with beach sand every Saturday. Heavy wooden shutters that hung at each window were painted green, presenting a sharp contrast against the white clapboard siding. A belfry dignified the primative structure and held what was probably the first public bell east of the Riverhead Courthouse. It was rung not only for school, but for church services, fires, and funerals. Not a Fourth of July passed that the old bell wasn't rung with pride and patriotism. In later years it was cracked and a piece broken from its side, which made its sound clearly distinguishable from other bells in the village.

Within ten years an increase in enrollment made it necessary to construct an addition which doubled the size of the place. The belfry was moved to the center of the building. A huge fireplace stood at each end of the schoolhouse, keeping it warm for classes and other community meetings held there during the winter months. In 1795 Jesse Hedges held the position of schoolmaster, with Samuel L'Hommedieu, Henry P. Dering, and Noah Mason as trustees. Of the approximately 60 students enrolled, many were members of the Jermain, Fordham, Latham, and L'Hommedieu families. Mr. Ishum, Mr. Hedges, Mr. Robinson, and Deacon James Nickerson were four of the teachers employed there.

The old schoolhouse continued to be used for about 85 years, until its dilapidated condition forced its closing. In 1872 Joseph Enos purchased the building and used a good part of the old oak timber, siding, and shutters for a dwelling he was building on Glover Street. The old broken bell, which had tolled for so many years, was sold for junk. In 1882 Stephen French owned the old schoolhouse lot and leased the property to Prentice Mulford and his sisters. The land was cleared and a new two-story house constructed on the site. One of the Mulford sisters lived in the house and carried on a private school there. A list of students who attended classes at the old schoolhouse in 1795 can be found in the Appendix.

THE MIDDLE SCHOOL

In 1804 the second schoolhouse in Sag Harbor was built. Situated on the corner of Church and Sage Streets, it was a private enterprise at its start, with Major John Jermain involved. The building stood two stories high, topped by a cupola with bell. It was known as the Middle School House. The building was later used for the primary department of the Union School. Mr. Aldrich, Miss Babcock, and Miss Terry were three teachers employed there.

The school, which stood in District 23, burned on a cold winter night in 1834. Snow had fallen and a strong northwest wind blew the night of the fire. It was believed that the blaze was caused by a candle left burning by the janitor. Another schoolhouse was built on the site and used until 1871. At that time the building was sold at public auction and moved to the west side of Main Street, on a lot next to Hedges Paint Shop, and became the harness shop of Henry Gillett. The law office of E. Carpenter occupied the second floor. On May 26, 1886 Hedges Paint Shop and the former Middle School building were destroyed by fire. It was, at that time, occupied as a saloon, with the Knights of Labor using the upper floor for their meeting room.

THE OLD YELLOW SCHOOLHOUSE

During the same years a third schoolhouse was built in Sag Harbor. This school stood on Division Street and in the East Hampton Town district of the village. It was known as the Old Yellow School House. After being used for only a few years, it was moved further up the street and remodeled for a private home. Mrs. Jessup, Mrs. Hedges, and Mrs. Merril were three of the teachers employed there.

Early Private Schools

In addition to the public schools in Sag Harbor in the early years, small private schools could be found throughout the village in which a variety of subjects were offered. Many classes were specifically geared to young men and women who wished to be instructed in subjects not available in public schools. Navigation, surveying, advanced mathematics, and languages could be taken for a nominal fee. Some of the classes were held in private homes, others in rented buildings, and some held during evening hours at the school house. Each year the local newspapers contained notices of the classes offered for those interested in furthering their education.

> Mr. Moody, in 1804, stated that if sufficient encouragement occurs, he would open a 4 o'clock school for young ladies at which composition, grammar, arithmetic, geography, etc. would be taught, with instruction in geography using a terrestrial globe to facilitate improvement on that very important and agreeable study. Those who wished to avail themselves of this opportunity of bestowing upon their daughters the most valuable legacy in their power, an education, will apply to Henry P. Dering, Asa Partridge, Thomas Ripely, or Silas Howell, for particulars.

Another private school was Miss Leigh's School For Young Ladies, held in the house then occupied by Augustus Sleight on upper Main Street. The following advertisement appeared in *The Suffolk Gazette:*

> Miss Leigh wishes to establish a respectable school in which young ladies may be instructed in both the solid and ornamental branches of an English formal education, and to limit the number of pupils so as to enable her to do strict justice to every patron, and effectually to promote the real improvement of every pupil. In the solid branches she will be assisted by a gentlemen whose qualifications for this undertaking are well known to be fully competent. Terms, which are moderate, and other

particulars, may be known when the school opens, or by going to Mrs. Worth's Millinery Store on the Main Street.

In 1807 Solomon Parker opened a school in the lower room of the new schoolhouse for the education of youth on Monday the seventh of September. The advertisement said:

> Solomon Parker will attend at the usual hours of teaching for the term of one quarter. He informs all those young gentlemen who are possessed of enterprise, and have a wish to render themselves qualified for the Navy of the United States or for the Merchant's Service, that on Monday the 5th of October, will open a school of mathematics, taught Monday, Tuesday, Wednesday, Thursday and Friday, six to nine PM. The true principles of Navigation and Surveying, Geometry, Trigonometry, the use of the Plain and Gunter's Scales. Also Navigation by inspection and by logarythms, both by Middle Latitude and Mercator's Sailing; both single and double altitudes, the use of the Nautical Ephemeris and the practical use of measuring the angular distance of the celestial objects for determining longitude.

Another private school advertised in the February 23, 1807 issue of *The Suffolk Gazette* stated:

> A School will commence on Tuesday in a room of the house occupied by Mr. William Hall, in which will be taught reading, writing, arithmetic, English Grammar, Geography, and Latin and Greek languages. It is confidently hoped that the strict and assiduous attending of the instructor will render the school an object worthy of the patronage of the public. Signed, C.H. Havens.

The April 14, 1810 *Suffolk Gazette* advertised two more private schools.

> Mr. Isaac Chapel will open a school in the east apartment of the Upper School House on Monday next. Mr. Chapel has recommendations from some of the most respectable characters in New London, Connecticut, as a good instructor.

> Also, Isaac Morehouse will begin a 4 o'clock school. To acquire correct grammatical habits and become familiar with the various other useful and ornamental parts of an English education, is incalculably correct. Impressed with this idea, the subscriber purposes to open a 4 o'clock school on May 1st in the upper room of the Union School House at which will be taught reading, writing, arithmetic, English Grammar, orthography, composition, etc. Price of tuition as low as possible.

In October 1847 a "Select School" opened in Military Hall over the Post Office, taught by Augustus Foster, past principal of Hill's Academy. The subjects offered were common and higher English branches, languages, and higher mathematics. One could register for these classes by paying five dollars per quarter.

Building Churches

Apparently the early settlers of Sag Harbor were not overly zealous when it came to religion, for although the settlement started its gradual growth in the late 1730s, three decades passed before there was any thought of building a church. In reality, it was a meeting house used not only for church services but also for town meetings, concerts, and any other community event that required a large meeting room.

THE OLD BARN MEETING HOUSE

Varied sources give slightly different accounts of the building of that first church, and three versions follow. The first is taken from the December 8, 1859 issue of *The Sag Harbor Express*.

> It doesn't appear that any church or religious society existed in Sag Harbor previous to 1791. It is true that a public building was erected for divine worship, but it will be recalled that our Puritan ancestors did not attach any sacredness to the place for public worship, but used it as sort of a town hall, for town meetings, elections, and all public purposes and called it the Meeting House. Over sixty years elapsed from the first settlement of the place before any religious society was organized and then it consisted of only four members. Nine years later it had increased to fifteen. In 1791 the present Presbyterian Society was formed by two men and two women. By 1800 there were only eleven additional members, and in 1809, thirteen members.

The second account, taken from Reverend Clarence Hall Wilson's *Historical Address of 1916*, stated:

> On February 24, 1766, a public meeting was held to consult upon the affairs of erecting a house for public worship at Sag Harbor. At this first meeting it was voted to "get timber and erect the house as soon as conveniency will admit." The church was founded in 1766, but as Reverend Wilson stated, "What does it mean to found a church?" Who its members and officers were, we do not know. There was no record

of a minister until 1789 when the congregation was called to worship by the beat of drum, and one of the members read a sermon.

The third account was copied from an ancient document printed in *The Sag Harbor Express* of July 12, 1866.

The start of a church: At a meeting of the inhabitants of Sagg Harbour, Hog Neck, and adjacent places, February ye 24th 1766, in order to consult upon the affairs of erecting a House for Publick Worship at Sagg Harbour. After solomn prayer and deliberation upon the important affair, the following conclusion was consented to and voted; viz:

1. That we erect a house as soon as conveniency will admit.
2. That a committee be chosen to inspect and direct as may be needful as to getting timber. Taking an account and making record of what labor is superscribed, and what timber produced and of whom and what in value as also to labor.
3. That in case any difficulty or dispute arise, the same shall be referred to and decided by Mr. Foster of Southampton, Maltby Gelston of Bridgehampton, and William Hedges of East Hampton as a committee for that purpose.
4. That a subscription paper be drawn in order for signing by the inhabitants of Sagg Harbour, Hog Neck, and adjacent places, to know what they contribute respectively toward erecting and finishing said house, either by money, labor or necessary materials.
5. That another paper be drawn up to request the charitable donations of friends abroad to help us by money or necessary materials for promoting and toward finishing said building.
6. Voted that this house be especially appropriated and improved for the public worship of God as designed for the ministerial labors of an Orthodox preacher regularly introduced and approved of such according to the Presbyterian plan and scheme of such government as now practiced upon in this county. The members of the meeting elected the following men: Joseph Conkling, James Howell, Captain Nathan Fordham, John Mitchell and Constant Havens.

The old Meeting House was a plain framed building without spire or tower, of ample dimensions, and covered with shingles. It stood on the northeast corner of Church and Sage Streets, with the southerly front on a green over which Church and Sage Streets now run. The interior was without ceiling or plaster, and swallows built their nests among the rafters and flew overhead during the lengthy sermons. Throughout the building were old-fashioned square pews. The pulpit, built on what was known as the "pepper box plan," had a huge sounding board overhead and a deacon's bench beneath. A gallery was built around three sides, and under the stairs leading to it were seats for the "colored" people, most of whom were slaves at that time.

A parishioner of those early days spoke of how the young people strolled about the woods on the Sabbath, picking blackberries and whortleberries that grew in abundance, and as soon as they heard the drum calling the people to worship, would scamper through the bushes up to the church and into the gallery where the ladies would seat themselves wherever they could find a clean spot left by the swallows overhead. Their beaus would climb to the more elevated seats above the pulpit and amuse themselves looking down at the congregation during the service.

For the first 20 years the church was without a pastor, and prominent members would read lengthy sermons to the congregation. The first preacher, John Taylor, arrived in 1789 and preached alternately between Sag Harbor and Shelter Island. About 1790 a revival took place, and a Congregational form of worship was soon established. For several years stated supplies—as the interim preachers were called—occupied the pulpit, James Richards and Nehemiah B. Cook, being two of them.

Reverend Daniel Hall, ordained in 1797, was the first settled minister to serve the church, remaining until the spring of 1806. Reverend Nathaniel S. Prime arrived in October of that same year, fresh from his theological studies. While in Sag Harbor he married Julia Ann Jermain, daughter of Major John Jermain. She organized one of the first Sunday schools in the United States. Prime left in 1809 and a year later the church adopted the Presbyterian form of government.

It was during those years discussions first took place concerning replacing the old Meeting House with a more substantial place of worship. In October 1807 an unidentified parishoner wrote a letter to the editor of the local newspaper, *The Suffolk Gazette*, hoping to stir up the residents of the village to consider it their duty to provide a new and decent place in which to worship God. He wrote:

> One meeting after another was held during the winter months of 1806, until all but four residents of the community agreed to demolish the old meeting house and build a new church. But when the weather broke the following Spring, and the ice on the bay melted, every man ran to his vessel or store and talk of the new church was drowned in the din of worldly business. After that, hardly a word was mentioned about building the church unless it was on a rainy Sabbath when drops of water

fell on the heads of those worshipping. No progress had been made at all.

The new frame, expected to be raised by that time had not even been started. Not a board! Not a shingle! Nothing! Why was it so difficult to raise money for the service of the Lord when $25,000 was obtained with little difficulty when it came to building a new whale ship? Many houses in the village were large, comfortable and stylish, but the house of God, inconvenient and leaky. Bats and swallows made their nests in the rafters. A new school house had just been built, neatly painted and furnished with a bell and tower that stood above the roof of the church. How shameful that the citizens of Sag Harbor felt unable to raise money for a new sanctuary. Let the material be sent for NOW, this Fall, before another year's delay. Let all the parishioners come forward with his pen in one hand and his purse in the other and make a liberal offering to the building of God's house.

Unfortunately, it was a plea that fell on deaf ears, for ten more years would pass before the new church became a reality. In January 1817 the local newspaper reported that on January 13th the citizens of the village tore down the old Meeting House for the purpose of erecting a new one. The job was done in two days without incident.

Mary L. Gardiner, wife of John D. Gardiner, pastor at that time, described her feeling of despair as she watched from her window in the manse on the corner of Madison and Sage Streets, as the building was demolished.

> I saw the first shingle torn from the roof. I watched the taking down of the building—heard the cheers when the last "long pull" told that the old fabric was demolished. As I sat by my window my tears flowed, for I felt the glory of the first temple dedicated to God in this village would never again be beheld.

The old Meeting House was gone.

THE 1817 PRESBYTERIAN CHURCH

A committee, consisting of Henry P. Dering, Asa Partridge, Silas Howell, Cornelius Sleight, John Osborn, Samuel Huntting, and Pardon Tabor, was formed to receive proposals for framing and raising the new church in the Port of Sag Harbor. The proposed building was to be 166 feet in length, 44 feet wide, have posts 26 feet high and a steeple 54 feet tall. The timbers were to be of oak, spruce, and chestnut, hewn and dressed on the spot. At the same time proposals were received to make windows, frames and sashes, with all work to be completed by April 1, 1817. The new building was to be constructed on the site of the recently torn-down Meeting House. The contract drawn up specified the following:

> Articles of agreement made and concluded this 10th day of January 1817 by Silas Howell and Cornelius Sleight in behalf of the Parish of Sag Harbor on the one part, and Samuel Schellinger, Eliab Byram and Pardon Tabor, on the other part, witnesses. That the said Schellinger, Byram and Tabor, for the consideration herein mentioned, have agreed and do hereby agree that they will frame and erect a church of the following dimensions—to say, one hundred sixty-six feet in length, forty-four feet in width, twenty-six feet in height and a steeple fifty-four feet high, in a way that such buildings are usually done in a good faithful workmanship manner, as is now fully explained in the draft herewith, also to make thirty-seven window frames and sashes to receive them to contain thirty lights of ten by eight glass each, also two circular windows and one oval window. The dimensions of which three are not particularly understood, but we agree to make them according to the directions of Silas Howell and C. Sleight, with pullies for the sash of each window for _____ , and the said Howell and Sleight in behalf of the appointed Parish on their part do hereby agree that they will furnish the timber for the said House, ready on the spot, but it is understood and agreed that all the timbers now in the old house is to be worked as far as is necessary in framing the new building, and the hewing and developing that it may require for the purpose is to be done at the expense of the contractor.
>
> And the said Schellinger, Byram and Tabor, agree to leave the said House framed and raised by the _____ with the frames and sashes completed by the same time.
>
> For the faithful performance of the several contractors and agreements the parties do hereby respectively bind themselves and their respective heirs and assignees each to the other in the sum of _____ and in testimony where of they have herewith set their Hand and Seal this day and a year before written.
>
> (No dollar amounts had been written in, so this may not have been the final contract.)

It was apparent that plans progressed more slowly than anticipated, and summer arrived before work was finally underway. To complicate matters, a quantity of lumber intended to be used was destroyed in the disastrous fire of

May 26, 1817—a fire that consumed the most valuable part of the village. Faced with this unexpected emergency, an appeal went out for financial assistance. Reverend Gardiner headed west and Deacon Augustus Sleight east, where they solicited aid from churches throughout the Island, New York City, and New Jersey. With those contributions and additional donations from local residents, work on the church resumed. When completed, it was said to have been the most elegant church on the east end of Long Island. Its total cost was $4700.

The text of Reverend Gardiner's dedicatory sermon on June 18, 1818, "Hitherto the Lord Hath Helped Us and the Fire Consumed it Not," was so appropriate that it was painted in gold letters over the south entrance of the church and remained there until the building was sold to the Episcopal Society and the door removed.

In 1833 the Presbyterians built a Session House on the northwest corner of Church and Sage Streets and directly across from the 1817 church. Used only briefly as their lecture hall and session house, the building was sold soon after the 1844 church was built on Union Street, and in 1856 it became the Village Hall. The ancient structure, in remarkably well-preserved condition, still stands on its original site. It is one of the village's earliest public buildings in existence and, today, is the home of the Sag Harbor Fire Museum.

THE METHODIST EPISCOPAL CHURCH
At first, Methodism was confined exclusively to the western part of Long Island, and it was not until after the American Revolution that traveling preachers ventured this far east. The earliest record of the Methodist faith being practiced in Sag Harbor was in 1807-08. At the beginning of 1809 Moses Clark and Stillman Eldredge of Sag Harbor and James Raynor and James Snowden of Southampton, having no other place than a private home in which to worship, united their efforts for the purpose of building a Methodist Church. These four men went about raising the money to build the church on a piece of land on Union Street donated by Moses Clark.

A Methodist Society was organized at Clark's home in March 1810, according to the order and discipline of the Methodist Episcopal Church in the United States. The first members consisted of Moses and Betsy Clark, James and Ursula Snowden, James Raynor, Stillman Eldredge, Charles and Dorcas Smith, James Halsey, Sally Latham and Ann Raynor. Five of the members were selected to act as trustees and carry out plans to erect the church. In May 1811 the frame of the building was purchased in Connecticut, and three months later it arrived at Sag Harbor. After enclosing the place, it was ready for worship. It was a plain structure and members of the congregation brought their own seats, foot stoves, and tallow candles. Later, when a cast iron stove was added, each member brought a stick of wood to feed the fire on cold wintery days. A circuit preacher served the needs of the congregation, the first regular one being Reverend Henry Redstone.

Membership grew slowly. In 1812 there were 22, and after five years, 16 more had joined. At a meeting of the male members held on January 12, 1818, it was voted to send out Stillman Eldredge on a tour to collect money to try to rid the church of its debt. Eldredge was allowed seven shillings each weekday as compensation for his services, and a horse was purchased for him to use while performing his duties. Apparently, the plan was successful, for the debt was paid, the interior of the sanctuary finished off, and galleries added to each side.

It was the custom in those days when evening meetings were held for each member to bring along their own candle in order to light the interior of the church. These "tallow dips" required snuffing every few minutes, and the brethren were constantly jumping up to the snuff them. As snuffers were not always handy, they sometimes used the more convenient but less elegant way of pinching off the wicks, and many a luckless brother had scorched his fingers trying to shed more light on the meeting. Occasionally, a gust of wind from the open door would blow them all out and leave the place in darkness till they could be lighted again. The story goes that certain suspiciously loud "smacks" could be heard in different parts of the building in the vicinity of whispering lovers' seats, until the place was no longer in darkness.

Organizations and Societies

Since early times Sag Harbor has been a socially active community with lodges, clubs and societies of all types and descriptions emerging throughout the years.

The first known society in Sag Harbor was a group organized before 1800, known as the Infidels. Their object: to attack Christianity. One would imagine that most of the early residents would have had a strong religious faith, but apparently there were some who did not. Reverend Clarence Wilson, pastor of the Presbyterian Church from 1887–1902, conducted a study on the religious beliefs of the early residents and stated:

> The founders of Sag Harbor were enterprising, energetic and capable, but not strong on piety. Very few of the businessmen and ship workers were professing Christians. Those who were aboard ship learned that

for them there was no Sabbath. The business of taking whales did not stop on Sunday—work went on the same as any other day. In fact, some of the seamen who experienced religion and refused to work on Sunday, lost their positions.

The Infidels held regular meetings in the village for several years until membership finally dropped, and at that time the society disbanded.

The Hampton Lodge No. 111 F & AM was the first fraternal organization in Sag Harbor. It was established on July 26, 1804 and at that time there was no other civic society in existence. The first officers were Elias Jones, Master; Ithuel Hill, Senior Warden; Joel Fordham, Jr., Warden; Moses Clark, Treasurer; Benjamin K. Hobart, Secretary; John Godbee, Deacon; Aaron Clark, Jr., Deacon, and John Morrison, Tyler. Five of those men were masters of vessels tied up at the wharf. The Masons were honored with special attention, and whenever they appeared together in public, schools were dismissed and places of business closed to see the Masons parade. After 1815 an anti-Masonic sentiment spread throughout the state. Politics had become unwisely linked with the society, and interest in the lodge declined. In 1819 the chapter was surrendered and the association disbanded.

For the next forty years no Masonic Society was found in Sag Harbor. Then in 1856 four former lodge members joined with others interested and started Wamponamon Lodge F & AM No. 437. The four were Jacob Leek, Thaddeus Coles, Nathan Y. Fordham and Noah Washburn. After much thought and discussion a name suggested by Nathaniel Dominy was selected for the lodge: "Wamponamon," meaning "to the eastward."

Meetings were held in the Odd Fellows' Hall on the west side of Main Street in the Lawrence Building. On July 1, 1869 they moved to the third floor of the Nassau House. After this building burned in the great fire of 1877, it was rebuilt and used until the Masons purchased the building that had been the second church of the Presbyterian Society and, later, Christ Episcopal Church. On February 7, 1884 the congregation of Christ Church held their last service in the place that had been their sanctuary for the last 38 years. The furniture and organ were removed from the building and put into storage. Near the end of February 1884 work had begun on the renovation under the supervision of George H. Post of Southampton, a member of the lodge. The alterations consisted of removing the steeple, installing new sills and stone, making lodge rooms on the gallery floor, building an annex on the north side for a stairway and entrance, reconstructing the main hall for public use, and laying a new floor, ceiling, papering and painting. The committee raised $4000 to cover the expenses. Luther L. Sherman was in charge of the outside work, and George Post, the interior work. On July 8, 1884 the newly remodeled hall opened with a festival celebrating the grand opening. This building was used by the Masons until they purchased the summer home of Mrs. Russell Sage for their temple. The sign on the front of the Masonic Temple was made in August 1922. Ivan C. Byram designed and painted the words "Masonic Temple" after George H. Cleveland cut the letters. Richard Smith of East Hampton gilded it with gold leaf, preparing it for the formal dedication on September 21, 1922.

A Literary Society was organized in Sag Harbor February 9, 1807. Its constitution stated that all members were to treat each other with decency and respect. The group was to "consist of disputation, composition, declamation and examination upon geography, astronomy, and such other exercises as a majority shall appoint." The treasurer's duties, along with handling the dues and other financial matters, included providing stationery, fuel, and candles.

Among the officers was a critic whose duties included criticising all compositions and declamations. An elaborate system of fines ranging from two cents to 12½ cents was set up, and members could be tried for gambling or intoxication and fined for each offense. They also stressed that no meeting would ever be held in a tavern.

A Moral Society formed in January 1817, the object of which was to promote morality and suppress vice, particularly intemperance, profaneness and Sabbath-breaking. Samuel L'Hommedieu was moderator, and Augustus Sleight, clerk. The first officials elected were: Stephen Howell, President; Thomas Ripley, Treasurer; Samuel L'Hommedieu, Moses Clark, Joseph Crowell, Stillman Eldredge, Hugh Gelston, Henry Packer Dering, and David Clark, the executive committee. This society may well have been the forerunner of the Temperance Society which was established in the 1820s.

5

SAG HARBOR'S PART IN THE WARS

In the late eighteenth century, life in Sag Harbor was good. Businesses prospered and the wharf had become the center of activity. As a seaport Sag Harbor had come into her own and was second only to New York City in importance. Products from farm, forest, and sea were shipped to major cities in the eastern United States and ports in the West Indies. Unfortunately, this rosy picture was not to last, as the country plunged into war, a war that was to have devastating effect on Sag Harbor and the rest of the Island.

The Revolutionary War

In February 1776 the Eastern Regiment formed, comprised of nine companies of men from the Hamptons and Sag Harbor. Colonel Mulford was in command. A regiment of Minute Men under Colonel Smith was also established, and a number of these volunteers took part in the August 1776 Battle of Long Island. After that disastrous confrontation, patriotism quickly diminished. The British gained full possession of the Island and held it tightly for seven long years. Many families fled to Connecticut to escape persecution, and Onderdonk's *Revolutionary Incidents* noted that on September 15, 1776 the wharves at Sag Harbor were crowded with immigrants awaiting passage across the Sound. Captain Zebulon Cooper made several trips across to Connecticut and on one such trip transported 63 persons, ten cows, two horses, 30 sheep, 17 hogs, and 33 loads of household goods. The local citizens left behind as few of their possessions as possible, knowing that what they left would be claimed by the British.

Those who remained in Sag Harbor and other places on the East End suffered tremendous losses as they were robbed, plundered and forced to feed and house the soldiers of the Crown. Homes and stores were taken over, and when money and supplies were demanded, the residents were obliged to provide them. Being subjected to British rule, they were forced to take an oath of allegiance to King George III or risk becoming prisoners of war.

The British set up a strong garrison and naval blockade preventing the Port of Sag Harbor from sending supplies to the American army. Their fort was located on Meeting House Hill and was described as "a breastwork, enlarged and strengthened by palisades." Officers were quartered in the house and tavern of James Howell, which stood on the site of the present American Hotel. Here they were close enough to have full view of their vessels anchored in the harbor. Barracks were set up on Madison Street, near Sage Street, and the village was held tightly and securely by the enemy. Sag Harbor was a convenient center for collecting supplies, and it was easy to distribute them from this point. The British Navy took over the port without resistance, and their presence in the village paralyzed commerce, discouraged industry, and impoverished the residents.

A quantity of provisions and material were collected at Sag Harbor by the British forces stationed here. In retaliation for the burning of Danbury and Ridgefield in Connecticut, General Parsons devised a plan by which they would surprise the British troops in Sag Harbor by making a swift attack and destroying the supplies held by them. Parsons discussed the plan with Lieutenant Colonel Return Jonathan Meigs, a veteran of Bunker Hill and a prisoner of war in Quebec for a year. The plan was put into effect on May 21, 1777.

Embarking from New Haven with 234 men in 13 whaleboats, Meigs proceeded to Guilford, Connecticut where they encountered a two-day wait due to rough seas. On the afternoon of May 23rd he left Guilford with 170 men and a convoy of two armed sloops. Upon arrival on Long Island about 6 o'clock in the evening, they carried their boats over a narrow neck of land at East Marion and to the bay between the north and south fork. They continued on across the bay, landing at midnight in the vicinity of the Noyac side of Long Beach. After securing their boats in nearby woods, 130 men marched toward Sag Harbor.

A stop was made at the house of Silas Edwards on Brickkiln Road, the place then being occupied by the British and used as a hospital. Two guards were captured and forced to lead the detatchment to the home of James Howell on Main Street, where the British commanding officer had been staying. There he was arrested as he lay in his bed.

At the fort on Union and Madison Streets where the Old Burying Ground stands, Meigs and his attachment attacked, and a small skirmish ensued in which six of the enemy were killed and 53 captured. From there they proceeded to the Long Wharf where they were exposed to fire from an armed schooner of 12 guns and 70 men. The raiders suffered no casualties and succeeded in setting fire to 12 British brigs and sloops which were anchored in the bay. Ninety enemy sailors were captured, along with 120 tons of hay, ten hogs-head of rum, and a large quantity of grain and merchandise. Accomplishing what they set out to do, Meigs, his men, and the prisoners marched back to the whaleboats and returned to Connecticut. The entire expedition took just 25 hours, and they completed their mission without a single casualty.

This raid of Colonel Meigs was considered of such great importance that General Washington, upon hearing the result, sent a letter of congratulations to General Parsons, and Congress voted that Meigs be presented with a sword.

Following the Battle of Long Island and the hostile occupation by the British, many of the active participants in the war thought it unsafe to stay in the area. Out of the 32 homes in the village, 14 of Sag Harbor's most patriotic men and their families left Long Island in fear of their lives. Nearly one-third of the fighting force fled from a weakened and falling Long Island to help strengthen the forces in Connecticut. Those who left were: Edward Conkling to Stonington, Daniel Fordham to Saybrook, Ephraim Fordham to Saybrook, George Fordham and Nathan Fordham to East Haddam, Obediah Gildersleeve to New Haven, Dr. Jeremiah Hedges and John Hudson to Stonington, Colonel John Hulbert to East Haddam, and also Obediah Jones, Samuel L'Hommedieu, Silas Norris and David Sayre.

Henry P. Hedges, in a speech before the Sag Harbor Historical Society on January 18, 1909, summed up the misery and oppression suffered by the citizens of Sag Harbor when he said:

> At what cost of privation Sag Harbor obtained independence; the victor's hostile flag floated before the eyes of her native born freemen. The victor's shout of triumph saluted their ears. Her wharves, stores, and houses held by her adversaries. Her shipping gone. Her trade ruined. The products of her fields siezed by her foes and often robbed by professional friends. The aged and infirm and sick, dying and dead, without

medical relief. Her sons fugitives in the armies of liberty and privateers, that heroically assailed their enemy, or in prison ships or dungeons. Her daughters subjected to the approach of soldiers of a garrison whose desire was their dishonor, whose every victory brought them nearer to the gate of dispair. All threatened with gaunt famine and all last to look on the returning ships of their country's foes and last to re-echo the glad hurrah for freedom and independence gained.

When the British sailed from New York they took thousands of royalists, born Americans, with them, but not one from Sag Harbor. Her sons and daughters remained true to the cause of freedom and independence. After the close of the war, the majority of those living in exile returned home to pick up the pieces of their shattered lives. Suffering heavy losses and encountering many changes, a great deal of time passed before a normal life was again possible. After seven long years of devastation under British rule, freedom and peace had finally been realized, and with grit and determination they united their energies and skills, revived commerce, re-established their homes and businesses, and began to look ahead to a new era of growth in the village of Sag Harbor.

Some local men who took part in the American Revolution were: Edward Conkling, Joseph Conkling, Daniel Fordham, Ephraim Fordham, George Fordham, Nathan Fordham, Joseph Foster, Jeremiah Gardiner, Obediah Gildersleeve, Philip Gildersleeve, Dr. Jeremiah Hedges, John Hudson, Colonel John Hulbert, Isaac Jessup, Zebulon Jessup, Obediah Jones, Samuel L'Hommedieu, Silas Norris, John Paine, Silas Paine, Silas Rugg, and David Sayre.

Early Military Companies

The residents of Sag Harbor survived the Revolutionary War, but peace was not to be theirs for long. In June 1806, with the threat of another war likely, the local citizens organized its first volunteer military company under the command of Major John Jermain. Officers elected were: Lodowick Post, lieutenant; Alden Spooner, Wickham Sayre, Franklin Davall and Ezekiel Jones, sergeants; Pardon T. Tabor, Erastus Glover, Elijah Simons and Eliab Byram, corporals; Henry B. Havens, drummer; and Lothrop Slate, fifer. With a great deal of pride and patriotism they marched in the local parades, and for the first few years carried their old muskets, as their new artillery cannon had not yet arrived.

The Suffolk Gazette of July 1807 carried the following notice: "Attention Soldiers. The uniformed artillerists are hereby invited to meet, complete with musket, at Eldredge's Coffee House in Sag Harbor, on the Fourth of July, 9 A.M., to unite in the celebration of America's Independence, by request of the Captain. A. Spooner, Sergeant." Fifteen years of service in the artillery company excused the volunteer from military duty for the rest of his life.

The military company of the 1830s and 40s was known as the Suffolk County Guards. This classy outfit was said to have been the crowning glory of Sag Harbor. It was, for the most part, made up of local men who didn't go to sea during the whaling years. The riggers, shipwrights, sailmakers, and others who worked land jobs took it upon themselves to form this company whose main duty was to care for the cannon that had been used in the War of 1812 and stored in the Arsenal.

When parades were held, they marched resplendent in their blue swallow-tailed coats with shiny brass buttons, white pantaloons and cockade hats. They paraded with drawn swords instead of muskets. Henry and Job Webb, gunners, rode upon the ordnance drawn by two horses. Captain Daniel Y. Bellows was in command, a rotund man who when dressed in uniform was the picture of martial pomposity. As they marched, they dragged behind them the little nine-pound cannon. To the Guards it was a piece of equipment held in reverence and awesome respect, and regardless of its size, they thought, in all honesty, their little nine-pounder would protect the village from any foe. Crowds would gather about when it was loaded and wait in anticipation for the moment of its discharge. Then a round of applause and cheers burst forth as the shot was fired.

Quite a group gathered when the Guards held their training drills. To watch them in action was a thrilling experience for the boys and girls of the village. A fife and drum supplied the music, the fife being played by Sidney Hallock, whose animated and persistant repetition of the march "Jefferson and Liberty" often provoked from the boys on the sidewalk the command, "Change that tune, Mr. Hallock!" After completing their maneuvers they would march through the village and around the liberty pole in single file, much to the delight of the spectators.

The artillerists disbanded in 1846, following the outbreak of the Mexican War, after almost 40 years of active service in Sag Harbor. The Suffolk County Guards were a proud and patriotic group of men who were ready to fight, but never did.

Remembering the Suffolk Guard

The following story is taken from the reminiscences of Sag Harbor's philosopher Prentice Mulford, as he recalled his boyhood fascination with the Suffolk Guards.

The crowning glory of our village in bygone times was its volunteer military company the Suffolk Guards. To miss seeing the training of the Guards was an incomparable misfortune in a boy's life. The Guard was an artillery company and used to drag after them on parade, a nine pound gun. In our estimation that gun could have prevented the largest fleet in the world from entering our harbor. It was stored in the Arsenal.

Sometimes we stole in that dark, dingy apartment where it was kept. That gun and carriage was no inanimate piece of machinery with us. It was a material connecting link between Bunker Hill, New Orleans and our own stale times, because there was no war and seemingly nothing to make any history. We touched it timidly and with reverence. So we did the balls lying about, with which it was loaded. What volumes of unwritten history, mystery and conjecture there are in the brains of a seven year old child. We ran away from school regularly on training day. It mattered not how hard the consequent thrashing might be, nothing could resist those bright swords, gilt epaulettes, blue coats, brass buttons and music.

For a boy to do any little service for the Guards; to be sent on an errand; to get a high private a glass of water; even to be addressed by a member in uniform was deemed an honor inexpressible in words. Some boys were allowed to help serve and fill cartridges. These, with us, had taken high degrees; had begun to leave the era of boydom and enter that of manhood.

The brass band always accompanied the Guard on parade. One air that the band used to play still lingers with me. It was called the "Swiss March." I think they could play it better than anything else. At all events they played it a great deal. They had a big bass drum. I have heard greater bands and greater bass drums since, but theirs after all was not the imposing performance of our band and bass drum. It intoxicated me.

A boy has a distinctive dislike for shams, he demands realities. We always wanted the Guards to go to war. We wanted them to go much more eagerly than the Guards did themselves. We didn't care what they warred with or what they warred for, but we knew those bright swords were made for cutting and that nine pound iron balls were cast to be shot into the British. In imagination we never fought any but the British in those days.

There was one English boy in our village. We regarded him with suspicion and hostility. He did get into our juvenile military company, but it was under protest of the most vigilant patriots. It was thought he might be a spy. He managed, however, to ingratiate himself with us by his skill and taste in the fabrication of paper military hats. Besides he said he had once seen the Queen and spoken to her, so we let him train. Those paper chapeaus were gorgeous with gilt and ribbon. The first I ever wore was taken off my head as I stood in the ranks by a mischievous gust of wind and deposited in a washtub nearby, half full of blue suds. It was irretrievably in a second. Military discipline was momentarily forgotten and the whole company, from the Captain, laughed — I cried. But I couldn't train any more that day. They put me out of the rank. Military honors depended largely upon the show a boy could make. The Captain of our company owed his position entirely to the possession of a scabbardless sword and a chapeau with gilt tassels. The legend ran that these trappings belonged to his grandfather who had fought a large part of the Revolution with them.

I suppose that most of the Guards are dead by this time, but they never surrendered. They disbanded with a suspicious suddenness at the breaking out of the Mexican War.

The Embargo and Fortification

In 1807, with war again looming on the horizon, a measure to place a ban on all foreign commerce was recommended by President Thomas Jefferson, and on December 22nd it was enacted by Congress. It stated that all American vessels were forbidden to sail for foreign ports but were permitted to engage in coastal trade after posting bonds equal to twice the value of their ships and cargo as a guarantee of the compliance with the embargo. Foreign vessels were allowed to depart from the United States carrying ballast only.

The principal intent of the act was to compel Great Britain and France to discontinue their interference with the trade of the United States. It had, however, little effect and brought the prosperity of the States to a precipitous halt. New York, including Sag Harbor, were hard hit, and freedom of the seas for American ships and their cargoes would be achieved only after America's victory in the War of 1812. The following notice appeared in the local newspaper, *The Suffolk Gazette*:

EMBARGO
United States Treasury Department
December 22, 1807

Mr. Henry T. Dering:
Sir: Congress this day passed an act prohibiting the sailing of ships or vessels from the ports and harbors of the United States to any foreign

port or harbor—copy of which is hereto annexed; and to which your particular and immediate attention is required.

Give notice of this act, on the day on which you will receive this letter, to all foreign vessels in your district; and take efficient measures to prevent their taking any additional cargo on board, such as provisions and stores as are necessary for their voyage only excepted.

No vessel whose departure for foreign ports is prohibited by the act and which are yet within the jurisdiction of the United States, must be permitted to depart, even though they had previously obtained clearance.

The instruction given in relation to the embargo of 1794 may, so far as they are applicable, be followed until you shall receive further instructions.

> I am respectfully your obedient servant,
> Albert Gallatin

A large meeting of the citizens of the Port of Sag Harbor convened on the 14th of January 1808 for the purpose of taking into consideration the dangerously exposed situation of the harbor and to ask the government for some means of defense in the event of war. At the opening of the meeting, Captain John Jermain addressed the chair.

Mr. Chairman: I rise to address you on a subject in which I feel sensibly interested and in which we are each and all of us equally concerned. We find from the measures of our government and the facts that have reached our knowledge, that there is just cause of alarm. We see those of our citizens who lie immediately exposed to the fury and devouring flames of an enemy, petitioning Congress for some means of defense. Are not our families, our lives and our property as dear to us as theirs to them? I admit that the city of New York lies exposed to ships of war but are we not equally exposed to those ships, tenders and barges, and yet without the least means of defense? I hope I feel in some degree a just sense of the trust and confidence which my country has placed me, in giving me the honor to command a company of Artillery; and in my humble opinion (if I may be allowed to use the expression of an honorable member of Congress) "as good men for war as ever God created," native Americans, whose bosoms are fired with the love of their Country, which will always prompt freemen to meet any danger or any enemy who attempts to invade their rights. But notwithstanding, we are blest with those principles and these nerves, you do not wish us to meet the mouth of our enemies cannon with these naked hands! No, Mr.

Chairman, you are perfectly sensible to the defenseless situation of our port, and therefore I move that we now appoint a committee to prepare a petition to the constituted authorities of our country, praying for some adequate means of defense. We have valuable property to protect. There is belonging to this port 6000 tons of shipping. During the last season there was brought into this port 7218 barrels of whale oil, 6600 quintals of cod fish and 150 barrels of fish oil. Our stores are within one mile of sufficient depth of water for ships of war. We cannot defend ourselves with muskets, and government have not furnished us with a single piece of cannon. Believe me when I assure you, sir, that if we can be placed in a situation to meet an enemy, I feel confident that we shall never disgrace the name of American soldiers, American seamen or American citizens; but we will endeavor honorably to discharge that trust which our country have right to claim, and afford that protection which our port or citizens look for and have a right to expect from us.

John Jermain, Captain

It was resolved that a committee of nine be appointed to contact the constituted authorities of the United States for assistance to protect the harbor, which was in a defenseless situation. The nine appointed were: Stephen Howell, Ebenezer Sage, Eliah Hones, Henry P. Dering, John Jermain, Stephen Mitchell, Cornelius Sleight, Samuel L'Hommedieu and John N. Fordham. A month later the committee was informed that the government ordered a survey of the harbor to be made regarding its fortification. It was decided that an arsenal should be built in Sag Harbor: a place to house a cannon and other stores to be used in the event of attack.

The Arsenal

Between the years 1796 and 1806 approximately 2000 American seamen were seized, subjected to illegal impressment, and forced to serve on British ships. With the arrival of the new century, threats of another war became greater and greater, and the Arsenal was built on Union Street next to the present Presbyterian Church at the north end of the Old Burying Ground.

The Suffolk Gazette of March 31, 1810 ran a notice stating that anyone interested in contracting the job to send in their bid. Proposals were accepted until the 20th of April. The contract read:

> Articles of Agreement, made this fifteenth day of June in the year of our Lord one thousand eight hundred and ten, between Henry P. Dering, Esquire, agent for fortifications at Sag Harbor for the United States of

the one part, and Henry B. Havens, master mason, and Eliab Byram, master carpenter, both of Sag Harbor aforesaid is as follows: (Viz) The said Henry B. Havens and Eliab Byram will erect, build and complete an arsenal in Sag Harbor. The dimensions of the said building to be fifty feet in length and twenty-three feet in breadth and two stories high, the foundations to be laid with stone and sunk six inches below the surface of the earth and twelve inches above the surface including the water table which is to be hewed and handsomely finished on the front or north side and on each end of the building.

The walls of the building to be of good brick; the building to have six projections in front of four inches from the main-body of the brick work, the two corner projections to be two feet and eight inches, and to be united at the top by arches or otherwise. The whole brickwork except the south side or rear to be laid in flemish bond.

The building to have five windows on the north side or front in the lower story and five windows in the second story of a sufficient size to receive a sash of twenty-four lights of six by eight glass. The building to be furnished with two large folding doors at each end sufficiently large to receive heavy cannon of 24 pounds caliber mounted on traveling carriages. The floor of the lower or first story to be laid with two inch plank and well spiked down on beams of nine by three inches, which beams are to be not more than eighteen inches asunder and to run the width of the building and to be supported by a string piece running through the middle thereof. The beams for the floor of the second story shall be ten by three inches and placed not more than two feet apart. The roof of said building to be made of good cedar shingles and to be supported by stout rafters not more than three feet asunder. The thresholds of the doors to be of gray stone.

The said Henry B. Havens and Eliab Byram do further covenant promise and agree to cause to be made one additional door of a common suitable size in the east end of the said building for a passage into the second story with a flight of stairs and passage or entry way into the second story. This door to be finished with a good substantial lock and key and hung with good wrought iron hinges.

And the said Henry B. Havens and Eliab Byram also hereby covenant promise and agree to and with the said Henry P. Dering on behalf of the United States will erect the said building and furnish and pay for all the materials, labor work and workmanship, provisions, liquors and all other objects of cost, charge and expense and that they will furnish and provide good materials of every description.

And the said Henry P. Dering on behalf of the United States doth covenant promise and agree to and with the said Henry B. Havens and Eliab Byram their heirs executors and administrators and every one of them to pay to them the sum of one thousand eight hundred and ten dollars lawful money of the United States and to make them convenient advances in money as the materials are furnished and the work progresses.

Sealed and delivered in presence of Henry P. Dering, Henry B. Havens, Eliab Byram. Witness, Thomas S. Lester and Jacob Parker.

A contract to paint the arsenal was awarded to master painter Nathan Skiff of Sag Harbor. For $60.50 the woodwork, window frames, shutters, doors, and cornices were to be painted with a durable white lead and linseed oil paint and the roof painted with a durable coat of Spanish brown and linseed oil.

On April 18, 1811 a letter to Charles Watson Payne contained a bill for $3.50 for teams and three yoke of oxen and two horses for drawing four 18-pound cannon with carriages from the wharf to the arsenal. On July 13, 1812, one month after war was declared, 500 muskets, 500 sets of accoutrements, 1000 flints, 10,000 rounds of fixed ammunition, and a nine-pound cannon on a field carriage, 100 nine-pound balls, 100 three-pound balls, 6 quarter casks of powder, and one coil of slowmatch were shipped to Sag Harbor. Henry P. Dering was placed in charge of the arms.

At the same time, a powder house was maintained as a supply depot near Fort Hill. It was located on Hampton Street and ran through to Division Street. Henry P. Dering owned all the land in that area and sold a 100-square-foot piece to the United States government on November 11, 1811, with privilege of a convenient way to pass and repass from the powder house to the public highway. The powder house was built by Henry B. Havens at a cost of $100 and was a stone building lined with seasoned boards, two doors with locks, and shingles.

Following the war the arsenal became an important building in the village. The Post Office and Custom House were located there, the Post Office remaining until 1829. At another time a school was held in the second floor rooms of the building. In 1816 a meeting was held there, at which time it was determined to build a new Presbyterian Church. During its construction, services were held in the arsenal. Guns, cannon, and equipment were moved out of the building and taken to Sleight's ropewalk near Division and Burke Streets for storage.

After many years, when the place became run down and no longer useful, Sag Harbor's philosopher, Prentice Mulford, wrote the following article which was published in *The San Francisco Bulletin* on February 14, 1875.

The Arsenal's Last Days

Something lives inside of any deserted building, something which the past has left there, something made up the lives, the acts, the events which in bygone days have been enacted there.

It is so with the old custom house. The walls are crumbling, the flagstaff is broken, its yard is choked with weeds. Many a year has passed and little stir or excitement has there been about the place, save twice a day the joyous outburst consequent on the dismissal of an infant school kept within its walls. But the school is no longer there. It is a tomb. The old custom house stands and broods over the past, and the tombstones in the graveyard adjoining seem also to be thinking over events gone by and every night, out of their graves, arise a crowd of ghostly whaling captains. They enter the ghostly old custom house, they take out a lot of ghostly papers and a fleet of phantom ships are cleared by a ghostly collector—an old Federal collector, arrayed in last century costume, in small clothes, stockings, a queue, a cocked hat—courtly gentleman of the old school, who firmly believed in the divine right of the Federal party and would have detested a Jackson man as an English nobleman does a Radical.

But those times are all gone. The vessel of our whale fishery is gone, We have no more oil, no more bone, no more money and we don't build any more churches and we don't fill those that are built and so the arsenal stand brooding over the past.

After the arsenal was torn down in 1885, the land remained vacant, with the question of ownership in dispute. In 1926 a government official arrived in town to dispose of the lot, and title was acquired by the village for $150. In December 1917 Frank Johnson, a contractor, unearthed the cornerstone of the old structure. The stone was 4 feet beneath the level of the sidewalk, a solid granite block bearing the initials H.P.D., placed in position in 1810.

In 1871 a bill authorized the Secretary of War to sell the 100-square-foot piece of land conveyed to the United States by deed from Henry P. Dering and his wife, November 11, 1811 on which the powder house stood. The proceeds of the sale went to the United States Treasury Department.

The War of 1812

As war again laid its paralyzing hand on all the industries of land and sea, the village, then consisting of about 200 dwellings, was once more subjected to a reign of terror. Preparations were made to protect the village against the enemy, and a small detachment of militia was stationed here. A fort, erected on the high ground known as Turkey Hill, overlooked the harbor. No regular garrison was established, however, until the summer of 1813 when British ships in Gardiner's Bay threatened to land at several points in the vicinity of the Port. At that time 3000-4000 men were stationed at Sag Harbor and remained until the end of the war. Part of the time there was a company of artillery; another time, regular troops; and in 1814, a company of sea fencibles. At no time, however, was the number sufficient to have actually defended the place effectively.

General Abraham Rose of Bridgehampton was ordered by the President to call together all the officers of the Eastern Regiment to prepare an alarm system to be used in the event of an attack. Rose made an urgent request for volunteers to defend the area, which resulted in many men offering to serve. Those volunteering from Sag Harbor were: Thaddeus Coles, Elias M. Cooper, Braddock Corey, John B. Corey, John Edwards, Stephen B. Edwards, Zebulon Elliot, Samuel Field, James Fordham, Nathan Fordham, David Hand, Hezakiah Jennings, Nathan B. Sweezey, Daniel Schellinger, Pardon Tabor, Wheaton Vaughn, Noah Washburn, Newton E. Westfall, Abraham Gardiner, John A. Holton, Henry Hatford, Charles Middleton, and Daniel Slate. Those exempt from military duty formed the uniformed Artillerist Citizen Soldiers under the leadership of Major John Jermain, Jesse Hedges, and Lodowick Post. They were stationed at the Arsenal ready to prepare the cannon at a moment's notice.

The British fleet, under Commodore Thomas Hardy, was sighted in Gardiner's Bay in June 1813. In fact, the British had already gone ashore at Gardiner's Island, where they removed cattle and other supplies. With the fleet a very real threat, General Rose dispatched a company of artillery, under Captain Post, and a company of infantry, under Captain Hedges, down to the harbor, where they were ready to march at the first sign of trouble. The British were determined to come ashore and burn the village, and the militia were just as determined that such a thing would never happen.

On July 11, 1813 the much feared attack took place. Accounts differ as to the exact details of the skirmish. One version stated that, in the wee hours of the morning, five British ships came ashore after taking three vessels and setting fire to a fourth. The alarm was sounded by Henry P. Dering, one shot a minute for three minutes, followed by a three-minute silence, and then repeated again. By dawn the roads leading into Sag Harbor were filled with soldiers from the neighboring villages hurrying down to the waterfront. Mr. A.M. Cook of Bridgehampton described the battle as follows:

Elisha Halsey of Hay Ground was drummer of his company. When he reached Sag Harbor he was ordered out into the street near the head of the wharf to call his company to form a line of battle. The enemy had already landed and held possession of the wharf and were firing cannon up the street. Limbs were falling from trees, solid shot were screaming overhead, houses were being shattered and pandemonium reigned generally.

The old Umbrella House in Sag Harbor bears the marks of the British cannon balls. The enemy met with such opposition when the cannon at the fort was turned on them that they made a hasty retreat. So fast, in fact, that in their rapid departure many guns and arms were left behind. Another account of the skirmish stated:

> A launch and two barges with about one hundred men from the squadron of Commodore Hardy attempted to land at the wharf in the night, but being timely discovered, the alarm was sounded and the guns of the fort shot off in the direction of the boats, that the enemy was thwarted in their attempt. They had time only to set fire to a sloop which they took from the wharf, when a shot from the fort led them to abandon the operation. The Americans went aboard, extinguished the flames and found a quantity of guns, swords, pistols, etc. which were left behind in their hurry to escape.

Abbey Latham Beaumont, who was born in Sag Harbor in 1802, recalled the state of affairs at that time and told this version of the battle.

> I assure you that I can never forget the last war between the United States and Great Britain. As a little girl I was sent more than once across the street in the night to tell Captain Parker's and Captain Sayre's folks to hurry up and get into our wagon to be carried up two miles on the Bridgehampton road. That was our lightning express train, loaded with women and scared children. Many times we carried trays of dough, clothes in wash and a tin oven. We wrung out the clothes and dried them on the bushes. When the war ships were made to back off word would be sent and we would all be carried home again. Six weeks one summer all the women and children went to bed without undressing at night and it was well they did, for many a night the alarm would be given, "The British are coming!" I can hear the cannon balls roar! The saucy British were determined to burn Sag Harbor. I suppose and hope there are many living now that remember the day news came that peace was declared between the United States and Great Britain. The news spread like wild

fire, women laughed and cried, men shouted, every bell in Sag Harbor rang out at once. Oh how the cannon at the fort on Methodist Hill and at the wharf would belch forth the noise.

The great illumination at night—a piece of tallow candle lighted and placed at every pane of glass in the front window of every home in Sag Harbor! More than once it happened when the British were in the bay that pedestrians on Main Street or on the old ropewalk, startled by the whirring noise behind them, would spring aside to find a spent ball rolling at their feet.

About this time, Admiral Sir Thomas Hardy, who with his fleet was blockading New London, sent some boats across the Sound to burn Sag Harbor. But a fort for the defense of the place had been erected on Turkey Hill, a high point overlooking the bay, and when the sentinel on the Long Wharf gave the alarm, Oliver Slate and Samuel Hildreth, hurrying with others to the hill, loaded the 'nineteen pounder' with spikes for lack of cannon balls, and as the boats came within range fired with so accurate an aim that two men were killed and the expedition put to rout.

Regardless of which account is more factual, Sag Harbor's troops thwarted every attempt the British made to burn the village.

In 1814 Congressman Sage commented on the miserable conditions that confronted the residents of Sag Harbor at the time of hostilities.

This place (Sag Harbor), consisting of about two hundred houses, has been built up since the Revolution by honest industry in catching whale and codfish. The people are not very rich, except a few, mostly mechanics and laborers with large families. The Orders in Council put an end to all our prosperity and war is fast making them poor and wretched. It is distressing to see the changes that a few years have produced among us. Perhaps near twenty of my neighbors who were formerly Captains, mates, sailors of vessels, carpenters, sailmakers, boat builders and in good circumstances, are now reduced to the necessity of doing garrison duty to get rations to feed, and a little money with which to clothe their families.

We formerly had twenty to twenty-five coasting vessels employed in southern trade and in carrying wood to market. Three or four of them remain, some have been taken and sent to Halifax, others burned and others so often taken and ransomed that the owners are unable to keep them in repair and sail them. They are either sunk at the wharf or laid up to rot in creeks and inlets. Our young men have generally gone into the army or flotilla service at New York, or emigrated in search of business; nothing to be seen but houses stripped of their furniture and, as we expect, to be burned, sent out of reach of the conflagration. Women who have seen better days are obliged to wash and billet soldiers to share with them their rations, no happy countenance among us, but children from the want of reflection and soldiers made happy by whiskey; but for our clam beds and fish, many would go supperless to bed.

When the war was finally over, Sag Harbor found that its greatest casualty was the loss of her ships, and the coastal trade was at a standstill for the next two years.

Some Court Martial Trials at the Sag Harbor Garrison

1. May 9, 1814 a Court Martial was held at the garrison Sag Harbor for the trial of Hervy Payne on a charge of absenting himself from camp and guard relief.

    Present—Lieut. Pardon Tabor, Lieut. Zeph Bailey, Ensign John Bassett
    He pleaded not guilty, his absence from guard relief was in consequence of being detained by assisting his neighbor in getting a cow out of the mire but acknowledged that it was more than a mile from camp. The court decided that if the accused had kept within the limits of the camp he would not have met with the causes of detention and do not consider it any justification, he having been engaged in the act beyond the limits when he had not leave or permission to go. The court accordingly sentenced him to pay the sum of four dollars, to be taken from his pay.

    Approved—Jeremiah Miller, Major Commander
    John Williamson, Judge Advocate.

2. June 1, 1814 a Court Martial was held for the trial of John Combs on a charge of going beyond the limits of the camp at an unreasonable hour of the night without leave and while there for committing acts of abuse toward Martha Petty and Prince Thomas, a free black, and otherwise disturbing the peace of the inhabitants.

    Present—Captain Denyse, Lieut. Tabor, Lieut. Van Cleef
    The charge being read he plead guilty. Whereupon the court adjudged that he pay a fine of eight dollars to be taken from his pay and to walk the parapet three days, and during the night to be kept in close confinement.

    Approved—Jeremiah Miller
    John Williamson, Judge Advocate.

3. June 23, 1814 a garrison Court Martial was held for the trial of John Tooker, a Corporal in Captain Haynes company, on a charge of refusing to do guard duty and using abusive language toward an orderly, Sgt. Baker.

Present—Lieut. Baker, Lieut. Burbis, Lieut. Abell

Plead not guilty. Sgt. Baker deposeth that at the sunrise parade of June 22, inst., said Tooker was absent and noted by the order of Captain Haynes was detailed for guard duty, as a punishment. I offered him a copy of the detail of guard for the purpose of mustering the guard, taking charge of them and marching them to the General Guard Parade. He refused to accept it and swore positively that he would not go on guard in consequence of which he was obliged to muster the guard himself and march them. That sometime after said Tooker came on the parade ground and made considerable disturbance in the ranks, called him a Negro rascal Mulatto, and abused him. Melvin Gardiner testified that he heard Tooker call Sgt. Baker a damned mulatto rascal and being reprimanded for it by him said he did not care a damn for Baker nor all the rest of them. John Pierson testified the same—John Stewart testified to the same. Whereupon the court adjudged him guilty and declared that for the first charge and offense that he be reduced to the ranks and no longer be permitted to serve as corporal, and for the second offense decided and determined that he ask the pardon of orderly Sgt. Baker in the presence of the officers of the company when on parade this afternoon—5 o'clock and refusal thereof to be liable for a second trial of disobedience.

Approved—Jeremiah Miller

John Williamson, Judge Advocate.

4. September 15, 1814 a Court Martial was called for the trial of Stephen Austin and David Liscomb.

Present—Captain Field, Lieut. Howell, Lieut. Mulford

Austin was called on a charge of quitting his post. Plead not guilty. Jasper Vail testified that said Austin came on board his vessel and asked of a watermelon and obtained it. Adjudged guilty and sentenced to hard labor two days in and about the fort and confinement during the night and seven days stopping of whiskey.

Liscomb was charged of sleeping on post, plead not guilty. Captain Haynes testified that he found Liscomb in the guard house asleep. Adjudged guilty and sentenced to pay a fine of four dollars to be taken from his pay and seven days stoppage of whiskey.

Approved—Jeremiah Miller

John Williamson, Judge Advocate.

5. November 7, 1814 a Court Martial was held for the trial of Smith Byram on a charge of firing a musket at an unreasonable hour in the night causing an alarm and thereby thrusting his bayonette into the door of Joshua Perry's house and losing his musket.

                Present—Captain Haynes, Captain Field, Lieut. Losee. Plead guilty. Sentenced to be chained six hours in the day to the flag staff for two days, remainder of the time to be chained in the barracks.

                Approved—Jeremiah Miller

                      John Williamson, Judge Advocate.

6

THE GREAT FIRES OF SAG HARBOR

Fighting fires was no easy task in early times. The bucket brigade and old hand-pumped engine stood little chance of controlling a blaze once it got underway. In the early days of Sag Harbor, three major fires consumed the business district: one in 1817, one in 1845, and one in 1877. At the time of the first fire, Sag Harbor had just begun to recover from the devastation of the war and was hardly ready for another setback. But misfortune, it seemed, was to be a frequent visitor to the growing port.

The Fire of 1817

The first of the great conflagrations occurred on May 26, 1817, when a small barn filled with hay was discovered to be on fire. Located in the most thickly settled part of the village, it rapidly spread along the waterfront igniting the nearby warehouses which were filled with whale oil. The winds blew a gale, and the tinder dry wooden structures at the foot of Main Street had little chance of escaping the spreading flames. In three hours about 20 of the best houses and most valuable stores were leveled to the ground. Most of the shops contained a large supply of merchandise and provisions, and the rapidity of the fire prevented the owners from moving their goods to a safe place. Three ships anchored at the Long Wharf and in the process of being fitted out for whaling voyages were detained due to a loss of provisions and casks.

Those who suffered losses in the fire were: S.& L. Howell, store; S. Huntting, store; C. Douglas, blockmaking shop; Hildreth & Son, store; S. L'Hommedieu, store; H. Crowell, house and blockmaking shop; H. Gelston, store containing ship sails and oil casks; J.T. Havens, store and oil vault; Gelston & Howell, store; S. Payne & N. Fordham, house and store; Jeremiah Hedges, house and store; and S. Raymond, T.P. Ripley, A. Partridge, J. Jermain, J. Halsey, J.N. Fordham, A. Gardiner, I. Hill, M. Stewart, E. Havens, C. Woodward, and Widow Bowman.

Immediately following the fire a meeting of the residents of the port was held for the purpose of adopting, "a means of relief for those suffering losses." With Samuel L'Hommedieu selected as moderator and Ebenezer Sage as clerk, a committee of seven was appointed to give the public a statement of the tragedy and solicit aid in the way of donations both at home and away. The committee was to adopt "any measure conducive to the relief of their distressed fellow citizens and that all donations be addressed to the commissioner for distribution."

On the corner of Church and Sage Streets, a new Presbyterian Church was under construction, and although out of reach of the flames, it suffered a setback as contributions to the building fund came to a sudden halt. Many residents who had liberally donated to its erection had lost everything in the fire and could no longer afford to give money toward the completion of the church. The entire village was in a state of shock, and much time would pass before things would get back to normal.

The Establishment of a Fire Department

Fires were prevalent in early times and part of the general order of things. Having a fire in one's home at least once in a lifetime was not uncommon, and because of the primitive fire fighting methods, the results were often disastrous. Bucket brigades and the old hand-pumped engine had little effect once a blaze had gotten underway.

When the first of Sag Harbor's major fires occurred in 1817, the flames were fed by whale oil and a brisk wind, resulting in a futile attempt to squelch the flames. Two years after this disaster occurred, a March 12, 1819 legislative act enabled the residents to form a fire company. It was hoped with this move that a recurrence of that dreadful event would never take place—that a fire company would be able to extinguish a fire before such a calamity could happen again. All persons entitled to vote assembled and chose by ballot "not

THE GREAT FIRES

less than three nor more than five discreet freeholders to be called the trustees of the fire company of the Port of Sag Harbor." Some of Sag Harbor's most prominent individuals were instrumental in organizing the first company, and it was considered an honor as well as one's duty to belong to it. Funds to aid in its operation came, for the most part, from donations given by the members. By 1829 one dollar was apportioned out of the yearly fines collected in the village to defray the expense of annual meetings.

The Otter Hose Company, established in 1819, had the distinction of becoming not only the first volunteer company in Sag Harbor but also the first in New York State. In 1832 a Hook and Ladder Company was organized with James Leonard in charge. A year later Engine Company #2 formed under Noah Washburn, and in 1837 Engine Company #3, under Lodowick F. Dering. Noah Washburn was later instrumental in forming the companies into a fire department.

Part Two

THE GOLDEN ERA OF THE WHALE FISHERY

1820–1850

1

THE GOLDEN YEARS OF WHALING

> I remember the black wharves and ships
> And the soft tides tossing free—
> And Spanish sailors with bearded lips
> And the beauty and majesty of the ships
> And the magic of the sea.
>
> *Author unknown*

In early times, before white men settled in the area, the Indians practiced a form of on-shore whaling. Long spears and harpoons were used to spear the "great fish," which was brought to the beach and tried out. Whale was plentiful along the coast at that time, and even into the years that Sag Harbor's first ships sailed from the port.

The Business of Whaling

In 1760 the first three vessels left Sag Harbor in search of whale. Named the *Dolphin*, *Success*, and *Goodluck* and owned by Joseph Conkling, John Foster, and others, they engaged in short cruises along the coast and returned with their catch to the water-front try works of Foster and Fordham. Here, the blubber was boiled down into oil. It was said that the process was so offensive it was soon declared illegal to do it within a good distance from the village, and in time the try works were built on the ship itself, saving much time, space and aggravation. Most of the products from these early whaling trips were shipped to New London and sold.

Before long the whale was so ruthlessly hunted it became difficult to find, and it was necessary to sail farther out to sea. Voyages to the West Indies and South America became commonplace. In 1785 a vessel owned by Colonel Benjamin Huntting and Stephen Howell sailed to a more southern latitude than had ever before been attempted, and her success laid the foundation for the profitable whaling days that were soon to come.

Between 1784 and 1809 the *American*, *Abigail*, *Minerva*, *Alknonac*, *Brazil*, *Warren*, *Washington*, *Lavinia*, *Jefferson* and *Abby* made up the growing fleet. Products with a market value of from $600,000 to $1,000,000 dollars were brought into the port. The *Hope* and the *Lucy* followed, sailing to the coast of Brazil, and experienced more profitable voyages than had ever been anticipated. It was said that in 1807 there was a rapid increase in wealth and population, and within a short space of three to four years its advancement had been beyond belief.

Unfortunately, with the onset of war in 1812, this surge in activity was not to last. With the Embargo Act in effect and the bay at Sag Harbor threatened by British vessels, the industry came to a complete standstill. It wasn't until the end of hostilities that whale ships once more sailed from the port and the industry again began to flourish.

Between 1816 and 1829 there were at least six arrivals annually, and by 1837 there were 13 arrivals and 29 departures, keeping the wharf busy with activity. More than 800 men and boys found employment on the ships and in related industries along the waterfront. In those golden years all branches of industry in Sag Harbor were contingent upon one pursuit, the whale fishery. Those who didn't go to sea were taught trades compatible with the enterprise: caulking, rigging, block and pump-making, sail-making, spar-making, coopering and blacksmithing.

The profitable years of whaling presented a time when wealthy ship owners built stately mansions that still stand along the tree-lined streets of the village, a time when money flowed as freely as the rum in the local taverns, and along the waterfront it wasn't uncommon to see Portuguese, Hawaiian, and Fiji Islanders selling their scrimshaw handiwork to the local citizens.

The year 1847 was the most productive year of the industry. Thirty-two arrivals that year brought 3,919 barrels of sperm oil, 63,712 barrels of right whale oil, and 605,340 pounds of whale bone into the harbor. The voyages often brought large returns to bold investors, yet not all who put their savings into the industry were successful. It was a risky business that played no favorites, some prospering greatly and others losing their life's savings.

How Sag Harbor Looked in 1834

An interesting description of Sag Harbor in 1834, published in *The Sag Harbor Express*, ran thus:

> In 1834 whaling was the chief industry of Sag Harbor. All the implements that were used for whaling were made in the village, such as whale irons, oil barrels, water casks that could hold from forty to fifty gallons. Shipowners furnished the crude material for making casks, barrels, etc. The material had to be hewed, dressed and jointed before being made into barrels. The ship owners also furnished the material for building whale boats. Each company owned a sloop that would carry between five hundred and six hundred barrels. The ships that came in from whaling usually anchored at "Indian Jail," between Hog Neck and Shelter Island. They had large floats that carried one hundred or more barrels of oil and the cargoes of the different ships were floated to the several company oil yards where each barrel was re-coopered before being shipped to New York. The barrels of oil were rolled together, bung up, and covered with seaweed to await the highest market price, which was about twenty cents a gallon. There were storehouses to store the whalebone in, the price of the same then was eighteen cents a pound, but later increased to about three dollars per pound.
>
> Different men owned different ships. The Hunttings owned five whaling ships, the Howells owned or were agents for seven. Mulford and Sleight owned about eight, the Derings owned four, Luther D. Cook owned or was agent for four, and Ezekiel Mulford was agent for two. Only a few ships that sailed from Sag Harbor were actually built here. The ships built at Sag Harbor were the Hannibal, the Panama, Arabella, Black Eagle, and the Mary Gardiner. The others were liners that were bought and made into whalers.
>
> Hundreds of men were employed on the docks and about the ships, amounting to three to four hundred. Charles Douglass kept the first shop which sold groceries, liquor etc.; next was the Sailor's Boarding House of Peter French. It was situated in two townships, being on the line that divided Southampton and East Hampton Towns, and in this house both towns held their elections. Going from the dock there were no other

stores until you came to S.B. Huntting's general store, then came Abraham Gardiner's general store, then the tavern kept by Charles Fordham. "Duke" Fordham also kept one on the opposite corner. Next was Josiah Douglass' general store followed by a tailor shop, Mr. Beckwith's store and then the jewelry store of Charles Conklin.

On the other side of the street was Major Hildreth's shoe store, and then the store of "Daddy" Ripley. Across the street was the store of Charles T. Dering, Robert Osborn's general store, Nelson's Lumber Yard, and Peleg Rogers' general store and Captain Chapman Rogers' hat shop, all in the same building. Next came the general store of George Brown and the Republican Watchman printing office. Next came the store of Charles Hedges, and next Albert Hedges' two stores. Mr. Bassett had a tailor shop in one and Albert Hedges kept a livery stable in the rear. Then came Noah Washburn's tin shop, Mr. Hildreth's butcher shop and then Seeley's bakery.

Next to "Daddy" Ripley's came Jennings' shoe shop, followed by Hunt's office that printed the Corrector. Next came Elliott's Jewelry Shop. Then there were no more stores until you came to Tinker's Cabinet Shop and Bill Simons' Oyster Shop. Close to Tinker's building was another shoe shop, then Ezekiel Mulford's general store and Van Scoy's. From Van Scoy's to the Mansion House there was a vacant lot. This is how Sag Harbor looked in 1834.

The Whaleship Thames

The whaleship *Thames* was considered one of the fastest, if not the fastest, ship belonging to the Port of Sag Harbor, and the ship held that distinction throughout her 12-year career as a Sag Harbor whaler. In 1818 Captain Noah Scovell built the 350-ton vessel at Essex, Connecticut, and for the first few years it was employed in the New London trade as a freighter and passenger ship. In June 1822 the New Haven Whaling Company remodeled and outfitted the ship for a whaling voyage to the Pacific. At the end of the three-year voyage, which resulted in considerable loss to the owners, the *Thames* was taken to New York. There it was sold to W.R. & C. Hitchcock for a small price and immediately sent down to Sag Harbor, where it became part of the whaling fleet.

The *Thames* sailed from Sag Harbor in the summer of 1826 with Captain Huntting Cooper, who remained master of the vessel for five consecutive annual voyages, most of which were very profitable. On his return in the spring of 1831, he turned over command to his first officer, David Hand.

In 1834 the cost of outfitting the *Thames* was $9,171, but a $30,000 profit, when the vessel returned to port with 500 barrels of sperm oil, 2,200 of whale oil and 18,000 pounds of whale bone, made the year-long voyage a very profitable one.

The last captain of the *Thames* was Henry Nickerson, who, unfortunately, had little success during his two voyages. The *Thames* was sailing her last voyage, her condition deteriorating. It was said that in bad weather she worked her frame and timbers so much that her crew was often alarmed to see her open seams about the plank shears. The entire frame of the old ship would twist and yield during the violent storms encountered at sea. She was 20 years old and unworthy of repair when she returned to port May 20, 1838 and was set aside from future service. After being condemned and broken up by her owners Mulford & Sleight, the skeleton of the ship was left to decay at Conklin's Point, east of the present Yacht Club. Here the keel could be seen for many years at the time of low tide. In later times, Ivan Byram, using dynamite, recovered a quantity of copper from the wreck of the old ship. In 1968, while dredging at the water's edge, the final remains of the *Thames* were unearthed.

It wasn't unusual throughout the years of the whale fishery that black and Indian seamen signed on for the lengthy voyages. The crew of the *Thames*, on all of her voyages, had a number of black and Indian men aboard. On the *Thames* first trip in 1826 were: Samuel Walkus, shipbuilder; Amaziah Cuffee, cook; James Arch, seaman; William Prime, Abraham Sack, Jerry Butler, Jason Cuffee, Aphy Cuffee, John Brush, and Josephus Wright. The second voyage of the *Thames*, in 1827, had Jason Cuffee, William Prime, Isaac Cuffee, Isaac Wright, Samuel Walkus, Simeon Tabez, Tobias Coles, and Silas Moore.

On the third voyage of the *Thames* in 1828–29 were: Jason Arch, Jason Cuffee, Harry Fordham, Pink, Peter Gabriel, Sam Eldredge, Simeon Tabez, John Warren, James Cuffee, Henry Killis, Sylvester Pharaoh, and Amaziah Cuffee. On the fourth voyage in 1829–30 were: Jason Cuffee, James Jones, James Cuffee, and Peter Coles. On the fifth voyage, in 1830, were Peter Coles and Henry Brown, and on the *Thames'* sixth voyage were Charles Garrison and John Paul Enos.

James Fenimore Cooper

When James Fenimore Cooper spent time in Sag Harbor, he was yet unknown in literary circles. The year was 1818, and Cooper had just resigned from the navy and married Susan Augusta Delancy of Westchester County, who was related to the Nicoll family of Shelter Island, New York. While visiting them, he and Charles T. Dering, a shipping merchant of Sag Harbor (and husband of Eliza Nicoll), decided to enter the whale fishery. With his first-hand experience with ships, it was only natural that Cooper had an interest in the industry.

James Fenimore Cooper and Charles T. Dering formed a company made up of several individuals, with Cooper holding the controlling interest. Cooper was said to have originated the practice of several people uniting and purchasing a vessel for a whaling voyage (at least in Sag Harbor). Thereafter, that practice became known as sending out "company ships." They outfitted the whaleship *Union*, for a voyage to the east coast of Brazil, and to fill his leisure hours while staying at Duke Fordham's Inn waiting for the ship to return, Cooper decided to write a novel.

Tradition tells us that after reading an English novel, entitled *Discipline*, aloud to his wife and her cousin Anne Nicoll, Cooper remarked that he could write a better book himself. Miss Nicoll expressed her doubts and challenged Cooper to do so, and *Precaution* was written to prove it, although actually it did not, for the novel was unsuccessful.

The circumstances which made one of America's literary geniuses out of the ex-naval officer have been frequently told in the Nicoll and Dering families. The facts appear to be that Cooper began *Precaution* while in Sag Harbor and completed it while living in Angevine, New York, for the late Susan Fenimore Cooper stated that, when a child, she heard her father read the manuscript of the novel to her mother while the family lived in Westchester.

James Fenimore Cooper's ship, *Union*, returned from her voyage on July 15, 1820 with only 900 barrels of whale oil, a poor catch for the size of the ship. Two successive voyages were made with similar results. During the years 1821 and 1822, Cooper spent a considerable amount of time in the area, both at the Nicoll mansion on Shelter Island and at the home of Mrs. Charles T. Dering in Sag Harbor. If the voyages had been more successful, it might reasonably be surmised that Cooper would have continued in the business.

About 1820-21 an important event happened in the life of James Fenimore Cooper, for although his first novel was a failure, such was not the case with the second. A person named Enoch Crosby, who lived in the vicinity where Cooper married his wife, played an important part in the American Revolution. Crosby kept General Washington supplied with information regarding the enemy, and his perilous adventures and narrow escapes provided Cooper with excellent material for his novel. In 1821 he wrote *The Spy*, which had a widespread popularity, was reprinted in England, was translated into many languages, and established Cooper as a new writer of fiction.

During the next seven years, James Fenimore Cooper devoted himself totally to the pursuit of literature and over that time published *The Pioneers*, *The Pilot*, *The Last of the Mohicans*, *The Prairie*, and *The Red Rover*.

Cooper, while residing in the Port of Sag Harbor, found that the whole industry of the settlement was connected with ships and shipping and certainly had its share of eccentric and colorful personalities from which a writer could avail himself to portray characters for his stories. The character Natty Bumppo, of the Leatherstocking Tales, was easily recognized as having been patterned after Captain David Hand of Sag Harbor. Captain Hand had been a seaman and privateer and, before the age of twenty, had seen Washington, been a prisoner of war five times, and was one of the exchange prisoners from the Jersey prison ships. Further distinguishing himself was the fact that he had five wives and outlived all of them.

Cooper's novel *Sea Lions* gives a description of Sag Harbor and the eastern end of Long Island during the years that he spent in the area:

> As a whaling town, Sag Harbor is the third or fourth port in the country and maintains something like that in rank in importance. A whaling haven is nothing without a whaling community. Without the last, it is almost hopeless to look for success. New York can, and has often fitted whalers for sea, having sought officers in the regular whaling ports; but it has been seldom that the enterprises have been rewarded with such returns as to induce a second voyage by the same parties.
>
> It is as indispensable that a whaler should possess a certain *esprit de corps*, as that a regiment, or a ship of war, should be animated by its proper spirit. In the whaling communities, this spirit exists to an extent and in a degree that is wonderful, when one remembers the great expansion of this particular branch of trade within the last five-and-twenty years. It may be a little lessened of late, but at the time of which we are writing, or about the year 1820, there was scarcely an individual who followed this particular calling out of the port of Sag Harbor, whose general standing on board ship was not as well known to all the women and girls of the place, as it was to his shipmates. Success in taking the whale was a thing that made itself felt in every fibre of the prosperity of the town; and it was just as natural that the single-minded population of that part of Suffolk would regard the bold and skillful harpooner or lancer with favor, as it is for the bell at a watering place to bestow her smiles on one of the young heroes of Contreras or Cherubusco.
>
> His particular merit, whether with the oar, lance, or harpoon. is bruited about, as well as the number of whales he may have succeeded in "making fast to," or those which he caused to "spout blood." It is true, that

the great extension of the trade within the last twenty years, by drawing so many from a distance into its pursuits, has in a degree lessened this local interest and local knowledge of character; but at the time of which we are about to write, both were at their height, and Nantucket itself had not more of this "intelligence office" propensity, or more of the true whaling *esprit de corps*, that were to be found in the district of county that surrounded Sag Harbor.

And so, after the three or four years that James Fenimore Cooper spent in the Sag Harbor area involved in the whale fishery, he moved on, but his fame as a literary genius remains, and the residents of Sag Harbor hold a special place in their hearts for the novelist who lived among them for a brief time.

The Whaleship Konohassett

The *Konohassett* was formerly a merchant ship sailing out of Boston. She joined the Sag Harbor whaling fleet in 1845 and set out on her first and only voyage on December sixth of that year, Captain James B. Worth in command. Nearing Hawaii, the *Konohassett* struck a reef and was lost at a place called Pell's Island, named in honor of Captain Pell, whose ship, *Holder Border* of Fall River, was wrecked in 1844. The *Konohassett*, insured for $30,000, was a total loss.

Captain Worth and the crew constructed a sloop from the wreckage which they called *Konohassett, Jr.*. Captain Worth, mate F.R. Cartwright, boatsteerers James Boilan and J.S. Horton, seamen William Baker and Nathaniel Payne, and cabin boy George Yellot boarded the sloop, with a small supply of bread and water, and set sail for Hawaii. They arrived at Honolulu on July 31st after 42 days at sea.

On August fourth the American Consul dispatched the Hawaiian schooner *Halileo*, and with Captain Worth aboard, they sailed to Pell's Island where the remaining members of the crew were picked up. Although the loss of the *Konohassett* was a terrible disaster, not a single life was lost.

The Whaleship Cadmus

Originally the *Cadmus* was a vessel of the Havre Packet Line and the ship that brought General Lafayette to America in 1824. Mulford & Sleight, Sag Harbor whaleship owners, purchased the vessel in New York in 1827, and for 20 years she sailed from the Port of Sag Harbor, cruising for whale. The *Cadmus* made a total of 15 voyages, sailing under Captains Henry Babcock, David Hand, Jr.,

David Smith, Henry Nickerson, Jr., and George Howell.

When gold was discovered in California, the *Cadmus*, under the command of Captain John W. Fordham, sailed for the west coast. She left port October 20, 1849 and arrived in San Francisco in 1850. Upon arrival the *Cadmus* was declared unseaworthy and was sold at auction. Purchased by a ship chandlery firm, she was converted into a storeship and for several years lay at the foot of Mission Street. In time the *Cadmus* was again sold to George Howgate and Frederick Howling, who broke her up in 1856. A portion of her timbers were used as planking for the streets in Montgomery, near Sacramento, using the "oaken walls" of the sturdy old craft. Simmons, who assisted at the demolition, saved a piece of her remains and crafted a model of the original ship. The shape, style, rigging, etc. was said to have been a perfect likeness of the *Cadmus*. The deck was made from the door frame of the cabin occupied by Lafayette; the forecastle, from a piece of the berth in which he slept.

Outfitting the Bark Pacific

To outfit the bark *Pacific* was no easy task, and the same could hold true for all ships in the Sag Harbor whaling fleet. From a paper containing instructions to the outfitter of the bark, bound for a three-year voyage, he was required to have: yards all up to topmast heads, spare spars, if any, on deck; jib boom rigged in; anchors on bows, both chains on deck and forward to windlass, or between windlass and bow; rigging all overhead, vizzers rigging all new, including backstays; all head rigging new, also for topmast and top gallant stays.

When ready, a crew of 22 men would be provided with three boats and their complements of harpoons, lances, lines and hatchets, together with two or three thousand well-seasoned barrels, fully marked with vessel's name, and provisions and cabin stores as follows:

> One barrel kiln-dried meal, 500 pounds pork hams, 100 gallons of vinegar, 2 quintals of codfish, 500 pounds of sugar, 400 pounds of coffee, 400 pounds of dried apples, 2 boxes of raisens, 30 pounds of beans, 20 bushels of corn, 100 bushels of potatoes, 200 gallons of lamp oil, 1 box of sperm candles, 3 boxes of hard soap. Also a chest of tea, 50 pounds of crushed sugar, 6 pounds of mustard, 25 pounds of black pepper, 20 pounds of ginger, 25 pounds of assorted spices, 30 pounds of saleratus, 1 box of peppersauce, 3 bags of table salt and 6 packages of preserved meats.

> The medicine chest carried 1 case of Holland Gin, 1 gallon of brandy, 1 gallon of port wine, and 10 gallons of whiskey. Among the miscel-

laneous items were: tar, 20 cords of wood, chains, head straps, old junk, white oak butts, boat knees, stems and timbers, 15 pounds of sand, 1 cask of sawdust, 1 cask of line, 3 whaling guns, 50 bomb lances, lance powder, spun yarn winch, 20 manilla lines, 2 tarred, 1 coil of lance line, 1 coil of marline, 4 coils spun yarn, 12 coils ratlines, ropes for the jib-stay and 8 coils of manilla rope.

The ship chandlery carried scrubbing brushes, chopping knives, lamp wick, coffee mills, brick, sieves, four sets of knives, beeswax, tacks, brass and iron screws, shovels, hoes, rigging leather, pump leather, matches and ensigns, 29 varieties of cooper's tools, an assortment of crockery and tinware.

In the ship's chest were: tobacco, reefing jackets, duck trousers, denims, Guernsey frocks, twilled jersey shirts, tarpaulin hats, southwesters, shoes and brogans.

The method of payment by ship owners was: Captains, mates and seamen all sailed on the "lay" method of payment, that is, for a certain percentage of the cargo secured. Usually a Captain received one-sixteenth; a mate, one-twenty-fourth; a boat steerer, one-nineteenth; and an ordinary seaman, one-one hundred and tenth of the catch. The remainder went to the owners, who bore the whole expense of the voyage. This system gave every man an interest in securing a big "lay," and it worked very well. An outcome of this plan was the system of "advance," by which they advanced to the men tobacco, clothes and money, often to the full value of their share in the prospective cargo. Those who were too extravagant taking advances often ended up with no pay at all at the end of the voyage.

Edward Cooper, the Cooper

"I am Cooper by name and cooper by trade" was the familiar greeting Edward Cooper gave as one entered his shop on West Water Street. His cooper shop, where huge oil casks and barrels were made, was a spot of continuous activity; men coming and going, both for business purposes and to catch up on the latest news.

Edward Cooper could be described as being a kindly and good-hearted individual with a loud commanding voice which he frequently used to keep the young boys out of his shop and away from the piles of staves and yellow pine planks he used in his business. The great oil cask was an essential item on every whaleship that left the harbor. Taken apart and put into bundles of "shooks," they took much less room aboard the vessel. The ship's cooper would set them up again as needed when whales were taken on ship and tried out.

Oliver Wade in his "Reminiscences of East Water Street" described the technique of barrel-making as follows:

> First the oak stave was hewn into rough shape with a cooper's axe, then put into a horse which held it while being further shaped by a draw knife, and then on long planes set on a decline, where the edges were finally smoothed and shaped ready for the final setting up of the cask.

> Under the head of a truss hoop the staves were carefully placed side by side. When the circle was complete a larger truss hoop was slipped over the first and driven down. The partially formed cask was then reversed and placed under the winch and the protruding ends of the staves encircled with a heavy rope and slowly drawn together as the hand bars turned the winch. It was now ready for the iron hoops. The hoop iron was measured about the cask and cut off. Then it was punched for the rivet and the rivet was firmed by pounding the end with an adz. The hoop was then slipped over the staves above the truss and driven down by a tool called a drive which had a grooved edge which gave it a hold on the hoop. The first hoop was then taken off and a second iron hoop was placed above the second truss which was then removed. Then came the making of the head and the fitting, then the cask was placed in a cradle and crozed which formed the chime and sunken rim into which the head fitted, the cooper's eye being the only guide.

Sag Harbor's dependence on the cooper during the whaling industry was immense. Several cooperages stood along the waterfront both east and west of the Long Wharf, and those in the business were: Abel Minor, at the foot of the village; Post & Sherry, near the bridge to North Haven; Michael Bush, D.Y. Bellows, Harry Tryon, Charles Seeley and Henry Stewart, all on West Water Street; Charles Ware on Spring Street; Thomas Pierson on Main Street; and John Budd on North Haven. Others working in the trade were James Bassett, William Bickerton, D. Atwood Eldredge, Samuel Fordham, John Gawley, Gilbert Horton, Charles Hubbard, James Nickerson, B. Reeves, and Thomas Wallace.

Making Needed Repairs

Many whaling vessels barely made it back to port at the end of their lengthy voyages. Badly in need of repair, they tied up at the Long Wharf where the caulkers, riggers, sail-makers and other workers related to the industry swiftly went to work restoring the ship and readying it for its next trip.

To repair the bottom of a ship was no easy task. The ship was hove down almost on her beam ends by means of large tackles, a set of huge blocks fastened to the masts and another set to the string piece on the opposite side of the dock. Through these, large ropes were woven as falls, with the end leading to a capstan on the dock. Through a hole near the top of the capstan a long bar was thrust, and then men at both ends would walk around and around, pulling the ship over farther and farther until, at last, the keel would come to the surface of the water. Then the old sheathing was taken off the ship's bottom, and the seams caulked with oakum, and then sprayed with hot pitch taken from a large kettle on the dock, heated and kept hot by some boy or disabled sailor who acted as foreman and received about 50 cents a day.

The pitch was then scraped off flush with the planking, the bottom sheathed over with thin planking, and over that a sheathing of copper to protect the bottom from worms that were very destructive to the wood planking in tropical waters. After one side was finished, the tackles were slackened up and the vessel allowed to right itself to an even keel. Then she was turned around, and the same operation repeated on the other side. This is how the ship's bottom was restored to good order.

2

WHALING ADVENTURES BEFORE THE DECLINE

There was only one case of mutiny aboard a Sag Harbor whaler, and that took place on the vessel *Oscar* in 1845. The ship's captain, Isaac Ludlow, shot a member of his crew, after four of them attempted to assault him during a fight aboard ship. Although the event caused quite a stir, Ludlow was exonerated after a Grand Jury found no evidence of misconduct on his part.

Mutiny on the Whaleship Oscar

The mutiny appeared to grow out of the drunkeness on the part of the crew, who managed to smuggle six bottles of rum on board, during the Captain's absence, while the vessel was lying off the coast of Brazil on August 18, 1845. The Captain went ashore, and shortly after, two of the three prisoners stripped themselves to swim ashore, contrary to the Mate's repeated orders. The Captain, when returning, picked up one of the prisoners and brought him back to the vessel. Captain Ludlow reprimanded the men for their misconduct and ordered them to go below. One of the prisoners, however, continued to talk about it and went aft, grumbling. Baker and Curtis (the man shot) told him to go ahead and they would back him, and upon this, Captain Ludlow, seeing there was a disposition to mutiny, went below, loaded a gun, returned to the deck, and summoning the crew, directed all who were with him to come aft.

The Mate and Second Mate, three Boatsteerers, and three Foremast men immediately joined the Captain, who then stepped on the starboard side, in front of the prisoners, and told them not to come abaft the main mast. He repeated this order several times, at the same time keeping the guns pointed toward them. Hoffman held the pump-break in his hand, and another of the prisoners, a marlin spike. The captain continued to warn them not to come more forward, and some of the prisoners opened their shirt bosoms and told him to fire, saying he could not kill more than one man. They still continued to press on toward the Captain. Curtis was foremost and dared him to fire, which the Captain at last did, and killed him on the spot. Captain Ludlow is said to be a very exemplary man and of good moral and religious character, and it is said that, prior to discharging the gun, he called upon the men to observe that he was perfectly collected and was only firing in self-defence.

The following account of the trial and its outcome appeared in the January 24, 1846 Sag Harbor *Corrector*.

UNITED STATES DISTRICT COURT

Before Judge Betts: Trial of Hoffman, Baker and Peake, two of the crew and the cook of the Bark Oscar, charged with endeavouring to create a revolt. Mr. Shepperd summing up for the prisoners, and Mr. Butler for the United States. The latter stated that whatever might have been the conduct of Captain Ludlow in taking the life of Curtis, the two cases must be kept distinct. The court in its charge to the jury explained the law bearing upon the case. In regard to the prisoners the charges are not of a serious nature, nor such as in any great degree to injure their reputations. The crew throughout, as shown by their testimony and appearance, seem to be men of intelligence and above the ordinary class of seamen. There appears to have been the greatest harmony between them and the officers until the day of this unfortunate occurrence.

The Captain's ill feeling was not shown, however, except by his looks, until he attempted to check the cook for talking loud to the steward. The cook would not obey, but continued talking. Curtis and Baker came up to near where they stood and looked angrily at the Captain who soon afterward went below and prepared his firearms and while doing so fired off a cap. Exclamations were made between Baker and the cook, and the former tying his suspenders round him said, "Let him come on with his bull dogs," and the cook throwing his hat on the deck in an angry manner and exclaiming, "I cannot die but once, and may as well die now as at any time." It was also said that Baker and Curtis had previously said something to the cook, but none of it in the hearing of the Captain.

The crew had been drinking freely that day and the jury must consider whether the Captain had ground to treat the temper they displayed as the result of such, or whether the state of the crew was really of a character calculated to create serious apprehensions on his part. One of the counts in the charge is for making a riot, which has reference to the time and its vicinity, when the man was shot down. Shouting and making a noise so as to overawe the officers, or impede them in the discharge of their duty, is an endeavor in the eye of the law, to create a revolt. The court does not consider, however, that some of the men crying to the Captain to fire, when he had his gun presented, came within the rule. If the men attempted to go abaft the mainmast when ordered by the Captain not to do so, with a view to intimidate the officers, and were armed so as to create apprehension, it was a mutiny, but if they acted merely from that care-nothing sort of way that may sometimes be pursued by seamen in the condition that they were in, it is different. It is said that after the smoke had cleared away one of the prisoners was seen with a hand-spike, another with a pump bolt, and another with an axe. It is also said that they caught them up for self-defense and after striking at a sharp whaling spade, held out by one of the officers, they put them down again. If these weapons were taken up with a view to self-defense, it does not come within the rule, but if intended to act against the officers it was so. As to the idea of riot, the others did not take any part of it.

The jury came into court saying they did not find the men guilty of a revolt. They found Baker and Peake guilty of riotous conduct and recommended them to mercy. They could not agree as to whether Hoffman was guilty or not. The jury were then discharged and two of the prisoners remanded. The third (Hoffman) is out on bail.

Judge Betts charged the jury in the above case; he told them that the charges against these men were not of a serious nature, nor such as in any great degree to injure their reputation. Now the words of Judge Betts, upon passing sentence upon these men. George Baker, one of the seamen of the Bark Oscar, found guilty of a riot on board the vessel at the time young Curtis was shot by Captain Ludlow, was brought up for sentence. The Court remarked to him, that the jury had recommended him to mercy, but the case becomes a very serious one from the consequences which followed his misconduct. From his previous good character, and apparently general intelligence, better things were expected of him than was shown at that time—you stimulated the crew, said the court, to acts of disorder, and your bearings towards the mate when he ordered the men to keep back was taunting and provoking to the highest degree. You got the crew in a state of commotion and it resulted in the death of one of your comrades. The sentence of the court is that you be imprisoned six months and pay a fine of $25.

Isaiah Peake, black man, the cook of the vessel, who was tried and found guilty of riot also, on the same indictment with Baker, was also brought up. The court stated to him that he had commenced the riot and continued disorderly and refractory. He was sentenced to eight months from the date of conviction.

The wind appears now to have veered to the opposite point of the compass; March 1846, the grand jury refused to find any fault for the killing of a mutineer and discharged Captain Ludlow. And so ended a case of mutiny aboard the Sag Harbor whaleship Oscar

Captain Royce and His Bomb Lance

Thomas W. Royce (Roys) came to Sag Harbor as a youth of 17, having been born in upper New York State about 1816. From early childhood he had a love of the sea, and while in his teen years shipped out as a greenhand aboard the Sag Harbor whaler *Hudson*. He was a strong and able seaman, surviving shipwrecks, cannibals and other whaling mishaps, and within eight years became the captain of his own ship.

In 1848 Captain Royce, sailing on the bark *Superior*, became the first American to pass through the Bering Strait into the Arctic Ocean. There he found the whale plentiful, tame and easy to capture. Returning a month later with 1800 barrels of oil, he opened the Arctic to the whale fishery. The following year 154 ships left for the Arctic whaling grounds, and the value of their season's catch was nearly $3,500,000. On subsequent voyages Royce commanded the *W.F. Stafford*, *S.S. Learned* and the *Highland Mary* (*Parana*), all out of Sag Harbor.

Captain Royce studied the various types of whales and discovered the bow head species in the Arctic. He designed his own whaling guns and lances in the mid 1850s. His weapons were cast at Liverpool by famous British engineer Joseph Whitworth. In one instance, while testing a new gun, he was seriously injured when the device exploded and shattered his hand. It was amputated aboard ship by the 1st mate, Roger Bishop of Westhampton. Upon arrival in port, further surgery became necessary when infection threatened his life.

A whaling rocket harpoon called the "Bomb Lance," fired from a shoulder mounted tube, was another of his inventions. In March 1861, after Captain Royce had returned to Sag Harbor, he tested his new whaling gun at the Long

The East Hampton Turnpike Toll House. *Courtesy JJML*

The Bull's Head Turnpike Toll House, late 1800s. *Coll. Otto Fenn*

The Long Wharf in the late 1800s. *Courtesy JJML*

Early wooden drawbridge, photo late 1800s. *Courtesy JJML*

The Beebee Mill, built 1820. *Courtesy JJML*

Two views of the waterfront after the fire of 1877. *Coll. Otto Fenn*

The first school building, photo ca. 1870. *Courtesy JJML*

The Arsenal on Union Street, photo ca. 1875. *Courtesy JJML*

The Atheneum, early 1900s, destroyed by fire. *Courtesy JJML*

e 1817 Presbyterian Church, late 1800s. *Courtesy JJML*

Henry Packer Dering, Collector of the Port. Painting ca. 1794 *Courtesy SPLIA*

e Custom House. *Courtesy SPLIA*

The Broken Mast Monument in Oakland Cemetery.
Courtesy JJML

Model of the whaleship *Daniel Webster. Courtesy Whaling Mus.*

The Sag Harbor Whaling and Historical Museum. *Photo: Richard J. Hornell*

James Fenimore Cooper, novelist and whaling entrepreneur. *Courtesy JJML*

Funeral print of Bark Oscar. *Courtesy SPLIA*

Captain Wickham Havens, portrait by Hubbard L. Fordham. *Coll. Whaling Mus.*

Mrs. Wickham Havens, portrait by Hubbard L. Fordham. *Coll. Whaling Mus.*

Captain Jonas Winters, portrait by Hubbard L. Fordham. *Coll. Whaling Mus.*

Captain Nathan Fordham, portrait by Hubbard L. Fordham. *Coll. Whaling Mus.*

Captain David Hand House, Church Street. *Photo: Otto Fenn. Courtesy SHHS.*

Captain Jared Wade House, 1797, Union Street. *Photo: Otto Fenn. Courtesy SHHS.*

Ephraim Niles Byram, clockmaker and astronomer. *Courtesy JJML*

The business district from the Methodist Church, ca. 1860s. *Courtesy JJML*

The Oakland Works from an 1854 map. *Courtesy JJML*

A young man on Long Wharf. *Coll. Otto Fenn*

Storeowner Louis Hertz with friends on Main St., 1890s. *Courtesy JJML*

Reimann's Pharmacy, ca. 1900, with Tooker (l.) and Reimann (c.). *Courtesy JJML*

Window of Muller's Market. *Coll. Otto Fenn*

Cook's Department Store on Main Street. *Author's collection*

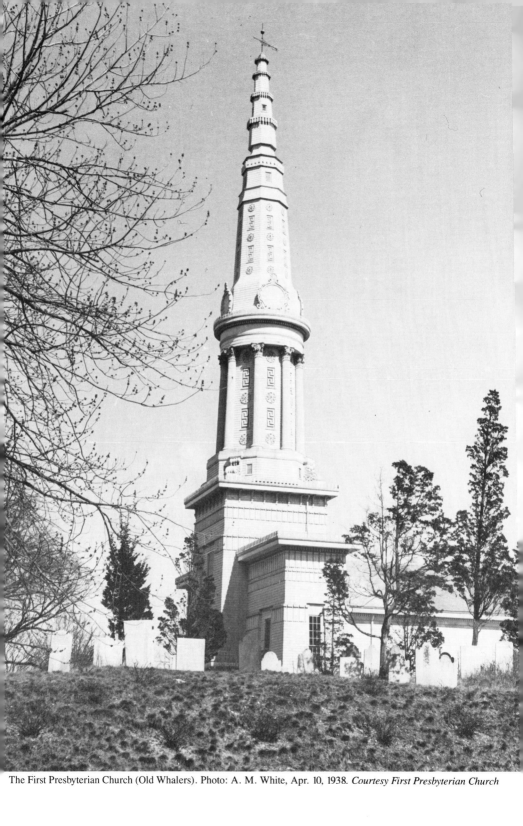

The First Presbyterian Church (Old Whalers). Photo: A. M. White, Apr. 10, 1938. *Courtesy First Presbyterian Church*

The Academy of the Sacred Heart of Mary, early 1900s. *Coll. Otto Fenn*

Temple Adas Israel, built 1900. *Courtesy Temple Adas Israel*

The Union School, ca. 1900. *Author's collection*

St. David A.M.E. Zion Church, built in 1840. *Courtesy ECHS*

The Bethel Baptist Church, ca. 1900. *Author's collection*

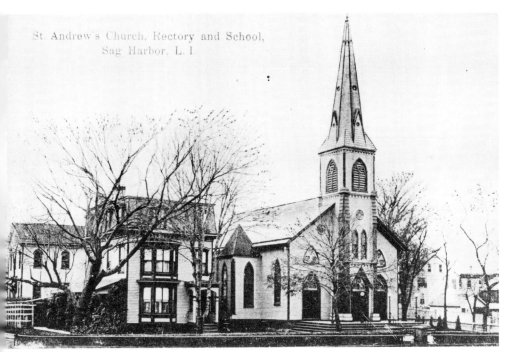

St. Andrew's Roman Catholic Church, early 1900s. *Author's collection*

St. Andrew's School on Union Street, early 1900s. *Coll. Otto Fenn*

The North Haven Chapel, ca. 1890. *Courtesy Eugene Hodenpyl*

Christ Episcopal Church, ca. 1890. *Courtesy Christ Episcopal Church*

Sag Harbor Cornet Band on Main Street. *JJML*

The Phoenix Hose Co., Washington St. *Coll. Otto Fenn*

The Methodist Church on Madison Street. *Courtesy JJML*

Waterfront with the Gardiner House. *Coll. Otto Fenn*

View of Main Street with Alvin Building, ca. 1900. *Courtesy JJML*

Hotel Bay View, Main Street, photo ca. 1930. *Coll. Otto Fenn*

Main Street with early street lights, ca. 1920s. *Coll. Otto Fenn*

Captain John B. Phillips, 1900. *Courtesy Patricia Donovan*

Phillip's trading schooner *Estelle*, ca. 1904. *Courtesy Patricia Donovan*

The steamboat *Montauk* built 1891. *Courtesy JJML*

Interior of the steamboat *Shinnecock*, 1895. *Courtesy JJML*

Charles Watson Payne III, merchant, ca. 1865.
Courtesy JJML

William Wallace Tooker, pharmacist, Algonquin authority, ca. 1910. *Courtesy JJML*

Stephen Talkhouse Pharaoh, a member of the Eastville Pharaoh family, 1879. *Courtesy JJML*

Momoweta Tribe #459 Improved Order of Redmen, ca. 1905. *Courtesy JJML*

The Sag Harbor Cornet Band, early 1900s. *Coll. Otto Fenn*

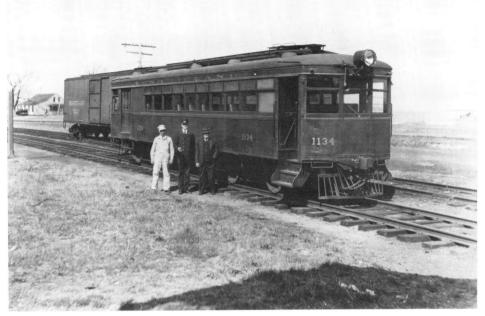

The one-car train known as the "Toonerville Trolley." *Coll. Otto Fenn*

he Brick Depot for the railroad, ca. 1910. *Courtesy JJML*

General view of the waterfront. *Coll. Otto Fenn*

Early 1900s view of Main and Washington Streets. *Coll. Otto Fenn*

Fahys Watch Case Factory, built 1881. *Courtesy JJML*

Alvin Co., early 1900s. *Courtesy JJML*; and after fire. *Author's collection.*

A house on Madison Street near Union Street, ca. 1910. *Coll Otto Fenn*

Margaret Olivia Slocum Sage, ca. 1910. *Courtesy JJML*

Interior of Library rotunda and reading room, 1910. *Courtesy JJML*

Laying the cornerstone for Pierson High School, 1907. *Courtesy JJML*

Mashashimuet Park flagpole dedication, 1913. *Courtesy JJML*

John Jermain Memorial Library, built 1910. *Photo James C. Ashe*

Sag Harbor Grain Company, early 1900s. *Author's collection*

E.W. Bliss Torpedo Barge in Noyac Bay. *Courtesy JJML*

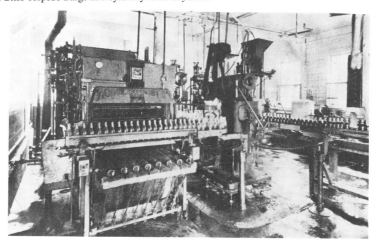
Inside Wilson's Bottling Works, ca. 1920. *Author's collection*

Camp Aldrich of the N.Y. Guards, 1918. *Courtesy JJML*

Municipal Building with World War I service flag. *Coll. Otto Fenn*

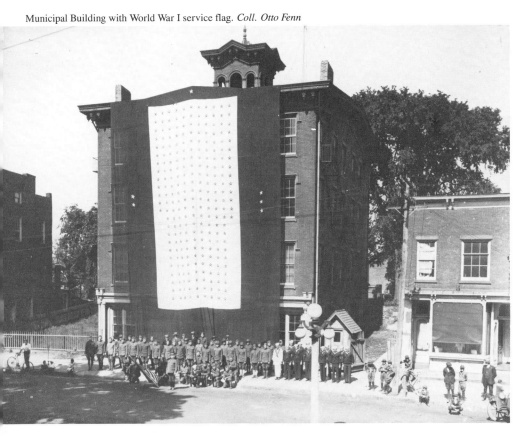

Poster for "Back Home and Broke," filmed in Sag Harbor. *Author's collection*

An early Sag Harbor police chief. *Coll. Otto Fenn*

Wharf. Whalemen from all around the area assembled in large numbers to watch the experiment. A cloth target, 3 foot square, was placed in the water 150 feet from the wharf. Captain Royce brought the gun to his shoulder and fired, striking the target near the center. The bomb exploded, scattering water in every direction. About 20 fathoms of line were taken out with the lance. The object of his invention was to lance whales which were not close enough to be harpooned by ordinary means. It was also thought that the explosion of the bomb inside the whale would generate enough gas to keep the carcass from sinking. The experiment was a complete success. Patents were secured in England, France, Holland, Norway, and the United States.

Captain Royce's whaling guns greatly improved the method of taking whales by providing a more humane way of capturing them. Although his inventions were widely accepted and modernized the whale fishery, they brought him no financial success. In 1866, with his health failing, Royce went to Mexico and died at Mazatlan on January 27, 1877 at the age of 61.

The Bark Highland Mary

One of Sag Harbor's notable whale ships had three different names at various times during her illustrious career. Christened the *Michael*, the vessel was a brig of 209 tons burden and launched under the Hanoverian flag for the Merchant Marines. Sailing with a cargo of sugar, the *Michael* ran aground on a reef off the east coast of South America. The crew of the schooner *Draco*, out of Sag Harbor, salvaged the ship, made temporary repairs, and brought the *Michael* to Baltimore, Maryland. The *Draco* had been on her way to the Pacific coast with a load of cargo consigned to a Sag Harbor shopkeeper who sailed to California with the Argonauts in 1849. When the *Michael* reached Baltimore, Captain Edward Smith, of Sag Harbor, arrived there to take command of the ship and sail her to our port. Here, it was partly rebuilt, outfitted as a whaling vessel, and re-named the *Parana*. Two whaling voyages under Captain Smith followed. On the first voyage the *Parana* cruised the South Atlantic, leaving Sag Harbor June 16, 1853 and returning June 15, 1854 with 29 barrels of sperm, 662 barrels of whale oil and bone, valued at $28,000. Two years later a 19-month-long voyage brought back 79 barrels of sperm, 359 of whale oil and bone, worth $15,000. This voyage brought the *Parana* to Patagonia (the southern portion of South America). Between June 1856 and 1860, Captain Thomas Royce, inventor of the bomb lance, made two voyages on the *Parana*.

In 1860 Hannibal and Stephen B. French bought the *Parana* from the estate of Thomas Brown, who had been agent for the ship, for $2250, and sent Captain

Green on a voyage to the South Atlantic. Upon its return, the vessel was rebuilt at Port Jefferson, New York and given a bark rigging. At that time the *Parana*'s name was changed to the *Highland Mary*.

During the Civil War, under charter and flying the English colors, the *Highland Mary* successfully ran the blockaded southern Confederate ports. Following the conflict, the ship once again joined the Sag Harbor fleet and sailed on July 3, 1867 for the South Atlantic, under Captain A. Smith French. At that time there was an unsuccessful effort to again change the name of the ship, due to the unsavory reputation the bark had gained as a blockade runner. On that same voyage most of the crew deserted the ship, and the *Highland Mary* was condemned at Panama. In 1868, after repairs were made, an Act of Congress granted the bark a new charter and the *Highland Mary* once again set sail.

In 1868 the *Highland Mary* assisted the British bark *Bogota* off the island of Tristan da Cunha, a volcanic island in the South Atlantic. The *Bogota*, sailing under Captain Jones from Glasgow to Penang (off the Malay Peninsula), was found to be on fire. Captain Jones threw overboard the cargo of powder and stood by his ship until actually driven from her by the flames. The captain and crew, manning small boats, reached the island and were picked up by Captain French, who agreed to take them to the Cape of Good Hope, even though the bark's course had been laid for New Zealand. On the way, they came upon the burned out shell of the *Bogota*, and Captain French ordered the derelict ship scuttled so she would pose no further navigational threat to other ships in the area. Before reaching the Cape, the *Highland Mary* met the steamship *City of Dublin*, bound for Capetown, and transferred to the ship the crew of the ill-fated *Bogota*.

For this service, Captain French received the following testimonial from the British Board of Trade through Her Majesty's Consul in New York:

> In transmitting the above documents I am desired to inform you that the Board has awarded a gold watch to Captain French in testimony of his services to the British seamen, which will be forwarded for presentation to him through his own government.

The Board of Trade also awarded to the owners of the *Highland Mary* a sum of 23 pounds sterling and 12 shillings, to repay them for expenses and losses sustained through subsistence and demurrage in connection with services rendered to the crew of the *Bogota*.

The *Highland Mary* was finally found unseaworthy, was condemned and sold at Tobago Island, a place about 30 miles from Panama. She was bid off

WHALING BEFORE THE DECLINE

for $820. Captain Davis C. Osborn of Shelter Island, New York had taken an interest in the vessel and had gone out to Panama to assume command. On arriving there, he found the bark advertised for sale and made efforts to have the sale stopped and the ship repaired. But upon investigation, it was determined that the ship was in such condition the cost of repairs would exceed the worth of the bark, so the sale went on. It was in 1873 that the end came to the *Michael-Parana-Highland Mary*, a Sag Harbor whaler that made six voyages, taking in products valued at $163,000, and it left the brig *Myra* the sole remaining vessel of the once spectacular whaling fleet of the Port of Sag Harbor.

A Voyage on the Henry Lee

One of the largest vessels registered at the Sag Harbor Custom House was the whaleship *Henry Lee*. She joined the fleet in 1842 and made two voyages: the first under Captain Charles Bennett, and the second under Captain Benjamin Payne. Sag Harbor historian Harry D. Sleight had the opportunity to contact George Dorsey of Wilmington, Delaware, the sole survivor of the *Henry Lee*, and obtained the following story from Dorsey, who sailed on that ship as a boy under the name of George Howard.

> Sag Harbor used to be a great whaling port. I have seen as many as fifty vessels lying there. Many of them were built at and hailed from Sag Harbor.
>
> Having been outfitted for the voyage by Douglas & Wade, under the name of (George Howard), on the 17th of June 1845, I sailed out of Sag Harbor on the ship Henry Lee. The Henry Lee was formerly a Liverpool packet called the Westchester. She was an old ship when I was in her and was one of the largest whalers sailing out of Sag Harbor carrying four boats, and I think the only one that did carry four boats. We had three on our port side and one, the captain's boat, on our starboard side. We cut in on the starboard side.
>
> The Henry Lee was owned by S. & B. Huntting and Company whose place of business was right on the Long Wharf. The Captain was Benjamin Payne (and a nice old man he was too—always treating all hands all right), the first mate, Mr. Rogers, and forty-two men in her forecastle.
>
> From Sag Harbor we went around the Cape of Good Hope and whaled around New Holland and New Zealand and thence up the Pacific, stopping at Pitcairn Island which was settled by the mutineers of the ship

Bounty. There was only one place on the Island you could land and it was called Bounty Bay. Then we went up the coast of America, stopping at the Sandwich Islands and from there across to the coast of Kamschatka. We had taken a few whales prior to this time but we took a great many here. As soon as it got too cold for us to stay there we went down the Pacific taking a few more whales. On our way down from Kamschatka, on the Malicious Bank, a whale struck our whale boat, knocking it to splinters and breaking and splintering my arm. The Captain did not often lower his boat, but he did this occasion. I was lying on a broken spar and piece of sail and the Captain said, "Oh the boy is all right, ain't you Howard?" I said, "Aye aye, sir." The Captain said, "I will go and kill the whale," and he did too. A couple of hours afterward we were picked up. To show you how long a way from home that was in those days, I will say that on the Fourth of July we spoke to the whaler, Harvest, of FairHaven, Connecticut, which was now homeward bound, with a keg up aloft to denote that she was "full." That was the custom. This day the Captain called that there was a chance for anyone who wanted to, to send letters home. I had one already written to my mother (I guess that was the only one that I wrote during the entire voyage) and I finished it up and sent it to her, and although the Harvest went direct home, that letter was eleven months in getting to her.

We took about 3500 barrels of whale oil and 150 barrels of sperm and came back to Long Island by way of Cape Horn after a three year voyage. When we got to Sag Harbor I drew $20 on my wages (I was on a 180th lay) and started home, intending to go back and get the balance of my wages, but I did not get home that trip, neither did I ever get my wages.

The next time I saw any of the crew of the Henry Lee was while laying at Rio de Janeiro on board the U.S. Ship St. Louis. Our captain, who had never been aboard a whaler, decided to visit one that was lying in the harbor. It was Sunday morning and I did not want to go as I was all togged out in white duck trousers and white shirt and I well knew the oily dirty character of a whaler, but as I was coxswain of the captain's gig, I had to go when he called for his boat. We took him to the side of the Phoenix of Sag Harbor. The Captain went on board and we lay at the gangway while he went to the cabin with the "old man" of the Phoenix. The crew of the whaler were looking over the side at us when I hard one of them call out, "Hello there Howard, what are you doing down there?" I looked up and saw the black face of Rugg—Adam Rugg—one of the members of the crew of the Henry Lee. The Captain of the bark coming from the cabin with the captain of the St. Louis said,

"Who are you hollering at, Rugg?" and Rugg said, "Why Howard is down there in the boat." The captain hurried to the side and looked over and I saw that it was Rogers, formerly first mate of the Henry Lee. Of course I had to go on board then, explanations followed and they were glad to see me.

About 1888 I visited Sag Harbor and vicinity. I stopped at the Nassau House because I was acquainted with the then proprietor's wife, who was a daughter of the woman with whom I had boarded for several weeks prior to sailing on the Henry Lee. I called on Captain Payne, who lived in a very nice place at North Haven, and met with a cordial reception. The next day was Sunday and we got a team and drove to East Hampton and saw George Bushnell, were cordially received and he gave me a book that was a journal of the Henry Lee and contained an account of every day's happenings on that voyage.

As I was by far the youngest member of the crew, you see, they must all be dead by this time, for that voyage was made over sixty years ago.

POLLY SWEET, PIONEER

Other than Mrs. Russell Sage, little has been documented about the women of Sag Harbor, yet, there were some whose courage and determination were outstanding and who overcame insurmountable odds to reach their goals. One such woman was a real pioneer and had the distinction of being the first woman from New York State to cross the Great Plains to the Pacific coast by prairie wagon in 1844-45. Her name was Polly Sweet.

Some historians believe Polly was born a Mackie or a Russell, but according to William Wallace Tooker, her maiden name was Cook. Tooker claimed her father was a Captain Cook; her mother Jane Taft; and her sister, Sarah Cook, wife of James Rogers of Sag Harbor. In any event, she was born in Sag Harbor in 1815, the daughter of a sea captain who made several voyages around the Cape to California in the years before 1800. When Polly was a child, Sag Harbor was already a port for vessels engaged in the coastal trade between here and the West Indies, and from her earliest recollections she listened spellbound to the tales her father told of his exciting experiences in California. She acquired a taste for adventure at an early age, and, while just a child, made up her mind that some day she would make the long and perilous journey across the country to the west coast.

Polly married in 1835 at the age of 20 and lost no time convincing Mr. Sweet that fame and fortune awaited them in sunny California. At the end of the first year of their marriage, Polly, her husband, and their infant son set out on an incredible adventure that would take them from Sag Harbor across this vast land to the Pacific coast.

Starting out by wagon, they traveled up to Albany and across New York State to Buffalo where they sold their horses and boarded a packet ship for the four-day trip to Chicago. They remained there for a year, during which time the second of their children was born. With two baby boys and all their household goods, the Sweet family proceeded on their journey. Traveling by wagon, their determination was increased by news brought back by hunters and trappers who had just returned from the coast with tales of excitement and challenge. It was during their stay in St. Louis that the Sweets met the famous Kit Carson and learned from him that a company of men and women were to start the following spring the long trek across the Great Divide. Throughout the winter they thought of little else but the forthcoming trip, in spite of warnings that the trip would take them through Comanche and Cheyenne territories.

Leaving Fort Leavenworth in May 1845, the group of 46 young men, seven married women, and 11 children started out on the expedition. It would be an undertaking in which they would endure suffering, deprivations, famine, and death before reaching their destination.

The wagon train crossed the Rockies through a pass which the Union Pacific Railroad was to use 25 years later. Enormous herds of buffalo were sighted along the way. Through Colorado and across the burning deserts of Utah and Nevada, they pushed on, losing several oxen due to the searing heat and the lack of water. Two wagonloads of household goods had to be left behind.

Several men fell ill with fever, and the women took over as teamsters, and Polly Sweet learned to handle the team with expertise. They finally reached the grassy slopes of the Sierras, but their troubles were hardly over, for an unfriendly tribe of Indians spent several days watching them, which resulted in posting guards at the campsite around the clock. Although in constant fear, only one actual confrontation occurred which resulted in the death of one white man and one Indian. On October 28, 1845 the group, exhausted and sick and with few provisions, finally reached Sutter's Fort. Eight adults and two children had perished along the way.

Polly Sweet and her family spent some time at Sutter's Fort, regaining their strength and trying their hand at cattle raising. They were, however, unable to accustom themselves to the calm and easy life, so on the advice of Captain Sutter, the family (which now had been blessed with a baby daughter) made plans to move north to the Oregon boarder. Along with a company of ten, they walked the 100 miles north to start a new American colony in that area. Polly became even more expert with a rifle than her husband, having to protect herself and her children on many occasions from the black bear that roamed near their campsite. They forded streams, slept in the forest, and lived on beans, berries, and deer meat.

The party pushed forward to the Siskiu Mountains where they encountered a tribe of about 2000 Indians who wanted to barter furs for their guns. When the Indians discovered that they couldn't make the trade, they attacked. Arrows flew thick and fast, and it was a miracle that none of the men in the group were hit. Four arrows hit the boards behind which Polly had taken refuge. The men of the party crawled back to camp to retrieve their loaded guns, and when they opened fire, the Indians took off. When the group arrived at their destination, the large number of unfriendly Indians and the total lack of law and order made it impossible to stay. They turned back to Sutter's Fort.

By 1848 news of gold having been discovered in central California sent the Sweet family south, and Polly Sweet became the first American woman at the scene of the discovery. The first week her husband tried his luck panning along the shore of the American River he collected $1600 in gold. Businesses shut down, farmers left their farms, and hundreds pulled up stakes to rush to the California coast. It wasn't long before the news reached the East Coast, and many of Sag Harbor's whaleships and their crews headed around the Cape for California, some never to return home again. They were the years of plenty, wealth and adventure, and the Sweets prospered along with the rest. Sag Harbor's Polly Sweet had finally found her fortune, after four years of a challenging and fearless experience that few other women would ever attempt to tackle.

Whaleships Sold for the Slave Trade

Most of the wealth, fame, and prosperity that came to Sag Harbor during the whaling years was from legitimate means. However, there were some who were out to capitalize on any get-rich scheme, including selling their ships for the illegal transport of human beings to be sold into slavery. A whaleship could be converted into a slaver without much effort and some of the ships that were sold or disappeared from the port might well have been used for that purpose. Many ships went undetected, and in 1859-60 some 85 ships in New York were estimated to be dealing in the slave market. Skippers who earned about $900 per year in the whale fishery could earn ten times that for a single slaving voyage. There were many instances where captains became affluent from a single voyage, with local investors also sharing in the profits from these illegal ventures.

The whaleship *Montauk* was probably the most infamous and well known slaver. For some months the vessel had been tied up at Long Wharf. In March 1860 it was sold to Captain Quayle, along with its gear, supposedly to be used in the whaling trade. The ship was previously owned by John Budd and added to the Sag Harbor fleet in 1853. Quayle lost no time in forming a company which included several prominent citizens of Sag Harbor, and then took the ship to New York where it was fitted out. Its supplies were somewhat suspicious, carrying a very large supply of fresh water, 130 barrels of bread, and 250 boxes of smoked herring. But because nothing illegal was found, it cleared from the Port of New York on April 28, 1860. The *Montauk* headed straight for the Canary Islands, where more provisions were taken on, and then sailed directly for the African coast. Eleven hundred and forty men, women, and children were taken aboard for the trip to Cuba where they were to be sold into slavery. One hundred fifty died on the journey, six of them infants. Before it reached Cuba the vessel was given a new name. "Lesbia of Toulon" was painted on a board and nailed to the stern. As the ship was about to land at Cuba with its human cargo, it was confiscated by the steamship *Ysabella France*, whose officials went aboard, put the crew under arrest, and towed the ship into Havana. The captain of the ship, however, was never detained, and before long all the crew were released.

The second ship, the *Augusta*, originally was a packet ship which sailed between Savannah and New York. In 1857 it was altered and added to the Sag Harbor fleet by W. & G.H. Cooper, and for four years cruised for whales. It was sold to Greenport in April 1861 and outfitted for its brief career as a slaver. The captain of the *Augusta* had taken on whale boats and a quantity of provisions at Sag Harbor, and the bark slipped away from Gardiner's Bay in November 1861. A revenue cutter, with a New York marshal aboard, was only an hour behind and soon intercepted the *Augusta*. The ship was condemned as a slaver and sold at public auction in New York City June 25, 1862, ending the *Augusta*'s brief attempt to enter the slave trade market.

There were also instances of whaleships disappearing after sailing from the port, and, in all likelihood, some entered the slave trade. Such may have been the fate of one missing Sag Harbor ship. In 1858 a mysterious bark was sold to New York and then to a well-known Spanish company where it was fitted out as a slave ship. The vessel, called the *Haidee*, sailed to the coast of Africa where it took on 1133 Africans and sailed for Cuba, where the 933 survivors were sold, 200 having died on the voyage. The bark then sailed out to sea, paid off the crew, and headed for the eastern coast of Long Island where plans were made to scuttle the vessel after nearing Montauk Point. Holes were bored in the ship's bottom and then plugged up. As soon as it was dark, the plugs were removed, and the officers and crew took to the boats. One headed for the Connecticut shore; the other, for Montauk, where the crew members told a tale of being shipwrecked. The bark took no time in sinking. Soon after, seven Portuguese sailors arrived at Sag Harbor, where they attracted much attention due to the large amount of Spanish gold in their possession. Rumors of slave trade spread through the village. During the night six were swiftly taken to Connecticut by a Sag Harbor resident of their nationality. One had died in Sag Harbor. On the same day the sailors had arrived in the village, a Deputy Marshal arrived in Montauk to make an investigation. Unfortunately, he arrived too late. The sailor that died was buried in Oakland Cemetery, his gold adequately paying for his funeral and gravestone which reads: "Tho Boreas' winds and Neptune's waves have tossed me to and fro, by God's decree you plainly see, I'm harbored here below."

How many other vessels escaped the swift sailing cruisers checking on slave ships? Only speculation can be made. But many did go undetected and delivered their cargoes of men, women, and children. It was a risky business to be sure, but the enormous profits to be made offered a tempting lure to the unscrupulous, and there were many who couldn't resist the temptation.

The Fate of the Whaling Fleet

After the peak of the whale fishery in 1847 the industry quickly declined. The scores of ships that once sailed to the four corners of the world were no longer useful and within 30 years had passed into oblivion. Some were sold, some condemned and left on distant shores, and others lost forever in the deep abyss of the sea.

A writer back in 1875 described Sag Harbor as "one deserted village, a seaport from which all life had disappeared...they are all gone; the ships, the oil yards, the coopers and the caulkers...all gone." His statement was close to reality, for within those years the village had undergone a transformation from a bustling whaling port alive with activity to a shipless bay with an abandoned wharf and an excessive number of unemployed residents. The end of prosperous times had come; the golden era of the whale fishery a thing of the past.

Discovery of gold in California, petroleum in Pennsylvania, and a general scarcity of the whale—all contributed to the decline of the industry. Because of that, one would imagine that after the voyages ceased the port would have been the scene of scores of derelict and ghostly ships silently dotting the shoreline, an ever present reminder of the flush times that had just come to an end. However, such was not the case. There were no ships left floating in the waters off Sag Harbor. Yet, how could a fleet such as sailed from here disappear in the course of only 30 years? What became of them? What was the fate of that magnificent whaling fleet that was known throughout the world?

Probably the largest number of the ships from Sag Harbor's fleet were sold to companies or individuals planning to sail to the West Coast. When news of gold being discovered in California reached the port of Sag Harbor, there was a general exodus of the men of the village. Many of the whaling captains, disillusioned by the scarcity of the whale, headed for San Francisco with their heads filled with dreams of making their fortunes.

The *Neptune*, *Sabina*, *Niantic* and *Cadmus* were but four of the many vessels that were sold and sailed around the Cape to the California shore, never to return again to Long Island. When the *Niantic* arrived in San Francisco in 1849, after a long and hazardous voyage, she became just another disabled ship along the waterfront. Quoting F.C. Matthews from his papers in the San Francisco Public Library, "As water lots filled up with sand hills which the steam excavators remove, it left many old ships that were beached a year ago as storehouses, in a curious pattern; for the tilled up space that surrounds them has been built upon for some distance, and new streets run between them and the sea." After fire in 1851 destroyed the San Francisco waterfront, the bottom was all that was left to the old ship. Gone was the *Niantic*, but a building erected on the site was named the Niantic Hotel, and even up to 1977, the place was called the Niantic Building.

In April 1978 the *Niantic* surfaced from her earth-filled grave as excavations in the area took place. An eight-foot section of her hull and the bottom of the ship were unearthed, and plans were made to preserve them. The old Sag Harbor whaler *Niantic*, who met her end on the other side of the United States, still lives on, a modern relic of the whaling era and the gold rush days.

The *Cadmus*, which brought Lafayette to America, sailed to California after her days as a whaler were over, and, like many other ships, would never return to Sag Harbor. The *Cadmus* was condemned as unsafe, broken up, and in 1856 portions of her timbers were used for planking the streets near San Francisco.

Other Sag Harbor whaleships met their end in quite a different and unusual way. The *Timor*, *Noble*, and *Emerald* did their part for the North during the Civil War by becoming part of the "Stone Fleet." Tradition tells us that Yankee genius conceived a plan to buy up the old ships, load them with stone, and fit their hulls with valves that could be readily opened. They would then be sunk

WHALING BEFORE THE DECLINE

in southern harbors, thereby establishing a blockade.

In 1861 one to six thousand dollars was paid by the Federal Government for each ship, which was then sailed to South Carolina and Georgia and sunk to prevent blockade runners from entering the harbors. The old ship *Timor* was barely seaworthy. Gone were the years when she earned $225,000 from the six whaling voyages she made, two of them circumnavigating the globe. She leaked so badly that the captain had to turn back and sail into port for repairs to keep her from sinking at sea. The *Timor* finally made the trip to Charleston, the valve opened, and down she went with the other ships.

The *Noble*, with a record of 12 whaling voyages, sailed the seven seas and brought back a catch valued at $260,000. The *Noble* was sunk off Savannah, as was the *Emerald*, one of Sag Harbor's largest whaling vessels. These ships served well and helped win the war for the North. At no time did they bring losses to Long Islanders, for when the whaling industry ended, they were sold for a big price.

Not all of the ships were sold. Wrecks at both near and distant shores took their toll. The *Governor Clinton* was destroyed by a typhoon off the coast of Japan, and the entire crew of 29 lost. The *Romulus* was lost at Honolulu, and the *Hamilton II*, near the Rio Grande. The *Concordia* and the *Thomas Dickason* were abandoned and lost with a great fleet of ships imprisoned in the Arctic ice in 1871. When the location was visited the following year, the *Dickason* lay on her beam end on a bank, bilged and full of water, and the *Concordia* had been burned by natives. The *Concordia* had been considered an unlucky ship, having made but one profitable voyage out of Sag Harbor.

Many vessels were in such a state of disrepair after making several long voyages that they were no longer seaworthy. The *Thames I*, once considered one of the swiftest whalers afloat, brought her owners about $200,000 in profits. She was condemned and lay in the water off Conklin's Point for many years, finally demolished, her bones covered in time by the shifting sands. Several other ships met a similar fate. The *Camillus*, in 1843, broke up and sank at a place called "Rotten Row" off Sag Harbor. The ship *Andes* was wrecked and burned to the water level at the east side of the channel off the Long Wharf. A sandbar formed over her keel and the place is still referred to as "Andes Shoal."

Mystery surrounds the loss of the bark *Ocean*, a 165-ton vessel owned by H. & S. French Company of Sag Harbor. On August 10, 1866 she sailed from port and was last sighted by two homeward bound ships as they rounded Montauk Point. There seemed to be no trouble at that time, yet the bark *Ocean* was never seen or heard from again. A poem was written about the unfortunate ship, *Ocean*, which must have gone down with her captain and crew.

> The Ocean's decks soon rang with songs
> That echoed o'er the bay,
> And through the breeze there oft was born
> The seamen's notes of praise;
> The trees upon the neighboring side
> Appeared to pass away,
> As onward through the rushing tides
> She left Sag Harbor's bay.
>
> The dark and dismal shades of night
> Soon hid her from our view;
> And when we took our last sad sight,
> And gave our last adieu,
> She passed with death upon her wing
> Who'd bent his bow and pulled his string.
>
> *Author unknown*

Sag Harbor's last whaleship was the brig *Myra*. Considered one of the smallest ships, weighing just 116 tons, she made several voyages. During one cruise a United States Cruiser detained the *Myra* off the coast of Africa, under suspicion of being a slaver. After much discussion, Captain Henry A. Babcock finally convinced the naval officers that his ship was peaceably and legally engaged in whaling only. In 1871 this last, lone, remaining ship was sent to sea again under the command of Captain Babcock. The *Myra*'s last voyage lasted three long years, and at the end of that time the wind and sea had reduced her to a useless wreck. The ship was condemned and broken up at Barbados in December 1874, the last of a proud and worthy fleet that sailed from Sag Harbor to the four corners of the world searching for the leviathan of the deep.

And so the end came to the spectacular years of the whale fishery, and although other industries came to Sag Harbor and provided employment for the local residents, Sag Harbor was never again to attain the fame, fortune, and glory it knew during its golden years of whaling.

A list of the whaling vessels that sailed from the Port of Sag Harbor, along with their captains, and details of voyages, may be found in the Appendix. Also in the Appendix are lists of industries related to the whale fishery and men employed by them in the 1840s.

3

THE GREAT FIRES OF SAG HARBOR

Sunday, November 13, 1845 started out like any other mid-autumn day. Indian summer had given way to crisp cool days and chilly nights, and thoughts of the approaching winter filled the minds of the local citizens. It was hard to imagine that within 24 hours Sag Harbor would once again be left in a state of confusion and disbelief as the result of another major fire. Nevertheless, by the next morning 45 families were homeless, 57 businesses wiped out, and nearly 100 buildings reduced to ashes.

The Fire of 1845

The fire broke out about 12:30 A.M. in a commission room for furniture in the Suffolk Buildings which housed Oakley's Hotel. Within minutes the building was engulfed in a sheet of flame. The three local fire wagons and their respective companies were called out to fight what was to be a losing battle. Strong winds fanned the flames, spreading them from shop to shop, home to home, and barn to barn, until it was virtually impossible to pass through the village. One description follows:

> It was terrific and appaling beyond the power of description, to behold some forty to fifty large buildings at the same time engulfed in fire; the

flames in their unrestrained and unconquerable fury bursting forth on every side and ascending up to heaven in one vast blazing pyramid of light, while volumes of black dense smoke shrouded the skies in gloom, hiding the stars from sight and covering with sack cloth the splendor of the full-orbed moon, was enough to fill every spectator with the mingled emotions of amazement and terror.

For 12 long hours the fire raged out of control, until nothing remained of the lower part of the village but rubble and ashes. From the end of the wharf to the brick buildings halfway through the business district, stores on both sides of the Main Street stood no more. The east side of Division Street as far as Rector Street was gone, and both East and West Water Street's cooperages, blacksmith shops, and chandleries were completely wiped out. Although through some miracle of Providence no lives were lost, the village was in an unbelievable state of chaos. The long bleak winter lay ahead, and with it, a period of hardship and despair. But through it all, the early residents' courage and determination prevailed, and two years later, Sag Harbor, phoenix-like, rose again from the ashes.

Following the second blaze, the fire department underwent a complete reorganization. The Gazelle Hose Company was formed and several pieces of new equipment added. Yet, even with such improvements and the growth of the department, the changes were not sufficient enough to protect the village from yet another major fire in 1877.

Those suffering losses in the great fire of 1845 were: B. Babcock, H.G. Bassett & Company, D.Y. Bellows, T. Brown, G.D. Chester, N. Comstock, D. Congdon, J. Conklin, J.A. Cook, Cook & Greene, H. Cooper, William Cooper, *The Corrector* Office, J. Crolius, Howes Crowell, Dering & Fordham, C. Douglas, Douglas & Wade, A.A. Eddy, Z. Elliott, T. Foster, I.C. Fowler, French, A.H. Gardiner, Gardiner & Seeley, S. Hallock, W.F. Halsey, J. Havens, S. Havens, A.G. Hedges, C.S. Hedges, J. Hildreth, J. Hobart, G. Howell, Howell & Havens, N.G. Howell, T. Howard, G. & H. Huntting, S. & B. Huntting, D.A. Jennings, T. Kiernan, P.P. King, Lawrence & Overton, J.G. Leonard, N.S. Lester, S. L'Hommedieu, G.R. Loper, Matthews, Miner, Mott & Street, Mulford & Sleight, W. Nelson, G.V. Oakley, Oakley's Hotel, Ocean House, A. Overton, Mrs. Pease, Pelon & Company, E. Phelps, Phelps Hotel, L. Pitcher, Mrs. Reeves, T.P. Ripley, Ripley & Parker, Robbins & Brown, E.C. Rogers, P. Rogers, E.L. Simons, W.A. Simons, O. Slate, C. Sleight, E.H. Smith, J. Smith, S. & G. Smith, Steam Mills & Pump, H. Stewart, Stewart & Crowell, William Taylor, N. Tinker and T. Vail, also Wady & Russell, William Wilcox, and Mrs. Wood.

Part Three

INDUSTRIAL GROWTH
AND BUSINESS OPPORTUNITIES

1850–1880

1
EARLY INDUSTRIES AND CRAFTSMEN

Along the upper cove where Green Street now leads to the water stood a windmill, a ropewalk, and a shipyard. The sheltered waters of the cove emptied into the bay, and ships built there passed through the drawbridge that connected Sag Harbor with Hog Neck.

The Industries at Peter's Green

In the early 1800s Benjamin Wade owned a shipyard where both whaling vessels and schooners were built. Among them were the *Marion, Storm, Sierra Nevada*, and *San Diego*. Captain Jared Wade sailed the little schooner *San Diego* around the Cape to California in 1849 during the gold rush. The ship was considered one of the swiftest vessels afloat. Oliver Wade described his uncle Benjamin's shipyard as a marvelous place for a boy to spend his idle hours. He recalled:

> Ship's carpenters busy with axe and adze shaped the ribs and beams of the vessels, which after a time grew from a skeleton into a shapely form. As the planks bent into place on her sides, they were pierced by the long worms of the augers, followed by driving into these auger holes the long yellow locust tree nails which fastened the planks to the ribs. Day by day the ship grew until the stagings that surrounded her were finally

114   INDUSTRIAL GROWTH AND OPPORTUNITIES

stripped away and she was nestled in the cradle which rested upon the greased ways by which she was to glide down into the dancing waters of the Cove.

It was said to have been an exciting sight, drawing large crowds of cheering people each time a ship slid down into the water, splashing a cloud of spray as she floated out into the Cove.

During the same years, a ropewalk, owned by Samuel L'Hommedieu, could be found near the shipyard of Benjamin Wade, where rope and cordage was manufactured with hand-operated tools. The business employed many men and, from time to time hired local boys as apprentices.

Ropewalks were long narrow buildings, their size estimated in fathoms. The length of the structure limited the length of rope which could be manufactured without splicing. L'Hommedieu's ropewalk extended some 500-600 fathoms but was only 15 feet wide. The rope made there played an important part in the outfitting of a whaleship, where it was used for rigging. Each whaleboat was equipped with a line of 300 fathoms of carefully coiled rope, stored in a tub and used in harpooning.

The interior of the ropewalk held a wheel of large proportions, usually made of oak, set in a spinning motion, which, in turn, rotated whirlers to which a bunch of hemp fibers were secured, to be twisted into yarn. Along the walk were horizontal crossbars with hooks over which the yarns were swung as the men walked backward from the whirlers, letting out the yarn. The rope winch, made up of three whirlers, was driven by a strap which twisted the three yarns into a strong rope. L'Hommedieu's ropewalk was a prosperous business throughout the whaling industry.

SAMUEL L'HOMMEDIEU

Samuel L'Hommedieu was born in Southold, Long Island on February 20, 1744 of French Huguenot ancestors who settled there in 1690. They moved to Shelter Island where tradition tells us that young Samuel built a raft to ferry his family and their guests to the South Shore, and that incident fired his interest in ships and shipping. While still a young man, Samuel L'Hommedieu moved to Sag Harbor to look for work at the port. This was prior to the Revolutionary War, and the village population consisted of only 40 families. L'Hommedieu owned and operated the ropewalk at Peter's Green on the cove, where rope and cordage for vessels engaged in the coastal trade was manufactured. This was before the off-shore whaling industry had gotten underway.

During the Revolution L'Hommedieu was commissioned as a lieutenant in the militia under Governor Tryon and soon fled to Connecticut with many other

EARLY INDUSTRIES AND CRAFTSMEN

prominent Whigs. When the war was over, he returned to Sag Harbor where he and his wife, the former Sarah White, built a house on the west side of Main Street. The place was soon filled with activity as their family grew, and with the exception of daughter Charity, Samuel Jr., Ezra, Sylvester, Phebe, Elizabeth, Sarah, and Mary all reached adulthood. His son Samuel built the impressive brick house on the corner of Main Street and Bay View Avenue.

Samuel L'Hommedieu became a prominent and successful citizen and, in later years, held the office of Justice of the Peace and was a member of the New York Assembly. A founding member of the local Presbyterian Church, he signed the covenant of the re-organized church in 1792 and gave bonds for 300 pounds in 1804, which were applied to the parish and the preaching of the Gospel. L'Hommedieu was known as the "angel" of the local church. He died at the age of 90 and is buried in Oakland Cemetery.

The third industry on Peter's Green was a spider-legged windmill owned and operated by Peter Hildreth, owner of the green. Only eight or ten mills of this type were to be found the entire length of Long Island. The millhouse, built thirty feet above the ground, was mounted on a pedestal of three-foot square timbers. The pedestal, topped with a brass collar and a shaft and axle, made it possible to turn the whole building, enabling the large sails to face the wind. Heavy bags of flour and grain were raised and lowered by a block and fall. The spider-legged mill of Peter Hildreth was in operation during the same years as the ropewalk and the shipyard.

The Oakland Works

During the mid 1800s, in the center of the property that is now Oakland Cemetery, stood a group of buildings known as the Oakland Works. John Sherry had them built in 1850 for his brass foundry, and soon took as his partner Ephraim Byram, noted local clockmaker and astronomer. They enlarged the place to make room for Byram's clock manufactory. They called the place the Oakland Brass Foundry and Clock Works.

Apparently the business was in operation for only 12 years, for in 1863 they leased the buildings to Abraham DeBevoise and B. & F. Lyon for a stocking factory. After installing new machinery, an advertisement placed in the local paper stated the business would "be of great benefit to the village, giving employment to idle hands." In September 1865 they enlarged the place by erecting a second building, about the size of the main one, and another bleach house. Steady employment was expected for 500 men, women, and children at the Oakland Hosiery Company, and 100 dozen pair of stockings per day were manufactured. Unfortunately, a drop in the market caused the factory to close after three years in operation.

During the next ten years two other industries occupied the Oakland Works. First, a barrel-head and stave factory owned by George Bush, followed by a Morocco leather business of Morgan Topping. Both were unsuccessful. A final attempt to operate a successful business on the site was made in 1880 when Edward Chapman Rogers opened a hat factory there. Called the Oakland Hat Manufactory and supervised by Samuel C. Pierson, the undertaking lasted but a few months.

In September 1882 the old wooden structures, which had been unoccupied for two years, caught fire and burned to the ground. At that time the uninsured buildings were owned by Mary A. Sherry. The Oakland Works were never rebuilt; however, the brick structure and clock tower, which were untouched by the flames, remained standing for some time.

Other Early Industries

Along with the major industries that located in Sag Harbor were a few lesser-known businesses worth mentioning. In the 1790s the Denison brothers opened a hatting factory in the building on Division Street now known as the Umbrella House. Samuel Tillotsen carried on the business in the 1860s.

In the mid 1800s an oilcloth factory, established by James G. Leonard, stood on the east side of Main Street above the Otter Pond bridge near Brickkiln Road. It isn't known how long the factory was in operation, but the building was later destroyed by fire.

A leather currying business, started by Abel C. Buckley in 1844, grossed annual sales of finished leather amounting to $18,000. Following Buckley's death, Samuel N. Davis took over the business.

Joseph Freudenthal's Cigar (Segar) Factory was located in the Huntting Building at the foot of Main Street. During the 1870s 75 people were employed there, and the business grossed over $100,000 per year. Freudenthal's factory was said to have manufactured the best Havana and American cigars on all of Long Island. He often found it impossible to fill all of his orders, even when he produced 70,000 cigars each week. Freudenthal manufactured a brand of cigar that he called the Enigma, in honor of the Enigma Club of Sag Harbor. The factory's supervisor was Henry Meyer and the store run by Julius Judell.

In 1875 Dr. William O. Ayres and Dr. C.S. Stillwell opened a factory in the Huntting building in which they refined crude cream of tartar. It isn't known if this business was successful.

EARLY INDUSTRIES AND CRAFTSMEN

A broom factory in the 1870s stood on Suffolk Street and was run by Thomas H. Vail. He advertised in the local papers that his brooms were of good quality and sold at reasonable prices.

Another early industry was the Sugar Manufactory of John Sherry and partners, located in the Huntting building. Preparations made prior to its May 7, 1863 opening included a corporation meeting to receive permission to use the public wharf west of the building. They called their business the Montauk Sugar Refinery, and the process utilized produced sugar from imported molasses. It isn't known how long the business lasted, but in all probability it was very short-lived.

Clockmaking was a craft in the early days that took mechanical skill, artistic ability, and a touch of genius. In colonial homes the clock was often considered a decorative as well as a useful instrument, the cases crafted of fine wood and intricately carved with figures and designs. Sag Harbor had the distinction of being the home town of two incredibly gifted clockmakers, Ephraim Niles Byram and Benjamin Franklin Hope.

EPHRAIM NILES BYRAM, CLOCKMAKER

Ephraim Niles Byram, born in Sag Harbor on November 25, 1809, was the son of Eliab Byram, one of the builders of the Arsenal. As a child, Byram's intelligence was so much greater than his classmates that it left him totally apathetic and bored with his lessons. He left school at an early age to pursue the things that interested him. Before long he became a self-taught astronomer, inventor, philosopher, and clockmaker, and without the advantage of family influence, formal education, or wealth, attained a goal that few persons ever reach.

Byram was skilled in making compasses, telescopes, and other nautical instruments, which he constructed with tools he had made himself. Living at a time when Sag Harbor was at the height of the whaling industry, there was always a ready market for his instruments. At the age of 25, after two years of work, Byram completed a mechanical model of the solar system, called an Orrey. After being on display at the Arsenal in 1836, it was taken on a tour around the country.

It was clockmaking, however, that Byram would best be remembered for, and in the factory next to his home on Jermain Avenue, he and John Sherry Sr. opened the Brass Foundry and Oakland Clock Works. There, in 1857 at the age of 26, Byram made his first tower clock. Built for the Methodist Church in Sag Harbor, it was said to have been such a finely precisioned instrument that the time varied less than three minutes a year. In 1844 he built a clock for the newly constructed Presbyterian Church on Union Street. Sadly, when it was installed in the tall steeple, swaying prevented the clock from keeping accurate time, so it was removed and taken to East Hampton where it was placed in their Presbyterian Church. Byram's clocks became so well known they were purchased for churches, schools, and buildings in Virginia, Georgia, Massachusetts, Connecticut, and Pennsylvania. The tower clock at West Point was one of Byram's masterpieces. It functioned effectively for 72 years! This unusual clock had a 5-foot dial, hands and numbers made of wood, and the spots between the numbers marked with cadet buttons.

As Byram advanced in years he made all kinds of instruments: chronometers, telescopes, etc., and although he hadn't learned the principles of arithmetic as laid down in books, they were noted for the mathematical accuracy of their movements.

Ephraim Niles Byram and his wife Cornelia were the parents of three children, Henry Eliab, who died in infancy, Loretta, and Ivan. Byram died June 27, 1881 at the age of 71 years and is buried in Oakland Cemetery.

BENJAMIN FRANKLIN HOPE

Sag Harbor's other noted clockmaker was Benjamin Franklin Hope, who lived on Main Street in the impressive looking house with the mansard roof. He owned and operated a watch and jewelry business during the 1860s and 1870s, with his shop at the rear of his house and facing Madison Street. In 1876, after five years of work, Hope completed a large chronometer clock of an exciting and novel pattern and displayed it in his store window for the public to inspect and enjoy. Its design was entirely original and consisted of a unique yet graceful arrangement on a skeleton frame and dial, without any case to obstruct a complete view of all the works. The frame and wheels were crafted of bronze, and the 14-inch dial made of a plate of brass taken from the wrecked steamer *Lavalle*. Benjamin Franklin Hope crafted the entire clock, dial, and engravings himself.

A spectacular example of a Hope grandfather clock can be seen at the John Jermain Memorial Library, along with one made by Ephraim Niles Byram. This exquisite piece of workmanship took Mr. Hope thirty years to complete. Seven tunes play, one every hour, and Westminster chimes strike on the half and quarter hours. Hope studied music in order to make the barrels for the tunes himself. The magnificent clock case is Benjamin Hope's work as well. On the dial of the clock the heads of Mr. Hope and his wife are etched on the moon.

On the ends of the minute hand, he etched his family coat of arms, and on the hour hand, a picture of his Irish terrier. The chime is the only part of the instrument that is not the work of Benjamin Hope. The tunes the clock plays are: "Old Hundred," "Old Folks at Home," "Within a Mile of Edinboro Town," "Auld Lang Syne," "America," "There's Nae Luck About the Home," and "Old Dog Tray."

Benjamin Franklin Hope and his wife Amelia both died in 1907 and are buried in Oakland Cemetery.

The Old Stationery Shop of Russell Wickham

Sag Harbor in 1842 was at the height of its spectacular whaling industry, with related businesses and shops lining the streets of the village, all sharing the profits of that lucrative time. In that year an obscure little stationery shop owned by Russell Wickham stood on Main Street, sandwiched between the larger and more well-known places of business.

Wickham's shop was the kind of place one would imagine the old cronies of the village met to discuss the news of the day and the local gossip. Not only did Wickham sell newspapers but also he specialized in book binding and repairing. A circulating library found on the premises served the public for many years. Early each morning Russell Wickham would open his shutters, unlock the door, and prepare for another day of business.

To look at Russell Wickham, one would easily compare him to a character right out of a Dickens' novel. His stooped appearance and rounded shoulders belied his 33 years. He was small in stature, clean shaven, and always garbed in a tall black hat and a black "claw-hammer" coat that was shiny and threadbare. He gave the impression of being a ne'er-do-well, yet he likely eked out a fair living selling slate pencils and quill pens, sealing wax and spelling books, testaments and toys. Local boys eagerly brought old rags and broken glass into the shop, where they were paid a penny a pound for their treasures. When enough rags accumulated, he sold them to the local newspaper printing office.

Year after year, Wickham puttered about his shop. He could usually be seen sitting at his desk in the store window enjoying a birds-eye view of the activities on the Main Street. It was said that he devised a system of strings running from his desk to the windows in the rear of his store, whereby he could raise and lower his shades without leaving his seat. A cot at the rear of his establishment served as his sleeping quarters, and he rarely left the store except to go for his meals, which he took at a nearby inn.

Russell Wickham operated the stationery shop right up until his death on

May 10, 1854 at the age of 45. On that spring day the shutters of his little shop remained closed and the door locked much past opening time. The local constable forced the door open and discovered that Wickham had passed away during the night. After relatives had come to remove his personal effects, the little stationery shop closed—but not for very long.

A few months later, George W. Tabor, an enterprising young man from Sag Harbor, seized the opportunity to purchase the shop and go into business for himself. He enlarged the place, added many new items, and installed gas lights. Tabor sold fancy goods, looking glasses, bird cages, and a variety of other items, and his clever advertisements and frequent sales made his business prosper. For the next 37 years George W. Tabor continued business at the same location. In 1892 he moved his entire stock across the street into his new store, ending a half a century of business in the little stationery store of Russell Wickham.

NATHAN TINKER, CABINETMAKER

Nathan Tinker was one of Sag Harbor's early craftsmen whose speciality was cabinetmaking and whose furniture was of such fine quality and workmanship that some of it still exists today. He lived at a time when life was simple and men took the time to create objects of distinction and beauty.

Tinker, born in 1792, grew up in Sag Harbor and married Hannah P. Woodward. He raised his family by supporting them from the profits of his furniture and cabinetmaking business. At the start of his career in 1819, he had a partner named Woodward, who, in all probability, was his father-in-law, and who may well have taught him the trade. They operated a warehouse opposite the drug and medicine store of Sage & Hedges on Main Street.

In 1822 Tinker opened his own establishment and advertised in the Sag Harbor newspaper *The Corrector* that he "continues his cabinet and furniture business at his old stand opposite the engine house." At that time he also had a large supply of furniture at William Griffin's and Israel Fanning's in Riverhead, along with supplying agents in Bridgehampton, East Hampton and Southold. Sideboards, secretaries, chairs, clock cases, candle and basin stands, tables, and desks were some of the items Tinker built. In addition, he specialized in wooden coffins of quality workmanship, which he guaranteed built in one hour's notice. He was skilled in repairing furniture and shipped to any part of the United States, free of charge. He accepted as payment, grain, country produce or lumber, but gave a ten percent discount for cash orders.

Between 1823 and 1826 Nathan Tinker supplemented his income by selling other products, including a labor-saving washing machine, a corn husker, and anti-dysenteric pills. A year later he established a milk delivery service and, twice, tried his hand at the blacksmithing trade. Although none of these ventures proved successful, he eventually made a name for himself as a fine furniture and cabinetmaker.

After suffering severe losses due to a fire on December 31, 1822, he constructed a new building on the east side of Main Street. Two years later he moved into that place, where he continued to maintain an active shop, often advertising for apprentices to help in the business and learn the trade.

Although there were other furnituremakers in the village during those years, Tinker regarded Henry Byram as his only major competitor. They battled verbally for several years, each trying to undersell the other. Both threatened to sell their businesses on numerous occasions, and in April of 1836 Tinker made good his threat and sold out to J. Lamb.

Trouble, it seemed, was no stranger to Nathan Tinker, who along with his business problems also had to deal with the untimely death of three infant children. However, not one to remain idle, in 1839 he reopened a cabinetmaking shop. During 1845 misfortune struck again when the the disastrous fire of that year swept through the business district. Although his brick building survived the blaze, much of its contents were damaged. Tinker took advantage of the situation by selling $2000 worth of new merchandise at greatly reduced prices. Following the fire, Tinker made his son Samuel a partner. They renovated the store and added a large brick structure that today is the American Hotel. They leased part of the space to other merchants in the village and hoped some day to convert the building into a double dwelling for themselves.

Nathan Tinker remained in the furnituremaking business for twenty-nine years, and in 1847 at the age of 55, he passed away. He is buried in Oakland Cemetery.

JOHN HILDRETH, SHOEMAKER

Throughout the years shoes were made on a molded shape called a last, traditionally of maple wood, and before machinery was invented to manufacture them, every step was done by hand. Often, this early craftsman was an itinerant worker who traveled from place to place selling his products. However, such was not the case with local shoemaker John Hildreth, who spent over 50 years in Sag Harbor making shoes and boots for the local residents.

Although born in Bridgehampton in 1795, Hildreth moved to Sag Harbor at an early age and, while in his teens, learned the trade as apprentice to master shoemaker Hezekiah Jennings. Jennings' expertise in the business was apparently well known, for shops in Cutchogue and Southold sold his handcrafted boots and shoes. He was one of the best, and John Hildreth learned the trade well.

In 1824 Hildreth ran an advertisement in the Sag Harbor newspaper, *The Suffolk Gazette*, informing the public that he had just returned from New York with 3000 pounds of sole leather, hammers, boot web and cord, shoe knives, shoe horns, and a quantity of fine morocco. Shoes and boots would be made at short notice, and leather was available wholesale to other craftsmen. Hildreth also accepted raw hides as well as cash for his services.

Shoemaking was not the only enterprise that John Hildreth was involved in. He was a noted citizen, devoted patriot, and a man influential in village affairs. At one time he was one of the largest real estate owners in Sag Harbor and built a large portion of the Brick Block on the west side of the business district. These brick buildings prevented the great fire of 1845 from spreading farther up the Main Street.

In 1849, four years after the blaze, an attempt was made to restore prosperity to the village by starting a manufacturing enterprise. A company was formed, with John Hildreth as president, which was instrumental in starting the cotton mill in Sag Harbor.

Although John Hildreth was financially successful, his personal life was filled with tragedy. His wife and seven of their eight children died during his lifetime. When Hildreth died on February 22, 1870, only one child survived.

John Hildreth was a man of many interests, but throughout his life was best remembered as the local shoemaker. In 1860, shortly before his retirement, the invention of a sewing machine for attaching uppers and soles together revolutionized the industry, but for the shoemaking business of John Hildreth, the invention came too late.

The Old Department Store

As Sag Harbor's rapid growth continued during the whaling years, the population swelled to a number that has never since been equalled. Some of the adventurous put their savings into opening shops and businesses to capitalize on the continuing expansion and became quite prosperous. One such budding entrepreneur was George B. Brown, who opened a department store in the village in 1832.

Brown was a likeable man, involved in village affairs and secretary of both the Union Band and the Temperance Society. He started his business at the Old

Stand on Main Street, and it grew into a profitable concern that survived for more than a century. George Brown made frequent trips to New York City to replenish his stock of groceries, dry goods, hardware, and crockery and was always on the lookout for new items to add to his inventory. In 1835 Nathan Tiffany joined the firm, becoming a partner, and the place was then known as Brown & Tiffany's. They enlarged the place and added a line of jewelry, medicine, shoes, and fencing.

In 1842 Brown moved his expanding business into a new building he had built at 45-47 Main Street, a few doors north of Washington Street. The large roomy establishment was stocked with a new assortment of goods on the ground floor, while the upper story held office space. In 1843 Brown's brother Charles joined the firm and the name of the place changed to G. & C. Brown. Throughout the next twenty years other partners would come and go as the business continued to prosper and grow under Brown's astute management. During those years business was conducted under the following names: G. & C. Brown & Company, George B. Brown & Company, George B. Brown & Son, George B. Brown Son & Company, and then back to George B. Brown & Son, the name that remained until the death of George B. Brown.

In the year 1886 a 13-year-old boy named William Cook took an after school job at Brown's department store as a delivery boy. Cook took his job seriously, and in the course of ten years worked his way up to manager of the store. Following Brown's death in 1896, his daughter Mrs. N.L. LaPlace inherited the business. Cook managed the department store for Mrs. LaPlace for five years, after which he purchased the business in April 1901. At that time he remodeled the store inside and out. Large display windows were installed on the street side and apartments as well as offices built on the second floor. The grocery department was done away with and replaced with other types of merchandise. When Cook reopened, all transactions were made on a cash basis, eliminating the credit system that Brown had permitted for so many years. Cook's motto was "The Always Something Doing Store," and business continued to prosper under his expertise and know-how.

Fire did considerable damage to the store in February 1916, but within a year Cook had rebuilt and business resumed. In 1932, on the 100th anniversary of the founding of the store, Cook celebrated the event by filling his windows with memorabilia from the past. A photograph of George B. Brown and a document stating the principles on which the business was founded were put on display. Other items were a model of a square-rigger ship made by a sailor on the whaleship *Phoenix* and owned by Luther D. Cook (William's grandfather), a carding wheel, a 1812 musket, a powder horn, bellows, and the lock and key from the original store that stood in the Old Stand.

The business continued until 1935, at which time William Cook held a huge going out of business sale before retiring. He had earned a well-deserved rest after 50 years in Sag Harbor's old department store.

JOHN FORDHAM AND THOMAS OVERTON, BLACKSMITHS

One of the most important tradesmen in the early years was the blacksmith. Sooner or later, whaler, homeowner, farmer, and ship owner would all require his products and service. John Fordham's expertise in iron forging was unequalled. Eel spears, harpoons, clam rakes, oyster tongs, blubber spades, anchors and scores of other wrought iron tools made by Fordham found a ready market not only in the Sag Harbor area, but along the entire eastern seaboard.

John Fordham, born at Riverhead, Long Island on May 29, 1831, came to Sag Harbor at the age of 12 and apprenticed to master blacksmith Jedediah Conklin. Young Fordham learned the trade well, becoming a master mechanic, which qualified him to earn a wage of one dollar a day. Fordham made axes all day long, and in the evening he sometimes put in another day's work to make a little extra money to support his new wife, the former Harriet Sweezey. In their little home on the corner of Madison and Union Streets, 12 children were born to the Fordhams, ten of whom survived. At their 50th wedding anniversary on September 26, 1902, all ten joined their parents for the celebration.

At the foot of the village on the corner of Main and Bay Streets, John Fordham opened his own blacksmith shop. His business prospered and, along with several apprentices, he employed a dozen men. In addition to this business, he had a contract with the village trustees to furnish fresh water for the village street-sprinkling wagon. Fordham erected a huge tank at the rear of his shop, and from that tank a long pipe extended out over Bay Street for the two-horse cart to drive under for loading and filling. The donkey pump, which drew the water, was also connected to a steam boiler used in his other enterprise. The well, although less than 6 feet deep and 4 feet across, stood on a natural spring which kept the water level high even after pumping continuously all day.

John Fordham was an outstanding citizen and well-liked individual. As an Elder in the local Methodist Church, he served as preacher in the absence of the regular minister. He was a good Christian in every sense of the word, and the Reverend George E. Bishop described him as "the most righteous man I ever met, as strong in character as in his manly arm." Fordham took his entire family to church every Sunday and was absolutely unyielding when it came to keeping the Sabbath. Saturdays he closed his shop and refused to do business

EARLY INDUSTRIES AND CRAFTSMEN

until the Sabbath was over. Even when he worked on steamboats in his later years and was responsible for keeping them in running order, he would wait until after midnight to go down to the wharf and get the boats ready for their early Monday morning departures.

John Fordham's interest in the village dramatic group led him to try his hand at acting. His tall rangy build got him the part of Abraham Lincoln in a local production, and it was said that, while splitting a rail, he overplayed the part and the axe went right through the stage floor!

John Fordham lived to the ripe old age of 82, passing away on April 29, 1913. He is buried in Oakland Cemetery.

OVERTON'S BLACKSMITH SHOP

Overton's Blacksmith Shop, a fixture in Sag Harbor for 81 years, was established in April 1835 by Thomas Overton. His shop at that time stood on the site of the Maidstone Mills property. After fire destroyed his shop, he moved to a building on Spring Street, where he carried on business under the name Thomas C. Overton & Son. After the death of Thomas, his son John Hull Overton took over the business, but in five years he sold the place to John Carroll, a blacksmith from East Hampton with six years' experience.

Other men who continued to ply the blacksmithing trade were John A. Cook, Charles H. Morris, David Schellinger and E.L. Simons in the 1840s; John DeCastro, Hildreth & Bennett, George D. Hill, Clarence C. Morris, Charles R. Morris, George C. Morris, Morgan O'Meara, and Robert J. Power in the 1880s. Blacksmiths in 1910-11 were H.R. Ruppel, Jerry Sullivan, C. Fordham, and H.D. Fordham.

The Mills at Trout Pond

Before the formation of Trout Pond, a creek called Noyack River flowed down through a natural flume and out into Noyac Bay. An abundance of shellfish and fresh water springs provided the Indians, who inhabited the site, with a plentious supply of food and water. After white men settled in the region, the stream was used as a mill site.

The Southampton Town Records tell us that as early as 1668 John Jennings was "given liberty to fence in a piece of the north side of Noyack River." In 1686 Obediah Rogers was granted permission to set a fulling mill on the stream. Subsequent owners of the mill during the 1600s were John Parker, Theophilus Willman, and Jonah Rogers. When a dam was built in 1738, a pond formed above the stream, and it was appropriately called Mill Pond. Charles Rugg,

126 INDUSTRIAL GROWTH AND OPPORTUNITIES

owner of the property at that time, constructed a small mill on the site. Rugg's mill was later replaced by a much larger structure driven by an overshot water wheel. During the years that Rugg lived there, the stream was known as Rugg's Creek.

The next owner, John Budd, built a windmill on the site and re-named the place Budd's Creek. Situated below the dam, it pumped the flowing water back over the dam and into the pond, to be used again. Budd's mill and the two houses that stood on the property were all destroyed in separate fires, one in May 1860.

George Barker built one of the last mills on the stream at Mill Pond, bringing all the chestnut lumber used to frame in his building from Connecticut. A turbine water wheel driven by the pressure of the water was installed on his mill. Later, Isaac Osborn, Henry Smith, and, finally, Thomas Eldredge owned the Mill Pond and nearby property.

Thomas Eldredge built a small house at the south end of the pond, gradually enlarging it to accommodate his growing family. By the time his tenth child was born, the house stood three stories high and contained 16 rooms. Eldredge leased the old Budd flouring mill and saw mill overlooking Noyac Bay and supported his large family by the profits from the two businesses. He purchased a boiler and engine from O.B. Lucas, making it possible to operate the mills by either steam or water power.

Henry Chadwick, of Brooklyn, purchased the mill in 1875 and employed Thomas Eldredge to run the place. A terrible calamity occurred in the winter of 1881, as heavy rains did considerable damage to the property. The pond overflowed, breaking the dam and sweeping away everything in its path. The main mill building was flooded, and the entire place moved a foot off its foundation. The engine house on the southeast corner of the mill was completely demolished, and the iron pump buried under a pile of sand. Huge rocks carried by the current partially destroyed the newly constructed stone bridge, and a 35-foot gap was made in the mill dam. Ephraim Eldredge, then miller of the place, estimated the damage at $1000.

The property changed hands again when George W. Thompson of California bought the pond and land surrounding it and erected a cottage there. Thompson made a garden spot out of the swampy wilderness by planting flowers along the many walks on his grounds. He stocked the pond with brook trout and renamed the place Trout Pond. Much to his dismay, the fish died by the hundreds. Whether it was the result of disease or poison was never determined.

Thompson married the second daughter of N. Prime of Sag Harbor, and, after his death, Thompson's widow married Charles M. Edwards of Noyac. They continued to live on the property and gave it the name Oak Grove Trout

EARLY INDUSTRIES AND CRAFTSMEN 127

Pond. In September 1905 the Edwards' sold all the property to F.E. Mellinger of Dayton, Ohio. Mellinger bought an additional 35 acres from Thomas Eldredge, increasing the size of his land to 55 acres. Mellinger operated a squab ranch and duck pond at Trout Pond. He built pigeon coops at an expense of $4000 to accommodate his 2500 pairs of brooding birds. He also stocked the pond with many ducks. After Mellinger's house and buildings were destroyed by a forest fire that swept through the area, the land reverted back to its swampy wilderness and remained in that state for many years.

Ice Harvesting at Round Pond

Another little freshwater pond found on the outskirts of Sag Harbor is Round Pond. In early years only wood roads led to the pond, the most widely used one branching off of Madison Street about one mile south of the business district. As one traveled the main road there was nothing visible to suggest that a few hundred feet away the sparkling waters of Round Pond called many varieties of wildlife to its shores.

The old wood road opposite Forest Street gently wound its way past a conglomeration of ancient apple trees, wild grape vines, huckleberry bushes, and a delightful assortment of wild flowers. Lady Slippers, blue lupine, and trailing arbutus bloomed profusely during the spring months, generating an aroma of indescribable sweetness. Approaching the pond, a large clearing appeared, and it was on this site that an Indian encampment stood during the woodland stage several hundred years ago. It was an ideal spot, protected on all sides by a dense oak forest. The freshwater pond teemed with perch, pickerel, and bass and provided food for those early native Americans. Even after the settlement of Sag Harbor in the early 1700s, a few Indians still lived by Round Pond.

During the 1800s the pond became a favorite spot for local civic and religious organizations to hold their meetings, picnics, and skating parties. In the year 1884 the site was in great demand, and land on the south side was leased by Louis Christman for a "German Picnic Ground" with seats and tables in the grove. The Baptist Church Society held a three-day oration at the northeast side of the pond on the Fourth of July weekend in 1884. The event included music by the Cornet Band, swings hung on sturdy limbs for swinging, boats for rowing, and, in the evening, fireworks lit from the center of the pond. The area on the south side was called Round Pond Garden, and each Monday night in the summer of 1884 concerts and dances were held from 7:30 to 11 o'clock with a first-class band providing the music.

128 INDUSTRIAL GROWTH AND OPPORTUNITIES

Round Pond, however, was more than a recreational spot, for a lucrative ice business was conducted there for more than 70 years. As far back as 1840, an ice house stood on the southwest side of the pond. Here, huge ice blocks were stored and later sold to the local residents and shopkeepers to preserve their food products. Ice boxes were filled as the iceman made his daily deliveries long before the refrigerator became part of our standard kitchen equipment.

Charles Sherrill Hedges built the first ice house, later selling it to Albert G. Hedges and, later still, to Little & Fields. *The Sag Harbor Express* of December 19, 1872 contained an interesting article about the old ice house at Round Pond;

> The old ice house used by Little & Fields, which had stood at the south side of Round Pond for upward thirty years, having been built by Charles Sherrill Hedges in 1840 and afterwards sold to Albert Hedges, and which has been a prominent target for many youthful sportsman at which to hurl his rifle ball across the pond, breaking from the door sundry padlocks on diverse occasions; whose downy bed of straw has been sought by many weather bound travelers as they took refuge beneath the roof or under the front piazza on rainy days watching the wild ducks as they paddled their own canoes on the glassy little lake, as well as those other "little ducks" who glided on its frozen surface as swift winged messengers on skates, and beneath whose sheltering roof the crystal lake has been stowed in mid-winter with which to refresh the inner man during the parching days of summer; was entirely destroyed by fire on Friday evening last, excepting the hole, which remains there still, through the agency of some reckless youth.

It is interesting to note that the entire article was written in one sentence!

In the winter of 1873-74 James T. Dodson built another ice house on the same site and the building remained there for many years. In 1901 tracks from the Long Island Railroad were extended to the ice house. A 1400-foot spur made it possible to ship blocks of ice to any part of Long Island.

There is evidence that things didn't always run smoothly for the ice companies, as the Southampton Town Trustees recorded, in their minutes, a dispute over the sections of the pond that ice could be removed from. In a case where an ice company cut ice upon the pond, it was sued by another owner for cutting in front of his land bordering the pond. The minor court found the ice company had trespassed in cutting ice beyond the lines of its own pond front. The case was never taken to a higher court, but the ice corporation thereafter paid for the privilege of cutting ice beyond a certain imaginary line of survey on the pond.

EARLY INDUSTRIES AND CRAFTSMEN

The record stated that the Middle Line, separating the Great South and the Great North Divisions, runs through the waters of this pond. Surveys of the pond show the Middle Line to be a boundary of owners of lands surrounding the pond. The allotments of land are surveyed upon what is known as the "eleven o'clock line," and the throughs are narrow, making several different persons the allottees of lands bordering the pond. It was apparent that property owners took their boundaries very seriously, and ice companies were not to take ice from in front of a person's land without paying for the privilege.

The last Round Pond ice house was destroyed by fire November 9, 1911, with the loss adjusted at $1200 on the main building and $125 on the elevator. Mr. Hildreth was the owner at that time. After the burning of the place, the era of ice harvesting came to an end and, in time, the pond reverted back to its natural state.

The Sag Harbor Savings Bank

As the village grew and began to prosper, a group of citizens met to establish a savings bank in Sag Harbor. They gathered in the village hall on April 25, 1860, with Thomas Crowell chairing the meeting. With 20 trustees in attendance, a proposed charter was read and accepted, and the board was organized. J. Madison Huntting of East Hampton was elected president, as were six vice-presidents: Jonathan Fithian, John Sherry, Alanson Topping, Charles N. Brown, Jeremiah T. Parsons, and Josiah B. Nickerson. William H. Gleason was elected secretary and bank attorney, and William A. Woodbridge, treasurer. Incorporation followed the submission of a bill to the legislature in 1864.

The bank opened for business on June 7, 1860 when 26 savings accounts were opened with deposits amounting to $733.24. The bank was located on the second floor of the DeBevoise building which stood opposite the Mansion House. In 1898 the Savings Bank moved to new quarters on the ground floor of the same building. A Marvin Combine Company fireproof and burglar-proof safe, with a patent time lock, arrived on the steamboat *Montauk*, and a sturdy wagon with tackle and gear brought it from the Long Wharf to the bank building.

In 1910, when larger quarters were necessary, the present bank building was built. For over fifty years, Harris' Bakery Shop occupied the northwest corner of Main and Spring Street, the proposed site of the new bank. The property was acquired for $10,000, and the old building cleared from the lot. The W.L. and G.H. O'Shay Company of Brooklyn submitted the lowest bid, $25,775, and was awarded the contract. Plans called for a two-story fireproof building with quarters for the Savings Bank on the south side and the Peconic Bank on the north side. Office space occupied the second floor. Built of fancy tapestry brick and terra cotta trim and limestone pillars in front, it was an impressive-looking structure. Concrete footings and steel floor beams were installed in September 1910, and the local newspaper advertised for brick-layers. The limestone pillars arrived at the site in October, and shortly thereafter the place opened for business.

Presidents of the Sag Harbor Savings Bank through 1940 were: J. Madison Huntting, 1860-68, Josiah Douglas, 1868-69, Henry P. Hedges, 1869-99, James H. Pierson, 1899-1914, Hervey T. Hedges, 1914-1918, and in 1918 William D. Halsey, who served in that capacity for the next twenty years.

A Business Directory of the 1840s can be found in the Appendix.

Mail Delivery and the Growth of the Post Office

With the arrival of 1861 a much needed improvement in the mail service was finally realized when a new route to the East End was established. Each Monday, Wednesday and Friday the steamer, *Massachusetts*, brought the mail from New York after an overnight trip down the Long Island Sound, and on Tuesday, Thursday, and Saturday the boat returned to the city with the outgoing mail. Although the railroad had been extended to the eastern part of Long Island in 1870, that means of delivery wasn't utilized for some time. For some reason, the manager of the railroad refused to accept the terms first offered by the postal department, so the mail was taken down the north fork to Greenport where it was transferred to stagecoach and then brought across the bay by steamer. It was an inconvenience, to say the least, and before long a committee of citizens from East Hampton and Southampton Towns met to discuss how to remedy the situation. Many meetings were held before an agreement with the railroad officials was finally reached, and about 1874 the south shore branch of the railroad began to transport the mail.

On May 1, 1890 the post office moved from the west side of Main Street to new quarters in the Alvin Building. It was said to have been the finest post office found on Long Island east of Brooklyn. The new building contained 160 lock boxes and 400 call boxes placed in an "A" shape, with all general delivery mail in the center. At that time Miss Genevieve French became Sag Harbor's first postmistress. The post office remained at that location for 26 years. When 1916 arrived, the Alvin Company decided to occupy the entire building, making it necessary for the post office to relocate again.

In May 1916, 16 representatives from the Post Office Department came

EARLY INDUSTRIES AND CRAFTSMEN 131

to Sag Harbor to look for a new site. The government accepted Arthur T. Brown's proposition to build the post office building on his burned-out property on Washington Street. Local residents protested that the location was unwise, due to the fact that Washington Street was a "mere lane" and that the corner of Main and Washington was one of the most dangerous corners in the village, especially since the arrival of the automobile. They claimed congestion was bad enough during business hours and couldn't imagine what it would be like at the height of the summer season. Their protests, however, fell on deaf ears, and the post office was built on the proposed lot. In October of that same year they moved to their new quarters, a fine modern building. It had spacious rooms with concrete floors. The first room on the east side was the postmaster's private office. Next to that was the money order and postal savings bank, then the registered letter department, then general delivery, a depository for letters, and, finally, the boxes (300 call boxes, 375 small lock boxes, 40 medium lock boxes, and 15 drawers). The business office was behind the boxes, and mail was received at the rear door.

The year 1931 brought about another move for the post office. Irving Ivans, spokesman for the Ivans Brothers Real Estate Company, informed the public that the government had selected the Ivans lot adjoining Alippo's Garage and the Hill property on the west side of Main Street as the site of the new post office building. The one-story brick and concrete structure, which measured 25 by 60 feet, was to be completed within 60 days.

When excavation for the basement began, workers discovered the remains of burned walls and foundation stones of an earlier building, which had to be removed before the job could be done. James McMahon, Jr. cleared the lot in preparation for Duryea and Baird to do the cement work. Samuel R. French of Hempstead, Long Island built the new post office, and after 14 years at its Washington Street location, the post office moved into its new quarters.

A list of the men and women who served as postmasters and postmistresses between 1794 and 1940 can be found in the Appendix.

2
HEALTH CARE IN THE EARLY DAYS

In 1804 Ebenezer Sage and Jesse Hedges operated one of the first drugstores in Sag Harbor. Residents of East Hampton and Amagansett came "down to the Harbor" to have their prescriptions filled, for no pharmacies had yet opened in those places. Dr. Sage advertised that, for the small price of one dollar, he would give inoculations of "Kine Pock," a guaranteed security against the dread disease smallpox. At the same time Daniel and Eden Latham opened a second drugstore. Their shelves were well stocked with vermifuge, ague remedy, blood purifiers and even leeches (for blood-letting). Many of the early residents depended completely on their druggist's expertise in medical emergencies. Although most of the products contained a hefty dose of alcohol or narcotics, including those intended for children and babies, the pharmacist was looked upon as a most vital member of society.

The Early Drugstores and Pharmacists

A few years later, the firm of Crouch and Worthington sold drugs and medicine in the store of A. VanScoy. An 1834 advertisement in the local newspaper, *The Republican Watchman*, stated they had their shelves stocked with a "general supply of the best quality medicines and that all prescriptions were filled with neatness, safety and at a price as reasonable as could be obtained in New York City."

HEALTH CARE

During the 1840s J.F. Chipman & Company could be found in their pharmacy at the Old Stand on Main Street. Chipman filled prescriptions and sold patent medicine, such as remedies for consumption, dysentery, and cholera, as well as expectorants, liniments, and balsams. According to *The Corrector*, S.B. Buckley also had a drugstore on Main Street during the same years, and George and Charles Brown advertised that they had for sale "cheap" drugs at the old depot. They sold turkey opium, sugar lead, arsenic, quicksilver, brimstone, tincture of myrrh, and other ominous sounding remedies.

On the northeast corner of Main and Washington Streets stood the village drugstore of Albert W. Goble, apothecary druggist and chemist. Goble came to Sag Harbor in the mid-1800s. He informed the public he would be available to serve them day or night. When the store wasn't open, he could be found at his residence across the street. Unfortunately, Goble's business failed after several years.

In 1862 John F. Daniel Lobstein came to Sag Harbor, representing his employer, Delluc & Company, Pharmacists, of 635 Broadway, to look after the company's interest in the store. Lobstein was impressed with Sag Harbor to such a degree that he purchased the stock and went into business himself. Lobstein, having worked in New York for the Delluc Company for fifteen years, was an experienced and competent pharmacist. On August 22, 1867 Lobstein moved into a new store he had built on the west side of Main Street, opposite the present Municipal Building, and conducted his business there for the next 22 years. After Lobstein's death in 1884, the pharmacy remained in operation under the management of his brother J.E. Lobstein of Maryland, with the assistance of C.F. Bollerman, a qualified graduate of pharmacology. In 1889 the business was purchased by Arthur T. Brown, who moved the complete inventory back to the old location at Main and Washington into his newly renovated store. Brown remained in business at that location well into the 20th century.

In 1897, on Madison Street, just south of the junction, stood Albert Pickard's Pharmacy. After three years he sold his business to Benjamin Babcock, whose Bridgehampton Pharmacy, house, and barn had recently been destroyed by fire. Babcock called the place the Madison Square Pharmacy. By September 1902, the drugstore was once again for sale.

The drugstore of William Buck was most unique, for it was a pharmacy at the same location for about 130 years. In 1844 Buck's old drugstore stood on the east side of Main Street in the shop of George W. Reeney in the Mansion House. Fifteen years later he moved his stock into a new store in the Brick Block on the opposite side of the street, just south of the alley that leads to the parking area behind the village. Today the Sag Harbor Pharmacy occupies the building. J.W. Burke, a native of Sag Harbor and pharmacist for nine years, took over Buck's old store in the Mansion House and opened another drugstore.

William Buck's new pharmacy was 20 feet wide, 63 feet deep, and finished off with Corinthian archwork. With counters of Italian marble, large flint-glass showcases, and yellow pine flooring, the place was an exceptionally fine and modern pharmacy. After four years, Buck took as a partner A.G. Bassett and continued under the name William Buck & Company. In 1866 a young man by the name of William Wallace Tooker was hired as a clerk and apprentice, and after learning the business, also became a partner. Tooker later became the next owner of the pharmacy.

The firm of William Buck & Company dissolved on March 31, 1873, and Tooker, with partner Arthur S. French, a recent graduate of the Philadelphia College of Pharmacy, purchased the firm. In 1886 Tooker hired William R. Reimann, a young man from Buffalo, New York who had been in the pharmaceutical business for eight years. In 1898, Tooker, who had been ailing for several years, sold to Reimann and devoted his remaining years to studying and writing about the Algonquin Indians and their place-names. Reimann remained at the store for the next 40 years, and, up until the present, the little drugstore, originally occupied by William Buck, still serves the community as a village pharmacy.

Another pharmacy belonged to William Deans, who opened the Sag Harbor Dispensary of Drugs and Medicine in 1839. An entire new stock of the choicest quality drugs were found on his shelves. Deans had the advantage of being a druggist of many years' experience and was acquainted with the most approved methods of compounding various pharmaceutical preparations. He stressed that no boy would be permitted to deal out medicine of a dangerous nature except under the careful eye of himself. In his pharmacy on Main Street, Deans served ice cream, lemonade, soda, cakes, and fruit in his Phoenix Room.

William Sternes' new drug and medicine store opened about the same time as Deans'. Sternes had been a surgeon in the United States Army prior to coming to Sag Harbor. In 1840 he rented a store on Main Street that had originally been the book store of Orin O. Wickham. The drugs sold at Sternes' store had all been selected by himself in New York and Philadelphia. He advertised in *The Republican Watchman* that all physician's prescriptions would be carefully compounded and put up at reasonable prices.

Dr. Edgar Miles, physician and druggist, had the distinction of being in the drug business for 50 years. In his office on the east side of Main Street, Miles practiced the eclectic school of medicine, with most of his remedies concocted from herbs and seeds. In later years his son Edgar L. Miles joined him in the business.

Arthur T. Brown was a native of Sag Harbor and a descendant of one of the early families to settle in the village. In 1888 he graduated from the New York College of Pharmacy and, upon his return to Sag Harbor, purchased the drug business of J.F.D. Lobstein. In 1890 Brown built the corner drugstore and named his business the same. He established a fine reputation in Sag Harbor and informed the public that the prescription department was under his personal supervision.

A few other pharmacists came to the village briefly, including Joseph P. Lowrey, who opened the Harbor Pharmacy in 1890 but, after five years, moved to Southold. James B. Harris came to Sag Harbor in 1892, having previously been in the pharmaceutical business in East Hampton. Albert Newins also arrived in 1890 and, apparently, both he and Harris were here for just a short time.

Strange Illnesses; Stranger Remedies

Quincy, ague, catarrh, dyspepsia, consumption: these and other strange sounding ailments were common complaints in the early days. Although the words may be alien to our present-day vocabulary, these maladies are no different from those we suffer from today. We know them better as indigestion, fever, and upper respitory infections. Before the introduction of antibiotics, opium, morphine, and alcohol were found in most prescription medicine and could be easily purchased over the counter by man, woman, or child. The remedies, along with herbal concoctions passed down from generation to generation, were the only means of treatment available.

Not all the early nostrums, however, were beneficial, and some, in fact, turned out to be quite deadly. For example, Mrs. Winslow's Soothing Syrup, a popular remedy for teething babies, was laced with sulphate of morphine, ammonia, and alcohol, and caused scores of infant deaths until the formula was modified. An advertisement in the 1850 *Corrector* read: "Reader! Take care about what medicines you buy. Our country is flooded with nostrums not fit to give a dog. Some do positive injury by debarring you from other means that would cure." The local newspaper devoted an entire page to medical advertisements and stories endorsing certain products and their magical cures. A few of the more interesting ones follow.

136 INDUSTRIAL GROWTH AND OPPORTUNITIES

Bilious Fever: Usually begins with yawning, stretching, pain in the bones, langour, giddiness, a swelling about the region of the stomach, bilious vomiting and other unpleasant symptoms. For relief: Wright's Indian Vegetable Pills.

Hedges Rheumatic Plasters: to be applied to the soles of the feet, and very effective in drawing disease from the system.

Gonorrhea, Gleet Stricture, Disease of the Kidney, Bladder, Etc.: Reader, do you have a private disease? Don't neglect it. Delay is dangerous. Take Dr. Baker's Specific. Price $1.50 per bottle.

B.A. Fahnestock's Vermifuge: Edward Silton certified that he had been afflicted with pain in his stomach and headaches occasionally for the last 17 years. He exclaimed, "Hearing about B.A. Fahnestock's Vermifuge, recommended for expelling worms, I was induced to try it. I took four viles of it and to my great amazement, passed about forty feet of tape worm with head and tail to it. I now feel like a new man since this reptile left my stomach."

Dr. Marshall's Headache and Catarrh Snuff: Will cure nearly all the common diseases of the head, except wrong-headedness. It purges out obstructions, strengthens the glands, and gives a healthy action to parts afflicted.

Elixir of Opium: To produce sleep and composure, relieve pain and irritation, nervous excitement and morbid irritability of body and mind.

Swedish leeches for sale: In the original cases and guaranteed fresh and healthy—some extra large. For sale by the druggist, S.B. Buckley on Main Street.

Cholera Morbus: Cholera morbus is contracted during the intense heat of the summer and before the process of digestion is completed. Food often spoils and causes bad breath, sour belching, costiveness and dysentery.

The Cholera Scare

Today immunization and modern methods of sanitation have all but eliminated cholera in the United States, but years ago the deadly infectious disease spread rampant through cities, villages, and countryside. No one was exempt. Young and old, rich and poor, black and white—all fell victim to the malady, and the death rate was alarmingly high.

A cholera scare in 1866 prompted the Board of Health of the Village of

Sag Harbor to take certain precautions to prevent its spread. The disease had reached epidemic proportions in other localities, and because of the frightening consequences, the following regulations were strictly enforced. People were told to remove at once from their premises all filth and other matter from their drains, cesspools, pens, yards, privy-vaults, and other places likely to spread disease, and to clean and purify with proper disinfectants.

A person was appointed by the Board of Health to inspect the premises of all residents of the village. Willful violators were judged guilty of a misdemeanor, and convictions were subject to fine and/or imprisonment, with such fine not to exceed $1000 nor imprisonment to exceed two years.

A treatment for cholera had been tried with moderate success in Bombay and was available locally.

> After administering an emetic and copious potations of hot water, give the following pills, one every quarter hour or half hour depending on the urgency of the case. The concoction was made up of 250 grams of aloes, 75 grams each of colocynth, scammony and gamboge, 12½ grams of opium and 125 grams of calomel. Powder fine and mix with 12½ grams of hard soap. Add muscilage sufficient to form a hard mass, add equal quantities of cloves and cajaput sufficient to soften mass, then divide into 50 pills and keep in a closed vial.

Although there were some deaths in Sag Harbor attributed to cholera, a serious epidemic never broke out. Probably the enforcement of the Board of Health's rules, not the prescribed medication, was the reason Sag Harbor was spared.

3

THE LIGHTS GO ON

When Sag Harbor's whaling industry provided spermaceti for candles and whale oil for lamps, they were the means of lighting homes and places of business. As the industry declined, another method became necessary. Kerosene was a more available product, and it was used extensively until the introduction of gas lights.

The Era of Gas Lights

Gas lights had been used in Europe since the beginning of the 1800s, but it wasn't until 1859 that they came to Sag Harbor. They were introduced by Captain David Congdon, who, after closing his steamboat lines, turned his attention to this new device. After obtaining a sufficient number of subscribers, Congdon proceeded with his enterprise and obtained a franchise on May 17, 1859 for the next 25 years. He purchased the old spermaceti candle factory of N.P. Howell, that stood on West Water Street, and made necessary alterations preparing the building for the new gas works. Because of the complicated machinery needed to produce gas from coal, Congdon substituted rosin which was converted into gas by running the melted substance into heated horizontal retorts. In August 1859, with the gas works nearing completion, the buildings in town were fitted with pipes and fixtures. Huge gas mains were buried under

THE LIGHTS GO ON

the village streets, with Main and Jefferson being the first done, and by the end of the year, Sag Harbor became the first village east of Brooklyn to have gas lights. When December 1859 arrived, the lights were turned on, presenting a spectacular scene. The local newspaper printed the following:

GAS LIGHTS! THE TOWN IN A BLAZE

Gas was turned on and the citizens had an opportunity to test the merits of the new lights. As darkness came gradually on, one after the other of the more eager experimenters drew near to their burners, carefully applied the match, and the deed was done.

The illumination spread rapidly up Main Street and along the entire line of the pipes. Every burner was called into requisition in every house and store and the effect can be better imagined than described. Troops of youngsters and some old people too, paraded the streets gazing with wonder at the brilliant display, giving vent to their enthusiasm in repeated cheers for the gas lights and Captain Congdon.

Most of the local citizens expressed their feelings in favor of the new lights with much enthusiasm and delight. One remarked that in passing through the village, "We couldn't but notice the great benefit our storekeepers will derive from the introduction of the lights. What was dark and gloomy before now becomes bright and cheerful, and wares and merchandise are displayed to much greater advantage." In the business portion of Main Street all the stores looked well, but those of Messrs. G.W. Tabor, Charles Baker, William Buck, and Tiffany & Rogers were especially noticed. Think of this ye men of olden time, to what have your children degenerated! Truly, no more can we boast of the simplicity and rusticity of the East Enders. The charm is forever broken and the community which was abandoned so far the customs of the good old times, as to introduce gas for lights, is ripe for anything. We presume that some will faithfully adhere to their old lamps and try to make themselves believe that they are better than any new fangled notions. We shall not be surprised at any change and confidently predict the speedy extension of the railroad, telegraph, and gas pipes into every nook and corner of Old Suffolk.

The gas works were damaged several times during the next few years, and on August 13, 1869 the old building was completely destroyed. A report at that time stated that it appeared the person in charge turned the faucet to the retort containing the burning rosin and let the boiling fluid run into the fire and under the building where it quickly ignited. It enveloped the whole place, which was totally destroyed along with its contents. Efforts to save the building were fruitless due to the highly combustible material. The gasometer was saved, but the loss sustained amounted to $6000, with insurance covering only $2000. At that time the gas works were owned by a company with Gilbert H. Cooper in charge. Plans were made to erect a new brick structure on the same site, with work beginning immediately. A month later the new building was finished, and on October 6, 1869 the gas turned on.

In 1885, with the franchise given to David Congdon expiring, it was renewed for another 25 years. The new franchise restricted the price of gas for lighting purposes not to exceed $2.25 per 100 cubic feet, and gas for fuel purposes not to exceed $1.75 per 1000 cubic feet.

Sag Harbor Gets Electricity

Gas lights were utilized in the village until about 1890. As the new century began, there was a conversion to electricity, and in 1902 the taxpayers of Sag Harbor voted to purchase the Electric Light and Power Company from the United Gas Improvement Company of Philadelphia. A mortgage of $20,000 on the property was attained, with $15,000 of the bonds owned by residents of the village, due and payable in 1927. In August 1903 the electric plant was sold to George Kiernan, who owned it for the next ten years. In 1913 Kiernan sold to Harry Butts, Percy Cunningham, and U.M. Muller of Brooklyn, who hired others to take charge of the plant.

The Power House of the Electric Light Company was destroyed by fire of a suspicious nature during an April night in 1913. Manager George Bloomburg shut the power down at 4:40 P.M. and left, leaving Thomas Collins asleep inside the building. Cornelius Cosgrove and Morris Meyer, both in different locations, noticed smoke and flames coming from the building. The fire department was alerted but upon arrival could see that the fire had too much of a head start, and they were unable to put out the flames. Mr. Collins lost his life in the blaze. A loss of $10,000 was claimed, even though three of the engines were capable of repair.

By 1913 the new owners had the machinery in good running order again and planned to install a new "Skinner" automatic steam engine for driving the electric generators. The 125-horsepower engine was ordered from Erie, Pennsylvania. In the 1920s the Electric Light and Power Company moved into its new building on the corner of Main and Washington Streets in the village.

4

THE GREAT FIRES OF SAG HARBOR

On a frigid mid-winter's night, Sag Harbor's third major blaze occurred; the most disastrous event to take place since the memorable fire of 1845. So vulnerable, perhaps due to its lack of protection from the brisk north winds, the village was doomed once more.

The Fire of 1877

It was one o'clock in the morning of February 24, 1877 when William Redmond, night watchman of the railroad property, noticed a familiar glow from the direction of the North Battery on the Long Wharf. (The North Battery was built after the '45 fire and occupied for many years by J.E. & E. Smith, grocers and liquor dealers. It was known as the rendezvous of the crowd of wharf laborers and boat builders during the days of the whaling industry.) Policeman Aldrich saw the fire and discovered it was actually located in the store of M.H. Gregory at the north end of the wharf. The flames had already spread to Gregory's storehouse and the adjoining property of Nickerson & Vail and had run up the corners of both buildings from the first floor. The fire alarm was sounded, and the department arrived at the scene and stationed the "Minnehaha" wagon near the foot of Main Street where a public well was located. It was evident that the blaze was to be another major one as the northwest wind increased to gale force and spread the flames to nearby buildings on both sides of the street. S.S. Crowell's spar and blockmaking shop, John Fordham's blacksmith shop, and the two storehouses of H. & S. French were soon ablaze. Then, the large building of W. & G.H. Cooper and the boat shop of Jared Wade caught fire. Captain Wade put all his tools in a boat he was building and, with assistance, launched the boat. Unfortunately, it, too, caught fire and he lost everything.

Soon the fire crossed Bay Street and reached the tenement house of George B. Brown and then DeCastro's stables and barns. The wind, holding its northwest course, blew furiously, wrapping a sheet of flame around the Maidstone Mills and the Chemical Works and continuing up the Main Street as far as the brick buildings of Douglas and Cooper. These brick structures prevented the fire from extending further south and thereby saved the rest of the village.

Conkling's blacksmith shop and the residence of John Kelly and Edward Murphy on Division Street were next to be consumed. In the meantime, the flames had crept under the roof of the music hall located in the large building of B.F. Huntting. Although supposedly fireproof, the place burned extensively. The Nassau House on the northwest corner was next to go before the fire continued up Division Street, igniting the homes of Mrs. Graham and Mrs. Lowen on Cross Street, then the shop and home of N. Matthews and the home of Mrs. Corcoran. S.B. Eldredge's brick house on the corner of Cross and Division was saved, as was the Mott house on the corner of Burke and Rysam. The fine home of Zachariah Rogers caught the flying cinders on the roof and started to burn. It was extinguished temporarily, only to catch fire again and burn to the ground.

Many of those who suffered losses in the 1877 fire were the same property owners who lost everything in the blaze of 1845, and although some decided not to rebuild this time, a majority of the residents cleared away the rubble and started from scratch again. They were a strong and hardy bunch, determined to face the future no matter what it should bring, and in spite of the fact that the golden years of the whale fishery were over, Sag Harbor would grow again as a period of industrial development began.

Recollections of a Fire Fighter

I recall vividly the great fire of 1877 and the bitter experiences of myself and all the others fighting that fearful blaze. A furious wind and snow storm were raging and the night was bitter cold. The water in the two street wells was soon exhausted and the boys backed the old 'Minnehaha' engine into the bay at the slip west of Huntting's block and stood in freezing water knee deep pumping for dear life, relayed by citizens, as the members dropped out one by one from sheer exhaustion. With little water, meager equipment and exhausted fighting force, the fire raged out of control.

The Hook and Ladder Company was no better off than the engine boys. The hooks and ladders were not only few, but comparatively useless. We tried to protect our outlying buildings from sparks and embers with little avail. I was ordered by foreman Sherman to try to save a large barn at Rector and Division Streets. My first exploit on reaching the roof was to step on the ice covered shingles and shoot down into the barnyard, a distance of twenty feet. It was a miracle that I escaped with bruises only.

My next order was to go to the house of Zachariah Rogers, an uncle, a half mile away, and help him out. When I arrived the roof and upper part of the house was enveloped in flames, with no water or ladders available. Several men were tearing down the front banisters, several others were forcing a square piano through a side window, which they succeeded in doing, only to have it topple over a retaining wall and into Mott's Pond. Mrs. Rogers "Aunt Fanny" was hysterically running about trying to get someone to save her plants, of which she had a choice variety. To pacify her, myself and others succeeded in saving a number of them and put them in Sleight's barn across the street, where Jack Frost finished the job. This house stood on Rysam Street where Mrs. Sleight's bungalow now stands.

Unsigned letter – 1925.

Other Serious Fires

Two short years after the 1877 fire destroyed so many homes and businesses in the village, the Montauk Steam Cotton Mill, Sag Harbor's largest industry, burned to the ground. The alarm, which had by then begun to send a shudder of impending doom to the local people, sounded once more. It was just after midnight on October 25, 1879 when Captain DeWitt Conkling of the schooner *Harriet* had arrived in Sag Harbor and noticed a fire in the west tower of the building. The blaze spread rapidly through the mill, igniting the many bales of cotton and the yellow pine flooring which was saturated with oil. The heat was intense, and the immense structure was soon engulfed in flames. The heavy cemented walls cracked, opened, and fell in great sections. The slated roof fell in with such a crash, while hundreds of people looked on in horror, probably wondering if this was to be the end of the village again. Although it destroyed the factory completely, it spread no further, and Sag Harbor breathed a sigh

144 INDUSTRIAL GROWTH AND OPPORTUNITIES

of relief that the village had been spared this time.

During the years ahead, other serious fires occurred, although of lesser magnitude than those which annihilated the village in earlier times. Several are worth noting.

On July 28, 1881 a block of stores burned on the west side of the business district. The buildings lost were: a two-story frame building north of Tooker's Drug Store belonging to Joseph Crowell and occupied by J.W. Edwards; next north, a one-story frame building occupied by W.L. Cook who sold fancy goods; next north, a one-story frame building occupied by A.D. Ludlow who had a saloon and store; next north, a two-story building owned by Elisha King who sold dry goods, clothing and groceries. North of King's store was a two-story building occupied by Mrs. Amelia Cobb, dressmaker, followed by a one-story building owned by Mr. J.C. Kelly and occupied by James A. Harris who ran a confectionery store there. Next was another two-story building also owned by Mrs. King and occupied by Ella T. Miller who sold fancy goods and hosiery. The next building lost was a one-story structure owned by B.J. Haurand and occupied by George A. Babcock's tobacco and cigar store. Three more stores were partially burned, north of Babcock's. Only an alley on either side of the burned out district prevented the flames from spreading further.

On August 20, 1881 the East End Pottery Works burned to the ground. The following year on September ninth, the Oakland Works were destroyed. The Electric Light and Power Company burned on March 13, 1911; seven stores were destroyed by fire February 14, 1916; and finally, the magnificent Alvin Silver Company building on Main Street succumbed to flames on New Year's Day 1925. More information on these businesses can be found in other chapters.

A list of other serious fires can be found in the Appendix.

The Growth of the Fire Department

A reorganization of the fire companies took place in 1846 following the devastating blaze of the year before, and the citizens of Sag Harbor raised $2200 to improve their fire-fighting equipment. The members, 100 in number, were uniformed in bright red shirts and heavy leather fire helmets. The Gazelle Hose Company was organized for the purpose of attending to the pumping engine; their motto, "We fight to conquer, we conquer to save." Gazelle Hose's first piece of equipment was built by Elbert Thorne of Sag Harbor in 1846. Thorne was a carriagemaker by trade and also a member of the company. A building opposite the Arsenal on Union Street housed the new engine.

Other pieces of fire fighting equipment were kept in various places throughout the village. Niagara Engine #1 was at West Water Street near the gas works, Protection Engine #2 on Madison Street opposite Sage, Torrent Engine #3 on Washington Street opposite Church Street, and Phoenix #1 in the Arsenal on Union Street. The fire companies, at that time, combined to form the fire department, electing William R. Post as the first fire chief engineer. Lodowick Dering was chief of the Gazelle Hose; Silas Loper, the Phoenix Hook & Ladder; Samuel "Trib" Hildreth, the Niagara Engine #1; D. Alden Jennings, the Protection Engine #2; and Edward M. Cooper, the Torrent Engine #3.

In 1861 the charter was revised permitting the fire department to protect North Haven, Noyac, and part of East Hampton Road outside the village limits in the event of an emergency. Funds were raised to purchase a more powerful and efficient hand-pumper, and with an additional $800 from village funds, the "Minnehaha" Engine was acquired. It came from Brooklyn, eight years old and condemned, but after a complete overhaul, it was put into service and remained part of the village equipment for the next 50 years.

The Phoenix Hook and Ladder acquired a new hook and ladder wagon in 1866. Built by Williams and Cullum of Sag Harbor, it was affectionately called "Old Hay Rack." It was given its name during a tournament celebration at which the firemen dressed up the big ladder with hay and themselves in overalls and straw hats. The machine, when fully equipped, weighed over 2000 pounds but was pulled with ease by some of the swiftest runners in the department. It was said that once the Old Hay Rack had built up momentum it was hard to stop.

In April 1868 an old defunct pump at the junction of Main and Madison Streets was removed and a new one put in its place. That same year a 12-foot-deep cistern was installed in front of the Methodist Church for fire purposes, receiving water from the church roof. In the 1870s a number of large wells were placed throughout the village.

In June 1873 a special corporation meeting was held to consider purchasing new fire equipment for the village. Their idea was to put a steam pump in the Maidstone Mills and to lay iron pipes and fire hydrants through Main Street as far as Garden Street. Five years later the idea became a reality, and in December 1878 hydrants were placed at Division and Burke, and Main and Washington Streets. The village by-laws at that time required every citizen who owned a house or store to provide an India-rubber or leather bucket of at least two-gallon capacity and marked with his name or initial, to be kept in a convenient place where it would be ready for use in the event of a fire. These precautions, along with the Maidstone Mills facilities, made the village reasonably fortified against future disasters. Unfortunately, even with the additional

146 INDUSTRIAL GROWTH AND OPPORTUNITIES

precautions, another devastating fire claimed 33 buildings in the business district on February 24, 1877.

When the 1880s arrived, the village residents were eager to obtain a more modern piece of equipment. A new carriage for the Gazelle Hose Company was purchased by the village trustees from Edward B. Leverich of New York City. The Long Island Railroad transported the carriage free of charge, and upon its arrival the department turned out and made the occasion one for a parade. The new carriage was of the "spider crab" pattern, lightweight, and of the best materials of the day. However, the local press reported: "What Sag Harbor needs is a steam engine, even at the cost of hiring an engineer, but the department shouldn't be too hasty in purchasing a machine without investigating its patent." On May 27, 1886 at a special corporation meeting, there was a running debate upon the various propositions to improve fire-fighting facilities. Waterworks, steam, and hand fire engines, and even a Japanese method, were discussed. The group eventually selected a committee made up of the Board of Trustees, Reuben E. Richards, and Henry Cook to take the matter in hand. Sentiments seemed to favor a steamer as against a hand machine. Despite considerable opposition, a "Button"-pattern hand engine was purchased, and in January 1887 the much talked about engine arrived via the Long Island Railroad. Two days after its arrival it was pulled to the well at Main and Washington to be tested. The hose was laid to the Union School and a thin stream turned on that managed to reach the eaves, a full force of men working the engine. The old "Minnehaha" was brought out for a comparison, but was found to be out of order and refused to "squirt." Remarks were heard, such as, "It really was surprising what violent and sudden attacks of illness the old machine was subjected to, for the day before it was in good working order and threw out a stream of water that was far better than the new engine's performance." The popular opinion prevailed that the old engine could do as much good as the new one, and the trustees who made the purchase were thereafter "marked men."

In 1899 the Murray Hill Hose Company built their new firehouse and meeting rooms on their Elizabeth Street property. Josiah Smith was given the contract to build the 18- by 28-foot, two-story structure. A 10- by 10-foot tower was erected on the roof.

The house of the Otter Hose Company was totally destroyed by fire in April 1911. Fortunately, the hose and carriage were saved. A new firehouse was built on the site in August 1912, Graham Hallock doing the masonry work and George R. Garypie the carpentry work. The 20- by 24-foot structure stood two stories and was topped by an 8- by 8-foot tower. At the rear of the building

THE GREAT FIRES

were two spools for drying the hose. The final cost was $1625.

Throughout the history of the fire department parades, tournaments and mask balls were elaborate and frequent. For a Suffolk County tournament held at Riverhead in 1887, three passenger cars and two flatbed cars were added to the excursion train to carry equipment. Gazelle Hose Company won the first of many prizes that the department would bring home. When the company arrived in Sag Harbor at 11 P.M., a procession led from the train station to the village. Bonfires blazed on the Main Street. Fireworks, rockets, and candles were shot into the sky, and the whistle of the train and the factory wailed long into the night.

By 1914 the fire department considered adding "motor" apparatus. Otter Hose voted to purchase a big Lozier car and equip it for their new modern fire car. In 1916 the Murray Hill followed, ordering their motor car.

Work began to transform the old Union School into the fire department headquarters and Municipal Building in December 1916, the work being done by George Cleveland. The Phoenix Hook and Ladder and Gazelle Hose moved their equipment into the place in 1917, and a sign indicating such was placed in front of the building. J. William Beebee, an ex-fire chief, carved out of solid wood a beautiful bas-relief representation of Gazelle's carriage. Originally, it stood under the central arch of the firehouse on Washington Street and later at the Main Street headquarters. Sag Harbor, by the year 1920, had finally come to a point in time where the village was reasonably well equipped with modern fire-fighting equipment and could be fairly sure that the village would be safe from further disasters.

A list of the fire chiefs of the department, from its start through 1940, can be found in the Appendix.

Part Four

EXPLORING THE SOCIAL SCENE

1820–1880

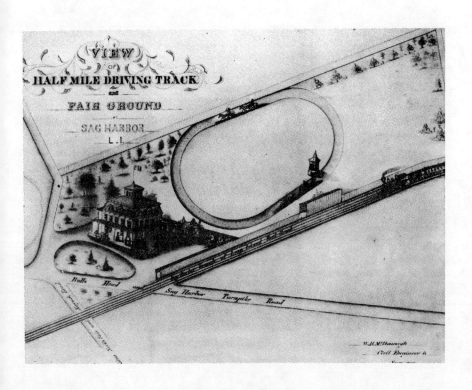

1

THE NEWSPAPERS PUBLISHED IN SAG HARBOR

Sag Harbor's earliest newspapers published little in the way of local news, concentrating instead on a story, sermon, and both national and international events. It is likely that folks learned all the local gossip and goings on at the general store, barber shop, or on the street corner; therefore, the publisher found it unnecessary to fill the four-page newspaper with such trivial things. Only by reading the shipping news and the classified advertisements could one identify the paper as being published in Sag Harbor, without looking at the title of the sheet.

FROTHINGHAM'S *LONG ISLAND HERALD*

The Long Island Herald, published by David Frothingham, was not only the first newspaper printed in Sag Harbor but the first one on Long Island as well. Frothingham set up his printing office in 1791 with the influential backing of Henry P. Dering, then Collector of the Port. Some historians place the location of his printing establishment on Main Street in the Herald House, while others, including author and historian, James Truslow Adams, claimed that his office, bookstore, and bindery were at the foot of Main Street near the landing. The July 26, 1860 issue of *The Sag Harbor Express* stated:

The Herald was printed in the building which stood in front of the lumber yard, now or formerly occupied by Major D.Y. Bellows; later in the chambers of the house afterward occupied by the late venerable Eliab Byram upon Main Street, which has long been replaced by their present commodious one and is still occupied as the family's residence. The printer's ink and posters were upon some of the upper rooms until it was taken down, and still later in his own residence which is replaced with the one now owned by the Reverend D.D. Lyons upon Main Street.

According to an old map, the Byram house stood on the east side of Main Street, south of the junction of Main and Madison. The Lyons house stood two doors from the Byram house, also on the east side of the street.

In any event, the first issue was printed on May 10, 1791 with the motto: "Eye Nature's Walks, Shoot Folly as it Flies—and Catch the Manners Living as they Rise." In the July 1791 issue, Frothingham informed his readers that the *Herald* was going to employ a post rider to travel throughout Long Island and take subscriptions for the newspaper. Samuel Isaacs was hired for the job. On the first anniversary of the *Herald*, in May 1792, Frothingham printed the following:

> This week completes twelve months since commencement of the paper, but as the printer was deficient (due to want of paper) it will be two weeks before the first volume of the Herald will be completed with grateful hearts. The printer returns, thanks to his customers, for the encouragement of the year past, and assured them that nothing shall be wanting on his part to render this paper a useful and entertaining repository. For the future, ten shillings per year will be the price and the first opportunity embraced to forward the packages. The paper will be sent on as usual unless ordered to the contrary.

Frothingham's *Long Island Herald* was printed for seven years and at least until the middle of December 1798. Beyond that date no copies have been located. After the demise of the *Herald*, all of Suffolk County was without a newspaper until 1802 when Selleck Osborn started printing Sag Harbor's second newspaper, *The Suffolk County Herald*.

THE SUFFOLK COUNTY HERALD
After the demise of *The Long Island Herald*, Selleck Osborn came to Sag Harbor from the New England States to start the village's second newspaper. Osborn gained the support of Henry P. Dering, and although inexperienced, he was dedicated to the newspaper business. The first issue of *The Suffolk County Herald* came out on June 19, 1802. Osborn told his readers:

I prefer the plain homespun name, Suffolk County Herald in place of the more high sounding Sun, Star, Universe, Globe, etc., as I cannot help comparing such pigmy fabrics on blue paper, with the fellow who kept a dram shop—who thinking to imitate the houses of entertainment, fixed a noble bunch of grapes over his door, while the poor oaf had no wine in his shop nor any other liquor other than whiskey and New England Rum.

It was stated that *The Suffolk County Herald* wouldn't please all political parties, but "those who are in, will grin; while those who are out, will pout." Whether Osborn's political ideas or his inexperience led to the failure of his paper isn't known, but just seven months after the first issue hit the press, the newspaper folded. Selleck Osborn soon left Sag Harbor to pursue a newspaper career in Litchfield, Connecticut, and the village was again without a newspaper until the following year when Alden Spooner started *The Suffolk Gazette*.

THE SUFFOLK GAZETTE

Alden Spooner was only twenty years old when he began publishing Sag Harbor's third newspaper, *The Suffolk Gazette*, on February 20, 1804. Like Selleck Osborn, Spooner was a newcomer to the business, and tradition tells us that his entire fortune consisted of only five or six dollars in his pocket and scarcely a decent suit of clothes on his back. Even the press and type used to print the *Gazette* didn't belong to him, but to about 20 individuals who agreed to lend the printing materials in return for free newspapers for the next four years.

For the first two years, Alden Spooner printed his paper without any assistance whatsoever. Every job, large or small, was done by Spooner, himself, in his printing office over the store of Jesse Hedges in the village. Spooner opened his paper with the following declaration to his readers:

> When a new paper is offered to the public, the general inquiry is, "What are the principles upon which it is to be conducted? What are the general and individual advantages which are to result from it?" These are objects of the first importance and to these inquiries duty demands that the public should have a satisfactory answer.
>
> It is a lamentable truth that the public newspapers of the present day, for the most part, teem with low invective and scurrility against the most dignified characters in our country. These are the fruits of a spirit of party which had unhappily arisen in our country, but which we now see rapidly subsiding; and we think, from convictions produced by repub-

lican measures. Such publications, although not confined exclusively to any party tend to inflame the public mind, mislead the understanding and retard the progress of political truth. All pieces of such a tendency will be carefully excluded from the Gazette, and it shall be the study of the editor that truth and decency alone shall appear. In the belief that the love of country no cold medium knows, the editor waves all pretentions to impartiality and had conscientiously adopted the principles of REPUBLICANISM.

Articles of news, foreign and domestic, will be faithfully and regularly detailed; and what, fellow citizens, can be more interesting to the inquiring mind than to learn from week to week the various events which are taking place, not only in our own country but thro' out the world? On one page we contemplate the melancholy and awful grandeur of conflicting armies, of thousands of honest, inoffensive men, led to the field of slaughter to gratify the ambition of a worthless tyrant. From these tragical scenes, the next page perhaps presents us with discoveries and improvements in those arts and sciences which increase our comforts, and make us wiser and better. In one hour we ramble over Europe, Asia and Africa, and then return home to our own domestic pages, and make a tour of the United States, into the state of parties, pick up improvements in agriculture and the arts, and see at one view the bustle of a busy world....

Alden Spooner's *Suffolk Gazette* lasted for seven years, its final issue printed on February 23, 1811. For the last six months, the *Gazette* was the property of a company that bought it from Spooner, although he remained editor. Alden Spooner then left Sag Harbor for Brooklyn, where he purchased *The Long Island Star*, and the village was once again without a newspaper for the next five years.

THE SUFFOLK COUNTY RECORDER

Samuel Seabury, a young man of 21 and a native of Sag Harbor, started the village's fourth newspaper on October 19, 1816. He named it *The Suffolk County Recorder* and charged $1.50 per year, which included delivery. The *Recorder* lasted but ten short months when it was substituted with another paper, *The American Eagle*, also published by Seabury. The August 30, 1817 issue of the *Recorder* informed the public that a new Republican newspaper, *The American Eagle*, would be on the newsstands each Saturday.

THE AMERICAN EAGLE

The American Eagle became the fifth newspaper published in Sag Harbor, and Samuel A. Seabury printed his proposals for a good Republican newspaper in the first issues.

> The object of the American Eagle will be, to maintain and vindicate the rights and immunities of the United States as a free sovereign and independent nation, against the pretensions, the violations, and the aggressions of any foreign power.
>
> To support the constitution and government of the United States and of the individual states, in their several and distinct provinces, and to sustain and uphold the liberties of the people.
>
> To defend the principles and measures of the general government as administered under Mr. Jefferson, Mr. Madison, and continued by Mr. Monroe.
>
> It will contain such mercantile, historical and agricultural information occasionally varigated with literary and miscellaneous pieces as shall best fulfill the usual purposes of a newspaper, and gratify the hopes and expectations of its patrons.

The American Eagle was printed on good paper and in handsome type and was issued to the subscribers at two dollars per year, payable quarterly. Those subscribing to *The American Eagle* were given the opportunity to advertise six percent cheaper than non-subscribers. The first issue of *The American Eagle* came out on October 18, 1818 and was said to have been a much better sheet than any of its predecessors. But regardless of its qualities, the paper lasted only three years, the last issue printed August 4, 1821. At that time, Seabury moved the paper to Huntington, New York, where it continued under the same name.

THE CORRECTOR

The Corrector, Sag Harbor's sixth newspaper, was established in August 1822 and became a fixture that survived for nearly a century. Harry Wentworth Hunt arrived from Boston, settled in Sag Harbor, and started his newspaper. Hunt had three sons, two of whom would play an important part in future local publications. *The Corrector* took as its motto, "Governed by Principle, Unwarped by Party; Oft we may Err, but Aim to be Just." *The Corrector* was published on a weekly basis until 1837 when it became a semi-weekly, published each Wednesday and Saturday until Hunt's death in 1857. The first issue contained the following information for its readers:

> The Corrector will be found a friend to Domestic, Manufacturers, the Arts and Sciences, Agriculture and Improvements; but under what cloak opinion, vice or corruption shall appear—bolstered or propped by

whatever power or authority, we will endeavor (at least) to tear a hole in the garment and expose it to ridicule of the honest part of society.

We wish the Corrector not only to be a welcome but useful visitor in every family, not only to the agriculturer, the man of business and the politician, but to the younger branches, for perhaps few other views or extends the ideas of young minds in so great a manner as a newspaper.

The Corrector was printed on a Washington Hand Press for 91 years. It was that very press that gave forth the first edition. It was said that "run off on a Washington Hand Press, a newspaper takes time to breathe; a pause between impressions gives ample opportunity for correction." Charles D. Daniels, foreman, continued in that position even after losing his hand. He devised an apparatus by which he could hold the compositor's stick, and he could set up a galley or two of type daily in the years before typesetting by machinery was introduced.

The printing office of *The Corrector* was located on the west side of Main Street, in the business district, and was one of the buildings lost in the great fire of 1845. Although most of the building's contents were safely removed, they were placed so close to the spreading fire that much of the type and furniture burned. Following the fire, *The Corrector* office occupied the rooms over the post office, which at that time stood opposite the Union School. Harry Wentworth Hunt remained publisher and editor of the newspaper for 37 years, and after his death on June 18, 1859, his son Alexander Hunt and Brinley D. Sleight took it over.

After Hunt and Sleight became editors, the paper changed from Republican to Democratic and, in 1860, was issued as a campaign daily. It was the first of its kind in Suffolk County. Unfortunately, the field was too small for it to be successful, and it again became a weekly publication. Sleight became sole editor of *The Corrector* that same year, following Hunt's move to upstate New York.

In January 1861 *The Corrector*'s office moved to the Brick Block and into the building of William R. Post. The third floor, formerly called Military Hall, was used as a press and compositor's room. The rooms on the second floor in the rear of H.P. Hedges office were used for the editorial office.

An interesting story relates that, during one unusually severe winter when the railroad was blocked with snow for ten weeks straight and the ferry was unable to run due to ice in the bay, copies of *The Corrector* were printed on common wrapping paper and on pink paper contributed by the local druggists. *The Corrector* was also the only paper in Suffolk County that published regular

THE NEWSPAPERS IN SAG HARBOR 157

telegraphic dispatches up to the time of going to press, and the March 9, 1861 Inaugural Address of President Lincoln was in print just three hours after being delivered in Washington, D.C..

When Brinley D. Sleight entered politics in the 1870s, he continued as editor of the paper. Even after going to Washington, the manuscripts and proofs were mailed to him for approval. Sleight remained in that position until his death in 1913, after which his son Harry D. Sleight took over. Sleight, who was also village historian, managed the paper until World War I, and at that time decided to sell *The Corrector*, due to his inability to find experienced help.

As *The Corrector* began its 97th year of continuous publishing, Charles Gilbride, foreman for the past three years, bought *The Corrector*. Harry D. Sleight remained on the staff as contributing editor. Unfortunately, after only one month, Gilbride contracted antimony poisoning of the hands from handling the type and ink and had to give up his work. *The Corrector* suspended publication immediately, and Burton D. Corwin, owner of *The Sag Harbor News*, purchased the name, and good will, and equipment of *The Corrector*. Corwin combined the two publications and called the paper *The Sag Harbor News and Corrector*. And so after nearly a century without missing a single issue, *The Corrector*, per se, ceased publication.

THE REPUBLICAN WATCHMAN

On September 16, 1826 Sag Harbor's seventh newspaper, a new Republican sheet, was introduced. Samuel Phillips called his paper *The Republican Watchman*; its motto: *Vincit Amor Patriae* – The Noblest Motive is the Public Good. Local shipping news, congressional, foreign and political current events, and a novel made up the contents. Competition and rivalry between *The Republican Watchman* and *The Corrector* were common and frequent, especially after *The Corrector* changed its format to Democratic. *The Republican Watchman* existed for 18 years and in 1844 removed to Greenport, Long Island, where it was taken over by Sag Harbor's Henry A. Reeves.

THE SUFFOLK WEEKLY GAZETTE

John Hancock began publishing the village's eighth newspaper in 1851. *The Suffolk Weekly Gazette* was printed at his office in the Exchange Building on Main Street. Hancock declared his paper to be a "family newspaper devoted to political and general news, agricultural, literature, etc." It was 11 by 18 inches in size, with its title printed in Gothic type, a change from the papers of the past. *The Suffolk Weekly Gazette* sold for $1.50 per year if paid in advance, or $2.00 if paid at the expiration of six months. After three years the paper folded.

EXPLORING THE SOCIAL SCENE

THE SAG HARBOR EXPRESS

Sag Harbor's ninth newspaper, *The Sag Harbor Express*, has the distinction of being the longest existing newspaper in the history of the village, still being published on a weekly basis after more than 130 years. The paper was established in 1859 by John Howard Hunt, son of Harry Wentworth Hunt, founder of *The Corrector*. The *Express*, during Hunt's years, was edited, published, and financed solely by himself. The first issue on July 14, 1859 contained this salutatory:

> We, today, present our readers with the first number of the Sag Harbor Express, while we apologize for many faults and deficiencies unavoidable in a new undertaking, we still venture to hope that the contents and general appearance of our paper will meet with the approval of our patrons....
>
> In conducting this paper, our great aim will be to promote the welfare of this village to the utmost of our ability and earnestly to advocate all such enterprises as are calculated to increase its prosperity.
>
> All educational, moral and religious organizations shall receive our hearty support, and full reports of their proceedings will be given in our issues.
>
> We take pleasure in informing our readers that we have secured the services of William H. Gleason, Esq., who will aid us in conducting the editorial department of this paper.
>
> Receive then friends, our warmest thanks for the kindness shown our new attempt—may our acquaintance be mutually pleasant and profitable. May you never have reason to regret the patronage you shall extend to us and may we never venture to present anything to you which, "dying, we should wish to blot," and thus with smooth seas and prosperous gales, we launch our little bark upon the ocean of Editorial Life.

The Sag Harbor Express was 100 percent Republican in its views throughout its life. During the Civil War the paper fought zealously for the Union's cause. After the war the *Express* became an active participant in political discussions.

In 1920, at the age of 85, John Howard Hunt sold the *Express* to Warren S. Gardner, who established the Sag Harbor Publishing Company. With the March 1, 1923 newspaper, Hunt's name was removed for the first time in

64 years. In January 1922 the *Express* office moved from the second floor of the Forester's Building, where it printed the paper for 40 years, to a new location north of the American Hotel on the ground floor of the former Cassidy Building. Mr. Gardner introduced labor-saving machinery to his publishing business, linotype, and self-feeding press, and electric motors for power. By subscription drives, the circulation increased considerably. Eventually, Gardner purchased *The Sag Harbor News and Corrector* thus combining three original papers. It then became the only newspaper in the village.

THE PASSWORD

The Password, Sag Harbor's tenth newspaper, was a weekly journal devoted to the interests of Masonic and Temperance organizations. George Latham was its publisher, and the paper lasted but a few short months in 1871. The old "Smith" press which stood in the *Corrector* office for 40 years was purchased by *The Password* to be used to print the newspaper.

THE FREE LANCE

The eleventh newspaper, *The Free Lance*, was also short-lived, but, unlike *The Password*, it created quite a stir in the village. William McFeeters, the editor, lived in Brooklyn and had a summer home in Sag Harbor. It was said that he was hired by some of the local residents who thought things were a little dull and wanted to stir up some action.

The first issue, published on August 27, 1887, started right out with a controversial column called "Town Topics or What the Tongue of the Gossips Find to Wag About." McFeeters told his reading public that "The Free Lance comes to remain but a few weeks this year, but during the short period of its existence it hopes to accomplish its unseen mission. If the paper is not spicy it will not be because there is not enough interesting matter under the surface to make it so." It seemed to be such a popular item that its circulation jumped from its initial 200 copies to over 1500 in just a few short weeks.

Editor McFeeters seemed to be an expert at causing problems and made a point of harassing the editors of *The Corrector* and *The Sag Harbor Express* as often as possible. In one instance he said of Editor Hunt: "Editor Hunt of the Express is said to have been upset during the recent boat race. If his ability as a sailor is equal to his ability as an editor, it might be taken as a matter of course."

Whether *The Free Lance* ever accomplished its unseen mission, we'll never know, but the few months the paper filled its pages with insults and gossip was enough to last the residents of Sag Harbor for a long, long time.

160   EXPLORING THE SOCIAL SCENE

THE RAPID TRANSIT

Sag Harbor's twelfth newspaper was *The Rapid Transit*. It, too, lasted only a few months during 1889. Charles S. Hedges, its editor, and William L. Cook, associate editor, took as the symbol on the paper, a bull chasing a boy. The first issue of the *Rapid Transit* hit the newsstands January 23rd of that year.

THE SAG HARBOR NEWS

In 1909 *The Sag Harbor News* began publication, the first issue making its appearance on January 29th. It was neatly printed, newsy, and sold for three cents per copy. *The Sag Harbor News* was published by R.C. Hallock of Bridgehampton, with Peter Hughes the local editor, and Burton D. Corwin, business manager. The office of *The Sag Harbor News* was located in the Reimann building, but the paper itself printed on the press of *The Bridgehampton News* in Bridgehampton. Corwin, who owned the *News*, later bought *The Corrector*, combined the two publications and called the paper *The Sag Harbor News and Corrector*. Eventually, Warren S. Gardner of *The Sag Harbor Express* bought *The News and Corrector*, and the three were made into one newspaper.

THE HARBOR PILOT

Peter F. Hughes, editor and publisher of *The Harbor Pilot*, began his newspaper in 1922. It was the smallest sheet in the history of Sag Harbor's publications, measuring only 11½ by 8¼ inches, but though its size was small, its pages contained a large variety of news. The column "What's Happening in Sag Harbor" took up an entire page and was filled with local happenings and gossip and, undoubtedly, was a popular item. Sports news and advertisements made up the rest of the paper. The first subscriber to *The Harbor Pilot* was Miss Louise Painter, and the first advertiser, Frank Metzer.

Hughes entered his new enterprise with a great deal of experience, having edited *The Sag Harbor News* for several years. The paper was printed at Peter Hughes' small office and printing shop on Madison Street and sold at three cents per week or $1.50 per year. After publishing *The Harbor Pilot* for two years, Peter Hughes and his newspaper went out of business.

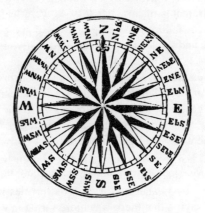

2
SCHOOLS IN THE NINETEENTH CENTURY

Young Oliver Wade was born in Sag Harbor, like his father (Oliver Sr.) and his grandfather (Captain Jared Wade). As a boy growing up in the village in the 1840s, Oliver witnessed the arrival and departure of whaling vessels, the training of the Continentals, the great fire of 1845, and the exodus of ships to California when gold was discovered in 1849. Oliver, like any boy, was mischievous and fun-loving, with a strong, vivid imagination. He probably ice skated on Mott's Pond, coasted on Sleight's Hill, played ball, fished, and went swimming in the bay. Oliver attended several schoolhouses during the course of his education, and he later wrote a delightful account of those years, a story that brings alive his experiences while attending school during the period 1845-1850.

The Schooldays of Oliver Wade

My school days were of three periods. The first was with a lady whose school was in the basement of the house of a Mr. Matthews whose sign read, 'Pump, Block and Sparmaker.' My teacher was Mrs. Post, the wife of William R. Post. She was an amiable sweet lady.

My second school period was with Miss Nancy Jessup at the school house at Church and Sage Streets. The room was the front upper chamber and was reached by an outside stairway. She was inflexible in her requirements of how her lessons were learned and her dreaded punishment for failure was being undressed and put to bed—your book given to you and the lesson so conquered that you could recite it before you could arise and dress and go home. In going to this school I went along the meadow by Morgan Ròger's house, through Burke Street to Hallock's Corner, where there was, set in the earth, the jawbone of a whale. On reaching this spot, my books were laid down while I leaped over the jaw. On returning, the same ceremony followed, and all the boys that went my way performed this act daily.

My third and last period of school in Sag Harbor was to that little yellow school house, otherwise known as the little yellow house of horrors, presided over by Leander Aldrich. His ferrules were whittled and he was fond of saying that there was more virtue in white pine than in any other wood. There was one boy, Henry Cooper, who lived in the only house on Love Lane, who took the torture, then thanked Leander, who visibly blushed from chagrin. Most all of the boys had a pair of boxwood combs and a small looking glass. Hair was allowed to grow long and was trained to curl under. Much attention was given to this in school. Leander was not in fashion and did not train his hair to conform with fashion. His forte was white pine ferrules.

While I attended the school of Mr. Aldrich I usually went from my home on the crest of Sleight's Hill. On the home side of the hill was a great gap in the fence. One third of the way over was a big grey boulder. Two thirds of the way was another boulder and then beyond that was a gap in the fence opening on Rysam Street. In March, when the high winds blew and great masses of clouds were hurried through the heavens casting dark shadows upon the ground, I was greatly troubled by imaginings that if one of those shadows overtook me between the first gap and the first boulder, I was in some mystical way cursed and blighted. Great was my joy if in calculating the speed of a shadow, I reached the boulder before the curse of the cloud. Waiting with heaving breast, I again sped away for the second boulder and finally from that to the second gap. After that I gave the clouds no thought. Their only power to harm was on Sleight's Hill.

It was during my school days under the domination of Mr. Aldrich that, theoretically, I played truant, the first and only occasion in my life. I say that my truancy was theoretical, and by this I mean that it was not premeditated in any way. I was simply led away by my love for music, "the sweet alarms of war." It was the occasion of the first public appearance of the company of Continentals of the village. They were in the church yard of the Presbyterian Church. It was at recess time of the school, and we all went to the church yard to see the soldiers. The recall bell had rung and all the boys returned leaving me with my excited emotions. Their orders were given to march, and Daddy Hallock, the fifer, struck up the "White Cockade," and Billy Winters trolled the sticks on the square drum, and the bass drum boomed in unison. Ah, what a rare drummer was Billy Winters. No drummer ever appealed to me as he, unless it was in later years the drummer in Seidel's Orchestra, who presided over the kettles. There was nothing in life that day for me but the soldiers—uniting came into my mind to accuse me. I was willing as the Pied Piper of Hamlin was drawing me on. Up Main Street we marched and down Glover Street to Peter's Green and all day long I marched and counter marched with the Continentals until they disbanded later that afternoon.

The next day my father was to start for California and after breakfast he called me into the sitting room and told me he had a note from Mr. Aldrich saying I had played truant. It was useless for me to try and explain the witchery of the drums and the fife which had lured me. I did the best I could and he finally said, "I am parting from you today for some years to come and I cannot bear to punish you. I will have to leave it for Mr. Aldrich to do." We were both in tears. That morning after school was in, Mr. Aldrich called me to his desk and dwelt upon the enormity of my offence. To him I could offer no explanation, for how could he comprehend my day of joy, so I stood before him and wept. He at last said to me, "Your father is going to California today and I shall not punish you."

The Sag Harbor Academy and Institute

In 1845 a two-story academy was built on Suffolk Street by a stock company, at a cost of $2500 to $3000. Known as the Sag Harbor Academy and Institute, it was established through the efforts of Reverend Joseph Copp, then pastor of the First Presbyterian Church. Four Ionic columns decorated the front of the building, and a belfry stood on the roof. Originally, a fee was charged to attend the academy. Later, the academic department of the Union School held classes there.

The academy opened September 2, 1845, offering classical and scientific subjects. In 1849 the building caught fire and partially burned. Although there was no insurance, the building was repaired, following the pattern of the original structure. In 1856 Principal George W. Dickerson became the director, and it was said that the school succeeded in a way never before realized. In 1858,

320 students attended the academy, 61 of whom pursued classical studies. The academy had the distinction of being the main educational institution in Sag Harbor for 24 years.

When the November 1860 term opened, discipline was described as "perfect, with an excellent order and regularity maintained, and with reading taught by theory and practice in order to make good readers." Charles B. Ruggles took over as president in March of 1862. Tuition costs were $400 for a program which included English, Grammar, Arithmetic, and Philosophy. If French were to be included, the cost was an additional $200, and if one wanted to learn Latin and Greek, it would cost an additional $600. Many who were pursuing careers in medicine, law, and government learned their basics at the academy before furthering their education.

After the organization of a Union School District, the place was used by the Academic Department, where students prepared to further their studies.

On February 10, 1864 the Sag Harbor Academy and Institute was completely destroyed by fire. A strong northwest wind blowing during the evening hours fanned the flames which consumed the structure. The entire library and consolidated libraries of the three old districts were lost. Up to 1000 books and textbooks valued at $1500 were destroyed. For several years following the blaze, classes were held in the basement of the People's Baptist Church and then in the Village Hall. The impressive academy, however, was never rebuilt.

The Union School District

The first meeting to consider consolidation to form a Union School District was held in February 1862, and on April 22nd of that year it was organized, combining the three former school districts. Charter members of the Board of Education were: Oliver Wade, Cleveland S. Stillwell, William H. Gleason, Jonas Winters, Stephen B. French, and Brinley D. Sleight.

In the fall of 1862, school opened in several buildings. The primary department was in the old schoolhouse on Madison Street, the intermediate department in the school on Church and Sage, and the academic department in the school on Suffolk Street. For the next several years, meetings were held concerning the purchase of a building large enough to accommodate all the districts in one schoolhouse.

The first teachers hired in the Union School District were: Miss S.C. Webster and Ellen M. Patrick for the Academic Department, Jehiel Raynor and Nancy Jessup for the Intermediate Department, and Sarah Jessup and Helen Hedges for the Primary Department. Charles B. Ruggles was the principal, and

Reverend C.H. Decker hired to teach the "colored children." Yes, segregation found its way into the Sag Harbor school system during the Civil War years.

Segregation in the Schools

Throughout the history of Sag Harbor's early schools all students, regardless of color or nationality, attended school together. It was during the Civil War years that the practice of segregation was introduced in the local school system. In 1869 it was voted to place the 31 black children in a separate room, although not all the local residents agreed. Even before that time, a black minister was hired to teach the black students. The following letter, written by the editor of *The Sag Harbor Express*, was published in his newspaper expressing his dismay over that shameful practice:

Democracy vs. Color
By the school census just completed in this village, it will be seen that there are now residing in this Union School District, between the ages of five and twenty-one years, 742 children, 711 white and 31 colored.

We always thought that the Democratic party were a more courageous set than they really prove themselves to be, for at the late school meeting they were so woefully afraid that the 31 colored children would "eat up" or otherwise damage the 711 white ones, that they voted to instruct the trustees of the Board to place them in a separate room. This is rather a new scare for the Democracy, for it has ever been a custom or practice in this place, even back in the old district school days, to have the white and colored in the same school. But the whole secret of this vote may be summed up in a nutshell, and it is this, that some of these colored children are smarter than some of the white ones, as will be seen by the proceedings of the last examination, when in the promotions from the Intermediate Department to the Academical Department, William Johnson, colored, stood first on the list, and Mary Consor, also colored, stood fifth. We should think that our Democratic friends would feel jealous. Since writing the above, we learn that there is a separate room for the colored children, but when they become so far advanced in their studies that they cannot longer be taught in that department, they are advanced to other departments, thus it is with these two of whom our Democratic friends are so jealous, not withstanding that they stood higher in scholarship than any other scholars in that department. The colored department of the Union School now numbers about nine scholars, sustained at an expense of about $300 per year. If our overburdened taxpayers, especially those who do not pay their taxes, really wish to lessen taxation, we would recommend to abolish this department and place the children in the other schools rather than crush the Academical Department which is of much more importance.

Subsequent issues of the newspaper fail to mention just how long the school was segregated.

The Union School

The Mansion House and the Baptist Church were two buildings considered large enough to house all the students of the district. Initially, both were turned down. But in 1871, when Dr. Frederick Crocker donated $5000 and the residents of the village raised $3000 more, the four-story Mansion House was acquired. In May 1871 the place underwent renovations to adapt it for school purposes, remodeling done under the supervision of Charles Hallett. The old battlement and fancy stone caps on the front of the building were removed. The roof was raised, and a three-foot overhang built, with John Chester doing the work. Three stores occupied the ground floor of the building, and the upper stories were used for the classrooms. Three hundred and seventy-five students moved into the place in 1871, and for the next 34 years the Union School served as the village's principal educational facility.

In 1893 an annex to the Union School was built at the rear of the building and facing Division Street. Completed in September of that year, it was ready for occupancy the following month. The building was painted dark red and heated by pipes which ran from the main schoolhouse. After the turn of the century, with the Union School building in great need of repair, the district was faced with the problem of finding another building or starting lengthy and extensive renovations.

A list of children attending Union School can be found in the Appendix.

St. Andrew's Roman Catholic School

Father Joseph Brunnerman founded a Catholic school for about 30 to 40 students during his pastorate in Sag Harbor, 1859-68. Originally, the old building in which school was held had been the Methodist Meeting House, then was bought by St. Andrew's for their Catholic Church. When their new sanctuary was built on Division Street in 1872, the building became their schoolhouse.

In 1872 the building was turned around, broadside to Union Street, and placed on a new foundation. This school building was used for 11 years, until a decision was reached to build a new school. The old structure was sold to

SCHOOLS IN THE NINETEENTH CENTURY 167

John McDonough, cut in two, and moved to Glover Street where it became a tenement.

In August 1883 the foundation was built, and by the end of that month, the frame raised. Payne and Whitney, contractors, built the 30- by 70-foot structure, completing it in March 1884. Classrooms for grades one through eight were on the first floor, and a Catholic meeting room, called St. Joseph's Hall, on the second. This parochial school was used well into the 20th century and later replaced by a new modern school on the northeast corner of Division and Union Streets.

The Academy of the Sacred Heart of Mary

Twenty-nine years after the founding of the Order of the Sacred Heart of Mary in France, a small band of nuns under the leadership of Mother Basil arrived in Sag Harbor on May 1, 1877. The luxurious home of Dr. P. Parker King on Hampton Street was purchased by the Monks family of New York for $5000 and turned over to the nuns. It was an elegant structure situated in an old oak grove and surrounded by spacious lawns, an appropriate setting for the establishment of their convent. The Very Reverend Bishop Loughlin consecrated the place, assisted by Reverends J.J. Heffernan and Michael Murphy, a native of Sag Harbor.

A chapel built on the grounds in 1888 held an angelus bell in the steeple which summoned both sisters and students to classes and to mass. Twelve nuns and a Mother Superior taught at the academy, where, in addition to academic subjects, instructions were offered in languages, vocal and instrumental music, drawing, and plain and fancy needlework. By the turn of the century the place was equipped with gas, electricity, steam heat, and running water. In November 1893 the convent received from the mother house in France a beautiful set of Stations of the Cross valued at $400.

At first, the majority of the boarding students came from Brooklyn, but in later years most came from Central and South America. After finishing eighth grade, many local girls continued their education at the academy, and for years it was the only Catholic secondary school in Nassau and Suffolk Counties.

At one time the academy housed the first American novitiate of the Order of the Sacred Heart. It opened, as such, in 1903 due to the enactment of laws in France that banned the training of religious orders in that country. The novitiate stayed at the academy until 1911, at which time it was transferred to Tarrytown, New York.

In September 1924 a two-story addition to the academy was built at a cost of $25,000. Seven years later, in March 1931, fire destroyed the new wing. The 4 A.M. blaze on that blustery March night miraculously spared the lives of 70 children who were sleeping in the building. The sisters proved to be the heroines of the disaster by herding the children together and calmly leading them to safety. The wing was rebuilt in December 1932, with the same builder, Edward Gay of East Hampton, hired to construct the building. Others involved were: J. Curtis Lawrence of East Hampton, architect; James Osborne of Amagansett, mason; Quogue Plumbing Company; Raymond Parsons of East Hampton, electrician; and Edward Willer of Bridgehampton, painter. The estimated cost to replace the addition was $25,000 to $30,000.

In later years a three-story brick building erected on the premises held classrooms and student housing. In 1968 a decision made by Mother Superior closed the academy, due to economic reasons and a decrease in enrollment. A year later the buildings were purchased for Sag Harbor's Elementary School and brought about an end to the Academy of the Sacred Heart of Mary's 90-year operation in the village.

3

ORGANIZED RELIGION IN SAG HARBOR

The second Presbyterian Church was only 28 years old when plans were initiated to build another. One would wonder why the local Presbyterians felt it necessary to replace the church they had so recently built. Reverend Clarence Hall Wilson in his historical address of 1916 said that, in his opinion, the great prosperity of the community during those golden years of the whale fishery prompted the residents to build a church in keeping with their homes and means. But even more likely was the great religious revival of 1842, when the membership swelled and the existing church became crowded. They thought of the future and imagined that the steady growth would continue.

Nathaniel Prime, in his *History of Long Island*, wrote that in 1842 a great religious revival took place in Sag Harbor. The first indication became apparent in the preceding autumn and continued with increasing power throughout the winter till the following spring. During a part of this season, religion became an all absorbing subject. In the streets and shops it was the general topic of conversation. Hundreds turned to the Lord, and the moral condition of the whole place improved.

The First Presbyterian Church (Old Whaler's)

After many meetings it was decided to build the third church, a magnificent structure that became affectionately known as the Old Whaler's Church. Built in 1843-44, it was designed by noted architect Minard Lafever. Property on Union Street, one block south of the early church, was purchased at a cost of $2000, and construction soon began.

An interesting letter, written in 1843 by one of the laborers, tells of the work's progress. Edward R. Merrall wrote the following to his mother:

> The church we are building will be a much more handsome ediface and considerably larger (than the Methodist). The steeple is to be 165 feet high. The original contract to build was $10,000. Since then they have added work to the amount of over $2000 more. Instead of my finding it enclosed as Mr. Lafever had told me, some of the window frames were not in when I arrived. The steeple was not boarded up over fifty feet high and there is sixty-five feet more of the form to go up yet. I do not expect the outside work will be done in much less than two months. There were seventeen men at work on it when I came, three have left, not much liking the job. The boss gives the old hands the preference for the inside work, all but two being from New York. An English man is getting out the stairs, they are a half circle going from the basement to the gallery. The pews are to be made in New York.

This letter is of great significance. It not only proves that Minard Lafever was the architect and often present during its construction, but gives the only known account of the job while in progress.

The facade of the church is one of the finest examples of Egyptian revival architecture to be found in the United States today. Blubber-spade trim decorates the cornices of the truncated pyramidal tower. The steeple, which was destroyed in the 1938 hurricane, stood as a welcome sight to the early whalers as they returned from their lengthy voyages. In the Greek Revival style interior, the pulpit is flanked by two gigantic Corinthian columns rising more than 50 feet from the floor to the coffered ceiling. Each ceiling square is decorated with egg and dart molding. A *trompe l'oeil* painting at the rear of the pulpit gives the appearance of a curved wall. Galleries on either side of the room are supported by fluted columns, and in the choir loft, at the rear of the church, stands a Henry Erben organ installed in 1845. It is the oldest organ in a Long Island church that is still in use today.

When Reverend Joseph Copp preached the dedication sermon on May 16, 1844, the church was filled with 1000 people. Several whaling vessels due to leave Sag Harbor that day were allowed to remain in port an extra day so the men could attend the service and receive the pastor's blessing.

The church was completed at a cost of $17,000, with wealthy businessmen, whaling captains, as well as men of lesser means all contributing what they could. The first step taken to pay off the debt was "hiring" the money and classifying the pews. They were divided into four classes and sold at auction, many bringing double their value. Fifteen thousand dollars was soon collected.

With such a magnificent new sanctuary, it is hard to imagine that not all of the parishioners were happy, but that seemed to be the case. In the spring of 1844 some members were so dissatisfied with the new church they returned to the old building to worship. They hired Reverend Alonzo Welton of Southold to be their minister, and at a revival meeting, others soon joined the group. They claimed they were the first Presbyterian Church, and those who built and worshipped in the new one were separatists and forfeited all rights to the property. The matter went to court, and after litigation, which lasted about a year, the case was decided against the claimants. There being no cohesive power to hold them together, they separated, and the attempt to establish a second Presbyterian Church failed.

In 1871 the church underwent extensive repairs and improvements. The old box pulpit, in which the minister was obliged to stand as he delivered his sermon, was removed, and a more modern one installed in its place. Some in the congregation looked upon the change as a sacrilege, to spoil the beautiful pulpit that graced the front of the church. However, most wanted to keep up with the times, and it was decided that a platform and desk not only would be a great improvement but would add to the symmetry of the structure as well. The fresco received a fresh coat of paint, the mahogany trim polished, and the exterior of the church, including the fence, were repaired and given three coats of paint. The entire job amounted to about $1600, with four individuals bearing the cost of $150 to remodel the platform and pulpit.

Ten years later, as the country mourned the death of President Garfield, the pulpit was heavily draped in black, relieved with black and white rosettes. The platform was festooned in plain black, and the two columns on either side hung from top to bottom with black. Behind the pulpit hung a large portrait of the late President, with the American flag in the background. The local daguerreian Mr. Warner had for sale three views of the church draped for the funeral obsequies, and every member of the congregation was advised to buy one.

In 1885 the ball and the 9-foot 10-inch weathervane were removed from the top of the tall steeple preparatory to painting, and a new vane was installed after George H. Hill completed the monumental task. In January 1902, Cox,

Sons & Buckley, a firm of New York decorators, were hired to refresco and paint the church interior; the contract price, $500. The design, considered artistic and modern, and rendered in ashes of roses, wasn't to the liking of many of the parishioners, and the general consensus was to have the old fresco restored. G.C. Callmander of Brooklyn did the restoration for $375 in May 1909.

Repairs to the tall steeple were made in November 1903, when champion steeple repairer of the world, Charles H. Kent of Brooklyn, came to work on the spire. Upon request, Kent presented a list of nearly 100 tall steeples in greater New York and vicinity upon which he had worked without scaffolding. The repairs were completed at a cost of $1600. The steps across the front of the church were built in August 1908, the lower concrete section done by master mason Edward J. Beckwith, and the wooden steps and platform by George Cleveland.

In 1926 J.L. Warner's steeplejacks, George and James Fenton, Ovilia Riel, and Edward Mansfield, of Northampton, Massachusetts, climbed the lofty spire to paint it and the weathervane that topped the steeple. The cost of this monumental task was $1875, quite a bargain when you consider that the year before Frank Havens was paid $1227 for painting the chapel!

A list of the ministers who served in the First Presbyterian Church and the earlier churches can be found in the Appendix.

THE MEMORIAL CHAPEL

Building a chapel for the Presbyterian Church had been discussed for some time prior to action being taken, but it wasn't until the annual meeting of 1893 that the project finally got underway. The Board of Trustees were appointed as a building committee with Pastor Clarence H. Wilson as chairman. The chapel was to be connected to the existing building at the rear of the sanctuary.

All necessary arrangements had been made and everything looked promising, when the effects of the panic of 1893 hit hard. Many who subscribed could not see their way clear to pay the amount they had "intended." Because of this situation, the matter of building the chapel had been postponed year after year. It wasn't until June 3, 1899 that the money was finally acquired. George H. Cleveland of Sag Harbor was the successful bidder, and the contract was signed with him August 25, 1899. Three days later ground was broken, and on September 20th the cornerstone was laid. Items placed in it were a copy of *The Sag Harbor Express*, *The New York Sun*, *The Sag Harbor Corrector*, *The Assembly Herald*, and *The Independent*, also a written account of the building of the chapel, an announcement of the death of Elder Samuel N. Davis, who died that day, a copy of the Prayer Meeting Topic Leaflet with a list of church officers, a photograph of Reverend Samuel King, a copy of William Guthrie Barnes' centennial sermon, a printed copy of a sermon by Reverend Edward Hopper, and a coin of 1899.

Built and furnished at a cost of $6225, the chapel holds five rooms and a hall, is 38 by 68 feet in size, with a portico in front over which reads "Memorial Chapel." The interior consists of two parlors, 21 by 16 feet each, and, to the east, the main auditorium which is 38 by 47 with 22-foot-high ceilings. Originally, over the parlors were the pastor's study and the infant school room, shut off from the main auditorium by rolling wooden blinds. It and the two parlors could be opened to the auditorium, making it possible to seat 500 people. The rooms were finished off in varnished oak with tinted walls above, carpeted in light green, with curtains to match, and seated with folding maple chairs.

Mrs. Alexander D. Napier of Brooklyn and Miss Julia King of Sag Harbor gave all the gas fixtures, pulpit furniture, an upright piano for the ladies' parlor, and furnishings for the pastor's study. Among the furnishings was a chair over 300 years old which was in a minister's family all that time. It was owned by Miss King's father, and prior to that, by her grandfather Samuel Lavington, and before that, by his grandfather Reverend Joseph Walker of Great Britain. The rooms were lighted with the Welsbach System, and one of the chandeliers was of 1200 candlepower.

The chapel was dedicated on December 15, 1899, with an elaborate musical program. Among the participating clergy was Reverend Robert K. Wick of Jamaica, New York.

The Bethel Baptist Church

Proof exists, in the form of a paper in possession of the Baptist Association, that Sag Harbor's Baptist Society was the second oldest religious organization established in the village. Among the minutes of the New York Baptist Association for the year 1792 appears:

> In 1792, October 31 and November 1, there was a Baptist Church constructed at Sag Harbor and united with the association the same year, and they sent as their messenger to the association, Jonathan Sizer. The church constituted with thirteen members and disbanded in 1800.

A note of 1793 tells of Elder Finch, pastor of the King Street Baptist Church of Connecticut, serving as pastor of the church in Sag Harbor during that year.

It isn't known how long this first church existed, but apparently it was short-lived, and it wasn't until 1843 that the church was re-established. For the first six months the congregation of eight to ten people gathered in private homes to worship. They later met in a room under the paint shop of Robert Roberts on Main Street. In November 1843 the first settled pastor, Reverend George F. Hendrickson, arrived. With the membership increasing, a lot on the corner of Madison and Henry Streets was purchased, and a temporary structure of rough pine boards was built. Services were held there for several months.

During the summer of 1843 construction began on a permanent building, and for the next two or three years services were held in the basement. The new church was "plain in design, neatly furnished within, and forty-two by fifty-six feet in size." It was completed at a cost of $6000 and designed as a Bethel or Seaman's church, one that preached the gospel to those involved in the whale fishery. The Bethel flag flew on the Sabbath, a silent invitation to enter and hear the sermon.

Under the leadership of Reverend Hendrickson, who was said to have been a fervent and impassioned revivalist preacher, the society grew. Almost every Sunday a public baptism of new converts took place in the waters of the Cove. This growth, however, was not to last, and with the decline of the whaling industry came a decline in church attendance. In 1857 the Baptist Church closed its doors and they remained closed for nearly ten years.

In November 1866 efforts were made to re-open, even though most of the remaining parishioners felt it wouldn't be practical with such a small number and lack of money to support a pastor. Horace Waters of New York City became the prime instrument in re-establishing the church, and through his contributions and solicitations, more than half of the salary for a pastor was raised. Reverend M.R. Barnetz, an eloquent and forceful preacher, came to fill the pulpit, and within six weeks after his arrival, he collected $300 from his congregation to make needed repairs and have a fence built around the church property.

Because of its size, the Baptist Church often became the meeting place for community activities. The Sag Harbor Literary Society held meetings there during the 1850s, and school classes were held there following the burning of the academy on Suffolk Street.

In 1882 a baptistry was added at a cost of $125, and although the membership once again began to grow, financial problems did as well. In March of that year the trustees of the church agreed to deed the property to the Long Island Baptist Association, which in turn provided funds to renovate the interior. A magnificent pulpit set of black walnut, upholstered in garnet silk plush,

ORGANIZED RELIGION IN SAG HARBOR 175

arrived on the steamboat *W.W. Coit* in July 1885. Money for it was generously donated by local furniture dealer O.B. Lucas. New carpeting was laid on the pulpit platform and the lecture room papered and painted. H.L. Topping installed two new furnaces to heat the church, and through the generosity of Leonard Richardson of Brooklyn, the place was painted.

Throughout the years the Baptist Church continued to have its problems, closing several times and re-opening when revivals took place in the village. Under the pastorate of Reverend J.R. Vaughn in 1913, the roof was shingled, with the Baptist Church Convention assuring the congregation that any financial obligations would be taken care of if the church was unable to pay their bills. In August 1917 ground was broken for the church rectory just east of the sanctuary.

As time went on, membership dropped to a point where it was no longer possible to keep the building open, and in February 1931 it was sold to the Independent Order of Odd Fellows and became known as Mechanic's Hall.

A list of the Pastors who served in the Baptist Church is found in the Appendix.

The Methodist Church

In 1834 the Methodist Church congregation had grown to 194, and it was apparent a larger church was needed. Thomas P. Ripley donated a lot on the corner of Church and Union Street, opposite the Arsenal, and stones for the foundation were delivered to the site. However, before construction had gotten underway, William R. Mulford offered a lot on High Street plus a $500 donation with the condition that the church be built there. It was a gift that was impossible to turn down, but as time went by it may well have been wiser for them to have accepted the first offer. The old church building was sold to the Roman Catholic Society for $1052.50 and was used for their meeting house and, later, for their school.

In May 1835 the cornerstone of the new edifice was laid by Reverend E.S. Merwin, presiding Elder of the district, and the following year the church was completed. The dedication took place March 31, 1836. Built in the Greek style of architecture and at a cost of $12,000, the structure was 53 by 68 feet, with the basement chiefly above the ground. The massive front doors were replicas of the famous bronze doors of the Baptistry in Florence, Italy. Two Roman columns on either side of the doors were copied from columns found in Rome and carved inward toward the top on one side only, creating an optical illusion of great height. Ephraim Byram, noted clockmaker, built the tower clock in 1839. A parsonage adjoining the church was constructed in 1843 at a cost of $1500.

There was one part of the building that didn't quite meet with the approval of some of the church members, and that was the tower. It was described as being "entirely out of style with the rest of the building. Its squatty proportions and dry-good-box shape with its immense dials, gives the appearance of an exaggerated Yankee clock." One of the earliest church bells in the village hung in the tower, and when it was broken in 1843, a new one was cast using the broken pieces.

Although the church was built on a high hill, with a beautiful view of the harbor, and proudly stood out as one sailed into port, its location proved to be quite inaccessable during the winter months. It was remote from the center of the village, exposed to the blustery winter winds, and the road leading to it steep and unsheltered. Many of the congregation were compelled to stay at home, or even worse, attend another church! Discussions were held regularly regarding the possibility of moving the building to a better location.

In May 1863 the Trustees of the church voted to move the building to Madison Street and, at the same time, enlarge it. The monumental job of disassembling the building, moving it to its new location, and then reassembling it, continued throughout the remainder of 1863 and into the next year. By March 1864 the exterior was nearing completion and the interior lathing and plastering well underway, the work done by Isaac Winters. A new gas-lighting system was hooked up, with the fixtures manufactured by I.P. Frink of New York City. Two sets of reflectors at each end, containing 16 burners apiece, were put into place, creating a reflected light that lit the building at little expense. A tall colonnaded open structure, built above the tower, gave the building a most elegant appearance. One year after the vote was passed to move the church to Madison Street, dedication ceremonies took place. It was held in May 1864, with Reverend H.J. Fox of New York City preaching the dedicatory sermon.

The church struggled under a great debt from the cost of moving and renovating the building. Mortgages in the amount of $12,000, with a high rate of interest, made for difficult times. The terrible strife of the Civil War created financial devastation; yet a small group of the faithful took on the responsibility of raising $10,000 which greatly reduced the debt. Over the next 25 years the remaining loans were paid off.

A new pipe organ was purchased in July 1883 at a cost of $1445, and the church refurbished to celebrate its 75th anniversary. The auditorium was redecorated, walls and ceilings painted, the old white woodwork replaced with stained

ORGANIZED RELIGION IN SAG HARBOR

black walnut, and new maroon carpeting purchased. The pews were neatly cushioned with maroon fabric, the ladies of the church cutting, stuffing, and sewing them.

Reverend William L. Douglas organized a Young People's Literary and Social Union in 1885, which sponsored picnics, church socials and musical programs. This group later merged into the Epworth League.

In 1891, during the pastorate of Reverend B.F. Reeve, Sylvanus H. Fordham built a new parsonage on the southwest corner of Madison and Amity Streets. Built at a cost of $3000, it was completed in the spring of 1891. At the same time, the exterior of the church received a coat of paint and a new lighting system. A handsome brass chandelier donated by Captain Jonas Winters made an exquisite addition. By the turn of the century, the parsonage received new furnishings, gas, water, and bathroom facilities. A two-manual Moller pipe organ was purchased in 1902, and in 1910 the beautiful stained-glass windows were installed. Purchased in New York, each window cost $100.

The 1938 hurricane toppled the steeple of the Methodist Church, and a year later a gift of $1800 from Richard Leonard Woodward of Montclair, New Jersey was given to the church for the purpose of rebuilding it.

A list of Methodist ministers can be found in the Appendix.

Reminiscences of the Methodist Sunday School

In April 1921 the Methodist Sunday School celebrated its ninetieth anniversary, and a letter of reminiscences written by Shamgar Babcock was read. In part it stated:

> My earliest remembrance of the school was about 1858 or 59, when Miss Wood, a daughter of the then pastor of the church was in charge of what was then the Infant Class. In fact, I think she was the organizer. Of her my recollection is indistinct, but of Mrs. Ripley, her immediate successor (the late Mrs. Julia Brown), I retain a vivid and pleasing memory. She was my first teacher.
>
> The outlines and equipment of the little class room in the old church on the hill are still pictured in my mind's eye....a fair sized room with a flight of stairs rising from the floor almost to the ceiling, with the children ranged in tiers according to length of life and limb; the little two by four melodeon which squeeked out, "I want to be an angel" and "Yes, Jesus loves me," the little cup-closet with its choice selection of Goody books; the little tinkling bell that was designed to rivet the attention of the children upon the teacher; all these things and others

range themselves in memory, and chief of all I recall the smiling, happy, handsome face of the assistant teacher, Miss Fanny Brown, now Mrs. Fanny Garaghan, a lifelong member of the church.

The test of promotion at that time was apparently based upon the same principle of length of life and limb. The steps, or seats, being but about eight inches high, when the boys and girls grew so tall they had to peer between their knees in order to see the teacher, they were promoted to the main school and the rest advanced a step to make room for the new recruits.

About 1860 I was transferred to the main school and John Gawley was my teacher. I think Henry R. Harris was superintendant at that time. The seats of the main school room were built upon lines of strict integrity, reminding one forcibly of the straight and narrow ways, seats flat and narrow, backs high and primly upright, so the pupils were forced to sit up and look up, as if set in stocks. Apparently the early architect had no conception of physical comfort or discomfort. The present generation who are enjoying more Sunday School advantages have no conception of the school of sixty years ago which had coal stoves, oil lamps, melodeon music and crudeness and discomfort at every turn.

In 1863 the church was removed from Methodist Hill to its present site, at a large and heavy burden of debt. But this is another story. During the removal and rebuilding of the church, the Sunday School was held in the Baptist Church, then not functioning. Not much of importance or comment can be recorded during this period other than the fact that the church bell was set up on the ground in front of the church, its clapper removed and the sexton required to use a sledge hammer to summon the worshippers. The old bell so placed was of course an invitation to all the boys and girls in the neighborhood to see how many times they could hit the bell with the stone without missing.

In 1863 the basement part of the church was so far completed that both church and Sunday School was held there. I recall the first pastor assigned to the church that Spring—Daniel O. Ferris—familiarly known as "Cinnamon Dan" on account of his ginger colored hair and illuminated Dundreary whiskers.

About the time of opening school in the new church, Mr. Gawley's class was broken up and I was placed in the missionary class taught by George B. Brown. Many of the boys were much older than I. The class was made up of "stray sheep," gathered from the by-ways without regard to race, color or previous condition of servitude, so I went on strike and was admitted to the class of Miss Anna L. Babcock.

ORGANIZED RELIGION IN SAG HARBOR 179

In 1876, against my better judgment, I was persuaded that it was my duty to take a class and 'teach the young ideas how to shoot,' presumably toward the stars. In time I gave up the task and went back to my first love, the Crusaders, taught by Miss Babcock.

St. Andrew's Roman Catholic Church

Twenty-eight year old Michael Burke came to Sag Harbor from his native London, England in 1820. He was a convert to Catholicism. Burke obtained work as a cooper, as the whale fishery was expanding and jobs in the trade plentiful. He married a local girl, and in 1824 went to South America where they spent the next five years. Upon their return to Sag Harbor, Mr. Burke became instrumental in starting a Catholic Society in the village. There were about fifteen families of the Catholic faith, many of them laborers and servants, and, with the exception of one Portuguese family, all were Irish.

In those early years a Catholic priest had never been seen on the eastern end of Long Island, and Burke, who was the most prominent Catholic in the village, assembled those of the faith at his home each Sunday morning. They recited the Rosary, the Litany of the Saints, the Gospel and Epistle of the day, and read a lesson from Bossuet's sermons. In the afternoon the group would meet again for the Stations of the Cross and prayers, and although they were without a church, in this manner Catholicism was kept alive in early Sag Harbor.

In 1835 Reverend William Quarter of New York visited Sag Harbor and ministered to the needs of the society, hearing confessions, baptizing, and performing other clerical duties. That same year an opportunity arose for the people to purchase a building for their church. When the Methodist Society built a new sanctuary, their old church building was put up on auction. Burke, making a bid of $1052.50, was able to acquire it and on February 10, 1836 took possession of the building. Many in the village, who were predominantly Protestant, didn't look too charitably upon a Catholic Church in Sag Harbor, but after William R. Mulford, a worthy Protestant citizen, gave a $100 donation toward renovating the church, there soon were better and more Christian-like feelings. An altar was installed in the church through the efforts of interested residents, and it became the first Catholic altar in Suffolk County. The church was painted white with green shutters and surmounted by a white cross. A row of cedar trees stood on either side of the door.

The fact that a new Catholic Church had started on the end of the Island prompted the Bishop to send a priest as often as possible. The first to come was Father John Burns in 1837. Father Burns was a missionary priest, having charge of the stations in Suffolk County and part of Queens. He visited the church once a month until April 1839, when Reverend Nicholas O'Donnell succeeded him. Others to follow were Michael Curran, Edward McGuinnis, J. McCarthy, and Michael O'Neil, all missionary priests. The house of Michael Burke was always their residence when they came to town, and in their absence Burke and his wife, who had by then been converted, led the devotions. They also maintained a Sunday School for 125 children, instructing them in Catechism and Scripture. In 1845 the parish consisted of 650 members.

In 1845 the parish acquired a plot of land on Brickkiln Road (formerly the old Northside Road) for a Catholic Cemetery. In 1900 the ladies of St. Andrew's gave a party in St. Joseph's Hall, and with the proceeds a fence was built around the burying ground.

Father Joseph Brunnerman became the first resident priest of the local Catholic Church in 1859. During his nine years at Sag Harbor he purchased a parsonage and established a school for 30 to 40 students, in addition to his regular duties. He was succeeded in 1868 by Reverend McKenna and Reverend William Kean.

On October 23, 1860 the Right Reverend John Laughlin, Bishop of the Diocese, bought a lot on the corner of Division, Sage and Union Streets for $950, with the intention of erecting a new church. It was sorely needed, as the Catholic population was growing rapidly and the old church building they had been worshipping in since 1836 was no longer suitable. However, it wasn't until 1872 that a Brooklyn architect by the name of Keeley was hired to draw up plans for the new church. Construction was soon underway, with Terry & Wells of Riverhead having been awarded the contract. The cornerstone was laid June 16, 1872 and contained various coins, a newspaper of the times, and a memorial written in Latin, which translated reads:

> The Corner Stone of this church dedicated to God in honor of St. Andrew, was laid in the year of our Lord, one thousand eight hundred and seventy-two, on the 16th day of June, during the Pontificate of Pius Ninth, the Right Reverend John Laughlin, being Bishop of this Diocese, the Reverend J.J. Heffernan, Pastor of the Church, George Kiernan and John Trihy, together with said Bishop, the Reverend John Turner, Vicar General, and the said Pastor being Trustees of this Church, Ulysses S. Grant being President of these United States, and John T. Hoffman, Governor of this State of New York.

St. Andrew's Church is 40 by 90 feet in size, with a steeple rising 100 feet from the ground. Beautiful Gothic windows of stained glass installed on either side of the sanctuary add to its elegance. They were presented by Dr. Sterling, Mrs. Eliza Murphy, the Misses Strein, Frederick G. Murphy, Mrs. Becker and her daughter Clotilda of Brooklyn, Mrs. Mary Murphy, Mrs. Sarah E. Regen, Gertrude Murphy and brother of New York, David Heffernan, James Heffernan, and Mrs. Ann Heffernan of Boston, who donated the chancel window.

The interior was designed with three aisles, one at each side and one in the center. The upper walls were made rough to resemble stone, and a wood finish was built around the interior as high as the tops of the pews. A beautiful chandelier hung in the chancel. The church was dedicated December 15, 1872, with the Right Reverend Bishop Laughlin preaching the sermon and a choir of professional singers from Brooklyn and New York providing the music. Two years later a 1400-pound bell, furnished by McShane Foundry of Baltimore, was hung in the steeple. Many contributed to the bell, and its official blessing was held September 10, 1874. The old carriage house and stable which stood at the rear of the church were moved to the northeast corner of the convent grounds on Hampton Street in 1877.

In 1892, under Bishop McDonnell, the edifice was enlarged and improved. The building was raised two feet, and a nine-and-a-half-foot-wide extension built on either side of the sanctuary. Both interior and exterior received a new coat of paint, and the ceiling was frescoed. While renovations were in progress, masses were conducted in the Catholic Hall and the Convent Chapel. Additional work was done in 1908. The old picket fence which stood along the front of the church was removed and a two-rail iron fence put up in its place. Cement sidewalks were laid from the steps to the street and cement posts built on either side of the entrance. Heavy wrought-iron gates were attached to each post and topped with electric lights. Inside, a new altar rail of heavy brass and scrollwork was installed. A handsome marble altar placed at the front of the sanctuary commemorated the services of the boys from the parish who were involved in World War I. The liberty pole on the grounds was presented by actor William Farnum, and the flag given by Patrick Foley of the United States Navy in 1917.

Many changes were made to the interior of St. Andrew's in 1929. In May of that year, E.B. Heath's crew of eight artists stenciled around the windows of the sanctuary, painted the walls and ceilings, and gave the pews a new coat of varnish. In August 1929 the church was decorated with rubber insert tile of mosaic design, a duplicate of the Catholic Cathedral in Buffalo, New York, and new light fixtures of a Gothic design were installed.

A handsome and spacious rectory, with a French-style roof and with 14 rooms, stands on the grounds of St. Andrew's, a home for the priests who served the Roman Catholic population of Sag Harbor over the years. A list of the resident priests of St. Andrew's can be found in the Appendix.

THE MARBLE ALTAR

A beautiful altar of the purest Gothic architectural design was built for St. Andrew's Church. In April 1922 a noted artist of the world-famous McBride Studios visited St. Andrew's, and while there took measurements of the church and examined its foundations. Designs were submitted and Father Peter L. Rickard, then pastor of St. Andrew's, selected the most appropriate and desirable plan. Orders were forwarded to the quarries and sculpture works of the McBride's, and following its construction at Pietrasanta, Italy, it was carefully crated and transported by steamship to New York City and then trucked to Sag Harbor.

Sag Harbor mason Ivan C. Byram installed solid concrete foundations and a base to support the altar's 20-ton weight. With the exception of the mensa (table) and the predella (platform), genuine Carrera statuary marble was used. Inlays and panels under the figures of the angels were of yellow sienna, and the two angels at either side, sculptured from Bianco statuary marble. A solid-gold lacquered door with steel safe, cedar lined, was installed with a crucifix indicated in the design. Verdi from the Alps for the green columns, side columns of Breccia Violetta, and center columns of Rubra from the Garfargna quarry completed the exquisite piece of work.

Choice of the Gothic design was made to conform with the Gothic interior of the church. The massive new altar was much lower and more compact than the previous one on which the cross blocked out part of the elaborately stained-glass memorial window placed by George Kiernan in memory of his parents.

Consecration of the beautiful altar took place May 13, 1923 at the church's golden jubilee celebration.

St. David A.M.E. Zion Church

Originally, the African Methodist Society was part of the Methodist Episcopal Church that was established in Sag Harbor in 1809. The group worshipped with them until 1839, when a considerable increase in their numbers caused them to organize a church of their own. Measures were taken, and in 1840 the association of St. David A.M.E. Zion was formed. It was organized by Lewis Cuffee, Charles Plato and William Prime, all outstanding members of Sag Harbor's black and Indian population. The committee bought a lot at Eastville and, with the aid of others, erected a small frame building on Eastville

Avenue at a cost of $700. The church was dedicated in 1840 by Reverend Christopher Bush, presiding elder of the district, and John P. Thompson became the first pastor.

The sixteen members who made up the congregation of the early church were soon joined by others who had not yet received their letters of dismissal from the Methodist Episcopal Church. In two years' time Thompson was succeeded by Reverend Richard Noyes, who during his pastorate saw the growth of the congregation reach 50 members. Reverend Noyes, a well-educated man, was a favorite among both black and white residents of the village.

During the 1850s membership decreased along with the decline of commercial property as the whaling industry began to slacken off. At that time the church could no longer afford a pastor, and for the next six or seven years, traveling preachers occupied the pulpit.

About the year 1859 the church split into two groups, due to a change in church government. Through the influence of Reverend Alexander Posey, the A.M.E. Bethel connection secured control. Subsequently, the Zion connection, by process of law and purchase, regained control. During the interim the followers of Zion, under the leadership of David Hempstead, constructed a new church and conducted worship there. This second black church probably stood on Montauk Avenue, as an 1873 map locates a church on the east side of the street, midway between Hampton and Hamilton Streets. The building was described as "a neat little edifice capable of holding about 100 people," and in May 1863 the church was dedicated. A notice in *The Sag Harbor Express* of January 7, 1864, placed by Nathan P. Cuffee, George Consor and David Hempstead follows:

> The attention of the public is called to the fact that in the separation of the Colored Church at Eastville, the part of the congregation, who seceded under the leadership of Reverend A. Posey (an expelled member of the African M.E. Zion Church of Sag Harbor) are advertising their church week by week, as the "Zion Church," a title they have no right to use as they are no longer connected with the Methodist Episcopal Zion Church, and the title, "Zion Church" belongs to the part of the church and congregation who are attached to the African Methodist Episcopal Zion connection.

DAVID HEMPSTEAD

David Hempstead, one of Sag Harbor's outstanding black residents, lived at a time when slavery was still practiced, when segregation in the local school took place, and at a time when people of color were generally looked upon as second-class citizens. Yet, David Hempstead was accepted, a man admired and respected in the village by both black and white residents alike. It was his kindness, generosity, and, most of all, his great faith that made him an outstanding leader in the black community.

Henry P. Hedges, historian, in his "Address on Early Sag Harbor" before the Sag Harbor Historical Society in 1896, wrote:

> David Hempstead was large of frame, of Afric type, uneducated and with little of this world's goods, but within there reigned an undwelling spirit in a soul born not of earth, nor of man, nor of the power of man, but an invisible presence that transformed him from the image of the earthly to the resplendent image of the heavenly. He was a living epistle known and read of all men. Who can deny that God made this man in his witness in the African Church.

Born in March 1808, David Hempstead and his wife, Mary, lived on Hempstead Street in the Eastville section. In 1840 Lewis Cuffee, Charles Plato, and William Prime organized the Association of St. David A.M.E. Zion, and they, along with David Hempstead, made up a building committee and erected a small frame church on Eastville Avenue. He was a great leader in the Zion Church, and when the A.M.E. Bethel connection secured control of the church building in 1859, he led a group of followers of the Zion connection, purchased a nearby private dwelling, and conducted worship there. The Zionists continued to worship there until the Bethels surrendered the original mortgage of $500, and Zionists were able to move back to the original church.

Throughout David Hempstead's lifetime his church played a most important role. On May 18, 1886 he died suddenly of heart disease. *The Sag Harbor Express* reported that, although not feeling well for two weeks, he had been down to the village a day or two before he passed away. Death came swiftly and quietly as he sat in his chair talking to his daughter. David Hempstead was buried from St. David's, where he had been a constant and faithful member, and laid to rest in the church cemetery on Eastville Avenue.

A newspaper article of 1868 notes that at that time there were still two black churches in the village, but by 1882 the second church, which had been closed for some time, had been sold and turned into a dwelling. Sometime between 1868 and 1880 the Zionists met on the grounds of the original church and were declared by the County Court at Riverhead to be the "rightful and legal trustees

ORGANIZED RELIGION IN SAG HARBOR 185

and custodians of the property." And so ended the split in the church.

In the early years, members of St. David held camp meetings and picnics at Round Pond Grove and at the Rye lot near Chatfield Hills. In August 1860 a highly successful picnic was given by the Sunday School, at which chicken, lamb, corned beef, hot buttered corn, and other vegetables of the season were served. Pie, cake, lemonade, fruit, and candy topped off the meal. Group singing added to the pleasant event, and George B. Brown spoke to those in attendance.

In 1891 St. David's underwent major renovations, with an extension added at the rear of the church and a vestibule built on the front. Miss Julia King of Sag Harbor presented the congregation with a bell to hang in their newly built cupola. A bequest of $500 to clear up the mortgage on the building was received upon the death of Miss King. With the old gallery removed, a raised pulpit and choir platform were built at the front of the sanctuary. It was surrounded by a chancel rail of polished brass, from which curtains were hung.

Various auxiliary societies donated money for six lovely stained-glass windows, which were acquired from Christ Episcopal Church. The Lyceum, organized in 1890, raised the first $100 toward the project. The Ladies Village Improvement Society, organized in 1889; the Sunday School, organized in 1840; and the Associated Sisters, organized in 1857, all assisted financially. One window was dedicated to Lewis Cuffee and another to David Hempstead. Professor Ashborn frescoed and stenciled the walls and ceilings, adding greatly to the beauty of the place. In July 1910 Mrs. Russell Sage donated the Joshua Eldredge house on Main Street to the church for a parsonage. It was moved from the Otter Pond grounds where it stood, in order to make room for a shore drive around the pond. In 1916 a furnace was installed at St. David's, and in 1922 electric lights and carpeting were added.

The A.M.E. Zion Cemetery, which dates back to the founding of the church, is located on Eastville Avenue, just a short distance from the sanctuary. Buried there are former pastors, Civil War and World War veterans, and other members of Sag Harbor's early black community.

A list of ministers who served at St. David's Church can be found in the Appendix.

Christ Episcopal Church

Early in 1845 a small group of residents professing the Protestant Episcopal faith assembled in a room on the second floor of the Arsenal on Union Street for the purpose of starting an Episcopal Church at Sag Harbor. Reverend Henry

Floy Roberts, hired as a missionary by the clergy of certain churches in Brooklyn, presided over the meeting. They made arrangements to move from the Arsenal into the old Village Hall (originally the 1817 Presbyterian Church) to hold services there for the next 12 months.

At that time they organized into a corporate body, according to law, under the name "Christ Church," with Reverend Roberts called to become the first rector. On the Monday after Easter Sunday 1846, the following officers were elected: Wardens Marcus A. Starr and William Fordred; Vestrymen Thomas Hallworth, Darius A. Nash, Erastus Osgood, Frederick Crocker, William Bickerton, John N. Schellinger, William Buck, and Cleveland S. Stillwell. Their primary objective was to make provisions for a permanent house of worship, and on August 25, 1846 they purchased the building in which they had worshipped the previous year, for the sum of $2100.

Marcus Starr, Darius Nash and Frederick Crocker were appointed as a committee to oversee all necessary repairs and alterations. Under their supervision a complete renovation took place, including removal of the old high pulpit in favor of a modern chancel and reading desk, papering interior walls with marbled print wallpaper, and applying oak stain to the woodwork. The old galleries were removed, leaving only the choir and organ loft. Carpeting, chancel furniture, baptismal font, and a $200 silver communion set were furnished by the ladies of the church. Chandeliers donated by one of the vestrymen hung over the center aisle. The renovations were completed at a cost of $2000, and the newly restored church consecrated on December 16, 1846. Right Reverend Levi Silliman Ives, Bishop of the North Carolina Diocese, led the ceremony, assisted by clergy from New York, Connecticut, and Long Island. Several persons were confirmed that same day.

When Reverend Roberts left in April 1847, Richard Whitingham replaced him. Thirty-two families regularly attended church at that time, although only 19 were members. During Whitingham's ministry the number increased to 27, and the Sunday School grew to 35 students and six teachers.

Reverend George O. Foot, the next rector, came to serve the parish on February 1, 1850, and during the three years of his ministry, 31 more were confirmed. Reverend Isaac Pardee took over on January 1, 1853. During those years a serious decline in membership took place, mainly due to the end of the whaling industry and a general exodus of many connected with the trade. Reverend Pardee worked diligently to build up the congregation, but, unfortunately, ill health forced his resignation shortly after one year. He was replaced in the spring of 1855 by Reverend William B. Musgrave.

In 1854 a new vestry room was built in a more convenient part of the church. Originally, it had been located near the front entrance. Two beautiful tablets in the chancel, inscribed with the Apostle's Creed, the Lord's Prayer, and the Ten Commandments, were donated by John Wallace of East Hampton. Dr. F. Crocker paid for the repairing of the foundation which was in a dilapidated condition since Sage Street had been cut through.

Early in the 1880s a decision was reached to build a new church. A lot on the corner of Hampton and Union Streets was selected as an ideal site for the church. The property and existing house belonged to the Winters family, and after the property was acquired, the house was moved further up the street. George H. Skidmore of Riverhead drew up the plans and the contract was awarded to E. Bailey & Son of Patchogue. Work started in July 1884, the anticipated cost $5000 to $6000, exclusive of foundation and stained-glass windows. Services were held in the Village Hall until the church was completed, and then the building sold to the Masonic Society for $1800. The Very Reverend A.N. Littlejohn, Bishop of Long Island, laid the cornerstone July 23, 1884, and by March of the following year, the church had been completed and consecrated.

The main body of the building measured 51 feet by 33 feet, and the chapel 30 feet by 24 feet. Built in the Gothic style of the period, the church was topped by a square steeple 100 feet tall. The steeple was successfully raised in November 1884, with Joseph DeCastro supervising the job. The slate roof was gabled, and each gable topped by metal or wooden crosses. The chancel, two steps above the nave, measured 15 by 11 feet. An Italian marble altar was built over the ancient wooden one that had been saved from the old church. The lecturn and prayer desk, of highly polished cherry, were donated by William Tooker and Reverend John Harrison, a former rector.

Through the generosity of North Haven summer residents Mr. and Mrs. James Herman Aldrich, many gifts and improvements were added. In 1890 they donated a new Bishop's chair, a marble baptismal font, a bronze lecturn, a Carrara marble altar, a brass pulpit, and a new chancel which extended 28 feet beyond the back wall of the church.

Shortly after Reverend Francis V. Baer came to Christ Church, the possibility of building a parish house was brought up. Various societies of the church worked and raised $2500 toward the project. A lot southeast of the church was selected and, following its purchase, an existing house moved off the grounds. However, when Mr. Aldrich met with the vestrymen, he proposed a new plan— to build the parish house at the rear of the church instead and use the newly acquired lot for the rectory. Mr. Aldrich pledged himself to assume all expenses and suggested that the money collected be used as an endowment fund. Arthur Wood, of Garden City (and formerly of Sag Harbor), was hired as the architect.

George H. Cleveland, who was responsible for building so many of Sag Harbor's structures, built the new parish house. The contract for heating went to Robinson and Wilson, the electrical work to Ivan C. Byram, and the masonry work to Graham Hallock, all of Sag Harbor. The parish house was presented to the church in 1912.

In 1914 Mrs. Aldrich called the rector and said she would provide the money to build the rectory for the parish. Arthur Wood, who designed the $10,000 parish house, submitted drawings. Planned was an Elizabethan-style house, two stories high, with cellar and attic, ten rooms, and two baths. Excavation for the foundation began in early May. Prior to the construction of the new building, the French House on Union Street and the Juliana King House on the corner of Latham and Division Streets were used as rectories.

On March 12, 1908 Mrs. Russell Sage had a new bell shipped from the Meneely Bell Company of Troy, New York. Measuring 46 inches at its mouth, the bronze bell weighed 2000 pounds. The old bell was taken to Pierson High School and placed in its tower. Mrs. Aldrich also donated the stained-glass window in the chancel of the church, in memory of her mother. The parishioners of Christ Church were fortunate to have had such generous friends and members during the early years. With their assistance the beautiful sanctuary, parish house, and rectory were kept in fine condition, and they still serve the Episcopal congregation of Sag Harbor. The rectors who served at Christ Church can be found in the Appendix.

Temple Adas Israel

The Jewish Association of United Brethren of Sag Harbor organized in 1883 "for the payment of a weekly benefit to sick members; to provide for attendance of a physician, for the payment of burial and funeral expenses and to provide a place for burial; to provide a place for the Association and a place of worship for its members; and to promote in all proper ways the social and moral welfare of its members."

In the years prior to 1883, it would have been difficult to find a resident of the Jewish faith living in Sag Harbor. The major influx came during 1886-88 when Joseph Fahys relocated his watchcase factory here and brought 40 to 50 Jewish men, some with their families, to work in his factory. Many were immigrants from Russia, Poland, and Hungary, and some had previously been employed at the Fahys factory in Carlstadt, New Jersey. Officers of the newly formed association were: Morris Meyerson, president; Samuel Heller, secretary; and Max Olswank, treasurer. Worship services were held at Crowell's Hall in the village.

As the Jewish population increased, so did the need for a synagogue. A lot was purchased on the corner of Elizabeth Street and Atlantic Avenue, and the land cleared. George H. Cleveland, Sag Harbor's noted master carpenter, built the temple at a cost of $2500. It measured 30 by 34 feet with basement and gallery, and it had a capacity to seat 100 people. A flight of stairs led to the front door, which opened to a 4-foot lobby and an auditorium 20 by 30 feet in size. An altar stood in the center of the room. A pulpit was on the east wall, in front of which were three gas jets representing candles. On the wall in back of the pulpit was the ark containing the Torah, and above it the motto, "Blessed be the name of and the Glory of the Lord for Evermore." Tall Gothic windows offered sufficient light during the day, and a Welsbach gas system was installed which illuminated the place at night. A mikva font, restrooms, and the janitor's quarters were located in the basement.

A very active Jewish community worshipped at the new temple. Only the men could sit in the main body of the synagogue, with women obliged to sit in the galleries, which was the Orthodox custom. Formal dedication took place October 28, 1900, with the doors opened by Jacob Meyer, former resident of Sag Harbor. The steps were tastefully lined with floral arrangements. David Sandman, of Riverhead (and formerly of Sag Harbor), opened the ark, while Hyman Meyer of New York carried the Torah to the ark as the procession marched around the altar. The synagogue at that time was called Temple Mishkan. A wooden altar piece consisting of the two lions of Judah flanking the Tablets of the Law was carved by Nisson Meyerson and presented to the temple.

Around the same time property was acquired on the outskirts of the village for a Jewish cemetery. With the death of the infant child of Morris and Sarah Spodok in May 1891, the first burial took place.

In the same years another Jewish society called the Independent Jewish Association was established. It consisted mainly of Hungarian Jews, about 50 in number, and a Rabbi from New York conducted services at "Engravers' Hall" in the village. Their officers were Max Grossman, president; Herman Schwartz, vice-president; Frank Jaffe, treasurer; and H. Treiheift, secretary. Their burial ground adjoined the United Brethren Cemetery, the two being separated by an iron rail fence.

During the early 1900s the two associations joined forces to save the financially-troubled temple, buying it back at public auction in 1918. A new stronger congregation celebrated the mortgage burning on December 8, 1920 with a gala parade, banquet, and dance. With the renewed interest, a Hebrew school started, taught by local school teacher Israel Heller. Now called Temple Adas Israel, the synagogue still serves the Jewish population of Sag Harbor and is the oldest temple in Suffolk County.

The People's Pentecostal Church of the Nazarene

The Pentecostal Society grew from a small group of worshipers, some of whom had withdrawn from the Methodist Episcopal Church of 1896. C.A. Reney, a lay preacher and native of the village, led the converts in this new form of worship. Reney later became an ordained minister and their first pastor in 1897. That same year a lot was acquired on the corner of Division and Latham Streets on which was constructed a house of worship. Built by the Brethren of the society, the handsome brick tabernacle, with its high-pitched shingled roof, was completed in May 1897. The 30- by 40-foot structure was lighted by gas and had a capacity to seat 250 worshippers. Dedication ceremonies took place June 3, 1897.

Reverend Reney resigned after serving the congregation six years and was succeeded by J.C. Bearse of Malden, Massachusetts. Upon Bearse's departure two years later, the church was without a pastor until the arrival of S.W. Fossenden in 1906. Reverend Bert Lewis and Reverend L.D. Keeler led the congregation in the years 1911 and 1912, and Paul Southard, for a short time.

With a small congregation and serious financial problems, the Pentecostal Church closed and reopened many times. C.B. Terry, Edward Beckwith, and William Holtz directed the services when there was no pastor. In later years the tabernacle opened only when gospel or revival meetings were held in the village, and in 1923 the place was sold to the New York District Board of Home Missions.

Nearby Chapels

THE NORTH HAVEN UNION CHAPEL

North Haven's Union Chapel was a small wood-framed building built in 1875 near the intersection of Ferry Road, Tyndall Road, and the road to Long Beach. It stood on the northeast corner, a one-story structure with a central front door, a window on either side, and a belfry on the roof.

Before its construction an appeal was made for financial aid, and any person contributing to the building fund before April 13, 1875 had his name placed on a roll deposited under the cornerstone. On April 19th the official cornerstone laying took place, and throughout the summer work progressed rapidly. October 3, 1875 the church was publicly dedicated as a Union Chapel, with

ORGANIZED RELIGION IN SAG HARBOR 191

members of Sag Harbor's Presbyterian, Methodist, and Episcopal clergy taking part in the ceremonies. Mrs. James Herman Aldrich, summer resident of North Haven, donated a fine Estey organ with a grand-organ attachment, pews, belfry, and bell. In April 1901 the trustees of the chapel voted to extend their thanks to Mrs. Aldrich for her generous gifts.

In April 1924, after being vacant for some time, the chapel was destroyed by fire. Some sources say lightning was the probable cause, while others claim it was arson. In any event, the place was never rebuilt, and in time the lot reverted back to its natural state, with nothing remaining today to suggest that the little North Haven Union Chapel ever stood on the site.

THE NOYAC CHAPEL

In nearby Noyac, quite close to each other, stand two little chapels, built for those who found it difficult to travel the few miles to attend worship in Sag Harbor. Very few families were fortunate enough to own an automobile in those days, and most relied heavily on their horse or their bicycle for local travel.

The Noyac Chapel was founded in 1913 through the interest and efforts of Reverend William Edds of the Sag Harbor Presbyterian Church. Mr. and Mrs. A.J. Edwards donated the land, and Mrs. Russell Sage, the money to build the chapel. Their generosity enabled the $3000 structure to be free of debt at its completion. The building measured 26 by 40 feet in size, with a basement beneath, a Sunday School room at the rear, and horse stables in the back yard.

Dedication ceremonies were held on May 18, 1913, with the Reverend Arthur Newman of Bridgehampton delivering the sermon. The chapel had been tastefully decorated with dogwood blossoms. The building has been used throughout the years, and services are still held there for the residents of Noyac and vicinity.

ST. JAMES EPISCOPAL CHAPEL

When Reverend F.V. Baer, rector of Christ Episcopal Church, visited Noyac in 1909, he held religious services in the little Noyac schoolhouse, which for 25 years had served as their church. It was his fervent wish that a more suitable place of worship might be built for the residents of Noyac. Four years later his wish became a reality.

In the spring of 1912 an organization was formed under the Episcopal Diocese of Long Island; its members were J. Miller Kenyon, David Wiggins, A. Frank Richardson, William Wilson, and D.C. Scoville. David Wiggins donated a plot of land along Noyac Road, and he and others cleared the lot on which the chapel would be built. Plans and specifications were drawn up by

W.E. Maran of New York, and on October 18, 1912 ground was broken by the rector of Christ Episcopal Church, assisted by Joseph H. Ivie of St. Andrew's Church, New York City. William Wilson of Noyac built the church at a cost of $1800.

The building measured 40 by 22 feet in size, the interior finished in plaster and wainscotting, and the ceiling covered in cypress. Double windows swung outward to let in ample light and air. The place, named St. James Episcopal Chapel, held opening services on June 1, 1913 and were conducted by Reverend Baer, Joseph Ivie, and Reverend Samuel C. Fish of Bridgehampton. Music was supplied by the Christ Church choir. The chapel was filled to capacity, with an additional number of worshippers standing outside. Five local children from the Scoville, Lewis, and Pugsley families were baptized. Frank J. Richardson donated a silver alms basin, in memory of his daughter Mrs. Hoyt. After a small debt on the building was paid, a formal dedication was planned. It took place on October 31, 1915, with the Right Reverend Frederick Burgess, Bishop of the Diocese of Long Island, in charge of the ceremonies.

The Temperance Societies

A Temperance society was established under the auspices of the Methodist and Presbyterian Churches. Believing that intemperance was one of the greatest evils in the country, the group took a firm stand against liquor being sold in the village shops. In September 1829 a group met at the home of Samuel L'Hommedieu to draw up the laws and select a committee to visit the local tavernkeepers. They pleaded that no liquor be sold to the village folk on the Sabbath, and a number of the tavern owners agreed, on condition that others would do the same. The committee also asked the local newspaper editors to publish the state laws imposing a duty on strong liquor and regulating its distribution in inns and taverns. In 1835, of the 25 stores and taverns where liquor was once sold, 16 no longer did, giving proof that the early Temperance Society had much influence in ridding the place of ardent spirits.

In 1841 Peletiah Fordham informed the public that his Suffolk Temperance House would open on the temperance plan. No intoxicating beverage of any kind would be kept in his place, "not even behind the curtain or in the closet." The barroom was refitted as a refectory where refreshments and relishes of all kinds could be found. Most of the prominent citizens of Sag Harbor supported the temperance groups, among them the Cook, Osborn, Dering, Hedges, Howell and Cooper families.

Other temperance groups also sprung up in the early times. Philander R.

Jennings organized the Young Men's Washington Total Abstinence Society on November 18, 1841. The Montauk Division Sons of Temperance started in 1844 and continued until 1865. It was succeeded by the Agawam Division of the same, instituted on April 5, 1867. They had a membership of over 100 people. In 1864 a Young Men's Social Temperance Club was organized by the Catholic Church and was named the St. Andrew's Total Abstinence and Beneficial Society of the Village of Sag Harbor.

The Burying Grounds

As each new settlement on Long Island grew into a village or town it became necessary to secure a piece of land for a burying ground. Early on, when a family member died, it was the common practice to bury them in a family plot on their property, often in the back yard. As the population grew, it was no longer practical to continue with this custom. Property divisions were small, with no space for individual cemeteries. It was time to open a community burying ground.

Little is known about the first burial ground which stood in the area of Madison, Church, and Sage Streets before 1767. Apparently, it was used for some 40 years before the Old Burying Ground opened on Union, Madison, and Latham Streets. Probably, the earliest settlers were laid to rest there. It is said that when excavations for foundations were dug on Madison Street, several graves were unearthed and the remains removed for re-interment. This burial spot was abandoned when the Old Burying Ground opened.

The Southampton Town Records state that in May 1767 William Rogers and David Woodruff came to Sag Harbor to purchase land near the Meeting House, not to exceed ¾ acres, for a village burying ground. In earlier times the site had been covered with a dense growth of oak trees, and children of the village found it a wonderful hill on which to play. During Revolutionary times the summit was "crowned with a breastwork and ditch and the space within armed." Several young men from East Hampton were forced to come to Sag Harbor with teams to assist in building the entrenchment. Prior to that time some burials had already been made at the old ground, then called "burying yard hill." Early deeds mention the Old Burying Ground in 1770 as "enclosed by a picket fence and set aside for a common burying ground."

In 1859 an elderly resident told of the burial of two children in 1767. She stated that, when the first child was buried, the mother mourned that her child should lie alone so far off in the woods, but before six months had passed a little brother was sleeping beside him. These early burials were the little son of James Howell, aged one year and three months, and his infant brother.

Walking through the old grounds, monuments with the names Howell, Fordham, Wickham, L'Hommedieu, Crowell and Wade predominate—all noted early citizens, all instrumental in the growth and development of Sag Harbor—shopkeepers, stagecoach drivers, innkeepers, boat builders, and rope makers.

The Old Burying Ground was used for about 75 years, and by 1840, with plots at a minimum, it became necessary to search for more property for a new burying ground. A 4-acre piece of land on South Street (Jermain Avenue) was acquired from Lewis, Nathan, and Harriet Howell. Organized and incorporated under the general laws of New York State, it opened for burials in 1840. Located in what was then an oak forest, it was given the name Oakland Cemetery.

Several years after the opening of Oakland, the citizens of the village called a meeting to discuss the deplorable condition of the Old Burying Ground. Apparently it had fallen into a state of neglect after it was no longer actively used. All attending the meeting felt it was time to act, as the old walls were starting to crumble and the fence had begun to rot away. They lamented that "herds of cattle and troops of unruly boys roamed its grounds, desecrating the ashes of the dead." The stone wall on the Madison Street boundary had deteriorated to such a degree that it was expected that, when erosion occurred due to the spring rains, coffins would be visible and, possibly, even tumble to the sidewalk.

Throughout the summer and fall of 1859, ideas were presented to the committee to help alleviate the problems. William H. Gleason suggested that the whole ground be leveled even with the Presbyterian Churchyard and laid out in walks with grass planted, and the remains of those interred collected and placed in a common grave in the center, with a monument erected over them. Another suggested leveling the ground and lowering each individual grave where it stood. Still another suggested they should remove the old wall, build a terrace, and place an entrance gate opposite Jefferson Street, with a gate and stone steps leading up to the cemetery. Enoch Eldredge was in favor of preserving the Old Burying Ground by enclosing it with an iron fence at a cost of $1000. In any case, it was decided to remove the graves of those buried in the front row on the Madison Street side, and in January 1860 approximately two dozen were taken to Oakland Cemetery for re-burial. Although work had started, it wasn't until January 1863 that the old wall was finally removed. The Methodist Episcopal Church, which was in the process of being moved from High Street to its present location on Madison Street, purchased some of the old stones to use for the foundation of the church. In July 1880 a new picket fence was built on the Madison and Union Street sides, and in later years it was replaced by an iron one. Sag Harbor's early residents were relieved that the graves of their forefathers were, finally, being preserved.

With the Old Burying Ground in better condition, we will look again at the development of Oakland Cemetery. At the start, the whole community showed an interest, and the plots were sold at moderate fees to village residents, with the proceeds to be used for upkeep and expansion. The original four acres were enclosed with stone posts and chestnut pickets, and after an additional three acres were added, a 140-foot iron fence with ornamental gateway was installed at a cost of $700.

In September 1884 the Oakland Cemetery Association bought the old Oakland Clock Works property for $400, and by April 1885 a third section opened, extending the boundary to Suffolk Street. This brought the total acreage to ten. A memorial gate was presented by the Ladies Village Improvement Society on October 22, 1903 and installed at the new section, which was called Oakland Rest.

In 1902 ground was broken for a large mausoleum for Joseph Fahys, made of rough granite blocks each weighing several tons. The marble-lined structure was 14 feet square and 12 feet high. Ivan C. Byram contracted for the job of digging and hauling the blocks, and for the mausoleum built by Charles B. Canfield of Manhattan and stonesetter Charles Seffert of Brooklyn.

4
INNS, HOTELS, AND BOARDING HOUSES

One of the earliest known hotels in Sag Harbor was an inn owned by James Howell. Built in 1730, it stood on the east side of Main Street on the site of the present American Hotel. British officers were quartered there during the Revolutionary Battle of Sag Harbor and captured by Colonel Return Jonathan Meigs during his daring expedition of 1777. In the early 1800s the hotel was called Eldredge's Coffee House. According to tradition, the cellar was capable of holding 1000 barrels of liquor. Eldredge's Coffee House was the meeting place of the old military group, the Suffolk Guards, and marchers would assemble there when parades were held in the village. When the great fire of 1845 took place, the inn, along with a good portion of the business district, burned to the ground. It was a great loss to the village, but following the blaze, Nathan Tinker built a sturdy brick structure on the site. In 1877 Addison Youngs exchanged his Bridgehampton farm for the building, and, with the assistance of his father-in-law, William Freeman, opened the American Hotel. Steam heat, baths, and electric lights were installed, making it one of the most modern hotels on Long Island. In March 1880 Freeman and Youngs bought the lot on the corner of Division and Leonard Streets at the rear of the hotel to build horse stables for their visitors. The following year the veranda on the front of the hotel was built by Josiah Smith.

INNS, HOTELS, AND BOARDING HOUSES 197

Peletiah (Duke) Fordham owned another early hotel which stood on the corner of Main and West Water Streets at the foot of the village. Duke Fordham's hotel was built before the American Revolution and known as "a roomy and convenient house that contained numerous rooms for lodging plus a bar that was well supplied to accommodate visitors." One early visitor was the famous James Fenimore Cooper, who began his first novel, *Precaution*, while staying at Fordham's Inn, waiting for his whaling ship to return from a voyage. The inn was later known as the Suffolk House and was a stop for the stagecoach that ran between New York and the East End.

During those years a great temperance movement took place in Sag Harbor, and along with many business men in the village, Duke Fordham was, apparently, deeply involved. In December 1841 he notified his patrons that as of that date his inn would be known as the Suffolk Temperance House, opened on the temperance plan. No intoxicating liquor of any kind would be sold in his establishment. The bar was fitted up as a refectory, where refreshments and relishes of all kinds were constantly on hand. The middle room was a saloon for ladies and gentlemen, where refreshments were served and suppers could be arranged if due notice was given. Fordham stated that he trusted all of his old customers would continue their patronage and believed the friends and members of temperance societies in other towns and villages would lend him a helping hand in what he considered a serious commitment. It isn't known if Fordham's temperance plan succeeded or not. Perhaps not enough time passed to tell, for during Sag Harbor's second major blaze in 1845, Fordham's Inn met the same fate as Howell's, as it burned with much of the business district.

Two other less familiar hotels of that era were; first, Gamaliel Bruen's Sag Harbor Hotel, a tavern and boarding house on the corner of Main and Washington Streets; and second, L. Hedges' Boarding House on the corner of Main and Howard Streets. Bruen advertised in the June 1840 *Republican Watchman* that he was ready to serve his customers at all reasonable hours with the best market affordable. Hedges advertised that their boarding house was a short five-minute walk to a safe saltwater bathing beach.

The Oakley family owned and operated another inn in the early days and called it the Nassau Hotel. During the 1830s and 1840s it was located in the Hedges Building. In 1847 Gilbert Oakley began construction on his new hotel but died before it was complete. His widow and sons, George and Alfred, later opened it after finishing the place. George Oakley, the first proprietor, advertised that he would "spare no pains to make it a pleasant resting place for the weary traveler." From the livery stable attached, travel could be arranged to any part of the Island. Oakley's new building stood on the east side of the business district, near the junction of Main and Division Streets.

In pre-Revolutionary times, Robert Fordham occupied a tavern on the site. That early house was later sold to someone who, tradition tells us, started to move it to Sagaponack. When it got as far as the south end of the village, the wheels broke, and the mover declared he would go no further with it. He bought the next lot and set it there. Dr. Wheeler moved it into the lot at the rear of the stores on Main Street's east side, and it was occupied as a tenement. When Fahys began its operation in 1881, the house, which faced Church Street, was moved to Glover Street and became a private home.

On March 27, 1854 the attic and roof of Oakley's Nassau Hotel caught fire, but due to the gallant efforts of the fire department, the wooden structure was saved. Financial difficulties in 1859 resulted in the place being put on the auction block at Riverhead. William Buck of Sag Harbor purchased it for $2400 and re-opened, hiring Lewis M. Ross, assisted by Alfred Oakley, to manage the hotel. The Nassau House remained in business until the fire of February 1877 destroyed it, along with many other stores in the village. A month later R.J. Powers remodeled the brick block of Douglass & Cooper buildings into a new Nassau House. The site of the wooden hotel which stood on the adjoining property was filled in, leveled off, and became the yard of the new hotel. Powers had windows and doors cut into the side of the building that faced the water and had verandas built on the first and second floors.

On January 1, 1892 Major Thornton bought the building from Powers and leased it to Charles E. Laws and J.A. Udall; Mr. Laws had been proprietor of a hotel in Greenport for many years. The two men purchased all the furniture and fittings and, after five years, took advantage of the option-to-buy clause and became the new owners. They remodeled it into a fine modern hotel. In March 1893 they added a fourth story to the building and topped it with a mansard roof. With this improvement, 13 new rooms were added. In October 1894 Udall hired J.H. L'Hommedieu & Company to draw up plans for a new wing to be built on the southeast corner of the main building. The first floor was used as a kitchen, butler's pantry, and servants' dining room, and on the second floor were the servants' quarters. In later years the name was changed to the Hotel Bay View. Udall bought out Laws' interests and hired Mrs. Ella Wallace to manage it.

After Charles Laws left, he leased a large house on Bay Street and opened the Laws Hotel or the Bay Side House. It stood on the corner of Bay and Rector Streets, and across from it a small pier and bathing houses were built for his summer boarders. A handsome veranda extended the length of the hotel front, with the main entrance and office on the east corner. Adjoining the office was a spacious dining room suitable for large gatherings. Fourteen large rooms, several with connecting parlors, were on the second floor, and ten rooms on the third. Each floor had its own bathroom. The place was later managed by Mrs. C.H. Gardiner and became known as the Gardiner House.

About the same time the Nassau House opened for business, the Mansion House was built. It was a brick structure, second to none, entirely new, and pleasantly located on the east side of Main Street, five minutes from the steamboat landing. The Mansion House, built in 1846 and owned by Ezekiel Mulford, could accommodate 60 individuals in its large, well-ventilated, and handsomely furnished rooms. From a bathing house on the premises, transportation could be arranged to Southampton, East Hampton, Montauk Point, or to the ocean. In addition, free carriage rides were provided between the hotel and the steamboat landing. Jedediah Conkling was proprietor of the Mansion House, and L.F. Dering, the business manager. This hotel later became the Union School house and was used for that purpose until Pierson High School was completed in 1907.

In 1817, almost opposite the Nassau House, Albert Hedges opened the Hedges House. It became a sailor's boarding house during the heyday of the whaling industry. Water for the Hedges House was supplied from a bucket well which was driven 40 feet deep. Even at that depth, at the time of the high tide the water was quite salty, so it was driven to 90 feet, but with little improvement. This wooden structure burned in the 1845 fire, and a brick hotel and livery stable was later built on the site. The second Hedges House burned in 1886. The place was rebuilt again, and in the 1890s John Glenn Jr. bought it for $4000. In 1920 Catherine Glenn sold the building to Joseph and Marie (Mary) Santacroce.

Betsey Jose's Boarding House, better known as "Betsey Jose's Fort," stood on Meadow Street during the last quarter of the 19th century. It was a simple boarding house, but got its unusual name from the vigorous opposition of its owner to the demands of Oliver Charles and his Railroad Company, and the decision of the railroad commissioners to take her property. Betsey barricaded the house and flew a flag of defiance from the roof and didn't surrender until terms were agreed on. Although Betsey retreated, she won the fight. For 17 years the house stood, a defiant fortress. It was described as a lively place in the past, and many a weary traveler found refuge there. The Railroad Company paid Betsey $3000 for her house and several months later sold it to John Battle. It was then moved to Cross Street and made into a tenement.

There were a number of other hotels and boarding houses in Sag Harbor near the turn of the century, many catering to summer tourists that came to the village each year. The East End Hotel stood on the corner of Main and Howard

Streets. In 1871 C.N. Bellows owned and operated it, and in 1877 the Polleys ran a boarding house there. The Lobstein House on Union Street, originally owned by Hannibal French and later purchased by Mrs. C.G. Vail, was another summer boarding house.

The Lily Pond House and the Lundhurst Hotel, both owned by John Lund, accommodated summer tourists. The Lily Pond House was a spacious mansion of 20 rooms surrounded by 90 acres of lawn, woodland and ponds with stables and bridle paths on the property. Both the Lily Pond House and the Lundhurst specialized in catering.

The Bijou Hotel was established on Main Street in 1877, a three-story wooden structure owned by Henry P. Porter. Porter advertised his lodging rooms as "cool, comfortable, and everything new and clean." A five-cent lunch and oyster counter satisfied the mid-day crowd, and dinners were served with the choicest wines and liquors. Following a brief period in which the place was closed, ex-conductor William Warner of the Long Island Railroad leased the hotel.

The Sea View Hotel, built in 1891 by William B. Collins, was located on Brickkiln Road. When first constructed it contained only eight rooms. In April 1892 J.K. Morris bought the place and enlarged it making thirty rooms. Morris was the proprietor of the Sea View Hotel for more than 35 years. In 1907-08 extensive renovations doubled its size. Twenty-two more guest rooms were added, the carpentry work done by Boss Edwards of Noyac and the masonry work by Edward J. Beckwith of Sag Harbor. The Sea View, with its commanding view of Noyac Bay, catered to the rich and famous. The inimitable Caruso spent time there in the 1920s, as did Governor Alfred E. Smith. In later years the hotel was called Hill Top Acres, and during a disastrous fire on December 19, 1970, it burned to the ground and it was never rebuilt.

5

INTERESTING PEOPLE AND PLACES

A philosopher of note was Sag Harbor's Prentice Mulford, a man ahead of his time, who was, in his love of nature, likened to Thoreau. A half a century ago he was described as:

...the strangest of men; a man who might have been called a crank or a seer, a foolish man or one who was wise beyond the measure of most men's wisdom. He visioned the airplane and the radio and in 1870 wrote much of the principles applied by the Wright brothers years later. He prophesied mental telepathy and practiced it. He was shy beyond belief yet had the keenest and most vivid interests in the affairs of men. He was full of the most out of the way information, mingled with much that was practical to a degree. His humor was delightful and his range of thoughts covered the widest and to many the most absurd dreams, yet he was also full of hard common sense.

PRENTICE MULFORD, PHILOSOPHER

Prentice Mulford, son of Ezekiel Mulford and the last in the male line of that old aristocratic family, was born at Sag Harbor in 1834 and spent his early years around the Mansion House where his father was then proprietor. At the age of 14 Prentice Mulford inherited the hotel but, for unforseen reasons, went bankrupt four years later. Restless and unable to hold a job, Mulford soon acquired the reputation of a ne'er-do-well. Little did anyone imagine at that time this shiftless young man would soon become a leading writer of his day. He spent a term at normal school in Albany, but found it difficult to concentrate on his studies, as his search for knowledge was not to be found in the classroom.

At 22 Prentice Mulford headed for California, rounding the Cape in a clipper ship along with other belated gold rushers on their way to San Francisco; however, he wasn't to make his fortune panning for gold, but rather by his interesting and imaginative articles and books. In 1860 Mulford wrote his first humorous sketch for a newspaper, and that article launched his career. Joseph E. Lawrence, editor of the weekly *Golden Era*, was so impressed, he asked Mulford to join his staff. Although his works were successful and won him a place in the literary society of San Francisco, he was, as in his youth, restless and unhappy.

In his search for peace, Prentice Mulford lived a lonely existence. His behavior became more and more bizarre, and he believed thought to be a tangible power. In 1865 he converted to spiritualism and claimed to have communicated with departed spirits and the ghost of John Wilkes Booth. An old whaleboat became his home, and he spent the next few years cruising San Francisco Bay in a strange one-piece knitted suit, turned rusty brown from the sun and the saltwater.

Mulford later traveled abroad, and London's literary circle received him as one of America's leading writers. He became personally acquainted with Mark Twain and other famous writers of that era. He accepted admiration for his works with extreme caution, thinking that some were ridiculing him. When he returned to America in 1874, he withdrew completely and lived for the next 17 years as a hermit in the swamps of Passaic, New Jersey. It was there, under those strange conditions, that he wrote some of his finest works on spiritualism, including the *White Cross Library*, dealing in such topics as thought currents and your forces and how to use them. Prentice Mulford seemed to have found peace at last and wrote 36 volumes on spiritualistic and theosophic science.

At the age of 57, Prentice Mulford made a decision to return to the place of his birth and write about Long Island after the gold rush. Leaving New Jersey in his boat laden with provisions and all his worldly possessions, he started home, but Mulford never reached Sag Harbor, as death overtook him on his voyage and, there, in his boat he died.

A great mind never fully understood passed on when Prentice Mulford died, and when his death was made known, the distinguished poet John Greenleaf

INTERESTING PEOPLE AND PLACES

Whittier wrote of him the following memorial verse of praise:

> Un-noted as the setting of a star
> He passed; and sect and party scarcely knew
> When from their midst a sage and seer withdrew
> To better audience, where the great dead are
> In God's republic of the heart and mind
> Leaving no purer, nobler soul behind.

After 30 years in an unmarked grave, Mulford's body was taken to Oakland Cemetery where a large stone was placed on his grave and inscribed "Philosopher," followed by his own words, "Thoughts are Things." It was a fitting tribute to Sag Harbor's own philosopher, Prentice Mulford.

Huntting's Spectacular Music Hall

When it came to impressive-looking buildings in the early years, Huntting's three-story brick structure was one of the grandest. Built following the fire of 1845, the large commodious structure stood at the foot of Main Street, facing the business district, and housed a sail loft, stores, and at a time the local bank. Huntting, a shrewd businessman and outstanding citizen, envisioned a spectacular Music Hall on the top floor of his building, a place where fancy balls, plays, and concerts could be held. After renting his place for 25 years, he finally decided to pursue his dream.

Huntting hired the firm of Hallock & Hart to draw up plans, and in November 1872 John E. Chester of Sag Harbor began the renovations. The third floor of the building was removed to create an 18-foot-high arched ceiling, from which hung a gas chandelier. The stage at one end of the room was complete with curtains and scenery, and constructed so it could easily be removed to convert this area into one huge room, large enough for the most elegant ball. Built at the other end was a beautiful serpentine gallery. Before opening to the public, the entrance was changed from the side of the building to the front, facing the business district. On February 19, 1873 the music hall opened with the most elegant reception ever held in the village. The inauguration program consisted of an instrumental concert until the supper hour, and the later part of the night was devoted to dancing. The hall, at that time one of the finest of its size in New York State, was tastefully decorated with 300 floral arrangements. Flags decorated the stage and surrounded a huge painting of "St. Cecilia as a Musician." The music, furnished by Papst of Brooklyn, consisted of six men who played selections from popular operas. It was noted that the national air of Faderland, "The Watch on the Rhine," with its martial strains and stirring melody, set the blood flying quicker through the veins of every listener. Nearly 100 ladies and gentlemen, dressed in all their finery, arrived shortly after 9 P.M. for a tour, examining the capacious gallery and dressing rooms, which were all modern and spacious. The quality of the woodwork, plastering, and painting was first-class, and the whole building a great acquisition to the village of Sag Harbor. Between 12 and one o'clock, supper was served in an adjoining building, under the supervision of Samuel Fordham. Later the Grand March of the evening took place, followed by dancing, until dawn, of the quadrille, valse, galop, schottische and polka.

Huntting's Music Hall proved to be the success that he hoped it would be, and it provided the residents of the village with many pleasant hours. Unfortunately, only five years after the hall opened, the great fire of February 1877 gutted the building. The brick structure, thought to have been fireproof, stood little chance as the blustery winter winds fanned the flames which crept under the roof shingles, putting a sudden and disastrous end to Huntting's spectacular music hall.

HUBBARD LATHAM FORDHAM, ARTIST

Hubbard Latham Fordham earned a reputation as one of the country's finest portrait painters of the 1800s, specializing in both life-sized and miniature work. Born in Sag Harbor on February 5, 1794, he was the first child of Jarius Fordham and Mary Latham. Hubbard Latham Fordham showed signs of his talent at an early age, but his practical-minded parents discouraged it, and much of his early work took the form of decorative signs for the local merchants. On November 26, 1817, at the age of 23, he married Hannah Frothingham, daughter of pioneer editor David Frothingham. Shortly after their wedding Fordham took up painting as a vocation.

Although Fordham maintained a home at Sag Harbor, he opened a studio on Chatham Street and, later, at Fulton and Broadway in New York City. He was listed in the city directories from 1830 to 1834 as a portrait painter. After he was commissioned to do a portrait of the Lieutenant Governor of Massachusetts, he opened a second studio in Springfield. Still later, with a growing demand for his portraits in Connecticut, he established a third studio in New Haven.

Hubbard Latham Fordham took up miniature painting prior to the Civil War and became one of the best-known American miniature painters of his day. He prospered financially and bought a farm in Iowa, where he spent some of his time painting. In April 1860 Fordham left to spend the summer at his Buffalo

County farm and met with sad disappointment. On arrival, he found fire had swept across the prairie and destroyed all of his buildings. Fordham returned to Sag Harbor via the steamboat and spent his later years in the village, semi-retired. At his studio on Hampton Street he did some of his finest work. His April 1861 portrait of Dr. Frederick Crocker of Sag Harbor was said to have been an exact likeness of his subject and a superior work of art.

Many of Hubbard Latham Fordham's paintings were displayed at Tooker's Pharmacy on Main Street. Examples of paintings done in the late 1860's were: *Triumph for Virtue*, *Christ Before the Chief Priests*, and *Toilet of Death—A Scene from French History*. His portraits included those of Mary P. Havens, Doctor Miles, Captain Edwards, General Floyd, and other notables. It was said that most of the old families in the village possessed at least one of Hubbard Latham Fordham's canvases.

In addition to his artistic talent, Hubbard Latham Fordham was a landowner in Sag Harbor and gave the property on which Spring Street was laid out. In his later years, with his eyesight failing to the point that he had to abandon his painting entirely, Fordham managed a tavern in Sag Harbor. On August 8, 1872 at the age of 78, Hubbard Latham Fordham's life came to an end, a brilliant and talented man, whose portraits can still be found decorating the walls of some of Sag Harbor's early homes.

The Atheneum

One of Sag Harbor's most interesting buildings was the Atheneum, an ancient structure with a lively history that spanned more than a century. Originally built by the Presbyterians in June of 1817 as their second church, it stood on the northeast corner of Church and Sage Streets. It was built by Eliab Byram, master carpenter, with Henry B. Havens doing the masonry work. Some of the lumber used came from the Old Barn Church, which formerly stood on the site. When the great fire of 1817 destroyed much of the new lumber intended for the building, an appeal went out for money to replace the lost material. Donations came in from all over Long Island and New York City, and the church was constructed as planned. Built at a cost of $4700, it was used by the Presbyterians until 1844 when the present Whaler's Church was built.

At that time, Christ Episcopal Church was in need of a larger sanctuary, and they rented the building for about two years. On August 25, 1846 they purchased it for $2100 and remodeled it to suit their needs. When a new church on the corner of Union and Hampton Streets was planned in 1880, the old structure was once again put up for sale.

Wamponamon Lodge #437 F.&A.M. bought it in May 1881, converting it into a Masonic Hall and entertainment center, and for 30 years all entertainment requiring a large hall was held there. In June 1900 the Masons sold it to Joseph Fahys & Company, who wanted the land to add to their factory property, and plans were made to move the structure to a new location.

In May 1903 the lengthy operation of moving the building began. Although its destination was but a block away, two long months passed before it reached the lot on the corner of Union and Church Streets and was placed on its new foundation. The basement measured 40 by 67 feet with 12-foot ceilings, in which a bowling alley, gymnasium, furnace room, dressing rooms, and bathrooms were located.

Plans for a complete renovation were submitted by local building contractor George H. Cleveland, which called for a main auditorium 43 by 67 feet, with 16-foot ceilings. A stage would be located at the west end of the hall, the box office at the east side of the main entrance, and at the east end of the extension, stairs would lead to the gallery. At the west end would be stairs to the Mason's lodge room built over the stage. A dining room and kitchen, 10 by 17, were also planned, and the existing gallery was cut back 10 feet, leaving a 24-foot-wide inclined floor. A covered entrance over the sidewalk to the curb line was built, with an open balcony above. Ceilings were constructed of stamped metal. The estimated cost of the renovation was placed at $9,000 to $10,000.

On November 18, 1903 a gala reception and ball, given by the Ladies Village Improvement Society, marked the re-opening of the hall, and it was known at that time as the Atheneum. The local newspaper suggested a different name be selected, calling the chosen one "jaw-breaking and misfitting." However, the name stood, and for the next 20 years the Atheneum was Sag Harbor's main recreation center, dance hall, and community theater. Its theatrical productions were popular throughout the entire East End and always well attended by local residents and those from nearby communities.

A disastrous end came to the Atheneum in 1924. It took but one hour to reduce the ancient structure to a pile of ashes. It was 10:10 in the morning of April 30, 1924 when the fire siren sounded, and within minutes the Sag Harbor Fire Department, soon aided by East Hampton, fought the stubborn blaze. At the height of the fire, 20 nearby homes caught fire from the flying sparks, but they were quickly extinguished before serious damage was done. Neighbors of the building had smelled pine burning the day before the fire, but thinking the smell was from a nearby forest fire, ignored it. When flames finally burst through the roof and upstairs windows, those who lived next door notified the janitor, Louis Kiselyak, who, although in the building, was unaware of the fire above him. Water from the Fahys factory pump provided an ample supply, but the blaze was too intense to be contained for the great wooden structure to be saved. Loss was estimated at from $75,000 to $80,000, an enormous amount for the times, and insured for only $20,000 by its owner, Joseph Fahys & Company. And so the end came to the Atheneum, a 100-year-old building that was used for many purposes: a church, lodge, entertainment center, theater, and bowling alley. It was never rebuilt and was a great loss to the people of Sag Harbor.

The Brass Band

The Sag Harbor Brass Band originally formed from a glee club which held meetings in the winter of 1857-58, and although the club was unsuccessful, several members showed an interest in forming a band. A subscription paper circulated, and raised $75 with which to purchase instruments. At a meeting held on March 3, 1858 the following men attended: Thomas H. Vail, Stephen Squires, William Winters, William R. Street, Leonard D. Hall, A. DeBevoise, C.A. Gardiner, G.H. Gleason and William L. Cook. Thomas Vail was elected chairman; William Cook, treasurer and secretary; and William Street, collector. Three weeks later motion was made that the treasurer be given authority to buy seven instruments and two pieces of music for each instrument. Two E^b soprano sax-horns at $18, one B^b soprano sax-horn at $10.50, two E^b alto sax-horns at $26, one B^b baritone horn at $20, and one B^b bass horn at $20 were ordered.

The band officially organized on April 3, 1858, and the 13 members met to rehearse three times a week. Along with those mentioned, the following were also members of the band: George H. Schellinger, Charles H. Fordham, L.C. Hedges, William Williams, E.P. Hedges, J.Q. Kelly and W.P. Schellinger. Vail and DeBevoise had resigned. In mid-June they acquired the services of John P. Stark of Middletown, Connecticut as an instructor, paying him $130 for 15 lessons. After only three, the band took part in the Fourth of July celebration, dressed in their new uniforms, and proudly marching in the village parade.

A room owned by John Stewart was rented for rehearsals, and missing practice made one liable to pay a 25-cent fine. Among the by-laws was a clause that stated each member was responsible for the care of his instrument. Dues of 50 cents per week were collected to help defray expenses.

A Fair Festival and Concert was held in the summer of 1858, at which $320 was raised. After deducting the cost of the uniforms, a balance of $15 was netted. On January 1, 1859 the Brass Band members exchanged their sax-horns for cornets and thereafter called themselves the Sag Harbor Cornet Band.

Apparently, the band didn't last too long, for in the June 25, 1874 newspaper a notice stated that the old Cornet Band, defunct for some years, had started up again. The village hall became their rehearsal room, and a teacher from New London was hired to give lessons. George R. Schellinger, director of the earlier Brass Band, became their leader.

There was a reorganization of the band again in 1898, and Professor Anthony Murphy became their director. New uniforms of army blue with red trim were ordered for the 17 members. Members at that time were: Murphy, who played solo B^b cornet; Peter Fischer, solo B cornet; Richard Drew, E^b cornet; August Dickel, B^b cornet; Joseph ("Midget") Murphy, B^b cornet; Alvin Kraemer, B^b clarionet; Martin Brown, E^b clarionet; John Meenan, solo alto; Numa Beynon, baritone; August Kluge, E^b bass, Albert Liniger, B^b trombone; Joseph Schwartz, 2nd trombone; Charles Bring, first alto, Theodore Biechele, second alto; William Schaefer, bass drum; John Wessel, snare drum; and Conrad Mellendorf, cymbals. Band practice took place every Tuesday, Thursday, and Saturday nights at the Fire Department Hall on Washington Street. Throughout the summer months band concerts were held weekly. Twelve-year-old "Midget" Murphy, the youngest cornetist on Long Island, was taught by his father and was an accomplished musician.

In June 1898 a bandstand was built on the vacant Huntting lot at the foot of Main Street. Octagonal in shape, with a peaked roof, it accommodated a band of 20 or more pieces. Years later, Mr. James H. Aldrich, of North Haven, donated money to repair the bandstand and have it moved to Mashashimuet Park, where weekly concerts continued to be held.

FANNIE W. TUNISON, EXTRAORDINARY LADY

Fannie Tunison was born in Sag Harbor in 1870, the only child of carpenter Abraham Tunison and his wife. To the grief and heartache of her parents, Fannie was unable to move from the neck down. Both local doctors and specialists were consulted, but no hope was given for her recovery. Fannie, however, blessed with an incredible sense of courage and determination, overcame her disability and became a self-sufficient, talented and positive person.

As Fannie grew, patiently cared for by her devoted mother and indulgent father, she learned early in life that with the use of her mouth she could turn the pages of a book and play with her toys. Strapped in her chair, she mastered the impossible. She learned to sew, write, draw, paint, and do needlework with her teeth, lips, and tongue. The work she produced was not only beautifully done but unique in the method it was accomplished. Fannie's father built a special chair for her, with a tray and work table attached to it at shoulder level. Every morning he would lift Fannie into the chair, strap her in, and leave her to spend her day making sketches, paintings in oils and water colors, and embroidering placemats and tablecloths. With remarkable skill, Fannie used scissors, thread, needles, and made knots at the end of the thread—all by the use of her mouth.

Fannie Tunison was well-read and had a keen interest in the current events of the world. Her mind was sharp and retentive, and she enjoyed a wonderful sense of humor. Not a trace of self-pity was evident as she spent hours chatting with friends or customers who stopped at her home to purchase her merchandise. She thoroughly enjoyed the ability to create beautiful things and ignored her obvious disabilities. In time, Fannie achieved economic independence and became the largest money-earner in her family.

The products of Fannie's skill were exhibited at the Riverhead Fair, New York City, and other places. She also supplemented her income by fortune-telling and "readings." Fannie lived to the age of 74, optimistic and cheerful to the end, a marvelous example of a beautiful person. She died in Brooklyn in March of 1944 and is buried in Oakland Cemetery, Sag Harbor.

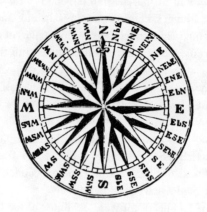

6

SAG HARBOR IN THE WARS

Although the actual operations of the Civil War were far removed from this area, Sag Harbor, nevertheless, was greatly affected. Most of her young men left to fight for the cause. During the war the citizens of Sag Harbor showed a patriotism never before equalled since the days of the American Revolution. More than 300 fathers and sons signed up to serve in the Union Army and Navy, with about one-tenth of them never to return home again.

The Civil War

In April 1861 the largest gathering ever held in the village took place, a meeting geared to attract volunteers and solicit contributions. Funds were sorely needed to provide supplies, uniforms, and to help out the families of the enlistees.

The 81st Regiment was formed, with Colonel Edwin Rose of Bridgehampton in command, and many from the Sag Harbor area served in his regiment. The Field and Staff Officers were: Major John McAmbley, Lieutenant Colonel Jacob J. DeForest, Adjutant Edward A. Cook, Quartermaster R.A. Francis, Surgeon William H. Rice, Assistant Surgeon Carrington McFarland, and Chaplin David McFarland. The non-commissioned staff were: Sergeant Major James L. Belden, Quartermaster Sergeant J.F. Youngs, Commissary Sergeant N.H. Gilbert, and Hospital Steward Charles S. Hart. William S. Winters of Sag Harbor was Drum Major, and Henry Hunt, Fife Major.

SAG HARBOR IN THE WARS

The monthly wage for those serving in the war was: Colonel, $211; Lieutenant Colonel, $194; Major, $175; Captain, $108.50; 1st Lieutenant, $108.50; 2nd Lieutenant, $103.50; Brevet 2nd Lieutenant, $103.50; 1st Sergeant or Orderly, $29; other Sergeants, $27; Corporals, $22; Privates, $20; and Musicians, $21. All other officers had to provide their own weapons and uniforms.

The following account of the Great Civil War Meeting was reported in the April 25, 1861 *Sag Harbor Express*.

THE WAR!!!
LARGEST MEETING EVER HELD AT SAG HARBOR. EVERY MAN READY. RECRUITING OFFICE OPENED! 43 VOLUNTEERS ENROLLED. OVER $3000 SUBSCRIBED!!
Sag Harbor in the Front Ranks!
Never in the history of our place has such excitement and enthusiasm been manifested as has been displayed since last Saturday. The news from the seat of war had enflamed the public mind to fever heat. On the Sabbath, the churches taught our citizens that they must act as well as think, and do as well as talk. All day long on Monday the streets were thronged with crowds of excited men discussing what was best to be done. A call for a public meeting in the evening was signed by all our leading men. The whole place fairly blossomed out with flags and many private homes raised the colors from the roofs. The band paraded the streets playing the National airs, and stirring up the hearts of every true American. But when evening came the enthusiasm became uncontrollable. Hundreds poured into Washington Hall, the largest public room in the place, crowding it to overflowing in every part. Never before had such an audience been convened in Sag Harbor, never such united feelings had been displayed by all classes and all parties. Difference, there was none. The past was forgotten and the future was only thought of.

Stephen B. French, Esquire, nominated as chairman the Reverend Edward Hopper. This was carried amid a perfect storm of cheers and the wildest excitement. The following persons were named as vice-presidents: John Sherry, Dr. Henry Cook, Stephen B. French, Thomas E. Crowell and Abel Buckley. Messrs. Charles W. Fordham and Walter S. Elliott were appointed secretaries.

The Chairman then set forth the objects of the meeting in an eloquent speech and said he considered it a great honor to be called upon to preside over a meeting of his fellow countrymen, convened to take action in this present crisis of our national affairs. He was greeted with frequent applause and vollies of cheers. A committee on resolutions was then made composed of Messrs. William H. Gleason, John Sherry and William A. Woodbridge. The following ode was sung, written by Reverend Edward Hopper, to the tune of "America." All joined heartily in the patriotic strains.

THE OLD FLAG
Flag of the brave and free!
Flag of our Liberty!
   Of thee we sing.

Flag of our father's price!
With their pure heart's blood died,
   Our pledge we bring.

We love each tattered rag
Of that old war rent flag
   Of Liberty!

Flag of great Washington!
Flag of brave Anderson!
Flag of each mother's son
   Who dare be free!

The Committee on Resolutions, through their Chairman, presented the following which were unanimously adopted.

Whereas a crisis has come in our history, unparalled in the past, overwhelming in its results, threatening the destruction of our Nation, our Union, our Government and our Liberty itself, therefore we, the citizens of Sag Harbor, patriots before we were politicians, Americans before we were partizans, and Union men first, last and forever—do hereby:

Resolve that we will stand by our Government, our Country, and our Flag, to the last, and will maintain for coming generations those priceless blessings which have been handed down to us from our forefathers, won by their sufferings and trials; and that we will, never, no never! desert the old ship Union, which has born us safely through so many perils, while one spar floats to which we can cling.

Resolved, that we urge upon our citizens as Volunteers in defense of their Country, and to show that the patriotic zeal which animated Old Suffolk in the wars of '76 and 1812 is still glowing, and still as ready to manifest itself as in the days that tried men's souls.

Lastly, for the perpetuity of our Nation, the Maintenance of our Government, and the protection of that "Old Flag" we do here in the presence of High Heaven, pledge to one another "our lives," our fortunes, and our sacred honor.

While the last resolution was being read, the whole audience arose and took the solemn pledge to one another.

Just at this moment our patriotic fellow citizen, Phineas Dean, raised the Star Spangled Banner aloft in front of the audience. An electric shock thrilled the vast assembly and it seemed as if the very walls would yield amid the tempest of cheers. Every man, woman and child hurrahed at the very top of their voices and strove to see who could outvie the other in the effort. Handkerchiefs, hats, bonnets, and shawls were swung in the air, while the old banners were waved on high. Again and again did the enthusiasm break forth, until it spent itself. Speeches on the resolutions now followed. The speakers were Messrs. Stephen French, John Sherry, William H. Gleason, John W. Burke, Brinley D. Sleight, Samuel W. Fordham, John M. Rogers, Edward B. Hill and P.R. Jennings. The choir then sang the Star Spangled Banner, all the audience joining in the chorus with splended effort. A quartet choir also sang the Red, White and Blue, joined by all present in the chorus. Then after a few more cheers from the audience, the meeting was closed—one of the greatest "Union" efforts our place has ever made—a gathering which warmed every patriot's heart.

The Sag Harbor Cornet Band, during the entire evening, played many pieces which were most thankfully received by the audience. We understand that they hold themselves ready to march as soon as their services shall be required. Out of doors cannons were fired and fireworks displayed during the meeting, and the patriotism of the village vent in a hundred different ways which we have not space to recount.

The recruiting office was opened on Tuesday morning and has been thronged ever since. Already forty-three have volunteered and there will doubtless be a full company of seventy-seven obtained. The volunteers held a meeting last night and elected their officers.

The following money was pledged by some of Sag Harbor's citizens and businessmen on April 23, 1861: N.P. Howell $300, J.S. Hitchcock $15, J. Winters $100, H.&S. French $100, J. Douglass $200, William Gleason $100, S.F. Brown $100, C.N. Brown $100, William Adams $100, William Buck $100, O.R. Wade $100, George B. Brown $100, J.B. Nickerson $100, R.M. Garretson $25, James Harris $25, John Budd $25, Benjamin Babcock $30, C.S. Stillwell $30, Benjamin Huntting $300, D.B. Wiggins $75, H.L. Topping $50, W. & G.H.

214   EXPLORING THE SOCIAL SCENE

Cooper $100, Elias B. Woodruff $50, E.C. Buckley & Son $100, Abel Buckley $100, John Sherry $100, W.R. Sleight $100, Huntting Cooper $150, B.D. Sleight $100, G.S. Tooker $50, French Smith $25, O.B. Lucas $25, B. & F. Lyon $50, J.W. Nickerson $30, Bassett & Terry $50.

It seemed that all the residents of Sag Harbor were caught up in an intense patriotism never before equaled in the history of the village. Reverend Edward Hopper, then pastor of the Presbyterian Church, was an ardent patriot and the most zealous advocate on all of Long Island. His sermons stirred the blood and fervor of his countrymen, and Reverend Hopper, perhaps, did more to influence the young men of this area to volunteer than did any other person. The American flag was raised to the top of the church steeple and was visible for miles around. Hopper's "Volunteer Song" inspired many local boys to head for the recruiting office to sign up.

In May 1861, 45 enrolled their names for the Revenue Service. In June a company of volunteers formed the 16th Regiment. By August a recruiting office was opened at the Mansion House by the officers of Colonel Perry's Regiment. Throughout the summer men enlisted for the Gun Boat Service, the Marine Artillery, United States Navy, Rose's 81st Regiment, the 127th New York Volunteers, and other companies.

The 81st Regiment recruits often camped at Ninevah Heights, Sag Harbor, where they drilled prior to being sent to the battlefield. When Edward D. Cook came to Sag Harbor to recruit men for Colonel Rose's 81st, he stated that those who wished to join and go to battle, under the command of one of Long Island's favorite sons, should do so immediately, as the regiment would soon be ready to leave.

In July 1861 a Relief Association was organized to assist in preparing necessary supplies for the volunteers. They sent to New York to be distributed: 100 sheets, 84 pillow cases, 13 bed ticks, 21 calico dressing gowns, six flannel dressing gowns, 34 handkerchiefs, 132 towels, 56 havelocks, 44 flannel bandages, 24 flannel undershirts, 60 bedshirts, 46 bed gowns, 84 pairs of drawers, 24 eye shades, and six pairs of stockings.

DISASTER AT THE WATERFRONT

During the Civil War a disastrous incident occurred at Sag Harbor's waterfront when the experimental testing of a new projectile weapon went awry and resulted in devastating consequences.

A rifled cannon for experimenting with General Charles James' new projectile was brought to Sag Harbor in August 1861. The two cannons were handsome rifles, one carrying a 13-pound ball and 12-pound shell, and one a 6-pounder of the United States standard. The other was calculated for 24-pound shot. These superior weapons were manufactured in Chicopee, Massachusetts, where workers labored day and night to supply the constant demand. General James and his assistant Charles B. Arnold set up the cannons on a bluff at the foot of the village near Conklin's Point, and various targets were fired at along the North West Creek area. On October 16, 1862 a tragic accident occurred when one of the projectiles exploded, killing General James, Captain James Smith, Henry Beverland, and injuring Orlando Bears, H.P. Byram and Captain Jeremiah Hedges of Sag Harbor. Bears died a week later from his injuries. He was only 17.

Beverland, who was leaning over the 24-pound devise and removing the cap with a pair of pliers, received the full force of the explosion and was killed instantly. James Smith died three days later, following the amputation of his leg by Dr. Cook. General James suffered mortal wounds to his head and died a day after the tragedy. His remains were taken to Providence, Rhode Island. A French officer named Kreutzberger also lost his life as the result of severe wounds.

Less seriously wounded were Jeremiah Hedges, Edward Allshaw (Aldershaw), P.R. Jennings, E.H. and Benjamin Carpenter, Joseph C. Harris, and a Mr. Phelps.

Antietam, Cold Harbor, Gaines Farm, and Richmond saw some of the bloodiest fighting of the war, with the North suffering heavy casualties. At least 46 men from Sag Harbor lost their lives, either on the battlefield, from sickness, or war-related injuries. Six were lost at Gaines Farm alone. Other local men were wounded or captured. In 1864 Charles H. Jessup and Joseph Pedro, of the 48th Regiment, were wounded in the Battle of Chester Heights, with Pedro taken to a hospital in Hamilton, Virginia. Stephen Crowell received wounds at the Battle of Honey Hill, and Edgar Z. Hunt suffered a saber wound at Red River.

Edward Jessup, of the 48th Regiment, reported missing, was discovered to be a prisoner at Andersonville. He later died. Charles D. Payne, also reported missing, was discovered to be imprisoned at Camp Ford in Tyler, Texas. Henry Wheaton Washburn served time at the same prison and was released in March 1865. George R. Sherman of the 7th U.S. Colored Troops was imprisoned at Danville, Georgia, and Nathan C. Fordham, of the 2nd Massachusetts Cavalry, held at the infamous Libby Prison in Richmond.

At the close of hostilities, all of the gallant soldiers and sailors from East Hampton, Southampton, Bridgehampton, Sag Harbor, and other neighboring communities were requested to meet at Washington Hall in Sag Harbor on the Fourth of July 1865. They were to act as an escort to the orator of the celebration and partake of a dinner given in honor of their return and in appreciation for the part they played in preserving the Union. Once again, Sag Harbor's boys did their village proud in helping to secure our most precious possession—freedom.

A list of the men from Sag Harbor who served in the Civil War can be found in the Appendix.

Slavery in the Sag Harbor Area

The holding of Indian slaves in New York was never a general custom. Although Indian slavery was continuous throughout the colonial period in New York, the number of slaves was small. Some were imported from the South and the Spanish Islands and were generally confined to the southern states. Actually, to state the exact number of Indian slaves in any colony would be mere speculation, and, in all probability, there were very few on Long Island. A rapid decrease took place due to the decline in the number of Indians, and a law in 1693 forbade trade and sale of them for slavery.

It was much easier to obtain Negroes, as the black population was so much greater. Yet, when we think of black slavery we seem to shift our thoughts to the South, to huge cotton plantations, where the unfortunate and indentured picked cotton from dawn to dusk under the whip of an often cruel and inhumane landowner. It is hard to believe that slavery was widely practiced on Long Island, and even here in Sag Harbor.

Slaves in New York generally lived in their master's home. Rarely did they toil in the field, but worked alongside of their master in what ever line of work he pursued. Many were household servants, with domestic duties left almost exclusively in their hands. In the 1746 census of Suffolk County, 1399 slaves were listed, serving a white population of 7855, a ratio of a little more than one slave to every 5.6 whites. It is safe to say that probably every family of moderate means had one or more slaves in their household. By 1790 the number had dropped to about one slave per 16 people, and by 1800, one slave to every 21 people.

In nearby Shelter Island the Nathaniel Sylvester family had many black slaves in their estate. When Sylvester died in 1680, 20 slaves were listed among his property ownings. Sylvester was known to have traded with Barbados, and it is likely that he imported them from that place. During the years of the American Revolution, slaves were largely in the hands of Nicoll Havens and William Nicoll, who between them owned 24.

A public sale of slaves at Whitestone in 1796 was attacked by a Sag Harbor newspaper as "disgraceful to humanity." Readers of the January 11, 1796 issue of Frothingham's *Long Island Herald* were urged to protest against the outrage by sending petitions to the legislature. It is interesting to note, however, that an advertisement placed by Mrs. Frothingham in 1804 and 1805 in another Sag Harbor paper, *The Suffolk Gazette*, offered a slave for sale! It stated: "In every respect suitable for a farmer, a negro woman 25 years old, with or without a girl 4 years old. A credit will be given if required. For information apply to Mrs. Frothingham." Strange that the seller of this slave was the wife of the editor of *The Long Island Herald*, the same newspaper that eight years earlier called slavery "a disgrace to humanity."

Another advertisement in the local paper of June 1806 read: "Wanted: a negro girl from 18-30 years old. Will be purchased for any time over three years. She is to live in a small family and must come well recommended for honesty." Worded as it was, the advertisement sounded much like a job offer, but it must be remembered that the person was not being hired, but bought, and would actually be owned by the family he or she lived with.

Another incident involving slavery in Sag Harbor comes to light with the following notice that appeared in a July 24, 1821 newspaper.

> Ran away from the subscriber on Wednesday the 14th, a colored man by the name of Isaac Prime, a slave, nearly six feet in height. Had on when he went away, a new blue broadcloth round-about and pantaloons of the same. Also on Sunday the 18th, Prince Prime, brother to Isaac, who was clothed in a blue jacket and trousers of blue broadcloth and a red flannel shirt, about five feet ten inches tall. Both belong to the estate of Samuel H. Jessup, deceased. Any person lodging either of both of them in the county jail, or returning them to James Post, administer, will be amply rewarded for their services.

During the Revolution a law was passed by which slaves enlisting in the army, with the consent of their owners, were entitled to their freedom. In 1788 an act of Congress freed the slaves, permitting the manumission of those under 50 years of age. However, the slave needed to prove that he was able to care for himself. Many could not, and it was obvious that slavery continued to be practiced in the area. In the year 1817 owners of slaves were taxed 50 cents for each one in his household. Nathan Fordham, Hubbard Latham, and Henry P. Dering, each wealthy and well-respected Sag Harbor residents, were taxed for one slave each.

The final and total abolition of slavery in New York State took place July 4th, 1827 and stated: "Each negro, mulatto and mustee within the state, born before July 4, 1799 be free. All negroes, mulattoes and mustees born after July 4, 1799 would be free, males at the age of twenty-eight and females at the age of twenty-five." It is more than likely that some of the offspring of the early slaves on Shelter Island were purchased by the affluent of Sag Harbor and, in later years, became some of the first black freedmen to live in the village.

Part Five

INDUSTRY, INNOVATION AND EXPANSION

1870–1900

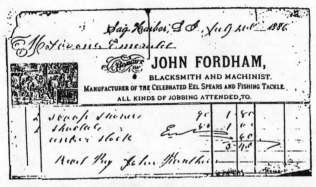

1
TRAVEL ON LONG ISLAND SOUND

Long Island Sound provided a means of travel far more superior and efficient that the land route between New York City and the East End. This was particularly true when the weather was agreeable and the sea calm. The dirt highway that ran the length of the Island was dusty and dirty in the dry season and rut-filled and muddy when the weather was inclement. Almost from the time Sag Harbor was first settled, the water route was utilized for both travel and shipping. Throughout the 1800s an extensive line of packets, sloops, and sidewheelers made the run between Sag Harbor, New York City, and the Connecticut shore, with much of the whale oil and associated products shipped to market on these vessels. Other ships sailed up the Hudson River to Albany to pick up lumber and other goods to bring to Sag Harbor, while still others ran solely for passenger travel.

Steamboats dock at the Long Wharf

In 1791 the sloop *Industry*, with Luther Cook master, sailed the Sag Harbor to New York route, "once a month, weather permitting." *The Rising Sun*, William Parker, master, and the packet ship *Peggy*, Stephen Satterly, master, also sailed the same route, while the *Speedwell*, captained by John Price sailed between Sag Harbor and Hartford.

In 1820 Captain Jeff Fordham's ship, *The David Porter*, sailing between Sag Harbor and New York City, carried 40 to 60 passengers, although it had berths for only one-quarter of them. At night an extra sail was spread on the main cabin floor for the men and boys to sleep on. All lights were out by nine, and although there was no extra charge for either stateroom or berth, not many were fortunate enough to get one. Meals could be obtained on board for 12½ cents, but most travelers brought their own.

It was the era of the steam-powered ship that really opened the tourist trade to the East End of Long Island. Sag Harbor on the South Fork and Greenport on the North Fork became meccas for vacationing city folk. The *Olive Branch* in 1839 sailed between Sag Harbor, Greenport and Jamesport, Long Island. It covered 50 miles in six hours and consumed one and a half cords of wood. The *Olive Branch* was built at a cost of $5000, with shares selling at $25 each.

In August 1875 the Greenmans of Mystic, Connecticut, owners of the steamboat *W.W. Coit*, organized a company called the New York and Montauk Steamboat Company. Several prominent citizens of Sag Harbor, Greenport, New Suffolk, Orient, and New York City were involved. Seven directors from the places mentioned were chosen, including H. French of Sag Harbor. The company planned to make changes and improvements in order to provide the public with the best service possible. The office of the Montauk Steamboat Company was located in the Alvin Building, and in 1898 a telephone connection to the Long Wharf was added.

The great fire of 1877, which started in a warehouse on the wharf, damaged the pier extensively. Following the fire, repairs were made under the supervision of John F. Foster, and after they were completed, the wharf was said to have been in better condition than when first built. The two narrow sections on the first section, known as the "old part," were widened so as to correspond with the new extension. The entire structure was cribbed on both side from 12 to 15 feet wide, which made it more substantial than in the past, and new piles were driven, replacing the old ones. After the pier was restored, the Sag Harbor Wharf Company was sold to Austin Corbin, president of the Long Island Railroad, for $20,000. As a result, the new Maidstone Pier was built to accommodate the steamers owned by the Montauk Steamboat Company, which plied between Sag Harbor, New York, and other coastal cities.

When the Fahys Watch Case Company came to Sag Harbor in 1881, they bought, from Captain George C. Gibbs, a controlling interest of stock in the steamboat line and negotiated for the purchase of Long Wharf. The railroad sold it at a sacrifice of $10,000. The Fahys Company then assigned the property to the steamboat company, but threw out the old charter, and divided the realty, reserving lots on Main and Bay Streets. A few years later the railroad extended their operation on Long Island and bought out the Montauk Steamboat Company, the Long Wharf property, and later the wharf lots held by Joseph Fahys and Henry F. Cook. They also leased the Maidstone pier and bulkheads, and this gave them control of the waterfront at Sag Harbor.

The Railroad Company ran a trestle down on Long Wharf so that their steamers could take on coal directly from the car. Also, they leased a portion of the pier to the E.W. Bliss Company of Brooklyn, who expended many thousands of dollars building a torpedo testing station. In 1896 the Long Wharf Company was dissolved, with ownership of the pier continuing in the hands of the railroad through the turn of the century.

The Shelter Island, *The Montauk*, and *The Shinnecock* were three of the sidewheelers built for the Montauk Steamboat Company to sail the Sag Harbor-New York route. The company ran a very profitable business for many years. Local religious and civic groups enjoyed many an excursion to Connecticut on these sidewheelers, and on Fourth of July each year, special sails were added to the regular schedule.

Steamboat travel continued to be a popular means of travel into the early 1900s. At that time, with the condition of the roads much improved and the train service extended to the east end, the era of the sidewheeler steamboat passed from existence.

A Description of the Village in 1875

An anonymous visitor had the following to say about the Village in 1875:

> Sag Harbor is delightfully situated on Peconic Bay near the narrow channel which connects it with Gardiner's Bay. It was once a thriving town, but today it is dead, dully and dreary. Like Nantucket, it rose and flourished and fell with the whale fishery. Fifteen or twenty years ago seventy whaleships were owned here and the streets of the town were alive with jolly whalers, some about to sail for the far-off fishing grounds—others just in from a three year cruise laden with gold and silver, and boiling over with anxiety to get rid of every penny of their hard earned wealth.
>
> Business of all kind was brisk and fortunes were rapidly made by the contented landsmen. Then the population of the town was four thousand, now it is barely two thousand. Then it contained two large cotton factories, two clock factories, large shoe shops and flour mills, and the cooperage business employed hundreds of men. Now the large buildings

once used by the coopers are empty and gradually going to pieces; the great stores which supplied ships and sailors with everything from tobacco boxes up to spars and spare ribs, no long resound to the din of the trade. There is one cotton mill in the town which cost $200,000 and was sold for $25,000, and there is a flour mill, but the once flourishing shoe shop is no more, the clock factory was closed years ago, and the laboring part of the population find little to do now except to sell dry goods and groceries, make cigars, fish and deal in clams, and a few subsist by dealing in beer. But, with the exception of the preachers and the barbers, of whom there are many, the breadwinners find it extremely difficult to make both ends meet at the end of the year.

There is one barber shop to every church; why this should be so I cannot tell; but I know that the knights of the razor are rarely idle and I am told that every preacher in town receives his yearly stipend with undeviating regularity. "You may not believe it," said Uncle Jack of the Nassau House, "but whenever a Sag Harbor man has ten cents in his pocket, he either goes to church or gets a shave. Nobody has ever been able to give a reason for this, but it's as true as gospel. If I was fool enough to go into business here, I'd have either a striped pole or a steeple for a sign, you bet!"

But you must not think for a moment that Sag Harbor is an uninteresting town. Far from it. It is a pretty place, well built and shady, and has something of the flavor of hallowed antiquity about it. Some of its private residences are very attractive. All of it churches, while not imposing, except for the Presbyterian, are creditable specimens of architecture. The Presbyterian Church has a very noticeable front and the steeple is one of the most graceful I have ever seen. Some years ago an attempt was made to set up a clock in it, but it was soon found that to time the vibrations of the steeple with those of the pendulum, would be too difficult a job. So the works were taken down and all that remains of the clock and its appendages are the four dials gazing blankly toward the four cardinal point of the compass.

I have just come down from the cupola of the Methodist Church, from which I enjoyed a glorious view of the water and the islands to the north, and of the dark brick hills to the south, with their thick growth of rich green foliage bathed in the bright beams of the morning sun and lazily rounding and swelling in many tinted waves as the soft touch of the morning breeze, that had just come up from the sea. You may travel a great many hundred miles before you enjoy a prospect equal to this in beauty. After my visit to the tower of the Methodist Church I took a walk over the bridge to North Haven and called upon Chief Justice

Charles P. Daly, whose beautiful country home overlooked the bay at this point.

...It is not altogether dead now for it boasts a dramatic and literary society of forty-five members, who give an occasional performance in a beautiful little hall belonging to B.F. Huntting, one of the enterprising citizens of the place. The hall is in the building once occupied as a depot for ship supplies.

I must not close without making mention of the fact that the clock in the tower of the Methodist Church was made by Ephraim Byram, who has since become celebrated. It was his first work and was done when he was nineteen years old. This was more than twenty-one years ago and the clock does not vary two minutes a year from the correct time. The tools which the young clockmaker used were all made by himself.

The W. W. Coit

The steam paddlewheeler *W.W. Coit* was essentially a summer service, running between New York, Greenport, Shelter Island, and Sag Harbor three times a week. After leaving New York, the overnight run arrived in Greenport at dawn and, during the day, continued on to Shelter Island and Sag Harbor. Its service started in the 1870s and by 1890 a stop at Block Island was included.

The following letter, written by an anonymous New Jersey resident, presents a descriptive account of both ship and voyage, as he sailed to Sag Harbor on the *W.W. Coit* in 1880.

I am off for my annual pilgrimage to Sag Harbor bound to get clear of the dust and heat and mosquitoes of Jersey, and breathe, in exchange, for a few days, the cooling breezes of Long Island Sound. The last barrel of freight, every empty fish box, and the high toned, high strung city horse is securely hid and has evidently made up her mind to make the best of it. The last passenger and his trunk are safely aboard. Promptly at 5 o'clock the order is given to let go of the tow line. In a moment the clear positive voice of the first officer, Ben Hobart, responds, "All clear, sir," then the bell rings to go ahead and the steamer, *W.W. Coit* slowly moves out of her berth and we begin to sniff the cool breeze of the East River. What a busy scene! Boats with steam and boats without. What a multitude of boats of every size and description.

Blackwell's Island is just ahead on the left, almost covered with massive stone buildings. The steamer *Massachusetts*, has just passed us almost as though we were at anchor. She is a splendid three decker and her immense hull has caused such a swell that the little *Coit* rocks like a cradle. Soon we will be in the Sound, as we pass Fort Schuyler. These works and some batteries on the East River shore protect the entrance to the East River. Signs with mammoth letters are warnings to master of vessels with their, "Torpedoes, Don't Anchor."

The *Coit* is a swift little side-wheeled steamer which will comfortably accommodate from fifty to seventy-five people. She has been on this route for some years and makes (except during the winter months) three trips per week, leaving Peck's slip, Tuesday, Thursday and Saturday at 5 o'clock PM, and leaves Sag Harbor, Monday, Wednesday and Friday at 4 o'clock PM. Although the Long Island Railroad takes a number of passengers, a great number prefer the boat, especially in warm weather. The fare is but $1.25, including berth. A room for two persons cost $1.00 extra.

The boat is neatly fitted up; clean, bright and cozy. Of course there is but little chance for exercise, the saloon covering about three-fourths of the promenade deck. There is, however, sufficient space at either end of the boat to comfortably seat the number of passengers named, while the saloon is neatly fitted up with an abundance of seating accommodations. A cabinet organ placed in the after part of the saloon is usually well patronized, on which occasion popular tunes are sung in a most vigorous and hearty manner. The officers are polite and obliging. Captain Gibbs, who has for many years been on this route, is not only an exceedingly careful sailor, but a pleasant and polite gentleman, and with the assistance of his experienced pilots, Mr. Hildreth and Mr. Banks, one can feel secure.

The moon, nearly full, is shining brightly in a clear sky. The waters of the Sound are smooth and our good boat is steadily steaming along. It is now after 10 o'clock and the music has ceased and the passengers have retired for the night. When we awoke at sunrise, the steamer is discharging freight at Greenport. Immediately across Peconic Bay on Shelter Island, stands the Manhanset House, king of hotels on the end of Long Island. There is a good wharf here and the *Coit* stops to let off passengers and freight. Further along on the same island is the Prospect, where more passengers are discharged.

We are soon off again and in the quiet clear waters of Gardiners Bay, and soon will reach the end of our route, Sag Harbor. Twenty years time has brought little change to the general appearance along the harbor of this beautiful bay. The steeple of the Presbyterian Church which for a generation past has welcomed the wanderer home, is quite as tall and

TRAVEL ON LONG ISLAND SOUND

wears the same old friendly look. So too the yellow sand banks of the "Neck" (Hog Neck). Aunt Jeanette's, the veteran poplars there, a full half century old, then Tindall's at the ferry. Next, Corwin's, then Uncle Sina Conklin's former humble house, so near the shore. Then White's amidst a friendly grove of cedars, then Captain Payne's, then the Point House, home of the ancient Paynes, the coolest spot of the Neck.

But now our boat is in, the gang plank out, and on the deck is a vast confusion of horses, hacks, country stages, and the horse and buggy of Charlie C., all waiting to accommodate the passengers that have just arrived to spend another pleasant visit here in Sag Harbor.

In later years the *W.W. Coit* became an excursion boat on the Potomac River and, in 1893, burned at its dock in Washington, D.C.

CAPTAIN JOHN B. PHILLIPS

Trade and commerce by sea was a method extensively used throughout the early years, with products unavailable on eastern Long Island finding their way to the Port of Sag Harbor by means of an active schooner trade. Not only were short trips made up the Hudson River and along the New England Coast, but a brisk trade was carried on with the West Indies and other southern ports as well. Sugar and molasses from Jamaica and Barbados, cocoa from Curacao, and lumber from Texas were among the products that arrived at the Long Wharf. It was a lucrative business with many local residents involved. One such young man in the business was John B. Phillips.

John Phillips was born on Bay Street, on October 7, 1867, to Nancy Filer Phillips and Captain Charles Phillips, a master of packet ships that carried freight between Long Island and Connecticut. It could be said that young John was born with a love of the sea and, at an early age, acquired work as a bayman. That was the start of his long career on the water.

John married Florence B. Field, whose father was keeper of the light at Gull Island, and in time four children were born to them: Francis, Dorothy, Elizabeth, and John L. Phillips. Captain Phillips became an associate of Hervey T. Hedges and others as owners of coasting vessels, bringing coal, ashes, gravel, and fertilizer to Long Island and returning to other ports with cargoes of wood and farm produce. In time Captain Phillips organized his own schooner company, at first owning the *H.T. Hedges*, the *Kate Scranton*, and the *Lizzie Vail Hall*. With daily experience he became a skilled navigator and earned the respect and admiration of all in the village with his expertise in handling ships. *The Sag Harbor Corrector* of June 25, 1898 gave the following account of his skill:

Captain John B. Phillips of the schooner Lizzie V. Hall on reaching this port, proved himself capable of handling a vessel under most critical and trying circumstances, being handicapped by a steam yacht and an electric craft which were anchored directly in the channel twenty yards off Long Wharf and at the new dock. The Hall is a large three masted schooner and the channel at this point very narrow. While working into his berth at the west end of the Long Wharf he had but about twenty yards room in which to work his vessel and was forced to make two tacks to gain the wharf. He was in a tight place but accomplished his task successfully and has established a reputation as a skillful and judicious skipper under most unfavorable conditions. Many flattering comments were made by spectators on the wharf who witnessed the maneuvering.

Captain Phillips commandered the *Lizzie V. Hall* for about eight years and then, in May 1904, went to Alexandria, Virginia and purchased the swift and graceful schooner *Estelle*. The 650-ton craft was comparatively new at the time, and after discharging its cargo at Boston, Phillips took over the helm. In nine and a half years the ship paid an average yearly dividend of 12 percent to its stockholders. It earned $31,500, despite a $5,000 expense when the ship went aground and had to be hauled off. The shareholders all received back their original investment at the time the *Estelle* was disposed of. The *Estelle* and his other craft, the *Carrie A. Lane*, were engaged primarily as lumber carriers, with runs between Texas and Providence.

In 1914 after an extremely rough trip from Galveston, the *Carrie A. Lane* lost about 12,000 feet of lumber from her deck, broke the stanchions on one side, and lost all her light gear to the heavy seas. Captain Phillips, however, brought his command safely to harbor. It was on that voyage the phenomenon known as St. Elmo's Fire—five balls—was seen on the spars of the schooner.

Captain John B. Phillips served his country during World War I as he ran his schooners through submarine-patrolled sea lanes carrying needed supplies. Freight was high and duty called. The *Florence B. Phillips*, last large vessel built and partially owned by the captain, was a large dividend earner, also running during the war years. None of Captain Phillips' schooners were lost, and as the war drew to a conclusion, he anticipated a drop in freight and depreciation of ship value and sold his fleet of schooners at top prices. When the *Florence B. Phillips* was sold in March 1920 for $80,000, there was over $76,000 left to divide among the owners after paying commissions. Captain Phillips commanded the *Florence B.* for two and a half years.

In 1926 Captain Phillips retired to his home on the corner of High and Bay

Street, a house which had been moved to its location from a site in the Northwest woods. When he retired, he became, with the exception of Captain James F. Davis, the only master mariner left in Sag Harbor, which years ago had numbered its navigators by the score. Phillips remained active in his retirement, being a member of the Sag Harbor Methodist Church, Wamponamon Lodge F & AM, and a dedicated member of the Sag Harbor Historical Society. He was responsible for setting up the great iron try pots and the jawbone of the whale that encompasses the front door of the Whaling and Historical Museum. Captain John B. Phillips passed away at the New York Medical Center on August 26, 1947, after a brilliant career as one of Sag Harbor's notable captains and highly respected citizens, and was laid to rest in Oakland Cemetery.

The Shelter Island

After the demise of the steamer *W.W. Coit*, a new ship was ordered to replace it. The Montauk Steamboat Company hired Harlan and Hollingsworth of Wilmington, Delaware to build a 175-foot ship. She had a 31-foot beam, 11 feet deep, and registered 618 tons. The new side-wheeler was named the *Shelter Island* by J.C. Hoagland, president of the Shelter Island Heights Association.

The *Shelter Island* had a vertical surface condensing-beam engine with 38-inch diameter of cylinder by 9 feet stroke, provided with a Stevens cut-off and properly proportioned throughout to sustain a working pressure of 10 pounds of steam, which carried her along at 18 knots per hour. Morgan's patent iron feathering paddle wheels, similar to those on the *Wyandotte*, were 20½ feet in diameter by 8 feet face, working a dozen wooden buckets.

There were 44 state rooms on the promenade deck, each one carpeted and furnished. The ship was well supplied with stationary wooden seats, lifeboats and life preservers, and was a model of beauty and splendor. The commander, Captain George C. Gibbs of Sag Harbor, was also one of the principal owners, along with his brother John C. Gibbs, George W. Hall of Brooklyn, and Robert J. Clyde of New York City.

The *Shelter Island* left from Pier 23 on the East River each Tuesday, Thursday, and Saturday evenings and arrived at Sag Harbor about seven A.M. the following morning. In 1896 the *Shelter Island* was chartered for the winter season to run between Key West and Miami. While in southern waters, the *Shelter Island* ran aground and sank, ending a 20-year passenger service for the Montauk Steamboat Company.

The Wreck of the Sloop David Porter

The following account of a dangerous venture into a storm comes from Maria Sayre in 1898, as she looked back at her childhood:

On the 19th of September 1827 the sloop David Porter left Sag Harbor for the city of New York, with a number of passengers from the former place aboard. Among them were Mr. & Mrs. Samuel L'Hommedieu, his sister Mrs. Joseph Crowell and myself, then a girl of thirteen. We were going to visit my uncle's brother Sylvester L'Hommedieu. There was also a party of merchants on board going to the city to purchase their fall goods: Asa Partridge, Benjamin and Henry Huntting, William Nelson, A. Hand and George Fordham; a young girl by the name of Esther Havens and an old colored man call "Old Brister."

It was about three o'clock in the afternoon when we left the wharf. The morning had been pleasant but at noon a south-east wind sprung up, the sky became overcast and by the time the vessel started, it was dull and misty with every appearance of a storm. The trip from Sag Harbor to New York was often a journey of three days and as there were seldom experienced cooks to be found on the sloops, it was necessary for the passengers to prepare the food at home and carry it with them.

The David Porter was a large class sloop commanded by Captain Jeff Fordham. She was loaded with whale oil; the hold and the lower deck, with the exception of a small place left vacant to reach the companion way, were filled with large casks. The vessel had gone out a short distance when the rain fell in torrents and the wind blew harder and harder. I was soon obliged to retire to a berth in the after cabin. The storm was continually increasing, the wind howled through the darkness, the vessel pitched and rolled, and we all realized that a rough night was before us.

In some means the glass in the binnacle had become broken and it was impossible for the pilot to guide the vessel correctly. Mrs. Crowell and my aunt Mrs. L'Hommedieu volunteered to take turns in holding the lantern so that he could see the compass and know in what direction he was steering. One of the ladies sat in a chair to steady it while the other stood on the top round of the back to make herself high enough to reach the compass.

My uncle came into the after cabin where I lay, still suffering from sea sickness, and carried me into the main cabin, hoping the change to where there was more air would benefit me. Thus the night passed. No one had thought of retiring but hoped that daylight would bring some relief to our fright and discomfort. But we were doomed to be disappointed and to meet with still greater danger. When daylight broke the storm was still raging and the vessel was tossed about on the waves like a shell. The men gathered together and consulted as to what was best to be done. The storm was so severe and the vessel in such a disabled condition that it seemed impossible for her to continue on her course much longer. Some suggested running the ship ashore, others objected saying that the tide was so low it would be destroyed on the rocks.

We were now at a place called Eaton's Neck, where a dangerous reef of rocks shaped like a horseshoe, with the opening toward the Sound, put out from the shore. But the majority had their way and the vessel was headed toward the land. It was fortunate enough to pass through the opening, the captain seeing the rocks on each side, as the vessel passed between them. Great excitement prevailed. Mr. Asa Partridge rushed into the cabin wringing his hands and shouting, "we are going broadside on!" The merchants brought their money to my uncle, who put it into his trousers pockets. He then tied a large silk handkerchief about his waist to keep the pocketbook from washing away.

My uncle took me, much against my will, from my berth and carried me above. The vessel was so much on her side that it was with much difficulty that he climbed up the companion way. When we reached the deck the sight that met my eyes proved a cure for my seasickness. The rain was still descending in torrents. The wind came in heavy gusts and the high waves dashed themselves against the sides of the boat. The boom was broken, the blocks swayed aimlessly back and forth with the motion of the vessel. The color of the water was a greenish-gray and it seemed to be covered with small mountains, each one having a crest of snow on top. I could not believe it was water, it seemed so high.

As the vessel moved forward her bow plunged under the water and it would be a foot deep on the lower deck. It was expected that she would founder any minute. Fearing that I would be washed overboard, my uncle carried me to the side of the vessel and standing me on a cask, tied me up in the shrouds as high as he could reach. The captain called to him advising him to take me down, for if the vessel foundered I would go down with it and there would be no possibility of my being rescued. He then fastened me slightly to one of the pumps by the side of the companion way. A pile of wood had been placed near here to be used on the vessel. As the waves dashed over the boat, the wood was washed against the passengers, who stood huddled together on the deck, bruising and injuring them. The mate, Henry Fordham, stood with an axe in his hand ready to cut away the mast. At this moment someone suggested knocking in the head of one of the casks of oil to still the waters. No sooner said than done. The waves that had been dashing over us were now changed to a smooth swell, covering us with oil, filling our eyes, and mouths, but we thought little of this. Soon after the vessel struck shore, breaking in two, the water rising in the cabin up to the two decks in a few minutes. It was planned that when the vessel reached the shore my uncle should assist the ladies, while the other men saved what baggage and freight they could.

The passengers, eager to escape, rushed to the side of the vessel nearest the shore and as the waves receded, two men jumped overboard and hastily threw a lady forward. She hurried to the beach while the men scrambled back on the boat to wait for the wave to recede again. In this way all the ladies reached the shore. Even that would not have proved a refuge save for the fact that the tide was low, for a steep bank rose perpendicularly from the beach and had the tide been high, there would have been no escape from the waters. The only habitation in sight was Eaton's Neck Lighthouse, which was possibly a half mile to the westward...

From this place it was easy to communicate with Hempstead, and my uncle hurriedly wrote a couple of notes, one to his father in Sag Harbor, and one to his brother in New York, and posted a man off on horseback to reach the coach which carried the mail through the Island, so that his friends could be informed of our safety. From here we journeyed on until we entered the village of Bedford, now a part of Brooklyn, and then to Fulton Ferry, where we left the conveyances.

The Long Island

In February 1893 the passenger steamer *Long Island*, built by Neafie & Levy of Philadelphia for the Long Island-New London Steamboat Company, made its trial run on the Delaware. Guests aboard the boat included Samuel Griffin, president of the company; vice-presidents J.B. Terry, G.C. Adams, William H. Beckwith, George Griffin; and Charles M. Griffing, captain of the *Long Island*. The boat burned pea coal, and its two 20-foot boilers, which were able to carry 130 pounds of steam, furnished the power. H. Konitzky, naval architect of the shipbuilding firm, designed the all-steel steamboat, and F. Matthews designed the engine and boilers.

The *Long Island* was 140 feet long and had a 28-foot beam; the depth of the hold, 10 feet 6 inches, with watertight compartments. Forward of the engine room, on the lower deck, was ample room for freight, and aft was a large passenger room, ladies cabin, and eating saloon. The upper deck extended the full length of the boat, with the 32-foot-long saloon located on the hurricane deck. There were accommodations for 300 passengers.

In the summer of 1893 the *Long Island* joined other steamboats carrying passengers between Sag Harbor and New London, with stops at Shelter Island Heights and Greenport. Nine hundred and sixty-six people sailed on the *Long Island* during the first six days it was in service. Two years later, the Long Island was sold at public auction, along with its freight house, coal bin, and contents, for $40,000 to a new company. It remained on the same route. In March 1901 William H. Baldwin, Jr. purchased the boat from the Montauk Steamboat Company. Three months later it was sold to the Central Railroad Company of Maine, where, after being fitted out in New London, it sailed to its new headquarters in Portland.

The Shinnecock

In 1895 another steamboat was specifically made for the Montauk Steamboat Company by Harlan & Hollingsworth of Wilmington, Delaware. The 238-foot steel sidewheeler's launching took place in March of that year, with little Edith Cook, daughter of the president of the company, christening her "Shinnecock." A special train took president Cook, secretary-treasurer George E. Fahys, and general manager French of the company, Frank Sherry of Brooklyn, and John Sherry of Sag Harbor to the scene of the launch, where they cheered as the new boat slid from its cradle into the adjoining waters.

The boat was fitted with steam-powered steering gear and windlass, and a 1700-horsepower engine. It was an elegant steamer, its interior painted white and gold, and the rooms furnished with red plush furniture and bright carpets. Ninety staterooms made it possible to carry 800 passengers with comfort. A dining room on the main saloon deck, a smoking room on the hurricane deck, and electric lights throughout made the *Shinnecock* one of the most modern and beautiful steamboats afloat.

The *Shinnecock* arrived at Sag Harbor in June of 1896 and made her first excursion trip to Block Island. The boat's regular route was the Sag Harbor to New York run, the fare, $1.50. In September 1899 the *Shinnecock* was temporarily withdrawn from the route and chartered for the Dewey Naval Parade. During 1905 the *Shinnecock*, chartered by the Joy Line, ran between New York and Providence, Rhode Island. In 1911 and 1912 she was back on the Sag Harbor route again.

234 INDUSTRY, INNOVATION, AND EXPANSION

Other Local Steamboats

The steamer *Mary Benton* - In May 1861 the *Mary Benton* arrived in Sag Harbor, and, after tying up at the Long Wharf, was visited by many of the local residents. The ship, a swift sailer, had been built expressly for the Sag Harbor-New London-Hartford, run. It was somewhat larger than the other ships in service, being about 12 feet longer than the *Island Belle*. Employed on the *Mary Benton* were Captain George W. Bates, Alvin Squires, and Mr. Vail, formerly of the *Island Belle*.

The steamer *Montauk I* - This boat was seized and sold at auction in July 1861. It burned after having landed a cargo of slaves on the coast of Cuba.

The steamer *Montauk II* - Built in Wilmington, Delaware in 1891, this sidewheeler joined other boats of the Montauk Steamboat Company. She was 175 feet long, 31 feet in breadth, and had a gross tonnage of 570 tons. She was a sister ship to the *Shelter Island*, which was lost off the Florida Keys. In 1902 the *Montauk II* was sold to the Algoma Railroad Company and the boat removed to Lake Huron, where she sailed under the British flag.

The steamer *Manhanset* - This boat was a 154-ton sidewheeler, owned by the Montauk Steamboat Company, and sailed the route between Sag Harbor and New London. She burned to the water's edge in her berth at New London in 1904. Captain Fred Youngs of Sag Harbor, who was asleep aboard the boat, escaped after awakening the rest of the crew.

The steamer *Massachusetts* - The *Massachusetts* ran between Sag Harbor and New York; Wickham Havens, captain. In June of 1862 the Navy Department chartered the boat for service in the Civil War. She later rejoined the Sag Harbor steamboat service.

The steamboat *Orient I* - In May 1862 this boat, formerly called the *Niagara*, was purchased for the New York-Sag Harbor run. Captain W.S. Havens went to Lake Ontario, where the 600-ton vessel was berthed, and brought it to Sag Harbor. The *Orient I* was 195 feet long and capable of carrying 300 passengers.

The steamboat *Orient II* - In February 1901 the new steamer *Hingham* was purchased by the Montauk Steamboat Company from the Nanta-Ket Beach Steamboat Company of Massachusetts, to run between Sag Harbor and New London. Enrolled and licensed at the Custom House, this wooden paddle-wheeler had 370-ton gross tonnage, was 142 feet long, and 25 feet wide. It was built at Chelsea, Massachusetts in 1896, and when it was brought to the village, the name of the boat was changed to the *Orient II*.

A list of schooners, steamboats, etc., along with their captains and routes, is found in the Appendix.

2
NEW INDUSTRY IN THE AGE OF DECLINE

As the whaling industry declined, it became apparent that some other means of making a living was necessary if Sag Harbor were to survive and grow. On October 25, 1847 a meeting was held at Mr. S.A. Seely's Counting Room in Washington Hall, for those interested in starting a steam cotton manufactory. "Turn out ye citizens of Sag Harbor! turn out ye mechanics, artisans and laborers, turn out ye capitalists, turn out ye farmers of East and Southampton. Come one, come all! and let the cause of Domestic Industry and Independence receive your countenance and aid," stated a notice in the local paper. Those in attendance had the opportunity to examine a report on the cost of putting such a mill into operation, as well as learning about the expense of running it and its productiveness as a stock.

Businessmen of the village and neighboring towns were assured that returns on their investments would be large, and they wasted no time in contributing money that might otherwise have been used to improve their own homes and stores.

The Steam Cotton Mill

So the mill was built at a cost of $130,000, an immense cost at that time, with work completed in 1850. The plant took up the entire block of Washington,

Church, Sage, and Division Streets. It was an impressive structure, four stories high, 250 feet long, and 55 feet wide. Its 44,000 square feet was filled with machinery set up for the manufacture of all kinds of cotton goods. A twin tower, 8 feet high, topped the building, and a 1400-pound bell that hung in it struck the hour throughout the day and night. A double flight of solid stone steps led to the main entrance.

The basement, or picker room, had walls of granite and brick, 3 feet thick, with a ceiling of iron which created a fireproof area in which to store the cotton. The engine room which adjoined the picker room held four large boilers and a 230-horsepower engine to drive the machinery.

The working machinery consisted of 48 cards, 9000 spindles, and 200 looms of three different types, which produced from 36 to 50 yards of cotton material daily. The spindles, rotating 6000 times every minute, spun out 14,000 miles of yarn every day. One hundred and seventy-five operators were employed at the cotton mill, providing jobs for local residents at a time when the economy was rapidly declining.

Not everyone, however, seemed to be happy with the new cotton mill. Some believed that Sag Harbor was not destined to become an industrial town but should remain a port with jobs related to whaling and shipping taking precedence. Some found it hard to imagine caulkers, coopers, and riggers spending their days working in a factory making cotton goods. Sag Harbor's philosopher and writer, Prentice Mulford, was one such resident who had little love for the mill, and in his own inimitable style had the following to say:

> When years ago we found the whaling business rapidly going down, and that we couldn't keep it up, we didn't know exactly what to do. We felt we must do something. When people are in this state they always do something ridiculous. So we did. We built a great cotton mill. We, the old Sag Harborites, were about as fit to conduct the manufacture of cotton goods as would be an old salt to make Geneva watches. (Watch spinning). With whaleships, tar, oakum, gurry, lances, harpoons, 30% dividends, and the 500th lay, we were thoroughly at home. So long as the whales were accommodating and lay around loose and convenient, to be killed, we flourished. Fitting out a whaleship was one thing, fitting out cotton mills quite another. We could strip an old craft from truck to keelson, put on new beams, new decks, new masts, re-sheath and copper, new yards, new sails, company ships owned by more or less caulkers, carpenters, riggers, blacksmiths and such — give them all a job, a good thing, good principle, this general distribution of labor and money — in the long run the community was more benefited than if the

INDUSTRY IN THE AGE OF DECLINE

cash had gone into the pockets of the few. So long as the whales were convenient, it paid. But cotton spinning was a more exact close-calculated business. It shaved a penny to the bare skeleton, it knew no friend and gave out no benevolent family jobs. It regarded men and women as mere machines, to be paid just enough to keep body and soul together, that they might furnish the intelligence necessary for manipulating the machinery.

How we worshipped that mill! How we watched the walls as gradually they rose from the ground. How we did fly around to the Hamptons to induce the farmers to take stock. How we argued, What benefits Sag Harbor benefits you all—sell more potatoes, eggs, garden sass. Those times are past and gone.

We saw Sag Harbor full of cotton factories—factories up to the bridge and down to the wharf, and on Sleight's Hill and Sagg Road; then long rows of factory boarding houses stretching along the beach; and crowds of cotton covered greasy operatives hurrying out at the earliest possible hour in the morning, and hurrying back to bolt their breakfasts in the shortest possible time, and ditto for dinner, and ditto, for supper, and still they work away in the close steaming atmosphere amid the glare of gas, the hum-buzz, patter and crash of cogs, pinions, all this from Monday morning to Saturday night. And we share-holders were eager and anxious that everybody's sons and daughters, SAVE OUR OWN, should leave their pianos, their embroidery, their legal, medical and theological studies and pull off their fashionable coats and roll up their fashionable sleeves and go to work from Monday morning until Saturday night, sixteen hours daily in our cotton mill.

The factory office stood behind the main building in a separate structure. Both places were heated during the winter months by steam heat conducted through pipes which ran throughout the buildings. Gas, manufactured on the premises, provided lighting. A rotary force pump, capable of throwing 1000 gallons of water per minute through a 300-foot hose, was installed to protect the cotton mill from the possibility of fire. The pump connected to a well on the grounds was fed by an inexhaustible spring of water.

Cotton goods production continued for the next seven years with little success. In 1857 Mr. C.C. Loomis, a New England manufacturer, came to Sag Harbor to take over the management of the mill. Try as he did to make the enterprise successful, it was not to be, and after ten years he was compelled to close the plant to save himself from losing everything. In a two-year period the price of cotton fabric had dropped from 27 cents a yard to 10 cents a yard.

In January 1861 employees of the mill, about 200 of them, struck for higher wages. Work resumed the following day after terms were reached.

Seven years passed, and in December 1874 Stephen Clark purchased one-half interest in the mill. Joseph Fahys and Sylvanus Lewis bought the other half, and an organization formed which made the ownership a stock company with a capital of $85,000. They re-named the place the Montauk Steam Cotton Mills. A vote passed to spend about $15,000 for new machinery, and within a short time production resumed with eight new spinning frames of the Sawyer patent and one Improved Kitson Picker. Russell Champlain of Norwich, Connecticut was employed as chief engineer.

Unfortunately, as fate would have it, Sag Harbor's cotton manufactory was not to be. On the night of October 25, 1879 a major blaze broke out, and the system devised to prevent such a calamity from happening had little effect in preventing the spread of the flames. The place was quickly engulfed, and in no time the Cotton Mill became little more than a pile of ashes.

A few months later the old iron shafting of the burned-out building was purchased by John Athens of Meriden, Connecticut. Charles Watson Payne bought up any old brick worth saving, and the rest of the rubble was spread on the upper part of Madison Street for a base under the new marl surface. The shaft and hub of the driving wheel from the ruins was removed from the site by John Homan, taken to the Long Wharf, and placed on board a vessel, the six ton of machinery having originally been brought to the village from Riverhead on a sled by Homan and Charles Thomas Smith.

Had it not been for that disastrous fire, the cotton mill may have succeeded. In any event, it did prove that manufacturing in Sag Harbor was not as impossible as some had thought, and within a year another factory would be built on the site.

The Maidstone Steam Flouring Mills

In 1862 Captain David Congdon, Hannibal French, S.B. French, and Wilson R. Cooper purchased the wharf and cooperage buildings of William R. Post at the foot of Division Street and formed the Congdon Company. Their purpose was to establish a flour mill at Sag Harbor. They bought the mill property of the Atlantic Steam Flouring and Grist Mill at Bridgehampton, and brought the milling machinery, with the exception of the steam engine, to Sag Harbor. A new 65-horsepower engine was acquired and installed in the mill.

The building was described as a fine frame structure, 80 by 34 feet and three stories high. On the grounds, James Beckwith built a brick engine and

INDUSTRY IN THE AGE OF DECLINE

boiler room and tall smokestack. The mill had five "run" of stone, with a capacity of grinding one hundred barrels of flour per day. During the years of its operation tens of thousands of bushels of wheat and other grains were brought to the village from neighboring towns to be ground. Thousands of bushels of grain were stored in bulk in the building's upper floors where feed, corn, buckwheat, graham, samp, etc. were constantly kept on hand. Its well-known brand of "Maidstone Flour" was ground from the finest Long Island amber wheat, and its "Mount Vernon Flour" from the best selected white wheat.

Following the Civil War the business continued under the firm of French, Cooper & Company. In 1874 improvements were made, the mill enlarged, and new bolts, stones, and cleaning machinery added. In February 1877 the mill was totally destroyed by fire, at a loss of $35,000.

The Hampton Flour Mill Company

To replace the Maidstone Steam Flouring Mills, a new four-story brick building was constructed on the site in 1878-79 and operated under the name Hampton Flour Mill Company. Ill feeling existed from the start, due to the fact that the mill had cost much more than first anticipated. The money that was to have been used for the mill's working capital had to be used, instead, to finish building the place, leaving no funds for its operation. The trustees, after calling a special meeting, decided to rent the mill to George Kiernan and Wilson Cooper at $1500 per year for one year, with the option of three. When mortgage payments failed to be met, the place was sold to a company consisting of H.P. Hedges, Hervey T. Hedges, and Robert J. Powers for $2000, subject to the first mortgage bonds, which made the price $10,000. It was a real bargain, as the mill initially cost $24,000.

In 1888 the Maidstone Pier took over the old mill dock, and it became the landing for the Montauk Steamboat Company's paddle-wheelers that plied between Sag Harbor and nearby cities. Several businesses leased portions of the building in the 1890s, including a tool factory, steam laundry, dial works, and a concrete-block factory. In the early 1900s the Sag Harbor Grain Company leased part of the premises. The company, incorporated under the laws of Connecticut, with a capital of $50,000, had as its directors Ernest C. Rogers, Cortland Palmer, W.J. Walden and C.W. Gildersleeve. A spur track of the Long Island Railroad ran down to the door of the building. Hay was shipped via the railroad all the way from Michigan to the Sag Harbor plant, where it was ground and sold locally.

Welz & Zerwick of the Highground Brewery of Brooklyn opened a branch depot in the old mill building in 1909, having taken over the brewery of Yetter & Moore of Sag Harbor and Riverhead. Welz & Zerwick intended to bring equipment to Sag Harbor for their operations.

In 1911 the old mill property was sold, along with its pier and bulkhead, for $30,000. At that time the East Hampton Lumber and Coal Company, the Sag Harbor Grain Company, and Welz & Zerwick occupied the premises and were assured that they wouldn't have to move. The new owner, Charles A. Carlson of Philadelphia, had plans to establish a marine engine factory in the building.

The Texas Oil Company leased part of the mill property in May 1916 and hired local carpenter George H. Cleveland to erect a building in back of the grain company to be used for their office, pump, and storage house.

In January 1920 the E.W. Bliss Company, who also had used part of the mill building for its machine shop, bought the old four-story brick building and the land on which it stood. The East Hampton Lumber and Coal Company, the Texas Oil Company, and the Sag Harbor Grain Company, all still located in the building, were told by Bliss that for the present time they would not have to relocate.

3
THE COMING OF THE RAILROAD

In 1870 ground was broken in order that the Long Island Railroad could be extended to Sag Harbor. The tracks ran through the woods from Bridgehampton, crossing Main Street at the west side of the park. From there it ran along the cove to the foot of the village and terminated in the area of the present post office.

Extending the Tracks

At the end of May 1870, with the tracks installed and the 60- by 70-foot engine house and freight house complete, the railroad was ready for business. An excursion train came to Sag Harbor, with officials of the railroad aboard, for the official opening on June 8th.

Originally, the ticket office was located in the Gardiner Building, at the corner of Main and Bay Streets, but soon after was moved into the freight house until the little wooden depot was completed. The depot was a rustic barnlike waiting room and ticket office, and served the public for forty years.

In December 1883 an accident occurred at the depot when the freight train was unable to stop, due to sleet on the tracks. It crashed into the bulkhead, tore up the platform at the north end of the building, and slid onto the sidewalk on Main Street, burying itself three feet in the sand. The platform was thrown across the sidewalk into the street, and sheer luck prevented anyone from being hurt. In May 1884 a new iron turntable was installed by J.B. Woodruff of Long Island City, making a great improvement.

The Brick Depot

Early in 1908, with the place sorely in need of repair, the matter of replacing the old depot was discussed by the Ladies Village Improvement Society. They petitioned the Long Island Railroad for a more modern station, like the ones built at Southampton, Water Mill, East Hampton, and other places in Suffolk County. Mid-October of that year the renovation began, and a new express office was built on a site to the west. As work progressed, the appearance of the building was subject to a great deal of criticism. Mrs. James H. Aldrich, who donated much time and money to help beautify Sag Harbor, claimed the building presented a squat and unattractive look. She suggested that covered platforms be attached to the depot on the south and east sides and a porte cochere built over the driveway to shelter passengers from the elements. She also suggested raising the height of the station to two stories, in order to make bathrooms and living quarters for the station master on the second floor.

After an unsuccessful effort to raise $500 from the local residents, Sag Harbor's other benefactress, Mrs. Sage, presented the village with a check of $1500, supplemented by $1000 from Mr. and Mrs. Aldrich. The Long Island Railroad president ordered the carpenters to stop work while he and other officials came to the Harbor to meet with Mrs. Sage. The conference resulted in a plan to do away with the old structure completely and build a new brick depot.

The first load of brick was carted from the brickyard on the Bulls Head Turnpike, south of Sag Harbor, to the site of the new station. A handsome sturdy building, two stories high and fireproof, was built and designated not only for the needs of the time but also with the growth and expansion of Sag Harbor in mind. The platforms and shelter that had been part of the old depot were taken to Bridgehampton to make covered platforms for their station. In September 1909 the new station was nearing completion, with the exterior work finished except for painting, and the interior well underway. At that time the tracks were extended to the end of the Long Wharf to facilitate deliveries and shipments to the Sag Harbor Grain Company.

A motor car, propelled by a 68-horsepower motor with gear shifts and built to accommodate 40 passengers, replaced the steam shuttle train in November 1927. Heated by an Arcola and operated by a motorman and conductor, the new car was affectionately called the Toonerville Trolley. Because it wasn't large enough for baggage and express, the American Express Company put one of its trucks into service between Bridgehampton and Sag Harbor. In 1929 the Long Island Railroad appealed to replace the trolley with bus service, but they were refused a franchise, and the train continued to be used until mid-May 1939.

The buildings that remained after the closing of the lines were later removed from the site. One building, moved to a lot on Spring Street, stood vacant for many years and is now a garden center.

The Pottery Works

A proposal to begin a pottery business in Sag Harbor gained interest in 1875. A November issue of *The Sag Harbor Express* reported that William Jones and Frederick Wood of New York City were interested in starting a crockery manufactory in the area.

Sag Harbor's George B. Brown, astute businessman and respected citizen, wrote a letter asking Jones and Wood to come to the village to look things over. A meeting held at the Nassau House concluded with the understanding that they would build the pottery works at Sag Harbor, providing land be given to them for the enterprise. The desired property was near the village business district, on West Water Street, and in earlier times the cooperage of Bellows and Green, and Howell's spermaceti candle factory stood on the site.

A committee consisting of Brown, S.B. French, Dr. C.S. Stillwell, G.H. Cooper, and Eleazer Latham acquired the property, and 145 local residents interested in the proposed business donated most of the needed $2200. Wood and Jones purchased a million brick, which arrived in Sag Harbor in January 1876. In addition to the existing buildings, their intention was to erect two or three more on the site. Three to four hundred jobs were to be available when the place opened for business.

Bricks, gravel, and sand arrived on the Long Island Railroad in early spring. By June the plans were put on display, showing the proposed buildings, dock, and railroad tracks. Bids opened for those interested in contracting the masonry and carpentry work, with preference given to workers from Sag Harbor and vicinity.

Samuel L. Gardiner drew up the deed and attended to other legal matters. Charles G. Douglass was hired as the boss carpenter and placed in charge of all the wooden frame buildings that were to be constructed. Edward J. Beckwith, boss mason, built a 50-foot chimney for the kiln which stood on a 3½-foot-thick foundation of firebrick. Progress was extremely slow, and work dragged on for several years. Much of the delay seemed to have resulted from the lack of experienced and licensed workers.

244   INDUSTRY, INNOVATION, AND EXPANSION

December 1880 brought the arrival of the main engine from New London, Connecticut and the potter's machinery from Trenton, New Jersey. By that time the masonry and carpentry work were near completion. The following June, mortgage bonds were issued to the amount of $12,000 for the purpose of raising monies to provide working capital and to attend to some last-minute details.

Captain P.C. Petrie purchased the entire interest of Frederick Wood and officially named the place the Eastern Long Island Pottery Works. He informed the public that they were ready to open, and the prospect of employment for many of Sag Harbor's unemployed was finally within reach.

However, misfortune, which was no stranger in the early days, struck again, and before the scheduled opening day, an arsonist set fire to the building. The August 1881 blaze, which started in three separate places, totally consumed all the wooden structures, with insurance only partially covering the $6000 loss. A $250 reward was offered for the detection and conviction of the person responsible; however, no arrests were ever made. Although there was talk of rebuilding, it never materialized and the Eastern Long Island Pottery Works was a complete disaster before it ever got started.

The Years of Brickmaking

Brickmaking was an industry that emerged from time to time in the early years of Sag Harbor's growth. The availability of sand and clay pits in the area made it unnecessary for the brickmaker to import his raw materials. There was always a ready market for the finished product, for the cost of locally made brick was a good deal less than that of imported brick.

Stephen Howell was the first known brickmaker in Sag Harbor. The site of his brickyard is uncertain, but in 1806 he placed an advertisement in the *Suffolk Gazette* to inform the public that he had locally made brick for sale. By 1823 H.B. Havens and James Parker had opened another establishment about a mile from the village and near the Cove. Captain Parker became the next owner of the brickyard, being in business between 1845 and 1850. As far as can be determined, for the next 30 years there was no brick being manufactured in Sag Harbor.

In 1885 William T. Graham, an experienced brickmaker from Southold, Long Island, came to Sag Harbor and leased the old Stanbrough place at Northside where some of the finest clay beds were found. They covered 20 acres and in some places were 32 feet deep. At the time of this new venture, brick was very expensive, owing to the cost of having it shipped to the area. Graham, who expected to begin production within three months after settling here, planned to sell his product at $6 to $7 per thousand.

He could see only one problem, and that concerned the bridge that connected North Haven and Sag Harbor. The draw in the old bridge had been closed for many years, and opening it would permit vessels to go through the Narrows to the old Scott Edwards farm where a landing could be built, cutting a mile off the shipping route.

The first year the new brickyard produced brick of inferior quality, one bake after another failing, but during the second year a much higher quality product was manufactured.

In 1891 the Sag Harbor Brick Company was established, with the yard located on the Sag Harbor-Bridgehampton Turnpike, about two miles south of the village. Officers elected were: C.A. Pierson, president; J.M. Hildreth, vice-president; and Charles Watson Payne, treasurer. The engines and boilers arrived on location, and work assembling the machinery began. The engine was first class, a Twin Patent 85-horsepower, and the two boilers were 60-horsepower each. A New Haven Brick Machine, which was the heaviest and strongest one made, and a Pott's Disintegrator and a sander were shipped from Indianapolis via the railroad and arrived at the Bridgehampton station. Julius C. Smith was in charge of assembling the machinery and building the new structures.

CHARLES WATSON PAYNE III, MERCHANT

Charles Watson Payne was the third member of the Payne family to bear that name. His father, Charles Watson II, noted whaling captain, lost his life at sea while in command of the whaleship *Fanny*. He was 30 years old when the tragedy occurred in the South Atlantic. Married five years, he left a wife, Maria, and two children, Maria and Charles Watson III. Charles Watson Payne I, an early settler in this area, owned and operated a farm on North Haven, as well as being a merchant in Sag Harbor. Charles III followed in his grandfather's footsteps.

Charles Watson Payne III was born at the family farm on North Haven, February 10, 1835. As a child he received his education at the local schools and graduated from the Sag Harbor Academy on Suffolk Street. In his late teens he left for New York City and found employment in the grocery store of E.R. Durkey & Company. After learning the business, he became manager of a wholesale outfit. At the age of 25 he returned to Sag Harbor and entered the grocery business with John Sherry, establishing the firm of Sherry & Payne. In addition to the grocery business, in which he was involved for over 40 years, he operated a coal yard and was instrumental in reviving the brickmaking

246 INDUSTRY, INNOVATION, AND EXPANSION

industry in Sag Harbor in 1891.

Along with his business ventures, Charles Watson Payne III was deeply involved in village affairs. He was a trustee for 23 years, acting President of the Board for much of that time. He served as secretary of the Sag Harbor Historical Society, president of the Board of Trustees of Oakland Cemetery, Chairman of the Business Aid Committee, and was a member of the Presbyterian Church. Very little took place in the village that Charles Watson Payne III wasn't involved in.

Charles Watson Payne III passed away on April 30, 1916 at the age of 81, after a lifetime of community service. He is buried in Oakland Cemetery.

The brickyard opened in August 1891, and within two months had fired one million brick. A giant kiln on the property held 400,000 brick. Connections with the Long Island Railroad were made, and a track leading to the brick plant anticipated easy shipping to all parts of the Island.

With production at an all time high, it is hard to speculate just what happened at the turn of the century, but the brickyard seemed to find itself in financial trouble, and in 1902 the place was sold to satisfy a $600 mortgage held by George Kiernan. The new owners, ex-Governor Thomas M. Waller of Connecticut and Arthur Griffin of Sag Harbor, also purchased the Fisher's Island Brickyard and planned to consolidate, calling the yard the Fisher's Island and Long Island Brick Company. In 1908 Charles Horn of Sag Harbor was put in charge of operations at the Sag Harbor plant, and business again flourished. This brickyard supplied all the brick for the construction of both Pierson High School and the new railroad depot building.

Fahys Watch Case Factory and Alvin Silver Works

The year was 1880 and the village was again trying to pick up the pieces after losing the Cotton Mill, its main means of employment. It was at this time the Business Aid Committee held a meeting to investigate the possibility of persuading Joseph Fahys to relocate his watchcase factory from Carlstadt, New Jersey to Sag Harbor. Fahys was interested in the idea and an agreement was reached. A new industry was about to come to the village.

Even the New York City newspapers carried the story of the move. *The New York Times* reported that Sag Harbor had been selected as the site for a large silver watchcase factory which would give employment to about 400 persons. Plans furnished by John A. Wood of New York City called for two main buildings 200 feet in length, three stories high, and connected by a 100-foot structure. Five separate buildings, each one story high, would be constructed to house a blacksmith shop, boiler and engine rooms, and rooms for annealing and melting the silver. They would be constructed of brick with granite trim, have stone floors and roofs of iron, making them absolutely fireproof. Steam would be used for heating the place and gas for lighting, which would be manufactured on the premises. A vault, 10 by 13 feet and made of 1½-feet-thick granite blocks, would be installed in the main building, and a high fence would surround the entire property.

Eleazer Latham, real estate agent, sold to Joseph Fahys the very desirable piece of land on the corner of Division and Sage Streets, formerly the residence of Abraham H. Gardiner, to be used as part of the watchcase factory complex. It was reported at that time that a large boarding house would be built on the site. Two contractors came to Sag Harbor in February 1881 to look over the grounds and make preparations for laying out the factory and arranging for living quarters for the workers.

In March 1881 the first load of brick arrived in the village from the Fisher's Island Brick Works, and soon construction began. Long and Barnes of Brooklyn was awarded the contract, with masonry work under the supervision of P.J. Carlin, also of Brooklyn. Mr. Carlin was assisted by several local masons. With the foundation completed in April, the cornerstone laying took place the 21st of that month. A platform was erected on Church Street near the northwest corner, and seats placed on it for the public's attendance. Stephen Clarke, a representative of Mr. Fahys, installed the stone.

In June 1881 the heavy stone vault, weighing 6 to 7 tons, arrived at the Long Wharf and after an arduous three-day journey, reached the factory yard. The same month the boiler arrived at the Bridgehampton railroad station, and Charles Henry Topping supervised the day-and-a-half trip to the factory. By August 1881 the place was nearing completion, the interior painting done by Hill and Strong. Robert Brockleheart installed a 2100-pound iron cap on the chimney, having hoisted it to the top in four sections. Machinery arrived in November and, after being set in place, was tested in preparation for the factory's opening day. In the meantime, the brick office of the old cotton mill was removed, giving the new factory a better front appearance. Many of the bricks from the demolished structure were used to build the foundations of homes under construction on Division Street.

With the arrival of the new year 1882, came the first workers, men whom Fahys had brought from his Carlstadt factory. The melting of silver began and Fahys Watch Case Factory was in business. By the end of the year, the work force had increased to 350 employees, with a weekly payroll of $3100.

248   INDUSTRY, INNOVATION, AND EXPANSION

After eight successful and productive years, the company expanded its facilities by purchasing a piece of property on the east side of Main Street in the business district, constructing a magnificent three-story brick building. Architects Carrere and Hastings of Bowling Green, New York City designed what was to be a masterpiece of architectural beauty. It was 80 by 50 feet and contained more than 300,000 bricks. Boss builder William A. Bassenden designed the front cornices and ornaments of fancy brickwork and terra-cotta. It was called the Central Building or the Alvin Building, and became a prominent place of business in the village for the next 35 years.

The Post Office occupied the south side of the building on the first floor, and the new Peconic Bank, the second. Both moved into their new quarters in the spring of 1890. On the north side of the building's ground floor was the Central Store, and on the second floor, the library and seven spacious offices. The third floor held an amusement hall and rooms for the janitor to live in. The vestibule on Main Street furnished an entrance to the bank, store, and to the stairs leading to the second floor. The entrance to the amusement hall was on Church Street, at the rear of the building. Offices on the second floor were occupied by the Sag Harbor Water Company, Meyerson's Ice Cream Parlor, and the law offices of Vermilye and Fanning, and, at one time, the United States Custom Office.

In 1911 the Alvin Silver Works, which until that time had been located in the factory, moved its main shipping office from New York into the Central Building, along with an office staff of 50 employees. Gradually, over the next few years, the businesses located in the building were forced to find new quarters, as the Alvin Company took over the entire place.

The upper floors of the building were remodeled into rooms to house the workers. Later, homes were built to accommodate those who brought their families with them to settle in Sag Harbor. Fifty houses with a monthly rent of $10 to $16 were needed, and the tenants in the Sag Harbor Real Estate Company grounds were informed they had to move out in order to fill the increased demand for housing. It was feared that the growth of Sag Harbor would come to a standstill if apartments weren't available for the relocating workers.

The Alvin Manufacturing Company comprised a solid part of the Fahys Watch Case Factory, carrying the name of Sag Harbor the length and breadth of the United States. Undoubtedly, the most novel and artistic work turned out by the company was known as electro-deposit goods. It met with great commercial success, being applied to decanters, perfume bottles, carafes, flasks, and other articles of crystal glass. A coating of silver was deposited on the glass surface by electric current, encasing the entire article with a coating of fine

THE COMING OF THE RAILROAD

silver. Skillful artists then traced intricate designs on the silver surface. The designs were of a continuous character, and the intervening spaces were, by another process, cut away to expose the crystal surface in the crevices of the design. The piece was then given to an engraver who finished the pattern by engraving scrolls, floral designs, etc., after which the surface was highly polished, producing a most beautiful piece of silverware.

The Alvin Company also turned out another line of products known as hollow ware, which consisted of tea sets, fruit dishes, sugar and creamers, and a complete line of flat and fancy tableware. A contract for 10,000 souvenir spoons for the Atlantic Cotton Exposition was awarded to the Alvin Company, with theirs the official and only spoon sold at the Exposition. A yachting award for the Harvard-Yale yachting race at New London in the early 1900s was designed and manufactured at the Alvin works.

In 1898 the Alvin Silver Company, along with nine other companies, including Tiffany's, vied to make a solid silver service for the new cruise ship *Brooklyn*. The Alvin Company had the prestigeous honor of being selected. The contract called for a 340-piece set which consisted of two candelabra, 22 inches high by 18 inches across and holding seven candles; a soup tureen bearing the likeness of the old frigate *Brooklyn*, with the new cruiser on the ends, and the seal of Brooklyn and the seal of New York State on the sides. Also included in the service were spoons, forks, knives, plates, a carving set, gravy boats, vegetable dishes, and other assorted pieces. The entire set called for 2350 ounces of silver. In 1936 the $10,000 silver service, which had been in storage, was presented to a new vessel also call the *Brooklyn*. Another unique item manufactured by the Alvin Company in 1896 was a silver mounting for bicycles which sold for $400.

Alvin's successful business continued in the village for 35 years, and then on New Year's morning January 1, 1925, a disastrous blaze put a sudden end to the silver company. The interior of the spectacular Alvin building was completely gutted by the fire. For many years the facade remained standing, a mute reminder of the profitable days when the Alvin Silver Works played such an important part in the industrial growth of Sag Harbor. (A detailed account of the fire can be found in Part VI, Chapter 6.)

The Fahys Watch Case Factory continued to grow, and in February 1911 a four-story wing was added to the part that extended out to Church Street, facing Washington, and separated from the turning department by a 30-foot air shaft. It was built to be used by the office force of the Alvin Company when they moved their wholesale rooms and clerical department to Sag Harbor from New York City. Survey for the addition was made by Sag Harbor's

Ivan C. Byram.
In February 1920 structural work began for the fourth story of the watchcase factory. To keep the newly poured concrete from freezing, peat fires were built on the site. When completed, the structure occupied most of the Division, Washington, Church, and Sage Street block.

WILLIAM WALLACE TOOKER, ALGONQUINIST AND PHARMACIST

Another of Sag Harbor's noted residents was Algonquinist William Wallace Tooker. By profession Tooker was a pharmacist, but his real love was the study of the local Indians and their language. William Wallace Tooker was born in Sag Harbor on January 14, 1848, the eldest of five children of William Henry Tooker of Old Lyme, Connecticut and Virginia Fordham of Sag Harbor. One of his great-grandfathers was David Frothingham, publisher of *The Long Island Herald*, first newspaper on Long Island and printed in Sag Harbor.

As a youth, Tooker spent much of his free time searching local sites for artifacts to add to his growing collection. The early aboriginal camp along the shore of Sag Harbor became one of his favorite spots. The local Indians belonged to the Algonquin tribe, and in the mid 1800s there were still a few living in the area. Tooker became well acquainted with "King" David Pharaoh of the Montauks and with members of the Cuffee and Bunn families.

William Wallace Tooker received his education at private schools and in 1865 attended the Sag Harbor Academy on Suffolk Street to prepare for Yale University. However, the destruction of the Academy by fire and the illness of his father disrupted his plans. Tooker spent the next year working in the family store, while his nights were filled studying old deeds, maps, and town records and familiarizing himself with all aspects of local history.

On January 15, 1866 Tooker entered the drug business of William Buck as an apprentice pharmacist, and after learning the business, became Buck's partner. On May 21, 1872 he married Lilla Byram Cartwright of Shelter Island. Three years later he became sole owner of the pharmacy and remained in business until illness forced his retirement in 1897.

Throughout the years Tooker spent his spare time studying and writing about the Indians. By 1895 his collection had grown to more than 15,000 specimens of pre-history relics, and his writings included 11 books and more than 50 pamphlets.

In 1887 the editor of *The Brooklyn Eagle Almanac* wrote to Harvard Professor N.S. Hosford, asking him to prepare a list of Long Island Indian place-names and their meanings. Professor Hosford, unable to spend the time on such an extensive project, recommended William Wallace Tooker as the man most qualified for the job. The *Almanac* started publishing the Indian place-names in 1888, and they became such a popular item they continued to print the lists in subsequent editions. In 1911 the John Jermain Memorial Library arranged with G.P. Putnam's Sons, prominent New York publishers, to publish the whole collection of names in a book called *Indian Place-Names on Long Island.* The book has become the most definitive work of its kind known.

Tooker often lectured on the Algonquins at the Brooklyn Institute of Arts and Science Department of Archaeology, the American Association for the Advancement of Science at Brooklyn, the Rhode Island Historical Society, and the Suffolk County Historical Society. In 1891 Francis P. Harper published his *Algonquin Series* consisting of ten volumes on the Algonquin Indians.

After his retirement, William Wallace Tooker opened an office in Sag Harbor from which he sold real estate and insurance. In his later years he was elected Police Justice for a four-year term starting March 1902.

For many years Tooker's artifacts were on display at his pharmacy on Main Street, until financial difficulties forced him to sell the entire collection to the Brooklyn Museum. William Wallace Tooker, in ill health, lingered on for seven years after his books were published, and on August 2, 1917 he passed away. Today the collection of William Wallace Tooker's books on archaeology, etymology, anthropology and ethnology can be found at the John Jermain Memorial Library, a lasting tribute to one of Sag Harbor's most fascinating and gifted early citizens.

Paving the Village Streets

Prior to 1898 the village streets were dirt, and few improvements had been made throughout the years. In March 1898 work began on Main Street with hopes of putting the road in better shape by plowing out both sides and building up the center of the street. At the same time, a bicycle path was made on the east side of the street. The sidewalk was widened and the curbing moved. Where there was no curbing, the road was lined with 2-inch hemlock planking. Nearly 7000 running feet was used.

In May of that same year a committee formed to discuss upgrading the deplorable conditions that existed. It was voted to buy gravel and spread it on the roads near the business district. Several local men volunteered to work on the project, each putting in two days' work. They were: William Schommer,

252 INDUSTRY, INNOVATION, AND EXPANSION

William Quail, Charles, Edward and Thomas Shaw, John Bloomingburg, Charles King, James McMahon, George Hildreth, William Stafford and Ivan Byram. In June 1898 the first cargo of Peekskill gravel arrived on the steamer *Lizzie V. Hall*, from Tompkins Cove opposite Peekskill, New York. The first roads to be surfaced with the gravel were Main Street to the junction of Main and Madison, from there up both Main and Madison to Union Street, and then Church and Sage Streets. Conditions improved considerably, although more gravel had to be added from time to time to fill in ruts that had formed. It wasn't until June 1914 that the village streets were covered with a surface of oil and 60 percent asphalt, finally ending the dusty conditions that had prevailed even after the gravel had been spread.

In the early 1900s New York State owned the highway that ran from East Hampton to the Sag Harbor Village boundary. In September 1913 plans were underway to extend the highway through the village via Hampton Street as far as the North Haven bridge, where, after crossing, it would pick up the State road leading to the South Ferry. Engineers McVey and Tuthill of the State Highway Department surveyed for the two-mile stretch, which also included straightening out the abrupt turn at the junction of Bay and Wharf Streets. Eight teams of mules, wagons, a large steam roller, concrete mixer, and sprinkler arrived in town in September, with work to begin as soon as it was approved at Albany. H.J. Muller, Contractors, of Jamaica, submitted the lowest of the ten bids received, $18,856. John T. Ehleider, State Engineer, was in charge of the project. The connecting link was completed in November 1914.

The permanent concrete paving of the entire length of Main Street was done in 1922 at a cost of $50,000 following a vote of the taxpayers, 255 to 96 in favor of the new surfacing. One hundred and nine women's votes were included in the decision. Sag Harbor had come a long way.

A business directory of 1888-89 can be found in the Appendix.

4
THE END OF THE ERA

John Emmel, proprietor of the Emmel Bottling Works, had what was probably the most successful bottling company in Sag Harbor. Established in 1891, Emmel bottled beer, ale, and soft drinks at his plant on the corner of Division and Burke Streets.

The Bottling Works

In February 1899, with his business expanding, ground was broken for a larger, more modern plant. The new building, which stood on the same property, was built by a Sag Harbor carpenter, George Cleveland. It was a two-story wooden structure, 72 by 24 feet in size, and fronted on Division Street. A stable was built at the rear of the place, with its access from Burke Street.

During the years between 1905 and 1909, when the local law prevented the renewal of liquor licenses, Emmel, along with other Sag Harbor bottlers, dealers and, saloon-keepers, was forced to bottle and sell soft drinks only — or go out of business. Emmel survived the dry years and prospered, manufacturing soda and ginger ale. In 1910 a new four-cylinder 35-horsepower Abresch motor truck was added to the business, in which Harold Emmel and Roy Dippel made deliveries.

254 INDUSTRY, INNOVATION, AND EXPANSION

In 1917 Fred W. Wilson took over the bottling works re-naming it Wilson's Bottling Company. He advertised that his plant had the most sanitary works on Long Island, with the latest automatic bottling equipment on the market. The syrup room was all white enamel, with glass-lined syrup jars and tin pipes to run the syrup through to the bottling machines. A Meyer Dumore soaker insured a 100 percent sterile bottle. Pure artesian spring water taken from a depth of 75 feet and filtered three times was used. Wilson's plant had a capacity of 24,000 bottles per day.

Wilson's Ginger Ale, Whistle, and Cherry Blossoms were the principle soft drinks bottled, and in 1920 Wilson called the place the Whistle Bottling Company. A branch distributing station opened at Bayport, Long Island, with Francis Scheider of Bridgehampton connected with that part of the business. The Wilson Bottling Company continued to manufacture Whistle until about 1930.

Others tried their hand at the bottling business in Sag Harbor, but with less success. William Schommer established a bottling works in 1892 and stayed until 1902 when he moved from the area. John Lellmann & Company bottled soda and beer at his establishment on the corner of Main and Bay Streets from 1891 to 1897. Lellmann had come from Greenport, Long Island, where he had been in the same business. Thomas W. Boyle, of Washington Street, bottled beer and liquor from 1895 to 1897, with William S. Wilson managing the place.

In addition to the bottling works in the village, a distribution center for Welz and Zerwick was located in the old flour mill building at the foot of Division Street. Prior to Welz & Zerwick, Yetter & Moore of Riverhead had a branch depot at the site. The Welz & Zerwick Company of Highground Brewery of Brooklyn came to Sag Harbor in 1909 and remained at the mill location for about two years.

Bailey's Cut Tool Company

In the spring of 1892, Mr. Bailey of Southington, Connecticut showed an interest in starting a cut tool factory at Sag Harbor. He met with village officials and proposed to subscribe $1000 and run the business for three years, taking no profit until the 8 percent per annum was paid to the stockholders. Bailey was notified that his offer was acceptable. Additional capital of $17,000 had to be raised, and the enthusiasm was so great that within two weeks half of the money had been collected. By-laws were adopted and officers elected: George C. Gibbs, president; George C. Raymond, vice-president; George Kiernan, secretary and treasurer; and C.A. Pierson, J.M. Hildreth, B. Lyon and Charles Watson Payne, directors. The first floor of the old mill property was rented for five years at $500 per year.

For the first four years the tool company grew and prospered. An order for 700 dozen chisels from a Philadelphia company was filled. The company prided itself on being the only tool factory that stayed in operation during the hard times of 1895. Unfortunately, this situation was not to last, for in July 1896 the factory closed its doors and remained shut until May 1897 when Superintendent Bailey bought all the stock of the company and completed manufacturing the tools that had been left unfinished when the plant closed.

The Montauk Steam Laundry

The Montauk Steam Laundry occupied the basement of the flour mill property. Harry Stevenson and George Gaffga installed the highest quality machinery and created employment for many practical and experienced operators. In 1893, a year after the laundry opened, they moved to the front part of the Lellman & Company Bottling Works, due to the inability to get enough power to operate their equipment at the old mill site. At the Lellman property power was furnished by the powerful engine of the bottling works. In July 1894 the plant was rented, with option to buy, to W.H. Baker of Greenport, who informed the public that he would continue the laundry and would open for business in August of that year.

The Sag Harbor Water Works

In the year 1889 sections of the village were hooked up to "city water." A system of pipes laid throughout the streets made it possible for homes and places of business in the village to have running water. Before this time individual wells and hand pumps provided the water supply for each family. Long Pond, which was spring fed, was the source of water for the new company. The Southampton Town Trustees recorded that a privilege was granted to the Sag Harbor Water company to use part of the water flowing from Long Pond through Ligonee Brook to the Cove, provided that sufficient depth of water be left for the passage of fish through the brook from the 15th day of February to the 15th day of April. The water flowed down a dreen, or man-made ditch, to the waterworks plant in the woods near Fore 'n' After Pond. There it was purified and piped to the water tank on the northwest corner of Suffolk Street and Jermain Avenue for storage.

The lot on which the water tank stood had been purchased in March 1889 for $200, and by June the 90-foot stack had been completed. The plant consisted of a brick structure in which a boiler, furnace, and filtering devices were installed. The October 12, 1895 *Corrector* reported that all the water was drained out of the tall tank for the first time since it was built, so it could be given a good cleaning.

The contract for installing the pipes through the village called for 20,000 feet of pipe to be laid and four wells to be built. Pipes and fixtures in individual's homes and businesses were left to local plumbers; a $3-charge to connect, $8 for the first faucet, and $1 for each additional faucet. George Merritt (son of Berlin T. Merritt), engineer of the steamer *Shelter Island*, ran the engines at the water works, and by the end of 1889 city water was available to many residents in Sag Harbor.

In June 1893 the Sag Harbor Water Works Company re-organized, and a controlling interest passed into the hands of Henry F. Cook by purchase from Dr. C.N. Hoagland. Cook bought the $40,000 in company bonds, with an accrued interest at par, and paid an additional sum which carried the controlling interest in the stock. Cook was elected president and George H. Fahys, treasurer.

The water mains were extended to North Haven in the 1890s. In 1910 several 500-foot-deep artesian wells were driven and a huge tank was placed at the Cook's home on North Haven by McMahon and Stafford, as an emergency reservoir.

When the water company built a new power house on its property south of Jermain Avenue, Ivan Byram laid the foundation. The structure, which measured 20 by 20 feet, was constructed of brick and iron. Two large powerful pumps driven by electric motors automatically controlled the operation and were supplied by the Worthington Pump and Machinery Corporation. The electric motors were purchased from General Electric Corporation. Workers from the Fahys factory installed the pumps, under the direction of the firm furnishing them. A chlorine sterilization process to purify the water was tested at the plant each week to keep the chlorine content stable. The new water station was completed in March 1924.

Thirteen years later (1937) another improvement took place with the construction of a purification plant to free the village from a high content of iron in the water, and which the ladies of the village referred to as "red water." Another building was erected at the existing waterworks to house the new turbine pump and aerator. The process used the existing pumps to force the treated water through sand filters and into the distribution system. John B. Ogden, chief engineer, informed the public that the place would be ready to begin operations in the fall. Ceremonies were held in November 1937, with school children, local dignitaries, and the general public all attending and being treated to a tour of the facility.

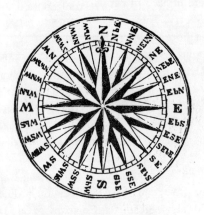

5

SAG HARBOR IN THE SPANISH-AMERICAN WAR

It was during the Spanish-American War that the citizens of Sag Harbor held a public meeting in September 1898 and resolved to do what they could to alleviate the suffering among the soldiers at Camp Wykoff in Montauk. The Government had leased 5000 acres of the railroad land until May 31, 1899, for $15,000, for an R and R camp. It was remote enough from the populated areas for an effective guarantee against the spread of yellow fever and malaria, but because the quarantine regulations were not strictly enforced, 257 of the 21,000 soldiers who passed through Camp Wykoff died. Money poured in freely, and more than $1000 was raised by the people of Sag Harbor. Items needed for the convalescing (those no longer in need of hospitalization but not yet well enough to return to battle) were taken to Montauk by the Montauk Steamboat Company free of charge. Four tons of goods were distributed.

As beneficial as this project was, people were needed at Montauk to do the distributing, and it was determined that a better plan would be to bring the convalescing to Sag Harbor, where they could be cared for by the residents of the village under special care of a delegate from the Red Cross. Henry F. Cook, president of the steamboat company, offered the Cook residence on Main Street as a soldiers' rest home. Within a few days enough cots to accommodate 20 men were placed in the house. When the train arrived from Montauk, 15 soldiers who were in need of care arrived at Sag Harbor, accompanied by John and Frank S. Sherry. They were all from the 3rd Regular Infantry, whose headquarters was at Fort Snelling, Minnesota.

Generous responses were made by the local residents in the form of clothing, nutritional food, medicine, and money with which to buy needed personal items. Mrs. Joseph Fahys was in charge of collecting the money. Volunteer physicians Dr. J. Richard Taylor and Dr. Robert Swan of Sag Harbor were assisted by Dr. Wells and Dr. Morton of New York, Dr. Edmund H. Cook of Flushing, and Dr. Charles Napier of Brooklyn, all summer residents of Sag Harbor.

At nearby Gardiner's Island Point, stone abutments were built, behind which guns were placed for protection of the entrance to Gardiner's Bay. The steamer *Shinnecock*, of the Montauk Steamboat Company of Sag Harbor, was chartered by the United States Government to transport soldiers from Camp Wykoff to New York City. Twenty-five hundred men were taken there during a 15-day period, and the *Shinnecock* was paid $1000 for each day it was used.

In April 1898 the students of the Union School took part in a school project in which they collected large quantities of clothing, vegetables, and other groceries for the suffering people of Cuba. From the deposit center at Lyon & Sherwood's store, all of the items were shipped to Havana. It was one small way that the young people of Sag Harbor were able to help.

The men and boys of the village were given a rare treat in August 1898, when 25 to 30 of Teddy Roosevelt's Rough Riders came to town and spent the day riding throughout the streets and relating incidents of the war to interested spectators.

By mid-October only five convalescents remained at the Soldiers' Rest. All men were required to rejoin their regiments by October 20. The government, at that time, released the citizens of Sag Harbor from caring for the sick. Fifty-four men had regained their health and strength in that temporary home and left with a feeling of deep gratitude to the people of Sag Harbor. Although the Soldiers' Rest was in existence for less than two months, it was Sag Harbor's small way of doing its part in the Spanish-American War.

Local men who served in the war were: George Cook, who enlisted as a private and fought throughout the conflict and was honorably discharged at the end of hostilities. Gunner Leonard Kuhlwein served aboard the ship *Olympia*; and George B. Zeis, aboard the *Baltimore*. They took part in the naval engagement at Manila. Eugene Smith French lost his life on the field of battle at Caloocan, Philippine Islands, February 23, 1899. Henry E. Curry served

THE SPANISH-AMERICAN WAR 259

as a sergeant in Company D, 47th New York Volunteers.

On the local front, the Sag Harbor Home Guard was organized with two companies of men. Those involved were: Carl Christman, William M. Cook, William Ellwood, William C. Greene, William G. Howard, Francis H. Palmer, A.E. Pickard, John L. Sherwood, C.S. Stillwell, John Tabor, and Reverend Clarence H. Wilson, all members of Company A. Company B was made up of Richard T. Aldred, Reverend Joseph Baird, William Blaiklock, Theodore Beigh, George Horle, Howell Leavitt, George C. Morris, William R. Reimann, Benjamin A. Sawyer, George Sprague, William Wessel, and A.M. Youngs.

Part Six

AN AMERICAN BEAUTY IN THE TWENTIETH CENTURY

1900–1940

1

ALONG THE WATERFRONT

The twentieth century brought about a new look along the waterfront. The long talked-about breakwater had finally been completed, the E.W. Bliss Company and their torpedo testing operation continued in full swing, the Yacht Club opened their new clubhouse, and the spacious Gardiner House overlooking the water found itself filled with tourists during the summer months. On the Long Wharf tracks had been extended to the end of the dock to facilitate the loading and discharging of coal and other products. Gone were the tall masts, the cooper shops, ships' chandleries, and other stores along the wharf. In their place, steam-powered passenger ships, which plied between Sag Harbor and other ports, tied up to the dock and used Sag Harbor as their home port and winter quarters.

At a meeting of the Sag Harbor Round Table Club on March 28, 1928 at the Hotel Bay View, members went on record as favoring the village's purchase of the Long Wharf and the Maidstone Pier from the Long Island Railroad and the Bliss Company. But due to the price asked, the project was soon abandoned. In May 1934, still interested in gaining ownership, the Round Table Club tried to persuade the Town Boards of East Hampton and Southampton to purchase and repair the wharf. Both rejected the plan. The village trustees then leased the Long Wharf from the Long Island Railroad for one year, and then renewed the lease in 1935 and 1936.

THE TWENTIETH CENTURY

The Breakwater

In 1829 four government engineers had come to town to survey the harbor as a preliminary measure to the construction of a breakwater and to deepen the channel through which vessels entered and left the port. It was hoped that the next session of Congress would appropriate funds for the project. Unfortunately, it wasn't to be, and 73 years would pass before the project finally got underway.

In 1902 the Businessmen's Association of Sag Harbor, represented by George Kiernan, took up the matter with Congressman Frederick Storm and W.H. Baldwin Jr. of the Long Island Railroad. For years the breakwater issue figured prominently in every First Congressional District campaign, and year after year representatives pledged themselves to do what they could to get necessary money for the work. But it wasn't until Frank C. Havens, wealthy summer resident, volunteered his services that things got started. Familiar with the methods of legislation at that time, Havens made a trip to Washington, D.C., where he appealed to the state senators for help. The needed appropriations were finally granted and the project adopted on June 13, 1902. It called for the construction of a 3180-foot-long sea wall to be built from Conklin's Point, northnorthwest, in water varying from four to ten feet deep at the high tide. Its estimated cost was $71,000.

The first appropriation was received in 1902 and the work began. Contractor Belding of Hartford, Connecticut, in charge of construction, built the first section of Connecticut granite. Work continued until the funds were exhausted, leaving the breakwater in a state of incompletion until more funds became available.

The second appropriation was granted in 1905 and work resumed. Barges of rock arrived. Heavy boulders were loaded from barges onto a shallow float, taken to the site, and placed in position. The work was slow, as it could be done only four hours out of 24, when the tide was at its highest. Nine thousand tons of heavy stone were used, most of it coming from Manhattan, where subway contractors placed the bedrock on the waterfront docks and offered it free for the taking. In the spring of 1906, a party of surveyors from the New York Branch Engineers Office of the War Department arrived to inspect the unfinished breakwater and take their report to the next River and Harbor Bill meeting. At that meeting they recommended dredging the channel and deepening the basin area.

The last appropriation was received in April 1908 and the breakwater finally completed. Its total cost was $61,946. It was a long wait from that first survey in 1829, but it was finally realized, and for many years has satisfactorily protected the wharf and harbor from the severe northeast storms that frequent the area.

The Frank Havens Mansion (Cor Maria)

On Bay Street, along the waterfront, stands the elegant estate known as Cor Maria. It was originally built in 1904-1905 by Frank Havens of Piedmont, California, as his "summer cottage." The wealthy summer residents of Sag Harbor and North Haven built huge homes on their waterfront property, each one more elegant than his neighbor's, and the Havens palatial residence was one of the most spectacular.

James McMahon and William Stafford, both of Sag Harbor, excavated the lot in October 1904 for the foundation, which was made with cement blocks manufactured at the Sag Harbor Building Block Company, located a few hundred feet west of the Havens property. Cement blocks, which had recently taken precedence over brick and fieldstone, were the latest thing in home construction. Plans for the house were drawn up by architect Leicht, of New York City, and called for a three-story wooden frame structure with attic and tower. Wide and spacious verandas surrounded the house, and a magnificently proportioned porte cochere covered the driveway on the south side.

The interior was finished in hardwood. The hall and grand stairway ascending to the attic received light through a large stained-glass window. Bathrooms were installed on each floor, and hot and cold water faucets supplied porcelain basins in each bedroom. The reception room had an ensconced fireplace and basket window embrasure. All windows were of French plate glass, and one great window, measuring 7 by 14 feet, afforded a spectacular view of the bay. Open fireplaces of decorative tile were installed on both floors, and wood for their use brought up on the elevator from the basement. From the tower room 65 feet above the ground, a magnificent view of Gardiner's Island, Plum Island, and Gull Island, with their fortifications and heavy guns which since the Spanish-American War stood guarding the Sound, could be seen. In the basement of the house was the laundry room, wine room, saltwater showers, and the furnace room.

A seawall and pier, constructed across the front of their property, provided easy access to the Havens family yacht. Beautifully landscaped grounds around the mansion made the Havens summer home one of the grandest residences along the waterfront.

The E. W. Bliss Torpedo Company

Beginning in 1891 the E.W. Bliss Company conducted experiments and tests with marine torpedoes in Noyac Bay. The location was selected because of the water's depth, lack of tidal current, and its land-locked environment. The torpedoes were manufactured at the Bliss factory in Brooklyn and shipped to Sag Harbor in four sections, where they were assembled.

The Bliss Company secured patent rights to build the Whitehead-Schwartkopf torpedo, a cigar-shaped device about 18 feet long. To assist in the testing operations was the steamboat *Sarah Thorpe*, which was refitted for the job. Originally, it was a passenger and freight steamer that ran between Sag Harbor and New London, Connecticut, and for several years, the *Sarah Thorpe* and its launch, *Stella*, were in active service. A crew of 13 men under Captain Thomas Corcoran lived and worked on board. In charge of the testing was Robert A. Hanna, United States Army, retired, who represented the Bliss Company. Hanna, at that time, was the government's torpedo expert and lived on Main Street in the village.

When a new torpedo was invented by Frank W. Leavitt of the Bliss Company, a larger barge was needed. The *Sarah Thorpe* was then used to supply the new barge, the *E.W. Bliss*, with food and water. The *Bliss* was 140 feet long, 40 feet wide, made of steel, and had four huge anchors, each weighing over a ton. Two fast sailing launches assisted the *Bliss*. The barge was used as a gun platform for charging Leavitt's new "dirigible" torpedoes with compressed air instead of a live charge. When shot from the platform, the torpedo sped toward the target at a speed of 45 miles per hour. The launch raced to the torpedo, recovered it, and towed it back to the barge. Originally, 120 pounds of gun cotton was the charge, but in the test, water equalling the weight of the gun cotton was substituted in the forward compartment. After the test, the torpedo would automatically float until it was recovered. It wasn't unusual for 20 shots a day to be fired.

The torpedo boat *Cushing*, which worked for the Bliss Company, was a 100-foot-long cigar-shaped ship with a 250-horsepower engine. It was said to have been the swiftest engine of nautical warfare afloat and "jumped through the water and under the waves." The *Cushing* was selected to go to New York in October 1892 to lead the naval parade in the Columbian Celebration.

The May 1, 1909 *Corrector* reported that an accident occurred in which the steam collier *John B. Dallas*, of New York, was rammed by an erratic moving torpedo and badly damaged below the water line. The boat had been discharging coal alongside the gunbarge *Bliss* in Noyac Bay when the mishap occurred and had to be towed to shore to prevent it from sinking. Another accident took place in September 1914, when launch number three of the Bliss Company was struck by a submarine torpedo and badly damaged.

A two-million-dollar order from the United States Government during World War I made it necessary to enlarge and expand the Bliss facilities. The Long Island Railroad leased the east side of the Long Wharf to Bliss, and a pier, office, storehouse, and room for the installation of machinery to adjust the torpedoes were built. In 1915 the steamer *Emblane* replaced the *Sarah Thorpe*, which for 20 years had served the company well. The new steamer was named for Emma B. Lane, daughter of Bliss' president, James W. Lane. Its size was 130 feet long, with Captain Fred Youngs of Sag Harbor in command.

Although the owners of the Bliss Company reported a net loss of $98,305 in 1923, two years later they re-opened their operations, with George Cary of Sag Harbor as superintendent of the station. Between 40 and 50 men were employed and put into service were launches 5, 7, 9, 11, 12, 13 and 15, which had all been equipped with motors. The contract for 1925 was designed for the South American government.

In all, 15 boats were used during the 30 years that torpedoes were tested in the Sag Harbor waters. In World War I a building was constructed to house the growing number of torpedoes tested during those years. The same building later held Agawam Aircraft, and still later, Grumman. Following the war, torpedo testing gradually diminished, and after a few foreign contracts were filled, the E.W. Bliss company's operations in Sag Harbor came to an end.

Local men involved in the torpedo testing were Leonard G. Kuhlwein, gunner; Captain James Brown, Commander of the launch *Ollie*; Captain Thomas Corcoran; and Captain Fred Youngs.

Saloons, Prohibition, and Rum Running

Sag Harbor, along with the rest of Southampton Town, was dry from 1905 to 1909. A great wave of reform swept over the village at that time, with Captain W.F. Kilgore of Sag Harbor one of its staunchest advocates. His conviction: "vote no licenses and every place selling liquor will be closed." There were about 15 hotels and saloons in Sag Harbor where ardent spirits could be legally bought up until the time that licenses expired. Then the town voted not to renew them.

It created hard times for the owners of legitimate hotels, which had to close their barrooms and sell only soft drinks. Many went out of business. Illegal trafficking was commonplace, with quantities of liquor coming over from Greenport, which was licensed. Dives and speakeasies sprung up, and Police

268 THE TWENTIETH CENTURY

Chief Higgins and his band of six constables were kept busy trying to keep things under control. The illegal sellers were fined or, in some instances, jailed, and in many houses "kitchen cabinets" were established.

These conditions existed for four years, until October 1909, when licenses were re-instated. A relief from the legal drought was heralded in with the arrival by railroad of large quantities of barrels, kegs and cases. One minute after midnight on October first, 14 sets of lights were turned on, revealing as many freshly painted bars and shiny sets of glassware, all ready for business. After four years of illegal trafficking and drinking in private places, it was again permitted to drink in public. The new law indicated that there would be fewer cases of drunkenness with the availability of draught beer instead of the turpentine and wood alcohol concoctions that had been prevalent during the dry years.

Eighteen licenses were issued yielding Sag Harbor $2500, with half going to the state. The lock-up, long filled to capacity, became cold, bare, and deserted. Chief Higgins and his troops found their jobs as sleuths a thing of the past. Once again Sag Harbor's bars, hotels, and liquor stores began to prosper. Their only complaint was a law, passed in 1910, requiring them to close at 11 P.M.

The following hotels, saloons, and bottling works suffered heavy financial losses during the dry years:

The Hoffman House: Premises at the corner of Washington and Division Streets was leased by William S. Wilson in 1896 and converted into a hotel which he called the Hoffman House. When his license expired in 1905, he closed the place.

The American Hotel: The bar was removed and billiard tables set up in its place. Soft drinks were sold throughout the dry years.

The Jetter Hotel: William Youngs purchased this hotel, which adjoined his American Hotel, to enlarge his place. Proprietor E.J. Hildreth went into another business.

The Dewey Hotel: John McNally, proprietor of this Main Street hotel, removed the bar until liquor licenses were re-instated.

The Glenn House: This hotel and saloon business opened in 1880 on the east side of Main Street, and after one year at that location, moved into the Glenn House, which he purchased from Daniel McCullen. He closed the hotel in 1905.

The Bayside House: William Nashold, proprietor, closed his hotel in September 1905 and moved to Jamaica to enter the hotel business there. In November the Bayside House was purchased by J. Cleveland Gardiner.

The Bijou Hotel: This hotel was established in 1877 by Henry B. Porter and stood on the east side of lower Main Street. In 1904 Edward A. Hildreth took a three-year lease on the property. In 1909 the hotel was purchased by Frank Jaffe, who converted it into a saloon.

The Railroad House: This place was owned by Elizabeth McGillicudy of New York and managed by Daniel McLain Jr. It was discovered to be on fire in 1904 and burned down. McLain then opened a saloon on the corner of Main and Bay Streets.

The Nassau House: J.A. Udall was manager of the Nassau House during the dry years. He decided not to bother with soft drinks and conducted the hotel business without a bar.

The saloons of Michael Cassidy, John Glenn, Michael Morouney, and Peter Silvey all closed.

William Schommer, bottler, gave notice to his customers that he could no longer serve them and moved from the area.

John Emmel of the Emmel Bottling Works ceased to bottle beer, but continued to bottle soft drinks.

After the law again allowed liquor to be sold in the village, some of the saloon keepers who had closed down their businesses reopened, but with the arrival of October 1917 came another change in the local licensing law. Inns in the Southampton Town side of the village were granted a two-year permit to sell wine and beer under the hotel section of the excise law. Several saloon owners, who were again being forced to close, discovered that by renovating their establishments into hotels, they would be able to continue to sell alcohol. On the other hand, the East Hampton Town side of Sag Harbor was bone dry. No liquor was permitted in any way, shape, or form, but those living in that part of the village had only to walk across Division Street to have their thirst legally quenched. Eleven bars received word that their places would be shut down unless they complied with the new law and made the necessary changes.

William McLain remodeled his saloon into a three-story brick hotel. Michael Cassidy of "Mike's Place," above the railroad depot, was granted his license after making the necessary alterations. Mae McNally of the Dewey Hotel on Main Street, Thomas Glenn on the east side of Main, William W. Wilson of the Hoffman House, William Youngs of the American Hotel, and E.W. Scribner of the Nassau Hotel, all received their two-year licenses.

The entrance of the United States into World War I added a great impetus to the prohibition movement, and in 1917 Congress passed the law which permitted the sale of only wine and beer. In December 1917 President Wilson issued a proclamation reducing the alcoholic content in beer, effective January 21, 1918. Several days later Congress passed a resolution to be submitted to the States within seven years, an amendment to the Constitution providing for national prohibition. The Volstead Act was passed by Congress, and although vetoed by the president in October 1919, it was overruled by Congress. In June 1920 the United States Supreme Court sustained the validity of the 18th Amendment and the Volstead Act, and so began nationwide prohibition, fifteen years after Sag Harbor first tried to stop the sale of alcohol in the village.

Rum Running During Prohibition

Although nationwide prohibition went into effect, it by no means stopped the flow of liquor through the village. An active smuggling operation existed at the east end of Long Island during the 1920s, with scores of private boats landing in the coves, creeks, and inlets with their illegal cargo. Montauk had a lucrative business that was closely scrutinized by the Federal Prohibition Agents and many arrests were made. Boats found their way to Sag Harbor, North Haven, and Noyac from "Rum Row," with brisk activity for several years.

February 1922 brought the arrest of three Sag Harbor men who had in their possession 25 bottles and five jugs of booze, but because no evidence of sale could be proven, the men were released. In August 1923 agents raided a private home in Noyac and confiscated 119 cases of hooch. The liquor had originally come from Scotland and the Bahamas. Although the haul was substantial, the house was empty and no arrests were made. During 1924 a lull in the illegal trafficking took place. Boats that formerly went out empty and came back loaded to the gunwales now lay quietly at the docks, but their engines were tuned up daily in hopes that business would soon pick up. They bided their time and made practice runs, and when business resumed, they were ready to go. Although activity did have another flurry, it never reached the intensity it experienced earlier in the decade.

In the winter of 1927 a reporter from *The Saturday Evening Post* came to Sag Harbor to investigate the alleged rum-running activities in the area. Liquor flowed in a tremendous stream from England, Bermuda, and the Bahamas on its journey to Sag Harbor and on to places west. Then it seemed that the hooch started to flow the other way, pouring out of those efficient bootleggers' plants in New York City and, according to several local residents, inundating Long Island with the "counterfeit stuff."

Eastern Long Island was once a land flowing with good scotch and plenty of it. The mellow British whiskey that used to be unloaded on the wharves and docks from the boats that ferried out to "Rum Row" was no more. But then "Rum Row" was no more, either, and thirsty natives of this place had to fall back on that "scotch made in Brooklyn." It was a terrible letdown after enjoying the real stuff for all those Volstead years. With rumors flying that the rum-runners were again landing cases of liquor in every cove and inlet, the reporter was sent to Sag Harbor to learn the truth.

The truth he learned was that no more did that potent beverage find its way to our harbor. He learned from the proprietor of the American Hotel that up until a year or two ago the docks had been crowded with motorboats bringing the stuff in from the Row, plus a steady movement of vehicles trucking it into Manhattan during the wee hours of the morning.

A caretaker of a North Haven estate overlooking Shelter Island Sound claimed that every night the sound of boats delivering their cargo to the North Haven shore at Hawthorne Manor could be heard. While being interviewed the caretaker remarked, "You see that gray stucco three-story house over there on the hill? That was their hangout. Hundreds and hundreds of cases of scotch were stored there." The reporter left to investigate the place on the hill but met with disappointment when he approached the house and found it to be deserted and the windows boarded up. He discovered a way to enter the place and found the rooms dark and bare and shivered at the thought of rum-runners' pistols blazing in the empty rooms. In the cellar were a few brown cardboard cartons (such as used to hold two pints of whiskey), a straw jacket for a bottle, cigarette butts, and a newspaper dated July 15, 1925, but not even a whiff of rum was to be found. And as he emerged from the house and gazed across the bay, not a boat could be seen, not a single rum boat, not even a clammer's boat. But then, it was February 1927, and he was a little too late.

2
NEW BUILDINGS FOR NEW BEGINNINGS

The Otter Pond

Below its bosky margin green,
With slender lines of light between,
The shadows sleep on Otter Pond.
While like a mother's radiant face
The matron moon with tender grace
Leans o'er the wooded heights beyond.

And list! A song! A boat glides by,
And youthful voices glad and shy,
Breathe words to which all hearts respond.
The glistening oars dip soft and slow,
And neath the bridge with quickening flow
The tide comes in on Otter Pond.

Mary B. Sleight

Otter Pond, one of a succession of small ponds that extend from Sag Harbor to Sagaponack, has a history spanning over 200 years. Its name was selected because in early days otters inhabited its shores in great number. Originally spring-fed and frequented by the Indians, it became a tidal saltwater pond after it was opened to the cove. With a depth of 35 feet at its deepest point, it

NEW BUILDINGS FOR NEW BEGINNINGS

is one of Sag Harbor's truly historic natural spots.

Back in 1792 Nathan Fordham, Ebenezer White, and David Hedges were given permission by the Southampton Town Trustees to dig a channel to connect Otter Pond with the Upper Cove and to build a bridge over the channel at least 12 feet wide, suitable for all types of carriages to pass over it. They failed to follow through with their plans, and a year later the same grant was given to John Jermain and his heirs. The ditch was dug, allowing saltwater to flow into the pond, and tradition tells us that the workers were paid off in New England rum.

In those early times a dense oak forest surrounded the southwest and northern sides of the pond, and John Jermain built his mill at the other end. The Town Trustees gave him permission to dig a mile-long trench connecting Long Pond and Crooked Pond to Otter Pond, in order to increase the flow of water needed to operate the mill. Unfortunately, it failed to solve the problem, and Jermain had to abandon his milling business. In 1803 Captain Stephen Mitchell purchased the place, moved the building to the village, and converted it into a store. It remained as such until it burned in the great fire of 1817.

Otter Pond was stocked with perch, striped bass and eels, and became a fisherman's paradise. After the mill was removed, fish were taken by seine, loaded on wagons, and transported to New York City to sell. On one occasion in 1806, 3600 fish were caught in one haul. In 1818 permission was granted to take eels from the pond. The local newspaper reported that most of the male population showed up in December of that year to eel through the ice, and 54 dozen eels were taken in a few hours' time.

By 1854 a blacksmith shop, carriage house, a store, and two houses stood on the shore of Otter Pond. It was a place where business was carried on up into the turn of the century. Mrs. Russell Sage purchased the pond and its surroundings in 1910. She had the existing buildings removed, the Joshua Eldredge house given to the A.M.E. Zion congregation and moved to Eastville for a parsonage. The grounds were added to the park property, and a shore drive made around the pond. Between 1910 and 1915 park director Robert Atkinson permitted swimming there as part of the summer program. Otter Pond was further improved in 1911 by the opening of a wading beach for small children, with a dock and float with springboard for the older children. Although the pond couldn't compete with the nearby beaches, it was a perfect spot for a quick swim, and many took advantage of the facilities. The greatest number using Otter Pond in a single day was close to 200 people.

During the winter months skaters from Sag Harbor and neighboring villages enjoyed showing off their skills in the well-lit evening hours, and occasionally the band gave concerts, much to the delight of all.

Now, benches around the neatly kept grounds provide an enjoyable spot to stop and reflect on the beauty of Otter Pond and to feed the many ducks and geese that call the place their home.

The Parks

For more than 100 years, the place now called Mashashimuet has been a park and recreation grounds for the residents of Sag Harbor. In November 1874 a meeting was held in the Corn Exchange Building in the village and an association formed to establish the Hampton Driving Park and Fair Grounds. Shares of stock sold at $10 each, and after 500 shares were sold, the stockholders designated a location for the park. The association was made up of Chairman Samuel B. Gardiner of Gardiner's Island, Dr. Edgar Miles, Dr. James W. Smith and Stephen B. French of Sag Harbor, and Henry P. Hedges and Orlando Hand of Bridgehampton.

In December 1878 the Sag Harbor and Hampton Park and Fair Grounds incorporated under the laws of the State of New York. Dr. Miles, Dr. Smith, and John M. Hildreth selected property on the southeast corner of Main Street and Jermain Avenue (then South Street), owned by the estate of Edward R. Merrall, William Buck, and others. They purchased the property with an assessment of five dollars collected from each person who subscribed to the project. Subscriptions in 1879 amounted to well over $2000.

Charles Watson Payne, chairman of the operation, hired local surveyor E.Z. Hunt to lay out a half-mile track. He cleared and graded the land, made necessary roads, purchased materials, and erected a temporary building in which to store the workmen's tools. The Park Association made arrangements with the Long Island Railroad to transport a large quantity of loam from the Hamptons to the park grounds for fill. Local volunteers assisted the 20 men who were hired to work on the track.

A large steamroller brought from Prospect Park, Brooklyn packed the loam firmly in order to make a good hard surface. A large pair of iron gates 17 feet long and 8½ feet high (a present from Captain Peck of the New Haven Steamboat Company) arrived and were placed in position at the entrance. A fence enclosed the park grounds along the turnpike, with a long row of maple trees in front. Cedar posts for the fence came from the North Haven farm of William C. White, and the lumber furnished by Nickerson & Vail of Sag Harbor. A fence of wooden boards (built by Luther L. Sherman) enclosed the track. Work continued throughout the spring and early summer, preparing for the opening

NEW BUILDINGS FOR NEW BEGINNINGS

on July 4, 1879. The park was officially named the Sag Harbor, Hampton and Shelter Island Park and Fair Grounds. All kinds of races took place that opening day, with seats set up for one thousand people in the grove adjoining the track. A judges' stand was erected nearby from which the winners could be determined.

In September 1879 an exhibition building, 30 by 50 feet and two stories high, was built. Each year a fair was held at which baked goods, preserves, flowers, art, poultry, and other farm animals were displayed and judged. It was a wonderful annual event that drew crowds from all over Long Island. Excursion trains and steamboats brought thousands to the festivities. Horsemen arrived to try their luck and skill in carriage team races, trotting races, walking races, and other contests.

The Fourth of July celebration in 1881 held trotting races, with the Suffolk County purse of $125, the East End purse of $125, and the Free for All purse of $225. Winners of the running races were awarded a $100 prize, and winner of the greased pole contest found a $20 silver watch at the top of the pole.

On July 3, 1890 the exhibit house was destroyed by fire. Arson was suspected, but no arrests were made. It put a veil of gloom over the events scheduled for the holiday, but the races went on as planned. Three years later, on July 4, 1893, a Great Bicycle Tournament was held at the track. It was estimated that over one thousand spectators attended, and bicyclists came from all over the Island to compete for the many prizes.

With all these events held at the park it would seem that it was one of the most popular recreation spots on the East End, yet as the turn of the century neared, it was used less and less. The grounds had deteriorated and become overgrown with weeds and brush. When Mrs. Russell Sage held a picnic there for the students of Pierson High School in June 1908, she was saddened to see the place in such a deplorable condition. She immediately looked into the possibility of acquiring the park property to build a children's playground. The Park Association accepted her offer of $5000, and after business transactions were completed, she hired the landscaping and architectural firm of Samuel Parsons of New York to renovate the place. In September work began, with J.F. Payne supervising the operation. The enclosure of the old track was made into an athletic field, and two tennis courts were built. A fine new house for the park superintendent was built.

In November 1908 work on the grandstand had begun. It stood 30 by 50 feet and was capable of seating 350. Edward Beckwith, Sag Harbor's master mason, did the masonry work, and Fred Edwards, the carpentry work. The foundation was laid in cement, the first story made of brick, and the grandstand seats and roof of wood. Restrooms and lockers were built under the steps, and the place was completed at a cost of $2500. In 1909 a large tank for the water system was installed by Ivan C. Byram. It held 225 barrels of water and was connected to a powerful pumping engine on the grounds.

In 1908 the bandstand, which stood at the foot of Main Street in the village, was repaired and moved to a hill site in the park. A donation of $75, given to the LVIS by Mr. James H. Aldrich of North Haven, covered the expense of moving the structure.

In October 1910 the Otter Pond and its surrounding land was added to the park property, having been donated by Mrs. Sage. As mentioned, the store, blacksmith shop, carriage shop, and homes around the pond were moved.

For the first several months the park was known as "Sage's Playground." Mrs. Sage announced that she had decided to call it Sagaponack Park in memory of her ancestors who lived at that place, but before the name was officially adopted, a change was made. William Wallace Tooker, local authority on the Long Island Indians, suggested the name "Mashashimuet," an Indian word meaning the "Place of the Great Springs." His suggestion was accepted, and the park was officially named Mashashimuet Park.

Robert Atkinson, newly elected park director, was placed in charge of the many activities that took place there in the early 1900s. During the years 1911 through 1914, baseball, tennis, track and field events, and other sports were held for the men and boys of the community. In addition, 144 children's gardens were planted, with separate little plots assigned to each child. Supervised swimming was allowed in Otter Pond, and, at the park house, children's games, story hours, and folk dancing were available. Band concerts became a weekly feature, with dancing permitted on an open-air platform, and on summer evenings motion pictures were shown. Daily attendance during the summer of 1911 averaged 275 people.

In 1913 the students of Pierson High School wanted a flagpole at the park so the flag could wave during their activities. They struck upon a novel way to acquire one. Each student contributed 10 cents toward the project, but had to earn the money themselves before contributing it. A pine tree was procured at Pine Swamp in the Northwest woods, and boss carpenter George H. Cleveland formed it into a 70-foot-tall flagpole. The bandstand was moved from the crest of the hill to a spot further south so that the pole could be placed at the highest point of the park property. A plaque, engraved in acknowledgement of Mrs. Sage's interest in the children of Sag Harbor, was secured to the pole.

In November 1917 Mrs. Sage turned the park property over to the Sage Foundation, which in 1920 deeded it to the Park and Recreation Association. The association, made up a board of directors consisting of nine local residents,

NEW BUILDINGS FOR NEW BEGINNINGS 277

attended to the varied duties of keeping the park operating smoothly over the years.

Before the turn of the century, circumstances found Sag Harbor in the throes of recovering from an enormous economic slump following the end of the whaling industry and the burning of the cotton mill. Joseph Fahys had built a new factory on the site of the mill and relocated his watchcase company from Carlstadt, New Jersey to Sag Harbor. Its opening provided many needed jobs for the unemployed. But with the arrival of the 1900s, the village had not yet reached the point where it was financially able to build a new schoolhouse (to replace the condemned Union School building) or a new library for the local residents—that is, until Mrs. Russell Sage came to the rescue.

MRS. RUSSELL SAGE

Margaret Olivia Slocum Sage, affectionately known as Lady Bountiful, Sag Harbor's benefactress, patroness, and philanthropist, is regarded by many as doing more for the village than any other one person. Although not native born, Sag Harbor was Mrs. Sage's summer home, the place of her ancestors, and she freely and lovingly shared her wealth with the people of Sag Harbor. Margaret Olivia was born in Syracuse, New York, on September 8, 1828, the daughter of Joseph Slocum of that place and Margaret Pierson of Sag Harbor, and the granddaughter of the celebrated Major John Jermain. She became the second wife of industrial tycoon Russell Sage in 1869, and while married to him, bought the Main Street homestead of her grandparents. Several summers were spent at that house before she purchased and restored the elegant Benjamin Huntting estate, now the Sag Harbor Whaling and Historical Museum. Dubbed "Harbor Home," it was referred to as Mrs. Sage's summer cottage. Upon her husband's death, Mrs. Sage became one of the ten most wealthy women in America.

Mrs. Sage loved Sag Harbor and its citizens, and that love inspired her to finance the building of Pierson High School, the John Jermain Memorial Library, and Mashashimuet Park. Help couldn't have come at a more opportune time. However, her generosity didn't stop there. In 1911 Mrs. Sage donated a sizeable check to help with the publication of William Wallace Tooker's book *Indian Place-Names on Long Island*, a book that became one of the most definitive works of its kind. That same year, the Gazelle Hose Company of the Sag Harbor Fire Department received money from Mrs. Sage with which to buy new uniforms to wear at the tournament in Sayville. In 1912 she gave $1500 toward the construction of the Union Chapel in Noyac and a large donation to finance the repair of the Presbyterian Church's tall steeple. More help came in the way of homes for the needy. While expanding the grounds of her palatial estate, several houses that stood on the property were given to needy residents, to be moved to other locations. Other dwellings surrounding the Otter Pond and on the park property also found new owners and were skidded to different lots. At least 13 families became the recipients of houses—gifts of Mrs. Sage.

Mrs. Sage's love for the children of Sag Harbor was evident from her frequent visits to Pierson High School and Mashashimuet Park whenever she came to town. A warm and caring relationship between them continued throughout her lifetime. Margaret Olivia Sage remained active into her 90th year, widely known and loved. On November 4, 1918 she died in New York City, and although her generosity extended to many, near and far, she will always be remembered in Sag Harbor as having had a tremendous influence on the village and its people.

Pierson High School

The following letter appeared in *The Sag Harbor Express* in February 1907, with the recommendation that a new school be built for the students of Sag Harbor:

> The Board of Education feels that the people ought to understand fully the situation connected with our new school building before they vote upon the question, therefore they publish this letter, that every citizen may be fairly and truthfully informed.
>
> The School authorities of the State complained of our school buildings nine years ago. They would have condemned them had they not known we were ourselves planning for a new and suitable school house. The question at issue has been a perplexing one. After much consideration we have arrived at a conclusion which we believe will be for the best interests of the school and the district.
>
> It is that we must have a new school, and that it would be unwise and impractical to attempt to enlarge or reconstruct the old one. The erection of this new building is the problem which now confronts us and has given the Board much serious thought. We are agreed that we must have a school house capable of seating and accommodating at least 900 pupils. It must contain 20 classrooms, be safe, substantial and of creditable architectural design. The area, air space and light must conform to the law...
>
> Why must we have a new school house? And, if so, why should it cost so much? The people of this state believe that the future welfare of this country demands that child labor shall end, and that the children of the

NEW BUILDINGS FOR NEW BEGINNINGS 279

poor, as well as those of the rich, shall be prepared for their life work by a reasonably good education, and knowing that many parents are not willing and others not able to educate their own, and that many of the wealthy are not public spirited enough to voluntarily assist their neighbors in this work, the Compulsory Education law had to be passed in order to make sure that those under 16 years of age would be sent to school.

The people also believe that the best part of the life of a child, if forced to be spent indoors in hard study, must be so spent in conditions that neither ruin the general health nor strain the eyes so that suffering should follow in all the after life, hence the law quoted above. The question has been how to best meet the conditions.

Fortunately for us, a lady of large means and sympathetic interests in our village has decided to donate $60,000 toward the erection of this building. It stands to reason that we must not expect this generous offer to materialize unless we meet it in the same public spirit and provide for the construction of the new building upon lines which shall fulfill requirements and be a credit to the district. Many claim that this is comparatively a poor village, yet it supports eight churches, a dozen or more saloons, and are able to fill regularly the amusement halls, but are too poor to have a public library or a good school. Of 900 children of school age but 23 over 16 years of age are in our Union School at the present time; ten percent are now absent on account of sickness mainly caused by poor ventilation, etc. This year but three are expected to graduate, and we have sent one to college, which is above the average. An architect of experience and high repute has submitted several plans. We have carefully examined them, rejecting those too elaborate and others not fully meeting our requirements. The plan chosen we consider the best adapted to our requirements, and the most economical, all things considered. It provides for a brick building of two stories and basement, with twenty classrooms and fireproof stairways. There is no question that brick is preferable to frame, and the additional cost can be offset in a few years by a savings in repairs, painting, heating and insurance. The greater safety, stability and appearance are things to be considered. We are not only building for today, but for years to come. The present school building has been occupied for 36 years. Fire-proof stairways are essential. No parent can object to them. The sewerage system may be deferred and cesspools utilized. Grading can be extended from year to year. The total cost of these items may not exceed a few hundred dollars. There will be no great demand for new furniture exceeding the annual appropriation therefor.

Is our building as planned too big? The 16 classrooms on the two main floors will seat 750 pupils under the requirements of the State laws. Our present school population, with the added attraction for school work should fill these rooms. As needed, the basement classrooms can be fitted up for 250 more pupils. The building will last for all time and for years should cost very little for repairs. It is especially designed so that additions may be made, if necessary, in future years without marring its architectural symmetry and beauty.

It is said that buildings have been erected in other places at much less expense; investigation shows if they were satisfactory buildings, they cost about the same in proportion to the size as our proposed school house. It is claimed by many that compared with other places, we are poor. If so, must it always be so? It is true that in the past we have been ready to meet half way those who have had an inclination to help us to better things? There are few places on Long Island having the natural advantages of Sag Harbor for a healthy, beautiful, thriving town. Have we done all we could to make it such a place as would attract people to become residents; if not are we to do so hereafter? The progressive towns are the ones that grow.

Mrs. Sage has made it possible for us to meet the State requirements in a new school building. Shall we meet her half way? If we should show a disposition to help ourselves we shall be in a better position to expect and receive help from others. Sixty thousand dollars is not a large sum of money to appropriate for our absolute requirements. The payment cannot be a severe burden, stretching over a period of twenty years in payment. About $4.50 on a thousand dollars and decreasing yearly.

This board has no desire to oppress a single citizen or taxpayer, or to go beyond the limit of jurisdiction and indispensible requirements, but it has reached the conclusion that the only solution of the present problem is to vote to build the school house and to bond the district in the sum proposed. And it trusts all the friends of the school and well wishers of Sag Harbor may feel the same way.

Charles E. Wels, President
Brinley D. Sleight, Secretary
William R. Reimann, Casper Schaeffer, Peter Dippel, B.O.E.

In 1905, when Mrs. Russell Sage had asked what Sag Harbor needed the most, she was told a new school. The old Union School building had been condemned by the State Education Department, and withdrawal of state aid had been threatened unless a new building was acquired. The village was extremely

NEW BUILDINGS FOR NEW BEGINNINGS 281

fortunate that a person such as Mrs. Sage was willing and financially able to provide Sag Harbor with a beautiful new school building.

The New York State Inspector suggested that at least seven acres of land be desired in order to provide ample space for future expansion. The construction of additional buildings, a spacious outdoor playground, a ball field, and enough room for a janitor's residence were all taken into account.

Before the purchase of the property known as Latham Hill was made, two other parcels of land were considered. A site on Suffolk Street and another on upper Madison Street were given serious thought, but the additional expense of having to remove existing buildings proved too costly. At a special meeting of the Board of Education in September 1905, William R. Greene and William R. Reimann were appointed to search the title of the Latham Hill property. They were favorably impressed, and the residents of the district approved their choice. Money in the amount of $18,000 was appropriated for the purpose of acquiring the ten-acre tract of land.

Board of Education member William R. Reimann soon received this letter from C.N. Talbot, who represented Mrs. Sage:

> Mrs. Sage wishes me to state that she is ready to cooperate with the Village of Sag Harbor to the extent of $50,000, in providing a school house; also leaving to the village the employment of an architect, the general details as to the size and general construction of the building. Of course, the building should be one sufficient to provide for the needs for which it is to be constructed.

Architect Augustus N. Allen, of New York City, was employed to draw up the plans for the school. It was to be an elaborate structure, second to none, with all modern conveniences. The submitted plans were approved by the Board of Education, Mrs. Sage, and the State authorities, but when specifications were given out to contractors, the bids greatly exceeded the amount Mrs. Sage agreed to donate. The plans called for a two-story, plus basement, structure, constructed of stone, brick and iron, and in every way modern, fireproof, and sanitary. The front of the building would be 250 feet long, with a tower and belfry at the top. The interior would have lavatories and closets on each floor, and classrooms to accommodate one thousand students. Two hundred and fifty thousand dollars was the estimate given for the original plans.

Considerable changes were made before the plans were accepted. Contracts were then awarded to A.J. Robinson for building, $89,487; Johnson and Morris for heating and ventilation, $18,900; and an additional $44,500 for the auditorium and for fireproofing, making the total cost $152,887. The architect's commission was $7,645.

The site was staked out in April 1907 and excavation soon underway. Three months later the first floor was closed over and the cornerstone laid. At 1:30 P.M. the school children formed a line of parade and marched to the site of the new building for the cornerstone ceremonies. A great crowd congregated on Latham Hill. The first floor of the building was used as a platform occupied by the speakers, the Board of Education, Ladies Village Improvement Society, representatives of civic societies, and other prominent citizens of the village.

Lawyer William C. Greene, chairman of the Arrangement Committee, called for order and made the opening address. "America" was sung by the school children, and a prayer offered by Reverend M.Y. Bovard. The Honorable Joseph M. Belford of Riverhead, who was scheduled to give the main speech, was unable to attend, and School Commissioner C.H. Howell substituted. According to the program, Colonel J.J. Slocum, brother of Mrs. Sage, laid the cornerstone. Historical data was read by Brinley D. Sleight, Secretary of the Board of Education. Music by the band followed, then a short address by Reverend J.J. Harrison.

Articles placed in the cornerstone were: a Bible, gift of Mrs. Sage; a souvenir of the 1896 Firemen's Fair; *The Corrector* of July 6, 1907; *The Sag Harbor Express* of July 11, 1907; a bag of 1907 coins; a photograph of the Main Street schoolhouse; a photograph of Pierson High School; a photograph of the Watch Case Factory; a photograph of the Central Store building; three views of Main Street; a view of the Upper Cove; a view of historic Sag Harbor, 1710; a view of Otter Pond Bridge; a view of Mrs. Sage's home on Main Street; views of the Methodist Church, Episcopal Church, St. Andrew's Church, the Convent of the Sacred Heart of Mary, the Atheneum, Cedar Island Light; a photograph of Mrs. Sage; a book of photographs of Sag Harbor; names of donors of the purchase of the four-story Union School, April 1, 1871; names of the present Board of Education and school faculty; names of the secretaries of the Board since 1862; names of all the members of the Board since the institution of the school, with the date of their first appointment or election and number of years of service; and the names of the Supervisors of the Town of East Hampton and Town of Southampton, 1907; and names of officials of the Village of Sag Harbor, local and federal.

The cornerstone laying took place on July 12, 1907. Eighteen hundred to two thousand people watched as Mrs. Sage's brother laid the stone with a silver trowel made by Fahys Watch Case Factory and Silver Works.

School Commissioner Howell spoke:

NEW BUILDINGS FOR NEW BEGINNINGS 283

Before us is a pile of brick, thrown together in a promiscuous mess. One by one the builders will place them together in their proper place and bind them together and these walls will rise in their grandeur and beauty until the "Home Sweet Home" of the donor's heart, through the architect and designers, shall stand out as an inspiring welcome to those who seek knowledge, and be an enduring monument to Mrs. Sage.

Alterations were necessary as the building progressed. Instead of having the auditorium and gymnasium downstairs as first intended, the two were combined into one room to comply with the required fireproofing methods. By the time the school was completed, $102,000 had been presented to the Board of Education by Mrs. Sage, leaving less than $60,000 for the district to raise.

Installed in the tower of the school were the old bell and clock originally in the Presbyterian Church on Meeting House Hill, and later in the Episcopal Church. Furnishings for the library, superintendent's office, and auditorium were gifts of Mrs. James Aldrich.

Mrs. Sage placed her own personal landscaper in charge of planting trees, shrubs, and flowers on the spacious grounds, readying the place for the formal dedication in June 1908. At that time keys to the newly finished school were presented to Commissioner Howell by the contractor.

Upon completion, the name was officially changed from Sag Harbor High School to Pierson High School, by an act of the State Education Department on May 15, 1908. It was so named in memory of Mrs. Sage's maternal ancestors, in particular, Reverend Abraham Pierson and Mr. Henry Pierson.

In 1925 Frank Havens was awarded the contract to stucco the school building. He purchased the material from Judson L. Banister to cover and waterproof the exterior, the material made of close-grained magnesite cement, which was guaranteed to bind perfectly with the brick. Havens' bid was $4,678. In recent years the stucco was removed, as the binding process wasn't as successful as expected.

The John Jermain Memorial Library and Earlier Libraries

Books were scarce in early colonial days, and it wasn't until after the American Revolution that the idea of a circulating library was instituted. Before that time many people had little time or money to squander on books, and when they did, the Holy Bible took precedence.

In 1791 the printing office of Frothingham's *Long Island Herald* in Sag Harbor had for sale *Gutherie's Grammar*, *Pope's Works*, *Sermons for Children*, and *Dilworth's Speller*. Those fortunate enough to attend school learned their lessons from these early textbooks. The weekly *Long Island Herald* usually consisted of a sermon or novel, along with world, national, and political news, and often was the main reading material found in the early home.

The start of the nineteenth century saw a few community libraries being organized, the more successful ones run by private individuals. Literary collections with volumes by Dickens, Cooper, Hawthorne, and Longfellow found a waiting public. However, it wasn't until the mid-1800s that the public library, as we know it, began to emerge.

In 1806 village librarian Ebenezer Sage, placed a notice in the *Suffolk Gazette* that the proprietors of the library in the Port of Sag Harbor would hold their annual meeting on January 14th at the home of Daniel Fordham. At that time five directors, a treasurer, and a new librarian would be elected. This was the first mention of a library in the village of Sag Harbor.

In 1836 Orin O. Wickham opened a circulating library consisting of 600 volumes. Those interested in becoming members paid $3.50 for a year's membership. That fee entitled them to borrow books, such as *Pilgrim's Progress*, *The Life of Aaron Burr*, *Pickwick Club*, *Modern Accomplishments*, and other literary masterpieces.

Another early library in Sag Harbor was the Seaman's Library, established in 1833 by the Methodist-Episcopal Church. It supplied many vessels engaged in the whale fishery with Bibles, Testaments, and other religious pamphlets.

In 1875 a circulating library of 200 volumes of miscellaneous works opened in the music store of E.M. Willard. Membership for one year could be had for a two-dollar fee. Although only one book could be borrowed at a time, one could change books as often as desired.

The first library of any consequence opened during the 1890s. Called the Sag Harbor Circulating Library, it was located on the second floor of the Alvin Building on Main Street. It was quite an improvement over the small collections that were previously found in the village, and an extensive collection of 1800 choice and valuable books were available for borrowing. The library remained at that location for several years until the Alvin Company took over the entire building. The books were then stored, and Sag Harbor was without a library until the John Jermain Memorial Library was built.

In 1909 Mrs. Russell Sage made arrangements to provide Sag Harbor with a beautiful new library building. She purchased a lot which belonged to John Osborn, on the corner of Main, Jefferson, and Union Streets, and had the old house taken down. Charles A. Frake and Morgan Hotchkiss, representatives of the A.J. Robinson & Company, contractors of New York, staked off the grounds in April 1909, preparatory to construction. For the contract price of

NEW BUILDINGS FOR NEW BEGINNINGS 285

$70,000, work was soon underway, with C.A. Frake in charge of building the 50- by 50-foot brick and granite building. Many described the impressive structure as resembling a Greek temple, with its massive stone pillars and unique dome. The dome was the work of the R. Guastavino Company, noted builder of domes for more than one thousand buildings in the United States. Mrs. Sage named the place the John Jermain Memorial Library in memory of her grandfather, Major John Jermain.

The library opened for inspection and the signing of applications on June 18, 1910. At that time the first floor contained a collection of 5000 books for borrowing, including many in Polish, German, Italian, French, and Hebrew languages. A magnificent winding marble staircase led to the second floor where the reading room was located. It was tastefully furnished with oak library tables and chairs of a classical design. Two smaller rooms were also open to the public. One, a museum room, displayed curios from all over the world, Indian artifacts, and scrimshaw pieces. The second room held several pieces of furniture that belonged to the Sage and Jermain families. Two elegant grandfather clocks crafted by Sag Harbor clockmakers, Ephraim Niles Byram and Benjamin Franklin Hope, stood in the library, both masterpieces of workmanship. Two granite urns, each weighing two and a half tons, were placed in front of the library on December 22, 1910 by George Gilman, John Gordon and Frank Frazer of the Robinson Company. The local newspaper reported they were sledded over the snow-covered streets to the library site.

On October 10, 1910, with Mrs. Sage present for the occasion, the library opened its doors to the public. After a prayer of dedication by Reverend William T. Edds of the Presbyterian Church, Mrs. Sage took out the first book. During the first month, 3868 books were borrowed, and at the end of the first year, 52 percent of the village population had become members.

Miss Cora H. Bunker, who arrived from Toledo, Ohio to become the first director, spent several months getting the place in order, but as opening day approached, she had a change of plans and returned to Ohio. Olive Pratt Young was then hired and became John Jermain's first librarian.

In 1912 the Alvin Company presented Mrs. Sage with the books and shelving from the Circulating Library that had been in storage since it closed. Some 2000 volumes were added, greatly increasing the collection. The library grew, and soon became not only a place that provided reading material but a place where exhibits, lectures, concerts, and other cultural activities were held. On Thanksgiving and Christmas holidays, a huge log was burned in the massive fireplace on the second floor, while community singing took place.

On October 18, 1917 the public was introduced to the library's new acquisition, a Victrola and records. It was purchased at Spitz's store. Seventy-five people assembled to hear both vocal and classical instrumental selections on the new machine. Records were made available to card holders, and during the year 1920, 1853 records were borrowed. In later years the library continued to grow and today it still serves Sag Harbor and the vicinity, providing services for young and old alike.

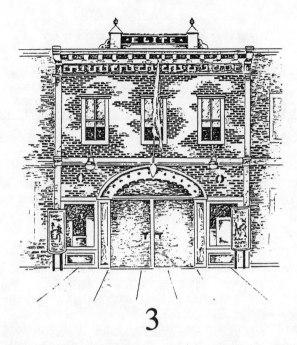

3

THE SOCIAL SCENE AND THE ARTS

Before motion pictures came to Sag Harbor the Trahern Company presented plays at the Atheneum. Appearing each Wednesday night during the spring and summer of 1907, the troupe consisted of 11 actors and a ten-piece orchestra led by Harry Masten. The following year, due to a controversy with Atheneum manager Ivan Byram over the sharing of profits, Trahern made a decision not to include Sag Harbor in his schedule. Although the loss of this professional group was unfortunate, a new kind of entertainment called motion pictures was about to be introduced to the public.

The Era of the Movies

In 1908 the Montauk Motion Picture Theater opened on Washington Street, a few months after an experimental film was shown at the Atheneum. Those in attendance were so delighted over the prospects of having a motion-picture theater in the village that the place became an overnight success. In July 1909 Carroll and Walsh, proprietors of the Montauk, added a brick extension to the place to accommodate the growing number of theatergoers more comfortably. In October 1910 Carroll and Walsh had the good fortune to secure the services of Leo Ormond, one of New York's leading tenors, to sing illustrated songs at both performances every evening of the week. He was accompanied by Mrs.

VanHoughton at the piano. VanHoughton was a local musician who also played for other singers and entertainers at the Montauk.

When John Carroll died in March 1911, the theater closed for a week, out of respect to the man who had provided such wonderful motion pictures during his three-year association with the theater. Walsh continued as proprietor, soon taking Frank Sexton as his partner. During the summer months motion pictures were shown in an airdome on Main Street, and when autumn arrived, they moved back into the theater building where a hot-air furnace had been installed.

The December 23, 1911 *Corrector* published the following schedule for the holiday season that year:

> A grand prize will be given away every Friday night at the Montauk Theater. This week it is a water set. Saturday night a Vitagraph picture will be shown. "The Black Chasm" an Indian tradition that tells in a most wonderfully picturesque way, an Indian romance that shows the Indian in all the dignity and wild natural grandeur of his race before it became dissipated by modern advancement and improvement. "Eagle Eye," the celebrated Apache Indian actor who is now connected with Vitagraph Western Company of players, will appear in the picture as Dark Feather's father.
>
> The special for New Year's Day at the 2 PM matinee is "Molly Pitcher" a page out of U.S. history, an incident in the battle of Monmouth. This picture is only out ten days, so don't fail to see it. It's a Kalem.
>
> The special for Tuesday January 2nd—three reels Vitagraph "Vanity Fair." Your wish is satisfied. At last you must acknowledge the supremacy of the Vitagraph art in this remarkable production from William Makepeace Thackeray's novel. Take it in at the Montauk Theater, Washington Street, and you'll come away satisfied and grateful.
>
> You will behold one of the marvels of moving pictures and of the age. Mr. Robert Tabor, better known as Stuart Tabor, a native and former resident of Sag Harbor, will appear in this picture as "aide de camp." The management of this inviting house deserves the heartiest praise for the high standard of their productions and refined character of their theater.

In 1909 Sag Harbor's second vaudeville and motion-picture theater opened in a building between Blaiklock's Garage and Shapiro's Restaurant, on the west side of Main Street. It was a one-story building which had been extended at the rear to accommodate 300 people. Known as the Star Theater, it had a box office, stage fittings, a fancy metal ceiling, and was managed by Ryland and Roberts. This second motion-picture theater created quite a stir, as some in the village questioned whether Sag Harbor could sustain two places.

The Star was described as a "comfortable little theater with an excellent program of music and films every night." In 1912 the place was sold to George Kiernan, and Walsh, of the Montauk, tried without success to obtain a ten-year lease on the place. Because this business deal fell through, Walsh ended his partnership with Frank Sexton and left Sag Harbor to open a theater in Southampton. Mr. Sexton then became manager of the Atheneum, and, apparently, the Montauk Theater closed at this time.

The Star closed for several weeks in May 1913, due to a fire that destroyed the electric power house. While it was closed, a fireproof booth was installed to insure patrons of the theater's safety. M. Tannenberg, of Sayville, took over the management of the Star in 1915 and signed a contract with Sobol of the World Film Corporation. For an admission of 15 cents, 10 cents for children, Shubert and Brady Broadway shows that had been made into movies were shown. On Saturday nights Charlie Chaplin films were featured. In June 1915 the theater presented *The Girl I Left Behind Me*, starring North Haven's popular summer resident and noted actor, Robert Edeson.

By November 1923 the Star Theater had closed its doors for good, and the property, which ran from Main Street through to Meadow Street and was then bounded by Alippo's Garage and Charles Hedges' shop, was purchased by Morris Meyer.

With nightly films at the Star, the Atheneum, if they wanted to keep a crowd, had no choice but to show movies as well. In September 1915 B.F. Porter, who had installed a Simplex Moving Picture Machine in the famous Strand Theater in New York, was hired to install the same in the Atheneum. For 5 and 10 cents on Tuesday and Thursday, and 10 and 15 cents on the weekend, Pathe News, a cartoon, and a feature film were shown. During 1915 and 1916 Sexton and Dippel brought major films to Sag Harbor. Theda Bara and William Farnum were two of the favorite stars, and in May 1916 Robert Edeson, starring in *Big Jim Garrity*, made a personal appearance when the film was shown at the Atheneum.

Now, with the Montauk Motion Picture Theater no longer open, George Kiernan purchased the Hennigar property on the west side of Main Street, opposite Washington Street, with the idea of building a new movie theater. In September 1913 Kiernan had the existing structure torn down and hired the Corwin Brothers of North Haven to start construction on the new building. George's Theater opened to the public in October 1915, but a notice soon appeared that all law abiding people should decline from patronizing the place, due to the fact that George had defied Ordinance #15 issued by the village trustees and kept his theater open on Sunday! A serious offense in some eyes.

In 1917 management of George's Theater was taken over by Dr. G.C. McKay, who had new machinery installed, providing better quality entertainment than had been offered in the past. Five refined vaudeville acts with new music, songs and dancing, opened at George's, along with America's greatest comedy trio, Charles F. Van, Aurelia Clark, and James M. Cole, in the musical comedy, "The New King of Tramps," accompanied by Cole's Red Hussar Concert Band and Orchestra.

Marshall Seaton bought the theater in 1919 and re-opened the place in October of that year with a new name, The Elite. On its first anniversary, The Elite, in collaboration with Mashashimuet Park, showed pictures suitable for children every Friday night, and in October 1920 a full week of special films were shown. After the retirement of Marshall Seaton in January 1924, the contract and management of The Elite passed to Samuel Rosenthal. That same winter Rosenthal made improvements by redecorating the interior, moving the ticket office to the center of the rotunda, and adding three new chandeliers. In August the front row of seats were removed and the floor leveled so the place could also be used as a basketball court and dance floor. By 1927 The Elite had been taken over by Mike Glynn, and at that time the name of the place changed to Glynn's Sag Harbor Theater. A new more powerful projector was installed, and Donald Fairservis of Patchogue became manager. Two years later a major development took place when the theater signed up for a sound and talking picture, the first in the history of Sag Harbor's theaters. *Kitty*, a film taken from a novel by Warwick Deeping, was shown on October 13, 1929. In September 1930 the Sag Harbor Theater closed for six weeks while a late model RCA Sound apparatus was installed, which provided theatergoers with a "perfect presentation and finest sound and talking pictures."

In 1936 Sag Harbor had a fine new $25,000 movie theater. Workmen began demolishing the main auditorium in order to erect a modern fireproof building of steel and concrete on the same site. Designed by John Eberson of New York City, the 600-seat theater became an elegant place of entertainment for the area residents. A new lobby eliminating the existing stairs, new restrooms, the facade transformed into a concave arc, and a box office in the center of the lobby were just some of the changes made. The decorating was done by Kenny Studios and Rambush Decorating Company of New York, decorators of the Roxy Theater in New York City. Local contractors involved were S.J. Lynch & Sons of East Hampton, masons; I.H. Fordham of Sag Harbor, electrician; and Frank Johnson

THE SOCIAL SCENE AND THE ARTS

of East Hampton, building contractor. The new theater had its grand opening on June 3, 1936 and charged the same admission prices as the old movie house; evening rates were 20 cents for children and 40 cents for adults, and matinee prices 15 cents for children and 30 cents for adults.

Sag Harbor's present theater still occupies the site on which these early theaters stood, and its name and exterior have changed little since its building in 1936.

MOVIES MADE IN SAG HARBOR

It is interesting to note that not only were movies being shown in Sag Harbor in the early years, but also portions of at least four major films were shot in the area. William Farnum, noted film star and summer resident of North Haven, was responsible for Fox Films Corporation shooting part of *The Bondman* in North Haven in 1915. A fishing village was set up and several cottages built near Tindall's Grove, and a bridge built over a stream near the ferry slip. Many local residents had parts as extras, among them: John McNally Sr., Patrick Kelly, Thomas Carroll, Jeremiah Sullivan, John and Hughie Brady, Alfred Bates, Louis Edwards, Mary Logan, Mae McNally, Lillian Henricks, Madeline Fordham, Angela Archibald, and Frances Smith.

Scenes for a second movie were filmed in June 1917. The William Fox Players arrived that summer to shoot *Major Charles Gordon, MD*, under the direction of producer Frank Lloyd. William Farnum, in the starring role, had as his leading lady the famous and talented Mary Martin.

Five years later the Famous Players Lasky Corporation selected Sag Harbor as location for all the exterior shots of George Ade's play, *Back Home and Broke*. When location manager Arthur Cozine, of Brooklyn, saw Sag Harbor, he immediately knew it was just the place he was looking for. The cast, headed by Thomas Meighan and Lila Lee, stayed at the Sea View House and other rooming houses in the village. A "Home Coming Parade" scene was shot on Main Street, with 40 local people having small parts. Pictured in the movie were William Cook's Department Store, Woodward Brothers Grocery, Fahys Watch Case Factory, the Masonic Temple, the bank, and the homes of William Crozier, George Cary and William Donohue.

In November 1932 Paramount Studios sent their camera crew to Sag Harbor to take street scenes for their upcoming film, *No Man of Her Own*, starring Clark Gable and Carole Lombard. They spent three days on Long Island looking for a suitable Main Street and decided that Sag Harbor was perfect for their needs. On March 8, 1933 the picture was shown at the Sag Harbor Theater, much to the delight of the village population who had a great time identifying familiar places and faces.

Later that year *Back Home and Broke* had a return showing on June 6, 1933. The arrival of the train in Sag Harbor with conductor Mercer flagging the train, the parade on Main Street with the local band and local drivers in the cars, and the employees of the watchcase factory leaving the building at the end of the day were all scenes that brought back fond memories to those who witnessed the making of the movie in 1922. At that return engagement of *Back Home and Broke*, manager Sullivan hired Mac Lewis and his orchestra to play throughout the silent feature, as the public now had a taste of talkies, and silent films were a thing of the past.

So, long before Alan Alda's *Sweet Liberty* was filmed in Sag Harbor in 1985, the village had already been the location for the filming of several other motion pictures.

The Public Golf Course

Cortland Edwards, B.D. Corwin, and other golf enthusiasts went to Russell's Neck, at Little North West, in the early 1900s and established a nine-hole golf course on land that was formerly the Edmund LaGuire dairy farm. Each member of this early club was responsible for the care and upkeep of one green. When the club disbanded, members were forced to use neighboring courses.

In 1929 a renewed interest led Mr. E.P. Eaton to contact Warren T. Diefendorf, owner of the property on which the defunct course stood, and learned that the 400-acre piece of land would be available in about two years. Redwood had recently been sold, and that 70-acre piece of property would have made a fine golf course, but the 18- to 20-thousand-dollar figure was too high a price for the club to consider, so they decided to wait for the Diefendorf property.

Twenty-five enthusiastic golfers and other interested residents attended an organizational meeting, in the Municipal Building on November 1, 1929, and elected a Board of Governors, consisting of town members and the following officers; C.H. Tillinghast, president; F.G. Thayer, vice president; A.M. Lewis, secretary; and C.H. Edwards, treasurer. Annual dues were set at $25 for men and ten dollars for women, one dollar per day or 50 cents a hole. It was also decided to create a junior membership, with a five-dollar fee entitling them to playing privileges.

When February arrived, club members burned the grass, which had grown tall during the years the course wasn't in use, and constructed a sample green of sand and clay on the west side of the property. A contract to build the course was awarded to James McMahon Jr., with work expected to be completed by mid-April. The greens were outlined, cedar trees removed, the mossy ground rolled, and the road leading to the course filled in and leveled.

During the first year, the existing house on the property served as a clubhouse. Two rooms were renovated, re-papered and painted to furnish a shop for the golf pro, Gilbert McCauley. A flagpole was donated and erected on the grounds, and the fairways cut and rolled, in preparation for the grand opening. The new Sag Harbor Golf Course opened to the public in May 1930.

In February 1931 Dick Wagner became the new golf pro, and at that time the greens were raised and surfaced with a mixture of oil and sand. New bunkers and traps were built, and a porch added across the front of the clubhouse. This house was later destroyed by fire, and in April 1933 plans were in the making to replace the clubhouse. After the new structure was built, the addition in February 1935 of a fireplace, office, and social rooms made it more comfortable to the members of the club. R. DiGate, of East Hampton, offered his services to build the fireplace, and Levi Bass volunteered to paint the place. Members of the club furnished the material. At that time George Dippel became president of the golf club, and Charles Staudinger, keeper of the fairways and greens.

The Yacht Club

Prior to the establishment of the Sag Harbor Yacht Club on March 27, 1897, two small clubs existed. The Maycroft Yacht Club, confined principally to the Cove, and the Harbor Yacht Club, on the Bay, were organized for the purpose of holding aquatic sports and races. In 1897 they merged and became one strong club, which they named the Sag Harbor Yacht Club. The earliest club pier was located near the old North Haven bridge.

A deed of conveyance for a waterfront lot on Bay Street, on which the new clubhouse and pier would be built, was given by Frank C. Havens, and a survey completed in June 1913 fixed the boundaries. The pier, built by Preston & Horton of Greenport, was 276 feet long and 6 feet wide, with a bulkhead 14 by 36 feet. It was completed in October 1913 at a cost of $1148, with an additional $850 to be used to construct a clubhouse the following spring. Howard Leavitt, a club member, filled in the lot and graded it.

When spring arrived, a clubhouse that formerly belonged to the New York Club of Shelter Island became available for sale. Rather than build a new one as previously planned, the club bought the Shelter Island building for $500 and the clubhouse furniture for an additional $135. It was moved across the bay to the end of the yacht club dock, where it was placed. A 4700-gallon gasoline tank was installed, and fuel for the boats piped to the pier. All Hampton yacht owners were invited to join the club, which boasted one of the finest landing floats in the area. The clubhouse also contained a reading room for its members and employed a full-time custodian.

In July 1920 a wooden pergola was erected on the yacht club property, with John Ward doing the work under the supervision of Eugene LaManna. Material for the pergola was donated by club member A.H. Ball of Watermill.

The Village Beach

The Ladies Village Improvement Society met in December 1922 and discussed the possibility of acquiring a lot on the Havens property to provide the residents of the village with their own bathing beach. Acting for the village, C. Augustine Kiernan accepted an offer from Lila R. Havens, of Piedmont, California, of a stretch of waterfront property off of Bay Street, which would be called Havens Memorial Park, in memory of the late Frank C. Havens, formerly of Sag Harbor. The village had to fill in the meadows behind the waterfront in order to build a road to the beach.

In July 1929 a long wooden picnic table, with benches and an attached roof, was constructed on the beach, electric lights leading to the park were installed, and plans to build a permanent bathing pavilion and bathhouses were considered. Wire safety pens were designed and built, which kept the very young children close to shore and in relative safety. A freshwater pump, driven by R.C. Barry & Son, provided fresh drinking water for those at the beach. Paul Hastman, associate director of Mashashimuet Park, gave swimming lessons to the children at a cost of 25 cents a day.

Mrs. Edna Dee Bunday opened a restaurant stand in 1936 on the Joseph Murphy property, at the rear of the beach, and sold five-cent ice cream cones and three-cent soda to beachgoers. During the evening, hot and cold sandwiches, cold drinks, cigarettes, and candy were available.

The beach continues to be used by Sag Harbor residents up to the present time. Barbeque grills, swings and other playground equipment, and a lifeguard on duty can now be found at Havens Beach, making it a safe and pleasant place for both children and adults to enjoy.

The Sag Harbor Historical Society and Other Organizations

A group of local citizens interested in preserving the historical integrity of the village, honoring their founding fathers, and endeavoring to keep alive interest

THE SOCIAL SCENE AND THE ARTS 295

in Sag Harbor's past, met in 1895 to establish a historical society. They congregated in the library room where organizational reports of various committees were listened to, a constitution passed, and the following officers elected: President, Reverend John J. Harrison; vice-presidents, David P. Vail and Henry F. Cook; secretary, Walter S. Elliott; assistant secretary, William C. Greene; and treasurer, Francis H. Palmer. Also elected were councilors for one year, Edgar Wade and Anna Mulford; for two years, Stephen H. Edwards and Charles Watson Payne; for three years, Dr. C.S. Stillwell and Mrs. Sarah Babcock; and for four years, William Wallace Tooker and Virginia Keese. Dues were set at one dollar per member per year or a payment of $10, which constituted lifetime membership. The society also had the pleasure of hearing historical lectures each month by the distinguished Henry P. Hedges.

For the first two years considerable interest was shown, and the society grew to number more than one hundred members. Monthly reports printed in the *Sag Harbor Express* described their meetings, programs, discussions, and planned activities. Some of the interesting happenings of the next few years follow.

At the December 1896 annual meeting, entertainment was provided by the St. Cecelia Society, after which secretary Elliott read an interesting paper on the prospective work of the society, and Mrs. Gilbert Cooper received a vote of thanks for two ancient papers she presented to the organization.

The February 1897 meeting opened with a piano recital followed by a Shakespearean reading by Charles Watson Payne. President Harrison then read a biographical sketch of the late Henry Wentworth Hunt that had been compiled by Mrs. Hunt in 1858 and read, in March of that year, before the Sag Harbor Lyceum. In connection with this was the reading of an address delivered before the "Sons of Tammany" by Mrs. Hunt at Setauket, Long Island in 1812, to welcome in the season of blossoms. On a more serious note, Reverend Gordon T. Lewis opened a discussion relating to the indiscriminate cutting down of shade trees in Sag Harbor and environs. A committee made up of Mr. Lewis, Charles Watson Payne, and Stephen H. Edwards were appointed to speak to property owners and urge them to make every effort to save their trees from further destruction.

At a historical society reception held in April 1897, Mr. and Mrs. Frank Beckwith held the audience captive by their delightful rendition of "See the Pale Moon." Miss Keese sang the "Minuet," while eight young ladies danced the same, costumed in gowns of "ye ancient days." John H. Hunt presented, in the name of Captain Daniel Atwood Eldridge, two oil paintings illustrating the Sag Harbor whaling industry. Those in attendance then participated in dancing the

Virginia Reel and enjoying refreshments from the chocolate table.

At the final meeting before their summer break in 1897, the society enjoyed hearing a lecture on the "Rise and Fall of the Sag Harbor Institute" and a historical sketch on *The Sag Harbor Corrector*. At the annual meeting, when they resumed in the early winter, elections were held, and Reverend Harrison was re-elected president. Henry F. Cook and Georgia H. Reeve were elected vice-presidents; Charles Watson Payne, secretary; and Francis H. Palmer, treasurer. A music committee made up of Miss Florence French, Georgia Reeve, and Mrs. Edgar Wade was formed. Dues at that time were changed to 50 cents per individual or one dollar for the entire family.

In February 1899 the society had the privilege of hearing L.J.G. Kuhlwein, gunner of the *U.S.F.S. Olympia*, which took part in the battle of Manila, speak about that eventful day, May 1, 1898.

At the April meeting that year, William Wallace Tooker brought one of his rare Indian relics to the meeting. It was an *uloo*, or Eskimo knife, found at Barcelona by a young man who sold it to Tooker. William Wallace claimed it was the first of its kind ever found in this area.

A very worthy project, taken on by the Sag Harbor Historical Society in 1901-02, proposed the placement of monuments to mark historic sites in Sag Harbor. A committee of Francis Palmer, Anna Mulford, Ida Miles, Mrs. Frank C. French, and Shamgar Babcock went about collecting donations. It was decided to place one stone at the site of the British Outpost on Brickkiln Road, the second at Sleight's Hill, commemorating the War of 1812, and the third on Union Street near the Old Burying Ground, where a British fort stood during the Revolution. Within a month $300 had been collected, with Mrs. James H. Aldrich donating $250 of it. The monuments were dedicated on May 30, 1902 at the 125th anniversary of the Battle of Sag Harbor.

By 1903 the Historical Society seemed to lose momentum. Reverend Clarence H. Wilson was elected president, replacing the retiring Reverend Harrison who had served in that capacity for seven years. Three months after assuming office, Reverend Wilson decided to leave Sag Harbor and resigned. Whether it was lack of leadership or lack of interest, meetings became sporadic, and finally stopped completely, and the November 19, 1903 issue of *The Sag Harbor Express* queried: "What has become of the Sag Harbor Historical Society? Is it sleeping the sleep of death or is it merely taking a long rest preparatory to full fledged life?" Apparently, it was the sleep of death, for the society disbanded at that time, after eight years of historical activities in the village.

Renewed interest in the Historical Society in 1936 brought about its revival.

THE SOCIAL SCENE AND THE ARTS

Kenneth Anderson and Thomas Bisgood were instrumental in its re-establishment. Membership was open to both men and women, at a yearly fee of 50 cents or a lifetime membership at the cost of ten dollars. The aim of the society was "to engender and develop an appreciation and regard for the historical background of Sag Harbor and surrounding areas and to collect and preserve records and objects of historical value, house them in the museum, offer historical thought and study, and to disseminate historical knowledge especially as it pertains to the whaling port of Sag Harbor and its environs."

One of the main objectives of the group was to open an historic and whaling museum. Initially the basement of the John Jermain Memorial Library was considered for that purpose, but through the efforts of the Sag Harbor Round Table Club and the generosity of the Masons, the ground floor of the Masonic Temple was acquired. William D. Halsey spoke at the February 1936 meeting on the subject of what type of articles would be the best to collect. He suggested that portraits by Hubbard Fordham, miniature portraits by Nathan Rogers, lusterware, pewter, brass, ivory, whalebone, lances, harpoons, blubber hooks, compasses, sextants, and log books were most valuable. Miss Helen Bennett, secretary to the late historian Harry D. Sleight, had the duty of arranging, protecting, preserving, and cataloguing the material.

Two rooms of displays were set up, including a collection of West Indies memorabilia loaned by Captain John B. Phillips. George P. Rackett, curator, reported that between opening day June 20, 1936 and September of that year, 5000 people visited the museum. The following summer the great try pots, donated by William D. Halsey, and the jaw bones of the whale were put in place by Captain Phillips.

Suffolk Lodge IOOF, Independent Order of Odd Fellows, was another early society in the village. Organized on June 29, 1843, with five members, it was the first of the order established in Suffolk County. By 1874 its members had grown to 90. An encampment, begun in 1859, was suspended ten years later. In May 1871 it resumed, with 25 men joining.

The Enigma Club of Sag Harbor had its first meeting on November 1, 1869, and its constitution adopted the following week. Only unmarried white males of good moral character, in sound mind and body, and at least 21 years of age were eligible for membership. Their motto was "Honesty, Brotherly Love and Mutual Enjoyment."

The Agassiy Club, Chapter 409 was established in 1883. At its first meeting on January 2nd, its constitution and by-laws were written up and were adopted May 11, 1883. Ivan C. Byram was president of the organization at that time. At their weekly meetings scientific articles were read. Insects, sea creatures, and animals were studied and discussed, and specimens brought in to be examined.

The Montauk Court of Foresters No. 85 was instituted on February 3, 1888. Meetings were held twice monthly in the Washington Hall Block, and membership grew to 190. Also organized at the same time was the Montauk Circle No. 1121 Companions of the Foresters of America. The Foresters tended to the sick and infirm, paying sick members $5 per week, and paying all physicians fees and medicine bills.

The Old Sag Harbor Village Improvement Society formed at the home of Dr. James H. Rogers on Main Street in the fall of 1879. Officers were elected, and an executive committee of 18 people was appointed, seven of whom were women. Dr. Rogers was elected president; Jonas Winters, vice-president; David P. Vail, treasurer; and B.D. Sleight, secretary. The constitution adopted was based on that of the Laurel Hill Association of Stockbridge, Massachusetts. At a meeting held in the Methodist Church on March 1, 1880, the proceedings of the society were accepted, and 50 public-minded citizens joined the organization, each paying one dollar. Although the society was credited with making considerable improvements in the village, the group disbanded after a short time.

On August 12, 1887 a new improvement society formed, one made up of women only, and they called themselves the Ladies Village Improvement Society. Its main function was to beautify and improve conditions in the village by keeping its woods, roads, and cemeteries in order, and to keep the trees trimmed so they wouldn't interfere with buggy traffic. Mrs. John Sherry, Mrs. Joseph Fahys, and Miss Anna Mulford were selected to elect officers, and from the 35 enrolled as members, Mrs. Charles Daly was elected president; Mrs. Edgar Wade, vice-president; Mrs. Blanche Sherry, secretary; and Mrs. H. Frank Cook, treasurer. An annual fee of 50 cents was collected from each member. The society planted willow trees, saw to it that the streets were improved with the spreading of Peekskill gravel, and had an iron fence placed around the Old Burying Ground. In 1907 they were responsible for having the name of South Street changed to Jermain Avenue. During World War I the society sewed and knitted articles and did other war relief work, aiding the Red Cross tremendously. Following the war the Ladies Village Improvement Society donated $100 toward the erection of the memorial at Otter Pond.

With the turn of the century, several new organizations and societies emerged. The Sag Harbor Council 584 of the Knights of Columbus was founded. It was instituted on July 7, 1900 and its 70 members met twice weekly in the Odd Fellows' Hall.

THE SOCIAL SCENE AND THE ARTS 299

Wegwagonock Council No. 64 Jr. O.U.A.M. was established February 21, 1903, with 85 members meeting weekly in Forester's Hall. Hogonock Council No. 46 Daughters of Liberty organized in August 1903 and was the only woman's secret society in Sag Harbor. Momoweta Tribe No. 459 of the Improved Order of Red Men was organized by George Farley, John Brogan, and William E. Jobe on June 20, 1904. The 53 members of the tribe met twice monthly in Forester's Hall. There was also a Sag Harbor branch of the Women's Political Union in 1914. The Campfire Girls Wegwagonock Chapter and a YMCA both existed in the village before 1920.

During the 1890s several of the wealthy residents of Sag Harbor and North Haven formed the Sag Harbor Lawn Tennis Club. The group consisted of about 20 young people from the Fahys, Aldrich, Sterling, Morton, Napier, Cook, and Sleight families. Lawn-tennis matches and business meetings were held on the grounds of Dr. Morton's estate on Redwood, where the grounds were rolled, fenced in, and kept in good order. At a meeting in 1893 the question of dissolving the club was brought up. Although there seemed to be a lack of interest and a declining membership, they decided to continue. In 1894 the Huntting property was secured for the season, and a court set up on the front lawn. It isn't known if this was the last summer the club existed. No further records have been found.

The Ku Klux Klan Meeting

The Ku Klux Klan, a secret terrorist society in the United States, had three consecutive movements; the first, in the south during the reconstruction period following the Civil War; the second, established on a wider geographical basis in the teens and twenties; and the third which arose after World War II.

The second movement was incorporated in 1915 in Georgia as a fraternal organization, under the name Invisible Empire Knights of the Ku Klux Klan, and was basically modeled on that of its 19th century predecessor. Following World War I the Klan expanded rapidly and became active in about 40 states. During its heyday in the early twenties, it numbered more than 1,500,000 members. The society projected ideas of super-patriotism and denounced aliens, liberals, trade unions, and striking workers as subversive radicals. Some Klansmen resorted to violence, but the majority at this period in history were non-violent. They marched in parades, paid dues, and voted for Klan-endorsed political candidates.

As the Klan spread north, it invaded the rural communities of America, preying on the gullible and impressionable, and Sag Harbor was not immune to the persuasiveness of the Klan. In fact, the residents of Sag Harbor showed a great deal of interest in learning what the Klan was all about.

In December 1923 a request was made to the First Presbyterian Church of Sag Harbor to allow its sanctuary to be used for a Ku Klux Klan meeting. The church was the largest building in the village for a public gathering. Reverend Sidney Barrett, pastor of the church, had no recourse but to put the request to the church session, who decided they had no objections as long as the speaker was an ordained minister, and the Klan had many. They sent Reverend Andrew Van Antwerpen of Sayville, Long Island, a Klansman and minister, to speak at the public meeting and explain the aims and objectives of the Klan. The overwhelming interest of the public packed the sanctuary, filling the main floor and the balconies. Scores stood in the aisles and 200 more, unable to gain admission, stood in the churchyard. It was said that not since the day Henry Ward Beecher lectured in the church had such a mass of people assembled. It was a crowd estimated at 1400 to 1500 and included not only Protestants but many Catholics, Jews, and Negroes.

Van Antwerpen's topics were: The Jew Opposed to the Acceptance of Christianity, The Catholic and the Parochial School, The Negro and the Klan's Opposition to Intermarriage, and Protestant America for Americans. Van Antwerpen stated that the Klan was expounded as one of the largest fraternal orders in America, standing for the tenets of Christian faith, patriotism, and law and order. After the lecture the meeting closed with the singing of "America."

Did this meeting have an impact on the residents of Sag Harbor? Well, it certainly stirred up the clergy of the local churches. The Sunday following the meeting, Reverend Raymond Scofield, rector of Christ Church, preached an anti-Klan sermon, entitled "The Cross or the Klan." Scofield spoke kindly of the Jew and Negro and pleaded for tolerancy against intolerancy. Dr. Burdette Brown, of the Methodist Episcopal Church, also spoke and stated that, in his opinion, Van Antwerpen didn't know his subject thoroughly and was not willing to tell the facts as they really were. He said, "Klansmen do not come out in the open; they are not known," and went on to say, "no one was able to identify any Klan members at the meeting other than the speaker himself." Three hundred people crowded into the Episcopal Church to hear the two preachers relate their strong anti-Klan feelings.

So, it seems that the Ku Klux Klan's meeting in Sag Harbor did little to change the attitudes and beliefs of the local people, and soon after this brief flurry of activity, interest in the Klan diminished. If any other meetings were held in the village, they didn't warrant news worthy enough to be covered in the local newspapers.

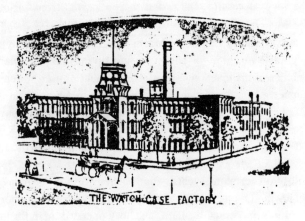

4

NEW BUSINESS ENTERPRISES

William S. Eaton, head engraver of Fahys Watch Case Factory, started his dial works in 1892 with a capital of $7000. He leased the second floor of the old flour mill property and, with his associates, George C. Raynor, Charles Pierson and B. Lyon, manufactured dials for watches and clocks. For many years he built and perfected a number of different engraving machines. In 1911 he formed the Engravers and Printers Machinery Company, incorporating under the laws of New York State. Edmund S. Eaton was elected president and general manager, and William Eaton, chairman of the board of directors and advisory committee.

Eaton's Engravers and Printers Machinery Company

At the Eaton property on Palmer Terrace, he opened an experimental shop and research laboratory, with J.F. Payne supervisor. There in 1913 Mr. Eaton invented his "Rotary Photogravure," a device of printing from a copper cylinder engraved by a photo mechanical process. His method engraved the roll by a single helical line of varying depth, starting from one end of the cylinder and running unbroken to the other. Edmund, his son, J.F. Payne, and W.J. Donovan, along with Eaton, attended the National Association of Steel and

Copper Plate Engravers and explained the function of his new machine. It proved to be very successful, and orders were received from various parts of the United States, England, and Australia.

Mr. Eaton's "Century Engraving Machine" was used extensively throughout the world. It was a machine for engraving inscriptions on silverware and fine jewelry. Another of his machines called the "Model C," used for engraving on steel and copper plates for business purposes, also met with great success. In October 1913 he leased a floor in the old schoolhouse as a demonstration room and again rented space in the old mill.

In 1918 Eaton's engraving machines were in such a demand that the old shop was no longer adequate. In the spring of that year, excavation began for his new factory on Jermain Avenue. Plans called for a brick building 40 feet square, with a wing on one side 20 by 50 feet. A Brooklyn contractor was hired to build the three-story structure. Eaton's factory operated there for many years, designing and building other machines, including one for the United States Treasury Department that played an important part in the printing of government currency. Another achievement attributed to Mr. Eaton was a geometric lathe. In April 1920 William Eaton resigned after 28 years as head of the company, and his son was then elected president.

C. Weidlog's Manufacturing Company

Charles Weidlog, a machinist formerly employed at Fahys Watch Case Factory, invented a device he called an "improved style of friction indicator," and which he patented March 27, 1903. The indicator, designed to show the depth of a cut or groove made by a drill press or lathe, was manufactured at his tool shop in the little brick building on Division Street, known as the Umbrella House. He called his new business the C. Weidlog Manufacturing Company. The indicator took little space and was a labor- and time-saving mechanism. Orders came in from machine shops all over the country, and by October 1903 the business had grown to such an extent that the Umbrella House was no longer big enough to handle the increase in his sales. Henry Meyer owned a building opposite the rear of the Union School Annex on Division Street, and Weidlog tried, without success, to acquire a ten-year lease on the building. No further mention of the business is noted, leaving one to speculate that Weidlog soon left the area.

NEW BUSINESS ENTERPRISES

The Suffolk County Building Block Company

Another industry located in the old flour mill building was the Suffolk County Building Block Company, a factory that manufactured hollow concrete building blocks for foundations. It was an ingenious new process patented by Harmon S. Palmer of Washington, D.C., and a decided improvement over brick or stone foundations. F.H. Palmer of Sag Harbor, no relation to the inventor, secured exclusive rights to sell the blocks and organized the Suffolk County Building Block Company.

Machinery was ordered and installed, and the factory opened in November 1903. Stock sold for 25 cents on the dollar, and in less than two days the entire $20,000 capital was taken up. Officers elected for the new business were: F.H. Palmer, president; William C. Greene, vice-president; and Arthur T. Brown, secretary.

The factory's ideal location at the waterfront made it possible to load and discharge with ease, using both the dock and the railroad, whose tracks extended to the factory. Sand for the block-making process came from property owned by the S.H. Realty Company on Bay Street, about a half mile away. Three large block-making machines manufactured the product, which was shipped to cities all across the United States.

The Bloch Hat Pin Factory

Mr. Emanuel E. Bloch, a former Sag Harbor resident, came from Manhattan to discuss the possibility of bringing his hat pin factory to Sag Harbor. The Board of Trade in the village granted Bloch permission, and in 1910 he made arrangements for the move. Bloch leased the annex of the old Union School on Division Street and anticipated providing jobs for many of the local people.

Emanuel Bloch, president of the company, once operated a butcher shop in Sag Harbor with his brother, and later he was employed at the Fahys Watch Case Factory as an engraver. David Meyer, vice-president, was a successful businessman in Sag Harbor, having been in the clothing business since 1883. Dr. W.H. VanNostrand, a Sag Harbor dentist for 14 years, was elected secretary of the hat pin factory.

The New World, under the caption "At Last! A Safe Hat Pin!" stated:

> The safety hatpin which we have all been expecting for a long time has come at last. Here it is, the invention of Emanual Bloch. Mr. Bloch does not say whether he invented this hatpin as a measure of self defense only, or as protection to the rest of the human race. No one who in a street

car jam has come within an inch and a half of having their eyes jabbed out by a protruding hatpin can fail to appreciate the benefit that lies in the production of the little balls on the ends of this pin. Different hatpins, somewhat on this order, have been seen but never been popular with the long-haired sex because the end of the pin was screw-shaped and difficult to ram through the hat—besides inflicting torture when it caught on the hair. Mr. Bloch's hatpin does away with the little screw and the sharp point of the pin is protected by a pretty little metal case of gilt or silver wire.

By June 17, 1910, with carpenters installing the work benches and attending to other last minute details, the place was almost ready to open. In July the machinery arrived from Rhode Island on the steamer *Wyandotte*, and John Mott, local trucker, delivered it to the factory where machinist Blaiklock hooked it up. The machinery consisted of a 25-horsepower Erie Center crank engine, presses, polishing heads and blowers, and a 35-horsepower boiler. J. Fran Cooper of Providence, Rhode Island was hired as superintendant.

Apparently the stores in Sag Harbor carried the new hat pin, for Davis' Department store advertised that they were having a special on Bloch's new safety hat pins, priced from ten cents to two dollars.

It appears that the hat pin factory was in operation for just a short period of time, for no other mention of it is noted in the local newspapers, and in 1912 the Kiss Pottery Company occupied the building.

The Kiss Art Pottery Company

In 1910 another attempt at pottery-making in Sag Harbor occurred when the Kiss family opened the Kiss Art Pottery Company. It was located on the east side of Madison Street, three houses south of Henry Street. Aaron, Charlie, and Coleman Kiss, along with their sister and her husband, operated the place, with Charlie Kiss elected supervisor.

A description of the facility provided by an individual who, as a young man worked there, tells us that:

> In the middle room of the house the spinning wheels were set up. The color was applied in the front room. Opposite the spinning wheels was where they put on the lead glaze. The wheels were on pivots or ball bearings and a table or bench ran along the wall, on which the clay was held. There were four or five wheels along the bench so there was always plenty of clay handy for the operators. A foot pedal was used to operate the wheels and a man hired to mix clay did it with his

NEW BUSINESS ENTERPRISES

feet...took his shoes and socks off and went to work. Outside the kitchen door, in the back yard, stood the kiln and other out-buildings.

The secret method of Mr. Kiss' process was to apply both color and glaze without firing between each step, thus requiring only one firing. The process, however, proved unsuccessful, as the glaze crumbled within a few years.

In April 1912 the Kiss Art Pottery Company moved from Madison Street into the annex of the Union School on Division Street. Machinery was installed at a cost of $3000, and in June it opened for business, employing 20 workmen. C.E. Fritts became president of the company. A large modern kiln was constructed on the site, and the business opened with a capital of $50,000.

A description of the operation at the new location tells us that the section where the pottery was placed was at ground level and the fire box below. Full-sized pieces of cord wood were used to fire up the kiln. Clay containers held the pots, each container holding several of them, depending on the size, and each container sealed with a ring of clay. A press with a plate full of holes made the long strings of clay, called "worms," that were used to seal the containers. A triangle with points was used beneath each pot to separate them and prevent the glaze from joining them together.

It took several days to fill the kiln, after which the brick door was sealed up with the clay worms. A small peephole left in the door permitted checking conditions during the firing, which took another several days to complete. Shifts were necessary, as the procedure had to keep going day and night. It took several more days to cool enough to open the door and remove the pottery. During the firing, cookouts were held for the employees, with corn, meat, clams, and other food, depending on the season.

In 1914 shipments of Kiss pottery were sent to New York City for export to Puerto Rico. Another shipment of 13,000 pieces was sent to New York and sold to the Grand Union Tea Company for stores in the city. Thomas Glenn was president of Kiss at that time, Charlie Kiss, vice-president, and F.E. Shelton, secretary. Large quantities of potter's clay were brought to the pottery works from the clay beds at Northside, Sag Harbor.

The Kiss Art Pottery Company remained in operation for about ten years, until the Kiss family moved from the area. With that move in 1921, the years of pottery-making in early Sag Harbor came to an end.

The Cloak Factory

As early as June 1902 representatives of the Brody & Funt Cloak Manufacturers of Brooklyn visited Sag Harbor, looking for a suitable building in which to open a cloak factory. A large place was needed with a gas engine to run their machinery, and at that time a suitable location was not found.

Eight years later, in July 1910, New York cloak manufacturer Harry Kittzinger & Company came to Sag Harbor and leased the old Union School building, recently vacated when the students moved into the newly finished Pierson High School. They installed machinery, and jobs for 200 machine operators were anticipated. The Sag Harbor Lighting Company installed a ten horsepower Kumberger gas engine, capable of running 50 sewing machines, and the first workers were hired.

A year later the Kittzinger Cloak Factory enlarged their plant, with the hope of increasing their work force and payroll to $100,000 annually. Things looked bright, but by May 21, 1912 *The Sag Harbor Express* reported that nothing was doing at the cloak factory. It stated, "What has become of the cloak factory industry that expected a weekly payroll of $1000?" Apparently, their expectations were never realized, and the cloak factory soon closed its doors for good.

The C.W. Butts, Inc. Factory

Another small business in Sag Harbor during the 1920s was the C.W. Butts Company, manufacturer of crowns, pendants, and bows for watchcases. Established by Charles W. Butts and E.P. Eaton, the factory originally operated out of a room in Eaton's Engravers and Printers Machinery Company. After the death of the founder, his sons carried on the business with Frederick S. Spencer and then Edward B. Hale, managing superintendents.

As the factory grew it provided employment for 11 operators, and its expansion led to its moving into rooms on the ground floor of the Municipal Building. In time Mr. Eaton sold his interest to the Butts brothers, and in August 1924 the factory re-located to East Orange, New Jersey.

B. Aptheken & Son — Rayon Factory

Another small industry that came to Sag Harbor was B. Aptheken & Son, Inc., manufacturers of rayon undergarments. In November 1933 the firm relocated from Brooklyn to Sag Harbor and set up business in the Municipal Building. Twenty sewing machines were installed, and when the call went out for seamstresses, 100 women and girls applied for the positions. Twenty-five girls were initially selected to begin a four- to six-week training session while permanent quarters in the E.W. Bliss Building were being readied for occupancy. The employees were paid $13 for a 40-hour week. Before a year had passed, production slowed dramatically, as strikes at the rayon supply companies resulted in a problem purchasing material to make the garments. The rayon factory struggled along until July 1937 and, finally, went out of business. Shortly after, Joseph Ross, who had come to Sag Harbor with Aptheken as chief cutter, opened the Harbor Underwear Company and began manufacturing ladies' rayon slips.

The Bulova Watch Company

When Fahys Watch Case Factory closed in January 1931, it left the village in dire need of a major industry to replace it and provide jobs for those left unemployed. Skilled polishers, engravers and machinists either moved from the area or found work in other fields, unable to pursue their trades. What Sag Harbor needed was another watchcase factory, and in June 1937 village officials devised a plan to have a branch of the Bulova Watch Company locate here.

In August 1937 the Village leased to the Sag Harbor Guild, Inc., a wholly-owned subsidiary of Bulova Watch Company, a portion of the second floor of the old factory, in which to open a watchcase factory. The village had previously leased the place from the Joseph Fahys Company. Before it was possible for any industry to occupy the building, repairs were necessary. A Citizens Committee, appointed by Mayor Kiernan and headed by A.T. Brown, was formed. The committee conducted a subscription campaign to which private individuals and local businesses would pledge money to pay for the renovation and purchase machinery for the new industry. When the machines were installed, a small group of men were hired to work on an experimental basis. After production had reached about 30,000 cases per week, jobs became available for 200 men and women, and this was the start of the Bulova Watch Company's long association with the village of Sag Harbor.

A business directory of 1910-11 and one of the 1920s can be found in the Appendix.

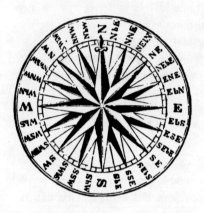

5

SAG HARBOR IN THE WARS

Nineteen seventeen saw the intervention of the United States into World War I. It was an event of monumental importance, the country coming of age as the world's greatest economic power, and by the end of the war, a major military power as well. With the declaration of war against Germany in April of that year, once again America's fathers, sons, and daughters were called upon to fight for the cause of peace.

World War I

In May 1917 the Selective Service Act required that all men between 21 and 30 must register, and when it became apparent that not enough men were available from that age group, it was extended to include those up to age 45. Suffolk County was required to furnish 871 men for the first army of 657,000. Sixty-four names were drawn from Sag Harbor, and those physically fit, with no just cause for exemption, were drafted. Any failing to report within ten days were treated as "slackers" and were subject to prosecution. The first 23 were called in August 1917, and many took their basic training at Camp Upton in Yaphank, Long Island.

A number of local boys served in the 77th Infantry, New York's own "Melting Pot" Division, a division comprised of descendants of 42 different nationalities. The Army, Navy, Marines, Coast Guard, and Aero-Force were well represented, and Sag Harbor's men and women served as machinists, signal operators, doctors, nurses, balloonists, mine-layers, wagoners, submarine chasers, and field artillerists.

As in past conflicts Sag Harbor's home bodies also proved to be a patriotic lot. Camp Aldrich, a local unit of the New York Guards, was established and held weekly drills, with Ivan C. Byram in command. An active unit of the Red Cross made hospital garments, bandages, knitted socks, and gave of their time and energies in numerous other ways. Local citizens saved everything from tin foil to fruit pits, from which carbon was extracted, an element necessary to combat Germany's poison gas attacks. They saved War Stamps, bought War Bonds, and donated money. In October 1918 Sag Harbor's donations to the War Department topped its quota by contributing $207,000. Factory whistles blew and church bells rang to celebrate the fete.

The village had a service flag, 35 by 55 feet in size, made of wool bunting, and which carried the initials of each veteran on a star. Donations were collected and several hundred dollars raised. The sisters of the Sacred Heart of Mary Academy also made a service flag of silk and satin, with over 100 blue stars and five gold stars. It was dedicated on December 12, 1918 and hung suspended from the arch in the sanctuary. The other flag hung from the top of the Municipal Building, and because of its immense size, it almost touched the sidewalk below.

At the end of the war a Victory and Peace Celebration took place at the Atheneum, where Sag Harbor's men and women were welcomed home. They, along with America's other sons and daughters, were the determining factor in the outcome of World War I.

Details of the men and women who served in World War I can be found in the Appendix.

The World War I Monument

After World War I ended and the veterans had returned home, a memorial committee was formed for the purpose of erecting a monument in memory of the men and women who served in the recent conflict. A public meeting was held in the Atheneum on January 16, 1919. One proposal considered was to erect a granite victory column surmounted by a large bronze eagle, with the base bearing two bronze tablets. One tablet would hold the names of those who gave the supreme sacrifice. It was suggested placing it at the north end of Main Street, near the Long Wharf, and calling the area surrounding it Victory Park. Another idea was to plant trees along the approach to the wharf, each one dedicated to one of the boys who died for his country.

Five years passed before the monument was erected. During those years $1300, or about half of the money needed for the project, had been raised. In the meantime, a different site had been selected. A decision was reached to erect the monument on a triangular green at the south side of Otter Pond, and permission was granted by the Sage Foundation. Ivan Byram located a native boulder, 14 feet tall, on the grounds of the Sea View House, and Joseph Miller, an East Hampton house mover, transported the massive rock to the site.

H.E. Bishop, local engineer, designed the monument, volunteering much of his time. A bronze plaque, made by the firm Gorham & Company and carrying the names of the veterans, was installed by Edward T. Archibald and his assistants. Stars were placed at the names of Sag Harbor's fallen heroes. The bronze eagle surmounting the memorial was crafted by John Williams & Company. Shrubbery, trees, and lawns were planted, and cement walks built around the area, making it a fitting tribute to the veterans who served in World War I.

Other War Monuments and Memorials

In October 1896 the Ladies Monumental Association, after years of work, had a monument erected at the triangular junction of Main and Madison Streets, as a tribute to honor the brave men from Sag Harbor who took part in the Civil War.

The statue, facing the business district, depicts a volunteer private at rest, and was acquired at a cost of $1200. It stands 15 feet 6 inches and weighs 10 tons. The pedestal, of Barre granite, is composed of three bases, surmounted by a polished disk on which is carved a shield and anchor, the emblem of liberty and union. Put in place by local marble workers Hill & Young, the inscription reads, "In honor of the brave men who from Sag Harbor, bore some loyal part in the Great Civil War," and, beneath it, in Latin, "Dulce et decorum est pro patri moria," which translated means, "It is sweet and glorious to die for one's country."

On October 24, 1896 a public unveiling took place, with a program that included a procession of veterans, firemen, school children, and the Sag Harbor Cornet Band. Assembled on a platform in front of the monument were the speakers, and trustees, and little Eva Parks, who unveiled the statue. Police Justice Greene, on behalf of the Ladies Monumental Association, officially presented the monument to the village. John L. Sherwood read a poem by Mrs. Julia Taft Payne entitled "The Soldier on the Monument," followed by several songs sung by the children and the formal address given by Reverend J.J. Harrison. The following veterans took part in the procession. Not all were from Sag Harbor. They were David J. Baker, Henry L. Baker, Thomas Bennett, Edwin Bill, L. King, George C. Morris, Oliver Oldershaw, Warren Overton, A.J. Blanchard, James Bunnell, Charles P. Cook, Edward D. Cook, F.J. Davis, Samuel B. Dutcher, Joseph Earle, William T. Gooding, S. Hudson, William Kelsey, E. King, Harvey B. King, Samuel M. Polley, William L. Polley, Edwin Roberts, H.H. Sanford, George R. Schellinger, James M. Strong, Richard M. Sweezey, Edward Thomas, James VanHoughton, Charles B. Wade, Charles Whitney, and Fred B. Williamson.

Sag Harbor's Historical Society met in December 1901, to discuss marking the historic sites in the village with granite monuments. Three places of historic importance were selected, sites that played a part in the Revolutionary War and the War of 1812. They were the British outpost on Brickkiln Road, the American fort of the War of 1812 on High Street, and the British fort captured by Colonel Meigs during the Revolutionary War on Union Street.

Orders were placed with local marble workers Hill & Young for the three granite blocks, the largest to be placed at the Union Street site. It was rough-hewn Barre granite 4½ feet high and 5 feet wide, with a bronze plaque inscribed: A BRITISH FORT—NEAR THIS SPOT WAS CAPTURED BY THE AMERICANS UNDER LIEUT. COL. MEIGS AT THE BATTLE OF SAG HARBOR, MAY 23, 1777. The monument cost $300.

The second monument, placed on Sleight's Hill, High Street, was a granite block 3 feet by 3 feet and inscribed: ON THIS SPOT STOOD AN AMERICAN FORT—1812. The third memorial was placed on Brickkiln Road, a 3- by 3-foot granite stone, marking the site of the British outpost captured by Colonel Meigs. On the polished face of the monument the following is inscribed: IN A HOUSE NEAR THIS SPOT A BRITISH OUTPOST WAS CAPTURED BY LIEUT. COL. MEIGS, MAY 23, 1777. The three historic monuments were unveiled at the 125th anniversary of the Battle of Sag Harbor, May 30, 1902.

6

THE GREAT FIRES OF SAG HARBOR

It was a frigid, blustery winter's night. The residents of Sag Harbor had just ushered in the New Year with celebrations and the customary whistle-blowing at the midnight hour. January 1, 1925 had arrived, and with it another disastrous fire. With the new year but three hours old, terror once again gripped the village, a ruinous blaze that resulted in $750,000 worth of damage.

The Alvin Silver Works Fire of 1925

About 3 A.M. fire was discovered in the Ballen store annex on Washington Street, a store occupied for the last seven years by Walter E. Seaman's confectionary and tobacco shop on the ground floor and by Ballen's storerooms on the second. A 40-mile-per-hour northeast wind prevailed, and it was evident that another major blaze would occur. Blasts of the steam siren on Fahys Watch Case Factory roused the sleeping residents, many of whom had just retired. As fire fighters arrived on the scene, the two motor-pumping engines of the fire department were quickly put into position and calls went out to Bridgehampton, East Hampton, and Southampton for assistance. By 3:30 A.M. Ballen's annex fell to the ground with a crash, sending sparks and embers into the air and onto the roofs of nearby structures. Ballen's main store and the new store of Morris Meyer's Sons were soon engulfed in flames.

Ballen's occupied an ancient wooden structure, originally a private dwelling dating back to about the time of the War of 1812. Remodeled into a store, it was first a cobbler shop and then two successive meat markets. When Ballen bought the place, he had J.O. Hopping raise the building and dig a cellar beneath the place. For a time the Ballen family lived on the second floor.

As the blaze progressed, Ballen's stock of ammunition, shells, and cartridges exploded, creating what was described as a scene from a war zone, and sending spectators scattering in all directions.

Plate-glass windows in stores across the Main Street and Washington Street cracked and fell from the tremendous heat, and although paint blistered and a few sparks ignited, they were quickly extinguished, preventing the fire from jumping to the west side of the street. Linemen from the Sag Harbor Electric Light and Power Company climbed the icy poles to cut electric wires and shut off the current. Shortly before 4 A.M. Southampton and East Hampton engines arrived in the village. Hoses were placed in holes cut into the ice, at the foot of Main Street, and stretched to the scene. It provided an ample supply of water but turned out to be no match for the gale force winds which fanned the flames.

By 4:30 A.M. it was apparent that the huge three-story Alvin Silver Company building was in jeopardy. Its yellow pine interior caught fire and burned furiously. The massive brick structure, with its built-in sprinkling system, stood doomed. Heat became too intense for the fire fighters to place ladders against the building, and they watched, in disbelief, as the place succumbed to the blaze. Its brick walls, however, did prevent the fire from spreading any further. At 6 A.M. the fire was finally under control. The front of the Alvin building stood intact, the other walls partly demolished. Insured for $25,000, it was considered a total loss and never rebuilt. For more than 20 years the decorative facade stood, boarded up, with the wooden panels beneath its graceful arches used for an honor roll to hold the names of those serving in World War II. In 1950 the place was purchased by the Bohack Company, the final wall of the old structure removed, and a Bohack supermarket built on the site.

EPILOGUE

September 21, 1938 started out much the same as any other early autumn day, although somewhat overcast and oppressive. Thunderstorms the night before brought little relief from the humidity. By noon an easterly wind picked up, and a falling barometer indicated that a storm was approaching. Long Islanders were accustomed to nor'easters, so no one seemed particularly concerned. As weather reports came in, strong winds were predicted, but not once was the word "hurricane" mentioned.

The Great Hurricane of 1938

By two o'clock in the afternoon, winds of gale force began to lash the seaboard, and eastern Long Island found itself right in the path of the impending storm. Within the hour trees started to fall, as the rain-soaked ground was unable to support their mighty roots. The wind gained in velocity, reaching a peak of 100 miles per hour at about 4 P.M., accompanied by a barometric low of 28.40 inches. As the eye of the hurricane passed, the winds diminished and the sun broke through. Many thought the storm was over and ventured out to survey the damage. Then the storm returned in all its intensity and caught an unsuspecting number of explorers in a grip of terror. When the winds subsided and it was finally over, it became apparent that Sag Harbor had suffered severe losses.

As the village emerged from the wreckage and debris, a brisk business in axes, saws, candles, and kerosene lamps took place. Hundreds of trees were lost, among them the largest elm tree in the village, which had stood on Bay Street. Porches, roofs, out buildings, automobiles, and homes were demolished. But these could be replaced. The trees, on the other hand, would take a century to attain the magnificence and splendor of the fallen ones that had shaded the village streets for many years.

One of the greatest losses was that of the steeple of the First Presbyterian Church, which had stood proudly for nearly a century, watching over the village, its beacon guiding the mighty whaleships back to port. The tall spire crashed to the ground, preceded by the melancholy tolling of the old bell. The Methodist Church suffered a similar loss, as their steeple also fell, part of it landing on a house and car in the next yard. The grounds of Pierson High School resembled a war zone—a jungle of twisted trees, limbs, and roots, and many windows blown in.

It took time to recover. The WPA allocated $11,778, to be used for clean-up, replacing curbs and sidewalks, and rebuilding catch basins. Sag Harbor village was responsible for 24 percent, or $2826, of the much-needed funds. So the landowners of Sag Harbor took on the monumental job of cleaning their properties of fallen limbs, trees, and buildings. In time things returned to normal, but the Old Whalers' steeple would never be replaced. Although a fund was started toward that goal, the needed money was never collected, and that majestic and awe-inspiring architectural wonder of Minard Lafever was gone forever.

History is forever being made, ever growing and never ending, an account of past events, a chronicle of the happenings of yesterday. But even as today will soon pass into the historical annals of tomorrow, a written account must at some point in time come to a close. Looking back, there is often a memorable time in life at which we tend to place incidents "before" or "after." For many in Sag Harbor and its surrounding communities, that time might well be the 1938 hurricane that devastated much of eastern Long Island. On numerous occasions we have listened to lifelong residents categorize events as happening "before the hurricane" or "after the hurricane." That storm was so intense, so violent, that 50 years later it still remains vivid in the minds of those who experienced its fury. It is very possible that the early citizens of Sag Harbor used the great fires of 1845 and 1877 in describing events of importance to them as happening "before the fire" or "after the fire." Each became a focal point from which the date of some particular event could easily be remembered. And so, this history concludes in 1940 just "after the hurricane." Hopefully, you have enjoyed reading and learning about Sag Harbor, a village that is small in size but abounding in history, a village that is truly an American beauty.

MAPS AND DIAGRAMS

The maps and drawings that follow show how Sag Harbor developed from swampy marsh to bustling settlement; and where people chose to live, work, play, and worship in the ensuing years.

MAPS & DIAGRAMS

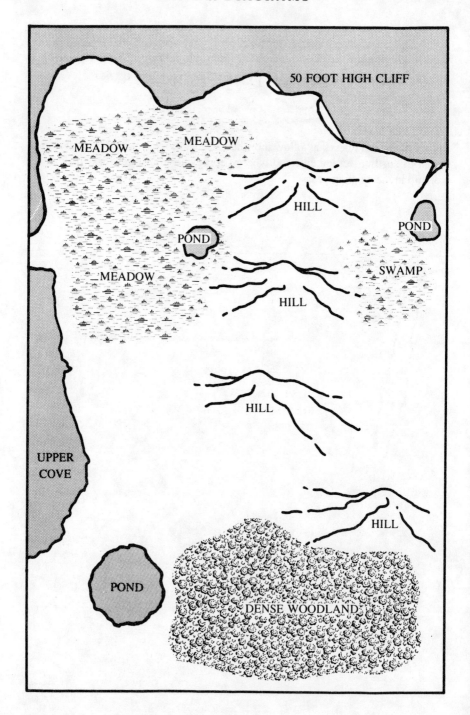

BEFORE THE SETTLEMENT • 1600s

MAPS & DIAGRAMS

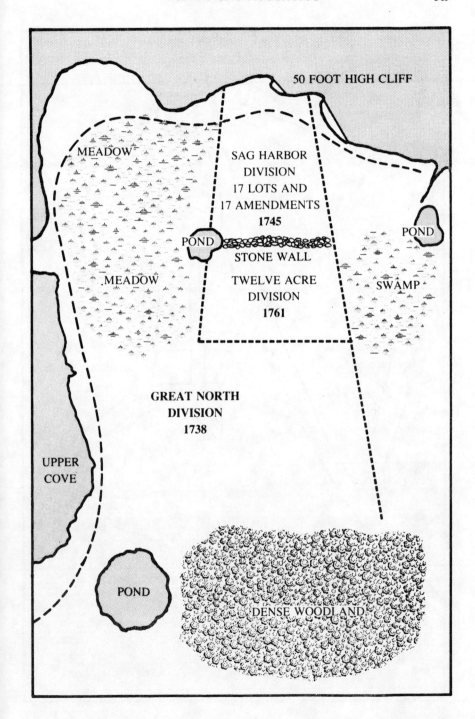

THE ALLOTMENT OF THE LAND • 1700s

MAPS & DIAGRAMS

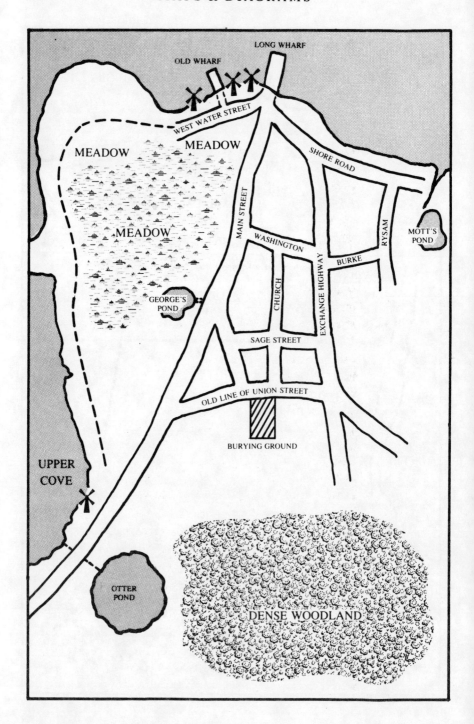

LAYOUT OF EARLY ROADS • LATE 1700s

MAPS & DIAGRAMS

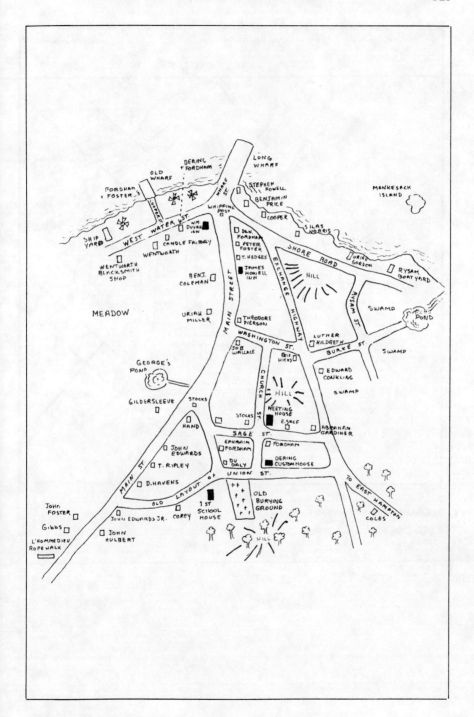

SAG HARBOR • APPROXIMATE LOCATIONS • LATE 1700s

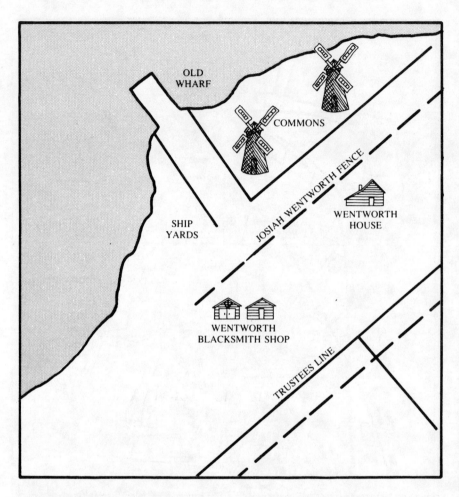

ALONG THE WATERFRONT, 1800

after a draft by Nathaniel Sherril, Jr.

MAPS & DIAGRAMS

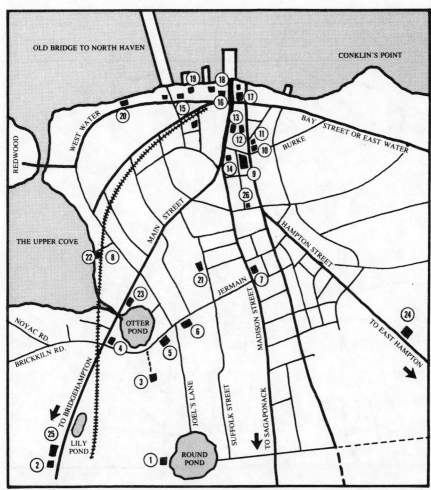

EARLY INDUSTRIES
1. Ice Houses 1840-1911
2. Sag Harbor Brick Co. 1891
3. The Sag Harbor Water Works 1889
4. Oil Cloth Factory ca. 1850
5. Eaton Engravers and Printers Machinery Co. 1918
6. Oakland Brass Foundry and Clock Works ca. 1850, Stocking Factory 1863, Barrel Head and Stave, Morroco Leather, and Hat Factories ca. 1870
7. Kiss Art Pottery Works 1910
8. Ropewalk, Windmill and Shipyard ca. 1800
9. Cotton Mill 1850, Fahys Watch Case Factory 1881, and Bulova Watch Case Factory 1937
10. Emmel Bottling Works 1891, Wilson Bottling Co. 1917
11. Denison Bros. Hat Factory ca. 1790, Weidlog's Mfg. Co. 1903, and Kiss Art Pottery 1912
12. Bloch Hat Pin Factory 1910
13. Cloak Factory 1910 and Aptheken Rayon Factory 1933
14. Alvin Silver Works 1890
15. Howell's Spermacetti Candle Factory ca. 1700, The Gas Works 1859
16. Cigar Factory ca. 1870, Cream of Tartar Factory 1875, and Montauk Sugar Refinery ca. 1860
17. Maidstone Steam Flouring Mills 1862, Hampton Flour Mill Co. 1878, Concrete Block Factory ca. 1890, E.W. Bliss 1891, Tool Factory 1892, Dial Factory 1892, Steam Laundry 1893, Sag Harbor Grain Co. ca. 1900, Welz & Zerwick Brewery 1908, Yetter & Moore Brewery 1908, East Hampton Lumber and Coal 1910, and Texas Oil Co. 1916

WINDMILLS
18. Mill ca. 1700
19. Homan Mill 1760
20. Mill ca. 1700
21. Beebee Mill 1820
22. Spider-legged Mill ca. 1800
23. Jermain Mill 1793

TOLL HOUSES
24. East Hampton Turnpike 1844
25. Bull's Head Turnpike 1840

CUSTOM HOUSE
26. Custom House ca. 1790

MAPS & DIAGRAMS

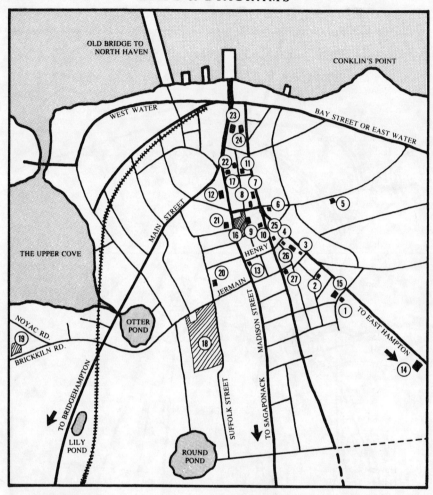

CHURCHES AND TEMPLES
1. St. David A. M. E. Zion Church 1840
2. Second Zion Church 1859
3. Chapel of the Academy of the Sacred Heart of Mary 1888
4. Temple Adas Israel 1900
5. Methodist-Episcopal Church 1835
6. Christ Episcopal Church 1884
7. St. Andrew's Roman Catholic Church 1872
8. Earliest Methodist Church 1811 and St. Andrew's Roman Catholic Church 1836
9. First Presbyterian Church (Old Whalers) 1844
10. People's Pentecostal Church of the Nazarene 1897
11. Old Barn Meeting House 1766, Presbyterian Church 1817, and Christ Episcopal Church 1846
12. Methodist Church 1863
13. Bethel Baptist Church 1843

BURYING GROUNDS
14. Jewish Cemetery 1871
15. A. M. E. Zion Cemetery ca. 1840
16. Old Burying Ground 1767
17. First Burial Site mid 1700's
18. Oakland Cemetery 1840
19. St. Andrew's Roman Catholic Cemetery 1845

SCHOOLS
8. St. Andrew's R.C. School 1872 and 1883
20. Sag Harbor Academy and Institute 1845
21. First School House 1787
22. Middle School 1804
23. Union School 1871
24. Annex 1893
25. Old Yellow School House ca. 1800
26. Academy of the Sacred Heart of Mary 1877
27. Pierson High School 1908

MAPS & DIAGRAMS

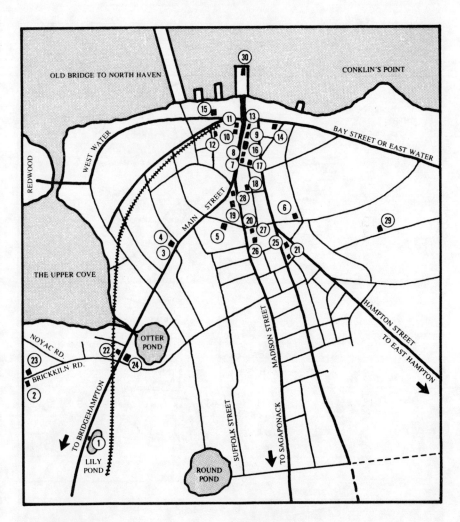

INNS AND HOTELS

1. Lily Pond House ca. 1920
2. Sea View Hotel (Hill Top Acres) 1891
3. L. Hedges Boarding House ca. 1840
4. East End Hotel ca. 1870
5. Vail's Boarding House
6. Lundhurst Hotel ca. 1920
7. Gamaliel Bruen's Sag Harbor Hotel 1840
8. Mansion House 1846
9. James Howell's Inn 1730 and the American Hotel 1877
10. Hedges House 1817, 1845, 1886 and Glenn House 1880
11. Duke Fordham's Inn ca. 1870
12. Betsey Jose's Boarding House ca. 1880
13. Robert Fordham's pre 1776, Nassau Hotel 1847 and Hotel Bay View 1892
14. Law's Hotel or Gardiner House ca. 1890

FIRE HOUSES

15. Niagara Engine #1
16. Phoenix Hook and Ladder and Gazelle 1917
17. Torrent Engine #3 1837
18. Montauk Hose Company
19. Protection Engine #2 1833
20. Phoenix Engine #1
21. Murray Hill Hose Company 1899
22. Otter Hose Company 1912

BATTLE SITES AND MONUMENTS

9. British Officers at Howell's Inn
23. British Outpost 1777 and Monument 1902
24. World War I Monument 1924
25. Powder House 1812
26. British Fort 1776
27. Arsenal 1810, and Monument 1902
28. Soldiers Civil War Monument 1896
29. American Fort 1812 and Monument 1902
30. Skirmishes with British on Wharf 1776 and 1812

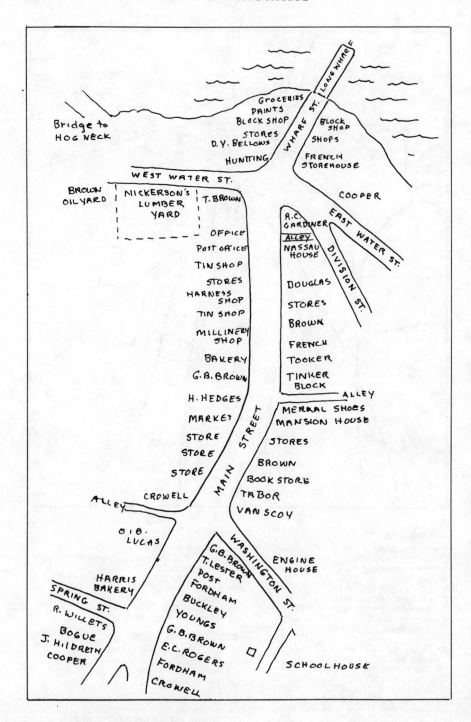

SAG HARBOR BUSINESS DISTRICT 1858

MAPS & DIAGRAMS

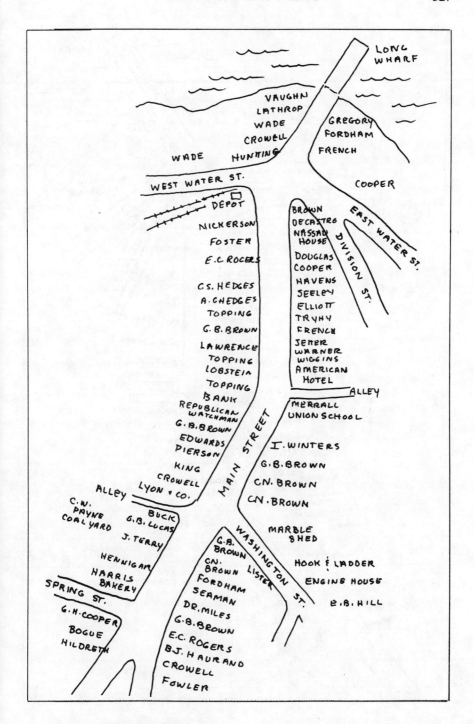

SAG HARBOR BUSINESS DISTRICT 1873

328   MAPS & DIAGRAMS

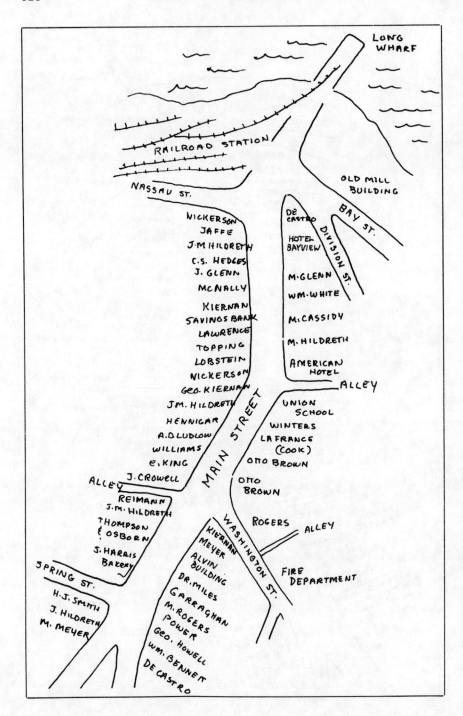

SAG HARBOR BUSINESS DISTRICT 1902

MAPS & DIAGRAMS 329

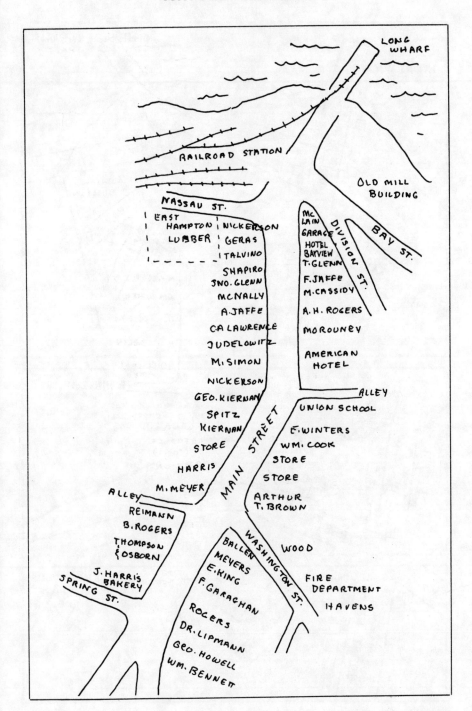

SAG HARBOR BUSINESS DISTRICT 1916

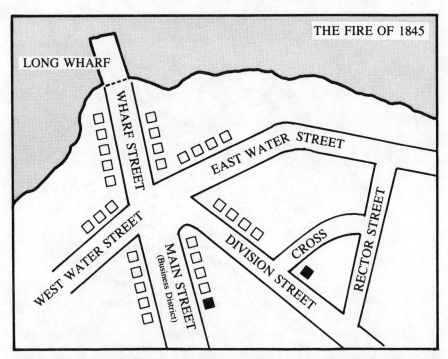

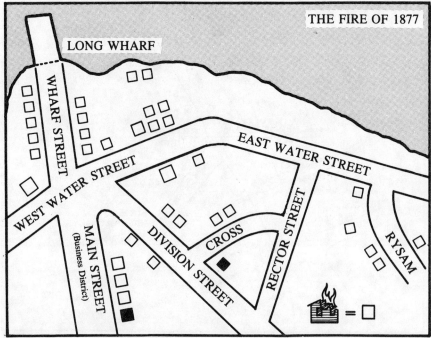

BUILDINGS LOST IN THE GREAT FIRES
Dark squares show where fires were halted by brick structures.

MAPS & DIAGRAMS

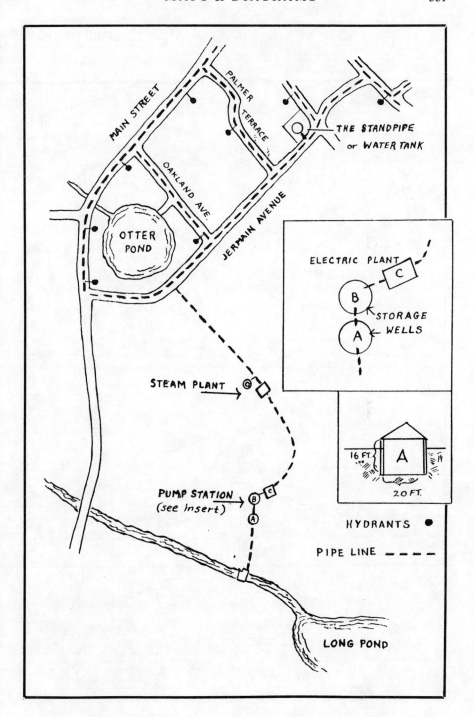

THE SAG HARBOR WATER WORKS ca. 1890

APPENDIX. SAG HARBOR NAMES

EARLY INHABITANTS

1775 Sag Harbor Village census

Bowditch, Widow Sarah
Butler, William
Coleman, Benjamin
Conkling, Benjamin
Conkling, Edward
Conkling, Joseph
Cooper, Silas
Cooper, Zebulon
Corey, Braddock
Duvall, William
Fordham, Daniel
Fordham, Ephraim
Fordham, George
Fordham, Nathan
Foster, Joseph
Foster, Peter
Foster, Widow Temperance
Fowler, George
Gardiner, Jeremiah
Gibbs, Joseph
Gildersleeve, Obediah
Gildersleeve, Philip
Hallock, William
Hand, David

Havens, George
Hedges, Timothy
Hicks, Widow Elizabeth
Hildreth, Peter
Hill, Jonathan
Howell, James
Hulbert, John
Hudson, John
Jones, Obediah
King, Benjamin
Latham, Widow Hannah
Latham, Hubbard
L'Hommedieu, Samuel
Matthews, Timothy
Miller, Uriah
Norris, Silas
Price, Benjamin
Satterly, John
Store, Joseph
Tarbell, Widow Sarah
Wicks, Silvanus
Wiggins, James
Woodruff, John

1775 North Haven census

Havens, Constant
Havens, Daniel
Havens, Joseph
Havens, Samuel
Havens, Dr. Jonathan
Mitchell, John
Mitchell, John Jr.

Mitchell, James
Paine, Ephraim
Paine, Jonathan
Payne, Peter
Sayre, David
Sayre, Nehemiah
Gardiner, Jeremiah

1775 Noyac census

Budd, Joshua
Edwards, John
Jessup, Isaac
Jessup, Nathan

Jessup, Silas
Pain, Daniel
Pain, Peter

APPENDIX. SAG HARBOR NAMES

PART I CHAPTER 4

SCHOOLS AND CHURCHES

Students of the Old Schoolhouse, 1795

Atwood, John
Bates, Lorenzo
Beebee, James
Cone, Reuben
Ells, Samuel
Duvall, Francis
Dennison, Edward
Corey, Asa
Corey, John
Crowell, Thomas
Fordham, Austin
Fordham, Latham
Fordham, Peletiah
Fordham, Sybil
Fordham, William
Foster, Phebe
Hall, Lucretia
Hall, Polly
Halsey, Eliphalet
Halsey, Nancy
Hand, Clarisa
Havens, Betty
Hedges, Howell
Hedges, Lodowick
Hicks, John
Hicks, Sylvester
Hildreth, Mehetable
Howard, Maria

Howell, Elias
Jermain, Alanson
Jermain, Julia
Jermain, Rebecca
Latham, Abagail
Latham, Ruth
Latham, Sally
L'Hommedieu, Polly
L'Hommedieu, Sally
L'Hommedieu, Samuel
Lincoln, Huldah
Lugar, George
Lugar, Christopher
Mason, Sally
Miles, Ephraim
Parker, James
Parker, Simeon
Rogers, Edward
Rogers, James
Rogers, Josiah
Satterly, Garrett
Satterly, Nancy
Satterly, Stephen
Stuart, Sayre
Topping, Jane
Topping, John
Topping, Sally
Woodruff, Abraham

PART IV CHAPTER 2

Students and Parents of the Union School District, 1865-66

Students	Parents
Albin, Charles, Clarence, Lenora, William	Edward Albin
Atkins, Inez	William Atkins
Barnes, Edward	Philip Barnes
Beckerton, Anna	Margaret Beckerton
Bebler, John	John Bebler
Bill, Eva, Frank, Frederick, Nellie	Edwin Bill
Bilson, David, George	George Bilson
Boyenton, William	John Boyenton
Brady, Anna, Hugh	William Brady
Brickel, Delia, Ida	Frederick Brickel

APPENDIX. SAG HARBOR NAMES

Students	Parents
Cary, James, Kate	Edward Cary
Chadwick, Charles, Myra	John Chadwick
Clayton, Patrick, William	William Clayton
Collins, Edward, Ella, James, Mary, Maggie	Edward Collins
Collins, Eva	Mary Collins
Collins, George, Maria	Samuel Collins
Colvin, George	Samuel Colvin
Conklin, Ethelinda, Herbert	John A. Conklin
Conner, Arthur, Helene	Hickford Conner
Cooper, Anna, Rena	Robert Cooper
Cooper, Leland	Wilson Cooper
Cooper, Eddie	William Cooper
Copman, Anna, John	John Copman
Corcoran, Hattie, Louise, Maggie, Sophia, Timothy	Mrs. Frank Corcoran
Corrigan, John, Rebecca	Mrs. Ella Corrigan
Crandall, Ella, Jennie	C.W. Crandall
Cunningham, William	James Cunningham
Curtis, Charles, Herbert	James Curtis
Curtis, Etta	William Curtis
Daniels, Emma, Ida, Willie	Jerome Daniels
DeCastro, Augustus, Henry, John, William	Joseph DeCastro
Dodson, Ellie	James Dodson
Dolan, James, Maggie	James Dolan
Douglass, Frank	Charles Douglass
Dowd, Ella, Nellie	Michael Dowd
Duffey, Lawrence	Mrs. Alice Duffey
Dutcher, Justina Edwards	Samuel Dutcher
Early, Sophie, Sylvester	John Early
Early, Mary, Willie, George	Patrick Early
Edwards, Lydia	Mrs. Lucy Edwards
Edwards, Ellie	Osborne Edwards
Eldredge, Ernest, William	Charles Eldredge
Eldredge, Addie, Ella	James Eldredge
Erwin, Kate, Lizzie	Martin Erwin
Field, William, Zachariah	William Field
Filer, Ada	Charles Filer
Fleiner, Charles, Mary	Mr. Fleiner
Fleming, Ida	Mr. Fleming
Fordham, Nathan	John Fordham
Fordred, Fannie	William Fordred
Foster, Fernando	William Foster
Fox, Mary, May	Peter Fox
French, Jennie	Hannibal French
Freudenthal, Frances	Joseph Freudenthal
Fuller, Ella	Mrs. Emily Fuller
Gawley, Delia	John Gawley
Gilbride, Joseph	Mrs. Ellen Gilbride
Glenn, John, Mary, Thomas	John Glenn
Glover, Charles	Mrs. Erastus Glover

… APPENDIX. SAG HARBOR NAMES

Students	Parents
Godbee, William	James Godbee
Halsey, Caddie, Maria	David Halsey
Handy, Wayland	Aaron Handy
Hennigar, Morton	George Hennigar
Hildreth, Ida	Nathaniel Hildreth
Hill, George	Edward Hill
Howell, Mary	Reuben Howell
Jennings, Lissie	Philander Jennings
Jetter, Mary	Gotleib Jetter
Keegan, Maggie, Mary	Edward Keegan
Kelly, Edward	James Kelly
Kelly, John, Maggie	John Kelly
Kelly, William	Patrick Kelly
King, Charles, George	Charles King
King, Addie	Elisha King
Lacy, Joseph	Thomas Lacy
Lacy, Catherine, Mary, Sarah	John Lacy
Ladd, Edith	Mrs. Arabella Ladd
Lafever, Gilbert	William Lafever
LaGuire, Edmund, Lafayette	Joseph LaGuire
Latham, George	Mrs. Sally Latham
Lawrence, Gilbert, Nellie	William Lawrence
Lister, Carrie, Emma	Thomas Lister
Littell, Ada Penny, Adella	Mrs. Amanda Littell
Loper, Frank	Thomas Loper
Lucas, Addie, Charles	Oliver Lucas
Lugar, Ella, Mary	John Lugar
Lyon, Richard	William Lyon
McCabe, Anna, Edmund, Ella, Kate, Mary	Lawrence McCabe
McCafferty, Ellen, Joanna, Libbie, Louisa	Henry McCafferty
McCullin, Arabella, Eugene	Daniel McCullin
McFarland, James	George McFarland
McGaraty, Ellen, Mary	James McGaraty
McMahon, Maggie	Patrick McMahon
McMahon, James, Jennie	Mrs. Elizabeth McMahon
Maloney, James, John	John Maloney
Matthews, Lilla, Wallenstine	Nathaniel Matthews
Maynard, Samuel	Seldon Maynard
Miller, George	George Miller
Miller, Ella	Hedges Miller
Miller, Anna, Gilbert Halsey	Mrs. Maria Miller
Miller, George	Mrs. Sophronia Miller
Miller, Ella, Jason, Mary	Samuel Miller
Montcalm, C.	Mr. Montcalm
Mott, Lizzie	Ethelinda Mott
Mott, Archie	Charles Mott
Murphy, Edward, John, Michael	Edward Murphy
Nickerson, Jennie, Kate	Watson Nickerson
Norris, Bertha, Hannibal, Lina, Olivia	James D. Norris

APPENDIX. SAG HARBOR NAMES

Students	Parents
Oakley, Ida	Alfred Oakley
Oakley, Hattie	Mrs. Charlotte Oakley
Oldershaw, Absalom, Samuel	Absalom Oldershaw
Parmental, Ella Miller	Joseph Parmental
Payne, Willie	Charles N. Payne
Penny, Ada	Mrs. Clara Penny
Perry, Charles, Frank	Joseph Perry
Peters, Gertrude, Sarah	William Peters
Phelps, Charles	Mrs. Mary Phelps
Pidgeon, Clara, Eleanor, Ruth, Ophelia	Stephen Pidgeon
Quail, Richard, William	Richard Quail
Richardson, Sylvester	Mr. Richardson
Reiger, Willie	Frederick Reiger
Reney, Susie	George Reney
Roberts, Clayton, Jennie	Peter Roberts
Schellinger, Arthur	John Schellinger
Schwartz,	Charles Schwartz
Seabury, Fannie	Sheffield Seabury
Shaw, Caroline, Ellen, Frank, George	George Shaw
Sherman, Louisa	Luther Sherman
Sherwood, Hattie	Mrs. Margaret Sherwood
Shreeves, George	George Shreeves
Simonds, Herbert	Charles Simonds
Simpson, Joseph, Willie	Job Simpson
Smadbeck, Gracie, Louis, Rosalie	Mrs. Henrietta Smadbeck
Smith, Henry	Abijah Smith
Spencer, Charles, William	Mrs. Eliza Spencer
Spencer, Ella Talmadge	John Spencer
Stakelam, Joanna, Thomas	John Stakelam
Story, John Kenigan	Mrs. Rebecca Story
Stratton, Lizzie	Thomas Stratton
Street, Ada	William Street
Strong, Henry	Phebe Strong
Sweezey, Mary	Mrs. Margaret Sweezey
Sylva, Emily, Mary, Thomas, Willie	Thomas Sylva
Tabor, Cleveland, Thomas	Cornelius Tabor
Terry,	Mrs. Lydia Terry
Tinker, Charles, Ida	Charles Tinker
Topping, Emma	Hyram Topping
Tooker, Eugene	William Tooker
Trammer,	Thomas Trammer
Trihy, Alice, Maggie	John Trihy
Tryon, Eunice, Martha	Henry Tryon
Tucker, Alice, Nathaniel	George Tucker
Vail, Charles	David Vail
Vail, Sophronia	Thomas Vail
Wade, Carrie, Hattie	Benjamin Wade
Ware, Jane	Charles Ware
White, Ella	William White

APPENDIX. SAG HARBOR NAMES

Students	Parents
Whitehill, James	Mr. Whitehill
Williams, Hannah	Mrs. Eliza Williams
Williamson, Ernest, Frank, Nettie	John Williamson
Winters, Clara, Fred, Henry, William	Isaac Winters
Winters, Addie	Thomas Winters
Wood, Charles, Josephine	Israel Wood

PART IV   CHAPTER 3

THE CLERGY: PASTORS AND PRIESTS

Ministers of the Presbyterian Church

John Taylor, 1789
James Richards, 1794
Daniel Hall, 1797-1806
Aaron Bogue, a few months in 1806
Nathaniel S. Prime, 1806-09
Mr. Gaylord and Stephen Porter, 1809-12
John D. Gardiner, 1812-32
Samuel King, 1832-33
Ithamar Pillsbury, 1834-35
Joseph A. Copp, 1835-51
Edward Hopper, 1852-63

John Lowrey, 1863-67
William Guthrie Barnes, 1867-72
Alexander W. Sproull, 1873-83
Edward H. Camp, 1884-85
Clarence Hall Wilson, 1887-1902
Frank Houghton Allen, 1902-07
William T. Edds, 1908-14
Walter A. Henricks, 1915-18
George M. Runner, 1918-20
Sidney H. Barrett, 1920-40

Pastors of the Baptist Church

Elder Finch
Elder Watrous
Rev. George F. Hendrickson
Rev. David W. Roland
Rev. Knapp
Rev. J.W. Ladd
Elder E.W. Bliss
Rev. Daniel D. Lyon
Rev. E.S. Wheeler

Rev. William B. Cullis
Rev. Still
Rev. Charles Edwards
Rev. Ringrose
R.J. Conklin
Rev. Nightengale
Rev. Andrew Heughes
Rev. J.R. Vaughn
William Rohm

Pastors of the Methodist Church

Henry Redstone and Coles Carpenter, 1810
Samuel Bushnell and Noble W. Thomas, 1811
Noble W. Thomas, 1812
Francis Ward, Theodosius Clark
 and Daniel Wright, 1813
Arnold Scofield and Charles W. Carpenter, 1814
John Reynolds and Oliver Sykes, 1815
John Reynolds, 1816

Luman Andrus and Fitch Reed, 1817
Fitch Reed, 1818
Aaron Pearce, 1819
Reuben Harris and S.D. Furguson, 1820
Reuben Harris and Eli Denniston, 1822
Humphrey Humphries, 1822-23
Henry Hatfield and Horace Bartlett, 1824
Horace Bartlett and John LeFevre, 1825

APPENDIX. SAG HARBOR NAMES

Noble W. Thomas, John W. LeFevre and Cyrus Foss, 1826
Noble W. Thomas, R. Morris, Cyrus Foss and Oliver V. Ammerman, 1827
R. Seaman, Oliver V. Ammerman and Charles W. Carpenter, 1828
C.W. Carpenter, 1829-30
Oliver V. Ammerman and John Trippett, 1831-32
Daniel Smith and John Trippett, 1833
Harvey Husted and C.W. Carpenter, 1834
C.W. Carpenter, 1835
Nathaniel Kellogg, 1836-37
J.D. Marshall and W.C. Hoyt, 1838
David Miller, 1839-40
J. Leonard Gilder, 1841-42
James H. Perry, 1843-44
Seymour Landon, 1845-46
William Dixon, 1847-48
A.S. Francis, 1849-50
J.A. Edmonds, 1851-52
Charles Stearns, 1853
R. Jessup, 1854
R. Jessup and R. Roberts, 1855
J.B. Stratton, 1856
J.W.B. Wood, 1857-58
John F. Booth, 1859-60
Charles Kelsey, 1861
Gad. S. Gilbert, 1862
Daniel O. Ferris, 1863-64
William Lawrence, 1865-66
John W. Barnhart, 1867-68
Edwin Warriner, 1869-70
Richard Rust, 1871-72
George H. Goodsell, 1873-75
Thomas D. Littlewood, 1876-77
John Rippere, 1878-80
John W. Barnhart, 1881
John S. Whedon, 1882-84
William L. Douglas, 1885-86
Barnabus F. Reeve, 1887-91
James Coote, 1892-93
Cornelius M. Pegg, 1894-95
Joseph Baird, 1896-98
Robert F. Norton, 1899-1903
Gordon Thompson, 1904-06
Dr. M.Y. Bovard, 1907-08
George E. Bishop, 1908-11
Mr. Hammold, 1912-15
T. Wagner, 1916-17
Lester W. Asuman, 1918-19
T.B. Miller, 1920
J.A. Macmillan, 1921-23
Burdette B. Brown, 1924
Harold G. Sabin, 1925-28
T.B. Miller, 1928-40

Priests of St. Andrew's Roman Catholic Church

J. Brunnerman
M. Carroll
J. McKenna
W.J. Kean
S. O'Callahan
J.H. Pollard
J.J. Heffernan
A. Albino
J.M. Galvin
W. H. Hand
M.S. Burke
M.J. Dennison
L.N. Martel
L.J. Guerin
W.J. Dunphy
J.L. Langan
C.J. Creamer
John Kelly
John A. Ferry
M.H. Carey
J.F. Higgins
T.F. Walsh
John J. Mahon
Bryan T. Burke
E.P. Flaherty
William J. White
H.C. Jordan
J.J. Doherty
W.L. Long
W.T. Conklin
D. Maloney
Edward A. Holran
Peter L. Rickard
Hugh Lynch
Francis V. Waters
Terence C. Sharkey

APPENDIX. SAG HARBOR NAMES

Ministers of the A.M.E. Zion Church

John P. Thompson, 1840–42
Richard Noyes, 1842–43
Thompson James, 1843
Thomas Hanson, 1844
John Spence, 1845
John Wells, 1846–47
William Bishop, 1847–48
John Wells, 1850
Cyrus Boohea, 1851
John A. Williams, 1852–53
Peter C. Conster, 1854–55
John P. Thompson, 1855–57
Silas A. Mitchell, 1858
Alexander Posey, 1859–63
James Meyers, 1863–64
William Brooks, 1864–65
G.L. Landale, 1871–73
Floyd Mills, 1874
Isaac Jenkins, 1876
James (or Jarius) Prime, 1877–82
Madison Milford, 1882–83
Charles Wathers, 1883–85
Ephraim Prime, 1886
J. Thompson, 1887

Clinton Leonard, 1888
Abraham Anderson, 1890–92
William J. Smith, 1892–94
Thomas Johnson, 1894–95
E.J. Miller, 1896–98
Lewis Day Williams, 1899–1901
Stephen Conrad, 1902–03
Charles Randall, 1903–04
Clarence Van Buren, 1904–05
Gordon Thompson, 1905
C.H. Lynch, 1906–08
G.M. Ray, 1908–09
R.R. Wilson, 1910
P.H. Jones, 1911–12
T.H. Edwards, 1913–14
E.O. Clark, 1914–19
J.H. Brockett 1919–21
S.N. Dunbar, 1922–23
A.E. Mann, 1924
Moses T. Smith, 1925–27
Rev. Douglas, 1928–30
R.F. Pile, 1931–32
H.J. White, 1937–40
J.W. Coleman, 1940

Pastors of the second church on Montauk Avenue

William Decker, Thomas Dana, Jenkins Williams, William Livingston, 1860–70

Rectors of Christ Church

Henry F. Roberts, 1845–47
Richard Whitingham, 1847–49
George C. Foot, 1850–52
Isaac Pardee, 1853–54
William Musgrave, 1854–55
Gordon Huntington, 1856–59
Charles S. Williams, 1859–61
William Mowbray, 1864–65
D. McDonald, 1865–69
Edward Hubbell, 1869–72
William Musgrave, 1872–73
William Mowbray, 1873–75
J. J. Harrison, 1875–84
William Fisby, 1884

William Walker, 1884–85
J. B. Jennings, 1885–87
J. W. Smith, 1888–90
Gordon T. Lewis, 1890–1909
Francis V. Baer, 1909–18
Wallace Thompson, 1918–19
Julian Wellwood, 1919–20
Raymond L. Scofield, 1920–24
Edgar E. Brice, 1925–27
H. T. Morrell, 1927
Frederick J. Compson, 1928
Herbert E. Martin, 1929–31
Herbert Covell, 1931–40

PART II CHAPTER 2

ALONG THE WATERFRONT

The Whaling Fleet

Abby — Entered the whale fishery 1809. Made the last voyage before the War of 1812.

APPENDIX. SAG HARBOR NAMES

Abigail	Entered the whale fishery in 1803. Made eight voyages. Captains: Barney Green, Barnard, Bunker, George Post, Joshua Topping. Broken up at Sag Harbor.
Acasta	Joined the fleet in 1831. Made 13 voyages. Captains: Samuel Dennison, James M. Havens, Henry Harris, Stratton Harlow, Sylvester Smith, David Hand, John E. Howell and Alfred Glover. Withdrawn in 1850 and sailed for California.
Alciope	Joined the fleet in 1842. Made two voyages. Captains: Benjamin J. Payne and Andrew Halsey. Sold in 1847.
Alknonac	Entered the whale fishery in 1805. Made four voyages. Captains: Elias Jones, John Hildreth, James Post, and Jonathan Osborn.
American	Joined the fleet in 1827. Made twelve voyages. Captains: Cooper, Frank Page, Daniel Havens, William Pierson, Wickham Jennings, George Post, and William Jones. Condemned at St. Thomas in 1848.
Andes	Joined the fleet in 1832. Made four voyages. Captains: Skinner and Tupper. Broken up and burned at Sag Harbor in 1830. Wreck covered with sand in time and created what is still known as "Andes Shoal."
Ann	Joined fleet in 1832. Made 14 voyages. Captains: J. Steen, Edward S. Hedges, Ezekiel Curry, James Hamilton, Samuel Leek, James Bishop, Charles Howell. Condemned at St. Helena in 1859.
Ann Mary Ann	Joined the fleet in 1842. Made two voyages. Captains: Jonas Winters and Richard Dering. Sold and sailed for California in 1849.
Arabella	Joined the fleet in 1827. Made eight voyages. Captains: Matthew Sayre, James Pierson, John Bishop Jr., Henry Babcock and Isaac Ludlow. Sold to New Bedford in 1849.
Argonaut	Joined the fleet in 1814. Made nine voyages. Captains: Isaac Sayre, Eliphalet Halsey, Uriah Sayre, William Jones, Absolom Griffing, and Oliver Fowler. Condemned at Sag Harbor in 1834.
Augusta	Joined the fleet in 1857. Made one voyage. Captain James M. Tabor. Sold to Greenport and condemned as a slaver in 1862.
Balaena	Joined the fleet in 1863. Made two voyages. Captain Andrew Jennings. Sold to New Bedford in 1871.
Barbara	Joined the fleet in 1842. Made three voyages. Captains: A. Smith French and William B. Howes. Condemned at Valporaiso in 1846.
Bayard	Joined the fleet in 1835. Owned by Greenport. Made nine voyages. Captains: Davis Miller, Jerome Graham, John W. Fordham, Francis Sayre Jr., and Ogden.
Black Eagle	Joined the fleet in 1851. Made two voyages. Captains: Jeremiah Ludlow and Joshua Edwards. Sold to New Bedford in 1859.
Brazil	Entered the whale fishery in 1806. Made three voyages. Captains: Oliver Fowler and A. Folger.
Cadmus	Joined the fleet in 1827. Made 15 voyages. Captains: Henry Babcock, David Hand Jr., David Smith, Henry Nickerson Jr., George Howell. Sold and sailed for California in 1849.
Camillus	Joined the fleet in 1835. Made seven voyages. Captains: Edward D. Topping, Ezekiel H. Howes, Wickham Jennings, Edwin Hedges, and Obediah Rogers. Condemned at Sag Harbor in 1843.
Caroline	Joined the fleet in 1843. Made five voyages. Owned by a company from Greenport. Captains: John Rose, Hedges Babcock, and Jesse Halsey. Condemned at Honolulu in 1859.
Charlotte	Joined the fleet in 1850. Made two voyages. Captains: Jonas Winters and Jesse R. Halsey.
Citizen	Joined the fleet in 1843. Made two voyages. Captains: David Lansing and Thomas Norton. Lost in 1853.
Claudio	Joined the fleet in 1828. Made one voyage. Captain A.K. Griffing.

APPENDIX. SAG HARBOR NAMES

Columbia	Joined the fleet in 1829. Made 17 voyages. Captains: John Sweeney, Hallock, Samuel Pierson, Jeremiah Hedges, Samuel McCorkle, George White, David Hand Jr., Lawrence Edwards, and Robert Hand. Withdrawn in 1847.
Concordia	Joined the fleet in 1837. Made 12 voyages. Captains: A. Smith French, Jeremiah W. Hedges, Loper, Thomas Cartwright, John Woodward, Samuel McCorkle, Rogers, Jonas Hamilton, Skinner, and Dunbar. Sold to New London in 1871.
Crescent	Joined the fleet in 1841. Made two voyages. Captains: Thomas Royce and Davis Miller. Withdrawn in 1847.
Daniel Webster	Joined the fleet in 1833. Made six voyages. Captains: Ezekiel Curry, Philetus Pierson, Stratton Harlow, E. Casey, and Edward Baker. Sailed for California in 1849.
Delta	Joined the fleet in 1832. Made 12 voyages. Owned by a company from Greenport. Captains: Isaac Sayre, Charles W. Payne, Treadwell Weeks, and Benjamin Glover. Sold to New London in 1856.
Elizabeth Frith	Joined the fleet in 1845. Made three voyages. Captains: John Bishop Jr. and Jonas Winters. Withdrawn in 1850.
Emerald	Joined the fleet in 1851. Made two voyages. Captains: William Jagger, Thomas Norton and Hallock. Sold to the United States Government and became part of the stone fleet in the Civil War.
Excell	Joined the fleet in 1857. Made three voyages. Captains: David Loper, Jetur Rose and Jonas Winters. Condemned at St. Helena in 1863.
Fair Helen	Joined the fleet in 1816. Made ten voyages. Captains: Robert Forrest, Hand, Howell, Uriah Sayre, Henry Harris and Howland. Condemned at Sag Harbor. Its remains could be seen for years at Conklin's Point.
Fanny	Joined the fleet in 1836. Made seven voyages. Captains: S. Woodruff, Silas Edwards, Charles W. Payne, Lodowick Fordham, James R. Huntting, and S.W. Edwards. Sailed for California in 1849.
France	Joined the fleet in 1837. Made four voyages. Captains: John E. Howell, W. Edwards, and Robert Douglass.
Franklin	Joined the fleet in 1832. Made seven voyages. Captains: Charles Griffin, David Youngs, Edward Halsey Jr., and Mercator Cooper. Lost off the coast of Brazil in 1850.
Gem	Joined the fleet in 1843. Made 11 voyages. Captains: Isaac Ludlow, James Worth, Theron Worth, Edward Halsey Jr., and Rogers. Lost in 1848.
Gentleman	Joined the fleet in 1852. Made three voyages. Captains: Frederick Cartwright and S. George Post. Withdrawn in 1856.
General Scott	Joined the fleet in 1822. Made one voyage.
Governor Clinton	Joined the fleet in 1832. Made two voyages. Captains: Samuel Ludlow and Joshua Rogers. Lost in a typhoon off the coast of Japan in 1834.
Hamilton	The "little *Hamilton*" joined the fleet in 1836. Made three voyages. Captains: Samuel Ludlow, Job Babcock, Shamgar Slate, William Jones, and David Hand. Sold and sailed for California in 1849.
Hamilton	The "big *Hamilton*" joined the fleet in 1839. Made two voyages. Captains: David Hand and Tut Loper. Lost near the Rio Grande in 1845.
Hannibal	Joined the fleet in 1818. Made 12 voyages. Captains: Lewis Bennett, Joseph Harris, James Parker, Henry Green, Huntting Cooper, John Canning, George Post, Robert Douglass, and Charles Bennett. Condemned at Rio de Janeiro in 1849.
Henry	Joined the fleet in 1828. Made eight voyages. Captains: David Youngs, Edward Topping, Frederick Cartwright, E.P. Brown, John Sweeney, Thomas Lowen, Sylvester Griffing. Sold and sailed for California in 1850.
Henry Lee	Joined the fleet in 1842. Made two voyages. Captains: Charles Bennett and Benjamin Payne. Broke up about 1849.
Highland Mary (Parana)	Joined the fleet in 1853. Made six voyages. Captains: A. Smith French, Henry Green Jr., Thomas Royce, Edward Smith. During the Civil War the ship ran the blockade of southern ports, sailing under the English colors.

APPENDIX. SAG HARBOR NAMES

Hope	Entered the whale fishery in 1784. Captains: Ripley and Silas Howell.
Hudson	Joined the fleet in 1833. Made eight voyages. Captains: Thomas Warren, Samuel Dennison, Henry Green Jr., Oliver Nickerson, and James H. Rogers. Sold to Mystic in 1848.
Huron	Joined the fleet in 1840. Made four voyages. Captains; Samuel Woodruff and Henry Green Jr.. Sold and sailed for California in 1849.
Illinois	Joined the fleet in 1843. Made three voyages. Captain: Daniel Jagger. Sold to New Bedford in 1849.
Italy	Joined the fleet in 1844. Made five voyages. Captains: Rowley and Frederick Weld. Broke up near Honolulu in 1858.
Jefferson	Entered the whale fishery in 1804. Captain Smith.
Jefferson II	Joined the fleet in 1845. Made five voyages. Captains: James R. Huntting, Sylvester Smith, James Post and John Godbee. Broke up in 1861.
John Jay	Joined the fleet in 1842. Made two voyages. Captains: Obediah Rogers and W. Harwood.
John A. Robb	Joined the fleet in 1861. Made three voyages. Captains: Barney Green and Andrew Jennings. Sold at St. Helena in 1868.
John Wells	Joined the fleet in 1843. Made two voyages. Captains: Jeremiah Hedges and A. Smith French. Sold to New Bedford in 1849.
Josephine	Joined the fleet in 1843. Made two voyages. Captains: Hiram Hedges and Thomas Royce. Sold to New Bedford in 1849.
Julius Caesar	Joined the fleet in 1820. Made one voyage. Captain Oliver Fowler. Sold to New London in 1821.
Konohassett	Joined the fleet in 1845. Made one voyage. Captain James B. Worth. Lost on a Pacific reef in 1847.
Laurens	Joined the fleet in 1845. Made two voyages. Captains: Atkins Eldredge and James Godbee. Sold at Rio de Janiero in 1848.
Lavinia	Entered the whale fishery in 1809. Made one voyage. Captain Oliver Fowler.
Levant	Joined the fleet in 1844. Made three voyages. Captains: Willaim Lowen, Jacob M. Havens, and Mercator Cooper. Lost in 1855.
Lucy	Entered the whale fishery in 1784. Made at least six voyages. Captains: David Squires, George McKay, and Jonah Rogers. Wrecked at Cape Cod in 1796.
Lucy Ann	Joined the fleet in 1844. Made three voyages. Owned by a company from Greenport. Captains: E.P. Brown and Benjamin Sisson. Condemned at Rio de Janiero in 1850.
Manhattan	Joined the fleet in 1843. Made one voyage. Captain Mercator Cooper. Withdrawn in 1847.
Marcus	Joined the fleet in 1825. Made between 15 and 20 voyages. Captains: David Loper, Benjamin Glover, Isaac Sayre, John Sweeney, M. Cartwright, Barney Green, Babcock, Andrew Halsey, Enoch Ryder and Eldredge. Condemned at Honolulu in 1850.
Martha I	Joined the fleet in 1815.
Martha II	Joined the fleet in 1844. Made one voyage. Captain George S. Tooker. Sold to New York in 1847.
Mary Gardiner	Joined the fleet in 1851. Made four voyages. Captains: Andrew Jennings, David Smith, Thomas Lowen, and Richard Nichols. Sold to New York in 1862.
Minerva	Entered the whale fishery in 1796. Made three voyages. Captains: Percy Russell, William Fowler, Francis Sayre and Job Parker. Sold to Nantucket in 1806.
Monmouth	Joined the fleet in 1836. Made five voyages. Captains: Richard S. Topping, Charles Bennett, Elkanah Smith, Lewis J. Corwin, James Sayre, and George S. Tooker. Sold at Valparaiso in 1862.
Montauk	Joined the fleet in 1854. Made one voyage. Captain A. Smith French. Sold and was active in the slave trade in 1860.

APPENDIX. SAG HARBOR NAMES

Myra	Joined the fleet in 1859. Made six voyages. Captains: Jacob Havens and Henry A. Babcock. The *Myra* was the last ship to sail from the port of Sag Harbor. Condemned at Barbados in 1874.
Nancy	Entered the whale fishery in 1804. Made two voyages. Captains: Nathan Sanford and John Godbee.
Neptune	Joined the fleet in 1827. Made 13 voyages. Captains: Philenus Pierson, Shamgar Slate, Richard Nichols, Edward Sayre, Jeremiah Ludlow, Mercator Cooper, George Post, Job Parker, and Rogers. Sold and sailed for California in 1849.
Neva	Joined the fleet in 1844. Made four voyages. The *Neva* was owned by a company from Greenport. Captains: Isaac Case and Isaac R. Hand. Condemned at Honolulu in 1859.
Niantic	Joined the fleet in 1844. Made one voyage. Captain Shamgar Slate. Sold to Rhode Island in 1847.
Nile	Joined the fleet in 1845. Made three voyages. The *Nile* was owned by a company from Greenport. Captains: Isaac Case and Charles T. Conkling. Broken up in 1857.
Nimrod	Joined the fleet in 1830. Made 20 voyages. Captains: Oliver Fowler, James Huntting, Albert Rogers, Wickham Jennings, James M. Green, Erastus Barnes, Job Parker, William B. Howes and Edward Halsey Jr.. Condemned at Sydney in 1860.
Noble	Joined the fleet in 1837. Made 12 voyages. Captains; Richard Nichols, William B. Howes, James Sayre, E.P. Brown, Wickham Jennings, William E. Fowler, Daniel T. Glover, and John Sweeney. Sold to the United States Government for the Stone Fleet in the Civil War in 1862.
O.C. Raymond	Joined the fleet in 1843. Made one voyage. Captain Samuel Dennison. Sold at Valparaiso in 1843.
Ocean I	Joined the fleet in 1822. Captain Weed.
Ocean II	Joined the fleet in 1864. Made two voyages. Captains: David Osborn and James Hamilton. Apparently lost sailing out of Sag Harbor in 1866.
Octavia	Joined the fleet in 1818. Made six voyages. Captains: George Post, Sylvester Griffing, Henry Green, and John Smith.
Odd Fellow	Joined the fleet in 1850. Made six voyages. Captains: Hervey Hedges, David Goodale, Jetur Rose, Selah Youngs and Frederick Weld. Sold to New London in 1869.
Ohio	Joined the fleet in 1844. Made one voyage. Captain Thomas Lowen. Condemned in 1848.
Ontario I	Joined the fleet in 1820. Made one voyage. Captain Smith. Lost at sea 1848.
Ontario II	Joined the fleet in 1834. Made eight voyages. Captains: Barney Green, Job Parker, Smith, and James Porter. Sold to New Bedford in 1850.
Ontario III	Joined the fleet in 1843. Made four voyages. Captains: Barney Green, George B. Brown, Josiah Foster, George S. Tooker, and Payne. Sold to New Bedford in 1854.
Oregon	Joined the fleet in 1853. Owned by a company from Greenport. Made two voyages. Captains: Nathaniel Case Jr., Ezra Terry, and Henry Babcock. Sold to Fair Haven in 1859.
Oscar	Joined the fleet in 1841. Made two voyages. Captains: Isaac Ludlow and Barney Green. Sold to Mattipoisett in 1849.
Pacific	Joined the fleet in 1864. Made three voyages. Captains: A. Smith French, Samuel Pierson, and Henry Huntting. Wrecked at the Sea of Kamakatka, Bering Islands in 1865.
Panama	Joined the fleet in 1838. Captains: Hallock, Thomas E. Crowell, and William Payne. Condemned at Valparaiso in 1851.
Parana	(See Highland Mary)
Phillip I	Joined the fleet in 1843. Made five voyages. Captains: Benjamin Sisson, Samuel Woodruff, and Joseph Case. Sold to New London in 1858.

APPENDIX. SAG HARBOR NAMES

Phoenix	Joined the fleet in 1830. Made ten voyages. Captains: Barney Green, Richard S. Topping, Briggs, and Cooper. Sold to Boston in 1849.
Pioneer	Joined the fleet in 1849. Owned by a company from Greenport. Made two voyages. Captains: Henry Babcock, Baldwin, and Treadwell Weeks. Sold to New Bedford in 1855.
Plymouth	Joined the fleet in 1845. Made one voyage. Captain Lawrence B. Edwards.
Portland	Joined the fleet in 1839. Made five voyages. Captains: William H. Payne, George W. Corwin, and Jared Wade Jr.. Sold and sailed for California in 1849.
Potosi	Joined the fleet in 1829. Made three voyages. Captain Charles Griffing. Lost off the Falklands in 1832.
Roanoke	Joined the fleet in 1836. Made 13 voyages. Captains: Hervey Harris, Benjamin Glover Jr., Jared Wade Jr., Isaac Hand, and Nathaniel Case Jr.. Sold to Boston in 1860.
Romulus	Joined the fleet in 1836. Made six voyages. Captains: Philander Winters, Joshua Rogers, Thomas Cartwright, Henry Fordham, and Joseph Case. Condemned at Honolulu in 1849.
S.S. Learned	Joined the fleet in 1856. Made four voyages. Captains: J. Madison Tabor, Thomas Royce, James Godbee, and Jeremiah Eldredge. Condemned at St. Catherine in 1862.
Sabina	Joined the fleet in 1844. Made two voyages. Captains: Shamgar Slate and David P. Vail. Sailed for California in 1849.
St. Lawrence	Entered the whale fishery in 1806. Made one voyage. Captain Edward Baker.
Salem	Joined the fleet in 1844. Made one voyage. Captain Edward Baker.
Sarah & Esther	Joined the fleet in 1843. Owned by a company from Greenport. Captains: Harlow and Charles Bennett. Condemned at Brazil in 1846.
Seraph	Joined the fleet in 1837. Made five voyages. Owned by a company from Greenport. Captains: Isaac Sheffield, George W. Corwin, Sherman, and Erastus Barnes. Condemned at Rio de Janiero in 1842.
Silas Richards	Joined the fleet in 1841. Made two voyages. Captain Richard Dering. Sold in 1847.
Superior	Joined the fleet in 1842. Made four voyages. Captains: Thomas Royce, John Bishop Jr., Frederick Cartwright, and Mulford. Sold to New Bedford in 1849.
Susan	Joined the fleet in 1856. Made four voyages. Captains: L.V. King and Edwin Smith. Sold to New York in 1863.
Telegraph	Joined the fleet in 1834. Made two voyages. Captains: John E. Howell and Edward Sayre. Lost off the coast of Japan in 1836.
Thames I	Joined the fleet in 1826. Made ten voyages. Captains: David Hand, Barney Green, Henry Nickerson, Huntting Cooper. Condemned at Sag Harbor in 1830; its remains were visible at Conklin's Point for years.
Thames II	Joined the fleet in 1841. Made three voyages. Captains: Edward Hedges, James Bishop, and William Payne, and Theron Worth. Sailed for California.
Thomas Dickason	Joined the fleet in 1837. Made four voyages. Captains: William Lowen, Wickham Havens, and Nathaniel Hamilton. Sold to New London in 1847 and lost in the Arctic in 1871.
Thomas Nelson	Joined the fleet in 1817. Made two voyages. Captains: Coffin and Gardiner.
Thorn	Joined the fleet in 1821. Made 15 voyages. Captains: Hervey Hedges, Stuart Tuttle, Robert E. Gardiner, Matthew Sayre, R. Hand, Wickham Havens, Richard S. Topping, Griffing, and Howell. Condemned at Bay of Islands in 1840.
Timor	Joined the fleet in 1842. Made six voyages. Captains: John Baker, Silas Eldredge, George White, and James Rogers. Sold to the United States Government during the Civil War to be added to the Stone Fleet.
Triad	Joined the fleet in 1831. Made two voyages. Captains: Horton and David Loper. Owned by a company from Greenport.

APPENDIX. SAG HARBOR NAMES

Tuscany	Joined the fleet in 1842. Made five voyages. Captains: Edwards, Benjamin Halsey, James Godbee, and White. Lost off Amsterdam in 1855.
Union I	Joined the fleet in 1819. Made four voyages. Captains: Osborn, Griffing, Sayre, and Edward Halsey. Last voyage made in 1829.
Union II	Joined the fleet in 1857. Made three voyages. Captains: Jeremiah Hedges, James Ludlow, and James Rogers. Withdrawn in 1868 to carry freight.
W.F. Stafford	Joined the fleet in 1856. Made one voyage. Captain Thomas Royce. Withdrawn in 1860.
Warren	Entered the whale fishery in 1809. Made six voyages. Captains: Francis Sayre, Edward Halsey, Oliver Folger, William Fowler, and James Post.
Washington I	Entered the whale fishery in 1808. Made two voyages. Captain William Fowler.
Washington (Brig)	Joined the fleet in 1853. Made two voyages. Captains: Hallock and Sylvester Brown. Lost at Shanter Bay, Ochotak Sea in 1855.
Washington II	Joined the fleet in 1837. Made 12 voyages. Captains: Corwin, Robert Wilbur, Hedges Babcock, Jetur Rose, Nathaniel Edwards, Sanford, and Sylvester Griffing. Sold to New York in 1862.
Wickford	Joined the fleet in 1841. Made two voyages. Captains: Davis Miller and David P. Vail. Withdrawn in 1843.
William Tell	Joined the fleet in 1843. Made six voyages. Captains: Benjamin Glover, Edwin Smith, James M. Tabor, James Austin. Lost in the Arctic in 1859.
Wiscassett	Joined the fleet in 1841. Made two voyages. Captains: Elkanah Smith and William Payne. Withdrawn in 1847.
Xenaphon	Joined the fleet in 1831. Made five voyages. Captains: Jesse Halsey, Andrew Halsey, Robert Hand, and Sylvester Griffing. Burned at the Sag Harbor shore during the fire of 1845.

PART II   CHAPTER 1

MEN EMPLOYED IN THE WHALE FISHERY, 1840s

Babcock, John	2nd Mate aboard the *Citizen*
Babcock, Hedges	Captain
Bassett, Albert	Seaman
Bassett, George	Mariner
Bassett, James	Cooper
Bellows, Daniel Y.	Cooper
Bickerton, William	Cooper
Bill, Erastus	Steersman aboard the *Citizen*
Bill, Edwin	Seaman
Briggs, Samuel P.	Captain
Carmen, Thomas	Caulker aboard the *Hamilton*
Cartwright, David	Coastal trade
Cartwright, F. R.	1st Mate aboard the *Konohassett*
Cartwright, Thomas	Captain
Cooper, Edward M.	Cooper
Cooper, William	Seaman
Dering, Richard	Captain of the *Silas Richards*
Douglas, Robert	Captain
Edwards, Lawrence	Captain
Edwards, S.W.	Seaman
Eldredge, D. Atwood	Cooper
Eldredge, Enoch	Rigger
Fordham, Charles	Mariner

APPENDIX. SAG HARBOR NAMES

Fordham, Lodowick	Captain
Fordham, Nathan	Steward aboard the *Hamilton*
Fordham, Samuel	Cooper
Fordham, William F.	Mariner
Gawley, John	Cooper
Gawley, Stephen	Seaman
Godbee, James	1st Mate aboard the *Hamilton*
Halsey, Walter P.	Cook aboard the *Hamilton*
Hamilton, James	Captain
Hand, David	Captain
Havens, James M.	Seaman
Hayes, Robert	Rigger
Hedges, Jeremiah	Seaman
Hildreth, Edmund	Mariner
Horton, Gilbert	Cooper
Howell, George	Mariner
Howes, William	Captain
Hubbard, Charles	Cooper
Isham, Joseph B.G.	Seaman
Jones, Edwin R.	Mariner
Jones, Elias W.	Captain
Jones, William A.	Seaman
Leek, Erastus	2nd Mate aboard the *Hamilton*
Loper, David	Captain
Loper, Henry D.	Mariner
Lowen, Thomas S.	Seaman
Miller, William	Shipwright
Miner, Abel G.	Cooper
Nickerson, Henry	Captain
Nickerson, James	Cooper
Nichols, Richard	Captain
Prime, William	Steward aboard the *Silas Richards*
Reeves, B.	Cooper
Reynolds, Edward	Seaman
Robbins, William	Cook aboard the *Citizen*
Slate, Shamgar	Captain of the *Hamilton*
Smith, Charles	Seaman
Smith, David	Seaman
Smith, George	Cooper
Smith, William H.	Seaman
Wallace, Thomas	Cooper
Wells, John	Steward on the *Hamilton*
Willis, William	Shipwright
Winters, Jonas	Captain
Worth, J.B.	Captain of the *Konohassett*
Worth, T.B.	2nd Mate aboard the *Konohassett*
Youngs, Selah	Captain

APPENDIX. SAG HARBOR NAMES

PART II CHAPTER 1

INDUSTRIES INVOLVED IN THE TRADE

Ropewalks — William J.Rysam's ropewalk stood on the northeast corner of Burke Street and ran to the northwest corner of Rysam Street.
Samuel L'Hommedieu's ropewalk stood off upper Main Street near Peter's Green on the Cove.

Cooperages — Abel C. Minor's cooperage stood at the foot of Main Street near the Long Wharf.
Post & Sherry had theirs near the North Haven Bridge.
E. M. Cooper and Michael Bush had a cooperage on West Water Street.
D.Y. Bellows, Harry Tryon, Charles Seeley and Henry Stewart all had cooperages on West Water Street.
Charles Ware's cooperage stood on Spring Street; Thomas Pierson had one on the west side of Main Street.
Captain John Budd's was at North Haven.
Others working the cooper's trade were James Bassett, William Bickerton, D. Atwood Eldredge, Samuel Fordham, John Gawley, Gilbert Horton, Charles Hubbard, James Nickerson, B. Reeves and Thomas Wallace.

Shipyards — Captain Daniel Sayre's shipyard was at Redwood in 1741.
Obediah Gildersleeve's was also at Redwood, 1760–70.
William J. Rysam's was at Conklin's Point.
William H. Cooper's stood at the foot of Main Street.
Huntting's was near the North Haven Bridge.
Post & Sherry's shipyard stood at the foot of Division Street near the Long Wharf.
Benjamin Wade had one at Peter's Green on the Cove.
Willis & Company had one on West Water Street.
John Budd and J. E. Smith's were on North Haven.

Ship Chandlers — S & B Huntting Company, L.D. Cook & H. Green, Samuel L'Hommedieu, N & G Howell and J.E. Smith & Brothers all were located on or near the Long Wharf.

Ship Carpenters — Elihu Edwards, James Gorham, Elisha Pryor, Captain Daniel Sayre, Benjamin Wade and Jared Wade

Riggers — Enoch Eldredge and Robert Hayes

Pump and Blockmakers — Nathaniel Matthews and Robert Rankin, Charles Douglas, Howes Crowell and Sylvanus Crowell

Blacksmith Shops — John Fordham's shop stood at the foot of the village.
Overton's shop first stood on the Maidstone Mills property and later on Spring Street.

PART V CHAPTER 1

SLOOPS, PACKETS, SCHOONERS AND STEAMERS

Year	Vessel	Route	Captain
1791	Industry	Sag Harbor-New York	Luther Hildreth
1791	Rising Sun	Sag Harbor-New York	William Parker
1791	Speedwell	Sag Harbor-Hartford	John Price
1791	Peggy	Sag Harbor-New York	S. Satterly
1792	Lucretia	Sag Harbor-New London	John Chase
1792	Fancy	Sag Harbor-Hartford	John Hicks
1819	Washington	Sag Harbor-New London	A. Parker
1819	Jefferson	Sag Harbor-Middletown, Ct.	
1819	Imperial	Sag Harbor-New York	
1819	Flash	Sag Harbor-New York	Charles Smith
1819	Maid of Cherry	Sag Harbor-Riverhead	Jasper Vail

APPENDIX. SAG HARBOR NAMES

Year	Vessel	Route	Captain
1820	David Porter	Sag Harbor-New York	Jeff Fordham
1824	Consolation	Sag Harbor-New London	William Moss, Jr.
1824	Bee	Sag Harbor-New London	C. Fosdick
1829	Expedition	Sag Harbor-Southold	Ephraim Overton
1829	Dandy	Sag Harbor-Southold	H.L. Jennings
1830	Dread	Sag Harbor-Southold	Ephraim Overton
1830	Boreas	Sag Harbor-Greenport	H.H. Horton
1830	Victory	Sag Harbor-New London	John Rogers
1840	Planter	Sag Harbor-New York	Cartwright
1840	Speed	Sag Harbor-Greenport	
1842	Victory	Sag Harbor-New London	J.L. Ryan
1842	Bee	Sag Harbor-New London	J.L. Rogers
1843	Cabinet	Sag Harbor-Albany	Henry Mott
1845	Emily	Sag Harbor-Albany	Henry Mott
1845	James Lawrence	Sag Harbor-New York	Henry Mott
1845	Expedition	Sag Harbor-Southold	Ephraim Overton
1845	Dandy	Sag Harbor-Southold	L.H. Jennings
1886	Emerald	Sag Harbor-Baltimore	F.L. LaGuire
1898	Lizzie V. Hall	Sag Harbor-Northern ports	John B. Phillips
1904	Estelle	Sag Harbor-Southern ports	John B. Phillips
1914	Carrie A. Lane	Sag Harbor-Galveston	John B. Phillips

STEAMBOATS

Year	Vessel	Route	Captain
1839	Olive Branch	Sag Harbor-New York	
1840	Maria	Sag Harbor-New London	Elliot
1841	Splendid	Sag Harbor-New York	Sanford
1841	Statesman	Sag Harbor-New York	D.A. Nash
1841	Express	Sag Harbor-New York	Geer
1842	Thorne	Sag Harbor-New London	Elliot
1843	Flushing	Sag Harbor-New York-Lyme	VanPelt
1859	Cataline	Sag Harbor-New York	Wickham Havens
1860	Albany	Sag Harbor-New York	
1860	Pioneer	Sag Harbor-New York	
1860	Naushon	Sag Harbor-New York	
1860	Island Belle	Sag Harbor-New York	
1860	Iolas	Sag Harbor-New York	D.C. Keeney
1861	Mary Benton	Sag Harbor-New York	J. Post
1861	Mary Benton	Sag Harbor-Hartford	George W. Bates
1861	Gypsy	Sag Harbor-New London	
1861	Sarah S.B. Carey	Sag Harbor-New London	
1861	Nantucket	Sag Harbor-New London	T. Burns
1861	Old Glory	Sag Harbor-New London	J.F. Smith
1861	Manhanset	Sag Harbor-New London	J.F. Smith
1861	Sarah Thorpe	Sag Harbor-New London	Mark Griffin
1861	Flushing	Sag Harbor-New London	VanPelt & LeFevre
1862	Orient	Sag Harbor-New London	T. Burns
1862	Massachusetts	Sag Harbor-New York	Wickham Havens
1862	Augustus	Sag Harbor-New York	Wickham Havens
1862	Niagara	Sag Harbor-New York	Wickham Havens
1863	Tiger Lily	Sag Harbor-Greenport	

APPENDIX. SAG HARBOR NAMES

Year	Vessel	Route	Captain
1863	Sprite	Sag Harbor-Greenport	
1863	Artisan	Sag Harbor-New York	Donaldson
1863	Suffolk	Sag Harbor-New York	Wickham Havens
1863	River Queen	Sag Harbor-New York	
1864	Sarah S.B. Carey	Sag Harbor-Hartford	George W. Bates
1864	Cricket	Sag Harbor-Hartford	
1864	L. Bordman	Sag Harbor-Hartford	
1864	Agawam	Sag Harbor-Hartford	Congdon
1864	Sunshine	Sag Harbor-Hartford	Bates & O.H. Clark
1873	J.B. Schuyler	Sag Harbor-New York	J.B. Edwards
1873	J.S. Underhill	Sag Harbor-Greenport	Charles Dixon
1873	Emile	Sag Harbor-Greenport	Lewis Ross
1873	Statesman	Sag Harbor-Greenport	A.D. Nash
1873	Dixie	Sag Harbor-Greenport	
1874	Daisy	Sag Harbor-New London	
1875	Port Royal	Sag Harbor-New London	Clark
1875	W.W. Coit	Sag Harbor-New York	George Gibbs
1877	Escort	Sag Harbor-New York	H.S. Ackley
1878	Gypsy	Sag Harbor-New London	James F. Smith
1879	George W. Beale	Sag Harbor-New York	J.S. Briggs
1885	Frances	Sag Harbor-New York	Youngs
1885	Greenport	Sag Harbor-New York	Carroll & Mitchell
1889	Shelter Island	Sag Harbor-New York	George Gibbs
1891	Montauk	Sag Harbor-New York	Joshua Gibbs
1892	Wyandotte	Sag Harbor-New York	
1893	Long Island	Sag Harbor-New London	
1895	Shinnecock	Sag Harbor-New York	A. Mitchell
1901	Orient	Sag Harbor-New London	T. Burns
1901	Long Island	Sag Harbor-New London	Beebee & Elton
1909	Meteor	Sag Harbor-New York	

PART I   CHAPTER 2 & 3

EMPLOYMENT AND INDUSTRIAL DEVELOPMENT

Business Directory, late 1700s

Boarding house	William Duvall, 1791
Dry goods store	Dering & Fordham, 1790
Goldsmith	Daniel Pierson, 1791
Hairdresser and bookbinder	Jonathan Hill, 1791
Miller	Mordaci Homan, 1760
Miller	James Mitchell, 1799
Physician and surgeon	James Sloan, 1797
Ropemaker	Samuel L'Hommedieu, 1792
Saddlemaker	David Eells, 1791
Sign, ship and house painter	Confider White, 1791
Storekeeper	Stephen Howell, 1786
Storekeeper	Uriah Rogers, 1786
Tailor	Daniel Gilman, 1791
Tailor	Silas Raymond, 1791
Tinsmith and coppersmith	Jonathan Sizer, 1791

APPENDIX. SAG HARBOR NAMES

Business Directory, 1804-10

Bookbinder	Jonathan Hall
Blockmaker	Charles Douglas
Boots and shoes	Amasa Patterson
Brickmaker	Stephen Howell
Butcher	Ebeneezer Beecher
Cabinetmaker	William Hall
Druggist	Daniel and Eden Latham
Dry goods	H. & D. Gelston
Dry goods	Asa Partridge
Gravestones	Ithuel Hill
Groceries	John N. Fordham & Son
Groceries	Jesse Hedges
Groceries	John Jermain
Hatter	Moses Bishop
Hatter	James Overton
Ladies fashions	Betsey Brown
Meat market	Hubbard Latham
Printer	Alden Spooner
Ropemaker	Samuel L'Hommedieu
Saddle and harnessmaker	Elias Howell
Ship chandlery	Samuel L'Hommedieu & Son
Tailor	S. Raymond
Tanning and currying	Hubbard Latham Jr.
Watchmaker	Elijah Simons

PART III CHAPTER 1

Business Directory, 1840s

Artist	Charles C. Douglas
Blacksmiths	John A. Cook, Charles H. Morris, David Schellinger, E.L. Simons
Butcher	John Schellinger
Cabinetmaker	Nathan Tinker
Candlemaker and Oil	S.A. Seely
Carpenters	John E. Chester, James T. Dodson, David Edwards, Charles C. Filer, William H. Gawley, Joseph F. Lamb, Gilbert Loper, Squires H. Miller, Joshua B. Nickerson, Charles Pierson, Luther Sherman, William H. Smith, Nathan Tabor, George W. Talmadge, George D. Terry, Samuel J. Terry, Jonas Williamson
Carriagemaker	Henry R. White
Clerks	John H. Fordham, Frederick F. Hildreth, Marcus Starr
Clothier	Gilbert B. Strong
Coastal trade	David Cartwright, Thomas Cartwright
Coopers	James Bassett, Daniel Y. Bellows, William Bickerton, Edward M. Cooper, D. Atwood Eldredge, Samuel Fordham, John Gawley, Gilbert Horton, Charles Hubbard, Abel G. Miner, James W. Nickerson, B. Reeves, Thomas Wallace
Dentist	Frederick Crocker
Druggists	William Buck, J.F. Chipman
Gunsmith	Zeb Elliott

APPENDIX. SAG HARBOR NAMES

Innkeepers	John Hobart, Henry Phelps
Laborer	John T. Silveria
Lawyer	Henry P. Hedges
Mariners	George Bassett, Erastus Bill, Richard N. Dering, Charles H. Fordham, Lodowick Fordham, William G. Fordham, Edmund A. Hildreth, George Howell, Edwin R. Jones, Elias W. Jones, Henry D. Loper, Richard J. Nichols, Shamgar Slate, J.B. Worth, Selah Youngs
Merchants	David Congdon, Gilbert H. Cooper, Daniel H. Douglass, Hannibal French, Henry L. Gardiner, John D. Gardiner, Robert E. Gardiner, Henry L. Jessup, Philander Jennings, Ezekiel Mulford, Lyman Pitcher, Abner D. Smith, Andrew J. Tabor, William R. Taylor, William H. Tooker, Calvin J. Wells
Painters	Peter Roberts, Robert Roberts
Photographer	E.H. Payne (daguerreotypes)
Physicians	Henry Cook, John Dayton, Edgar Miles
Pump and blockmakers	Nathaniel Matthews, Robert Rankin
Riggers	Enoch Eldredge, Robert Hayes
Sash and blindmakers	Oliver B. Lucas
Seamen	Hedges Babcock, John Babcock, Albert Bassett, Edwin Bill, Samuel P. Briggs, William H. Cooper, Robert Douglass, Lawrence Edwards, S. Woodruff Edwards, Nathan Fordham, Stephen Gawley, James Godbee, Walter P. Halsey, James Hamilton, David Hand, James M. Havens, Jeremiah Hedges, William B. Howes, Joseph Isham, William A. Jones, Erasuts Leeks, David Loper, Thomas S. Lowen, Henry Nickerson, William Prime, Edward B. Reynolds, William Robbins, William J. Rodgers, Charles Smith, David Smith, John Wells, Jonas Winters, T.B. Worth
Shipwright	Stephen Baker
Shoes and boots	Abel C. Buckley, Isaac C. Fowler, David A. Jennings, N.S. Lester, Henry T. Williamson
Stonecutter	Stephen Baker
Suffolk County National Bank	John Hand
Tailors	Erastus G. Bassett, William Fordred, Charles W. Hedges, Samuel A. Redfield, Joshua Terry
Tinsmith	James H. Robin

PART V CHAPTER 4
Business Directory, 1888-89

Amusement Hall and Park	Augustus Meyer, George E. Thompson
Auctioneers	Henry Hyman, C.H. Vaughn
Bakers	James E. Dickerson, James Harris
Barbers	John Battle, Schmid & McCullin
Bartenders	Adelbert Pierson, William S. Wilson
Blacksmiths	John DeCastro, John Fordham, Hildreth & Bennett, George D. Hill, Clarence C. Morris, Charles R. Morris, George C. Morris, Morgan O'Meara, Thomas C. Overton, Robert J. Power
Boat and ship agents	George Babcock, John Burbank, Hannibal French Jr., clerk on the steamer *Shelter Island*; Joshua E. Gibbs, agent for the Montauk Steamboat Company; John Gray, John Homan, steamboat agent and Captain; William Jeffries, pilot; Lewis Ross, pilot; John Saggers, pilot; James Smith, Captain of the *Manhanset*

APPENDIX. SAG HARBOR NAMES

Bookkeepers	Peter Dipple, Edward Fields
Boots and shoes	Sherman W. Barteau, Robert O. Cooper, John H. Fields, Isaac Harvey, Patrick Keating, James C. Lawrence, Patrick Mulligan, Herbert F. Nickerson, Henry T. Williamson
Carpenters	William A. Bassenden, Charles A. Parks, Charles W. Payne, Thomas Vail
Cigar manufacturers	James M. Dolan, Henry E. Meyer, Egbert S. Williams
Clerks	William Bassenden, Joseph Burns, Edward B. Dennison, Charles Dorflinger, Charles George, Frank Glover, Frederick Kuss, Charles Warner, Casper Shaeffer
Coal and lumber	Hedges & Wade, Elisha King, Oliver G. Nickerson
Dentist	Elbridge G. Howard
Deputy Sheriff and Justices	Henry Hyman, Philander Jennings
Doctors	Edgar Miles, William H. Perdomo, John Rogers, A.S. Schiller, Adolph Schlosser, George A. Sterling, Cleveland S. Stillwell
Druggists	J.F.D. Lobstein, Edgar Miles, Albert Newins, William Wallace Tooker
Editors	Brinley Sleight, Cornelius R. Sleight
Engineers	Michael Collins, Stanley Dyer, Edward Fulton, Henry Irving, Benjamin Merritt
Engravers and printers	Richard S. Aldred, Lewis Austin, William Eaton, William Godbee, Emma P. Hallock, Grace Preston, Frederick Pulver, Max Sontheimer
Factory workers	Shamgar Babcock, William Blaiklock, James Brobeck, William W. Calkins, Henry F. Cook, Charles Daniels, Charles Metzer, Frank A. Parks, John W. Pierce
Fish	Edward A. Hildreth
Hides and tallow	Gabriel Halsey
Hotels	Freeman & Youngs, American Hotel; Peter Gaffga, The Gaffga House; Charles D. Harris, Bijou Hotel; Samuel Kipp and Allen C. Dalzell, The Cove Hotel; Robert J. Power, George B. Warner, The Nassau House
Ice, wood, and trucking	Charles N. Hildreth, George H. Hildreth, Herbert Hildreth
Insurance and real estate	Charles N. Brown, George H. Cooper, Greene & Raynor, John N. Hunt, George A. Kiernan, John Sherry, John Sherry Jr.
Laundry	Peter Gaffga, Sam Wing
Lawyers	Thomas F. Bisgood, Everett Carpenter, Greene & Raynor, Henry P. Hedges, John Sherry Jr.
Library	August Meyer
Marble and granite	William J. Beebee, Hill & Young
Millers	Edward M. Cooper
Musical instruments	George W. Reney
Painters and paperhangers	John W. Meyer, Horace P. Emanuel, John H. Spencer
Photographers	William G. Howard, Jonathan Warner
Post office employees	Genevieve French, Hannibal French
Railroad employees	Emmet Crawford, Frank French, Anson White, John P. White
Reporter	William McFeeters
Salesmen	Francis H. Palmer, Augustus Tooker
Saloonkeepers	Thomas Boyle, John Glenn, Nichols S. Herbert, Frederick Jetter, Arthur D. Ludlow

354 APPENDIX. SAG HARBOR NAMES

Shopkeepers and storekeepers	Richard Aldrich, George B. Brown, Michael F. Cassidy, Gilbert H. Cooper, Thomas Cunningham, Samuel L. Davis, Mrs. Samuel Dutcher, Edwards Brothers, Eliza Edwards, John Emmel, Samuel Fordham, Henry French, Arthur M. Havens, Charles Hedges, Frank Hennigar, S.P. Hertz, Hildreth & Bennett, Benjamin F. Hope, Meyer Hyman, George Kiernan, James C. Lawrence, Thomas Lester, John Lobstein, Oliver B. Lucas, Lyon & Sherwood, Meyer Brothers, Edgar Miles, Morouney & Job, William Naul, Albert Newins, Charles Watson Payne, Henry P. Porter, George W. Reney, Reuben E. Richards, Clive Riseman, William T. Robert, Edward E. Scott, L. Seaman and Company, Smith Brothers, George N. Tabor, Wilbur N. Tabor, Seymour L. Tooker, William Wallace Tooker, H.L. Topping, James Tucker, Carl L. Vaughn, Paul Weilbacher Jr., Edwin T. Winters, Mitchell Wise
Steward	Joshua Terry
Surveyor and civil engineer	Edgar Z. Hunt
Tailor	Joshua Terry
Telegraph operator	Gilbert W. Penny

PART VI CHAPTER 4
Business Directory, 1910–11

Accountants	S.W. Barteau, Frank W. Bill, Thomas F. Bisgood, C.S. Elder, Lloyd Jeffrey, John N. Talmage
Assistant Postmaster	Genevieve French
Autos and bicycles	Harry M. Youngs
Bakers	L. Epstein, Elwin Harris, F.H. Warner
Banks and bankers	The Peconic Bank, William E. Denison, president; F.W. Corwin, cashier. Sag Harbor Savings Bank, James H. Pierson, president; E.L. Tindall, secretary and treasurer; John Y. Corwin, assistant treasurer; Richard Lyons, clerk
Barbers	Stephen Alioto, Philippe Bano, Nicholas Battle, Joseph DePasquale, Vincent Florimo, Mariano Viscuso
Blacksmiths	C. Fordham, H.D. Fordham, T.C. Overton, H.R. Ruppel, Jerry Sullivan
Bliss Company	William O. Amman, C.M. Davis, Charles Donohue, Edward B. Logan, Harry J. O'Brien, Alfonso Sauer, E.W. Scribner
Boat builders	George Higgins
Bottlers	Emmel Bottling Works, John Emmel, prop.; Schommer's Bottle Works, William Schommer, prop.
Boots and shoes	D. Meyer, M. Meyer, D. Harris & Son, S. Klein
Brick manufacturers	Long Island & Fishers Island Brick Co.
Butchers	John H. Aldrich, George Browngardt, Thomas Griffing, Lafayette Halsey, Sam Heller, George J. Howell, King & Wade, L.E. Halsey, Thomas Lister, Mrs. J. Eisenberg, Clarence Pulver, Harry E. Wade
Captains	Thomas Brewer, Thomas Corcoran, James H. Brewer, J.F. Kelly, F. Lafayette LaGuire, Joseph McFarland, J.B. Phillips, James T. Pidgeon, Edward C. Reeve, David Grossman, L.N. Ross, J.M. Wallace, Augustus Wallace, Fred Youngs
Carriagemakers	H.H. Hildreth

APPENDIX. SAG HARBOR NAMES 355

Chauffeurs	Frank N. Howell, Ralph Halsey, Paul Venmoos
Chief of Police	George F. Payne
Clergymen	F.V. Baer, Episcopal Church; George E. Bishop, Methodist Church; William T. Edds, Presbyterian Church; A.C. Goldberg, Pentecostal Church; William L. Long, Roman Catholic Church; George N. Ray, A.M.E. Zion Church; Raymond J. Vaughn, Baptist Church; and Edwin Winters, Methodist-Episcopal Church
Clothing	David Meyer, Morris Meyer, D. Harris & Son, E. Spodick
Coal and wood	East Hampton Lumber & Coal Company, J. McMahon, C.W. Payne, W.H. Stafford, Charles Shaw
Confectionery	Keating & Jones, The Fair, N. Meyersohn, propietor; The Ideal, Dalzell & Gibbons, proprietors; Mrs. E.S. Williams; P. Katz
Contractors and builders	George H. Cleveland, Calfer & Tench, Charles H. Payne, Charles E. Bassett, H.D. Cleveland, James Bennett, Harry H. Bramble, James E. Bunnell, Joseph Corwin, Nathan S. Corwin, Alfred J. Edwards, Oscar B. Edwards, Ralph J. Eldredge, Benjamin F. Field, Edward F. Field, Wilson K. Field, William E. Fordham, Charles King, George Page, Nathaniel Perkins, William Renkens, William P. Rohm, James Simms
Crockery and hardware	P. Ballen, E. Efron, M. Simons
Dentists	C.H. Tillinghast, W.H. VanNostrand
Department stores	William M. Cook, James F. Davis, Lyon & Sherwood Company
Dressmakers	Hazel M. Bassenden, Grace C. Bogue, Nettie Fenelon, Sarah Field, Mary E. Greene, Alice Havens, Mary Hughes, Bessie Meyer, Margaret Mulligan, Pearl Walsh
Druggists	A.T. Brown, William R. Reimann
Dry goods	William H. Cook, James F. Davis, Lyon & Sherwood, Edel Spodick
Electricians	William H. Bloomingburg, Ivan Byram, Louis Sands
Engineers	William H. Quackenbush, H.T. Tuthill
Fishermen and baymen	Charles H. Aldrich, George R. Babcock, David R. Bennett, George L. Bennett, Henry C. Bennett, Herbert W. Bennett, Cornelius Bennett, Edwin E. Flynn, Peter Fournier, Peter Gunning, A.W. Pugsley, John Slowey, Samuel Terrel, Addison Thompson
Fruit dealers	Max Grossman, Julius Cohen, P. Katz, George Fick, Benjamin Schocket
Garages	Ferris Andrews, William Blaiklock, Michael Marouney, Harry G. Wallace
Gas Company	Joseph L. Ehret, Robert H. Palmer, Peter Silvey
Grain, feed, and flour	Charles Watson Payne, W.J. Walden, R.J. Smith
Groceries	Stephen Alioto, Adolph Disch, Edwards Brothers, Fischer & Bury, S. Klein & Son, C.F. Miller, William Naul, Charles Watson Payne, Edward Scholtz, R.J. Smith, Annie Schwartz, C.H. Vaughn, Woodward Brothers
Hardware	P. Ballen, E. Efron
Harnessmaker	Robert Gerlach
Hat pin manufacturers	Bloch Brothers, J. Frank Cooper, supervisor
Hotels	American Hotel, A.M. Youngs; Gardiner House, Mrs. C.H. Gardiner; Nassau House, J.A. Udall and H.G. Ham; Seaview House, J.K. Morris; Vail House, Mrs. Frances L. Vail; Anna Babcock, Catherine Glenn, Cora Bennett

APPENDIX. SAG HARBOR NAMES

Ice	Hildreth & Company, George and Herbert Hildreth
Ice cream	The Fair, N. Meyersohn; The Ideal, Dalzell and Gibbons; Dick's Restaurant, Richard King; Keating & Jones, Mrs. E.S. Williams
Insurance	George Kiernan, C.R. Sleight, James E. Early, Thomas F. Lachall, C.W. Thompson, E.J. O'Halloran
Jardinier manufacturer	Kiss Brothers (Aaron, Charles, Coleman Kiss)
Jewelers	C.E. Fritts, F.S. Hand
Junk dealers	Morris Ginsberg, Nathan Eisenberg, Samuel Cohen
Lawyers	O.F. Fanning, William C. Green, Daniel Vermilye
Lifesavers	Frank Field, George W. Sears
Library	Cora Bunker
Light and Power	Sag Harbor Electric Light Company
Milkmen	Joseph O'Brien, F.W. Payne, John Soah, George E. VanScoy Jr.
Millinery	Frank Hennigar, Jennie L. Vail, Carrie Nickerson
Miscellaneous	Henrietta Bauman, actress; George Gaffga, assayer; Anna Healy, bathing station attendant; William Boyington, chemist; Frank Maier, caretaker; John F. Nolan, coachman; W.F. Youngs, duck farm; Fannie Tunison, fancy work; Herman Ballrich, farm supervisor; Jesse Payne, park supervisor; Howard Yecker, pigeon farm; Grover C. Hart, principal; Harry Restofski, telegraph operator; Henry M. Payne, weaver; John F. Schumann, instrument maker
Monuments	Charles N. Archibald, William Young, Thomas Duffy
Newspapers	*The Corrector*: B.D. Sleight publisher & editor, *The Sag Harbor Express*: John H. Hunt publisher & editor, *The News*: Corwin & Hallock publisher, Peter Hughes editor, George Densing journalist, Frances Harris compositor, William R. Sleight compositor; Mary Hughes typesetter
Nurses	Sadie Bates, Kate McQuade, Marie Slate
Phonographs	Herman Spitz
Photographs	Louis Eister, W. G. Howard
Physicians	M.B. Lewis, T.C. Lippmann, C.S. Stillwell, C.E. Wells
Plumbers	Clarence Anderson, E.J. Ewertson, Raymond A. Lyons, C.H. McGowan, H.C. Morris, Charles H. Redfield, Howard Reney, Walter Halsey
Postmaster	Genevieve French
Railroad employees	A.C. Adams, William Y. Bath, C.A. Birs, Joseph J. Brooks, E.B. Hubbard, William M. Miller, Edward Murphy Jr., Fred L. Payne, Paul Rogers, Harry Rundy, Stephen Swayzey, Albert A. Wassell, William Wassell
Real Estate	Eleanor Raynor, A.H. Rogers, B.D. Corwin, John Snyder
Restaurants	Dick's Restaurant, R.C. King, Home Restaurant. Mrs. James Hill, Joseph Shapiro
Salesmen	George W. Finckenauer, Charles Podowitz, W.S. Somers, W.S. Wilson
Saloonkeepers	M.F. Cassidy, Michael Dorsky, J.T. Emmel, Daniel McLane, Frank McNally, Manuel Rosenthal
Sea tool manufacturers	H.D. Fordham
Shoe repairs	L. Crowitz, J.H. Field, Frank Fisher, J. Judelowitz
Stables	A.S. Douglass, Seymour DeCastro, George H. DeCastro, John DeCastro, Frank Jaffe, Jerry Sullivan
Tailor	John Karl

APPENDIX. SAG HARBOR NAMES

Tax collector	William T. Vaughn
Theaters	The Atheneum, The Montauk, The Star
Tinsmiths	Ralph Sweezey, D.E. Youngs
Trucking	George Stafford, W.H. Stafford, W.F. Hultz, Harry L. Mott, John Mott, E.P. Roberts, James McMahon, George H. Champlain
Undertakers	Edward Archibald, Thompson & Osborne, Frederick Yardley, Jr.
Veterinary surgeon	W.W. Bennett
Watchcase manufacturer	Fahys
Water service	Sag Harbor Water Works
Window shades	G.A. Halsey

PART VI CHAPTER 4
Business Directory, 1920s

Banks	Sag Harbor Savings Bank, Peconic Bank
Barbers	Stephen Alioto, Nicholas Battle, Augustus Scarlato, Tony Oro
Beauty parlors	Lucille's Beauty Shop
Billiard parlors	R.G. Nichols, William Scarlato
Bottlers	Fred Wilson
Builders	Garypie Brothers, John Ward
Cleaners	I. Friedman
Clothing	Betty Shop, Harry Meyer's, George McFarland, S. Raff, A.W. Basile
Coal	Andrew Gilbride, East Hampton Lumber & Coal, C. Augustine Kiernan
Department stores	Cooks, Simons
Druggists	A.T. Brown, William Reimann
Electricians	Herbert M. Dutcher
Farms	Leander Aldrich
Funeral directors	Thompson & Osborne
Furniture	Thompson & Osborne
Garages	Bay View Garage, Gilbride Brothers AEF Gas Station, Maier's Garage, Michael Morouney, Joseph Sherry, Jr., H.M. Youngs, Tabor's
Grain	Sag Harbor Grain Company
Groceries	A & P, H.C. Bohack, Edward Brothers, C.E. King & Son, Joseph Klein, Laspesa Fruit Store, Madison Market, Charles Podewitz, Raulston's, Ralph Raniolo, Sag Harbor Bake Shop, Sanitary Market of Joseph Korsak, William Shocket, Walter Seaman, H.E. Wade, Woodward Brothers, Mueller's Market
Hardware	R.C. Barry & Son, Philip Ballen
Hotels	American Hotel, Hotel Bay View, Lundhurst House, Sea View House, Lily Pond House
Ice	Kenneth Olejnik
Ice cream	Chandler's, Jaffe, Ken Olejnik, Joseph Santacroce
Jewelers	Calvin Fritts, E.H. Scribner
Laundry	H.G. Ham, East Hampton Laundry
Lawyers	Harry M. Leek
Millinery	Vail Millinery Parlors
Painters	E.B. Hill

APPENDIX. SAG HARBOR NAMES

Paints	William C. Bates
Pianos	Stephen Bediance
Plumbers and heating	Frank Jose, William Trimpin
Radio and electronics	C. Mortensen, H. Spitz
Restaurant	Candy Kitchen, Elm Restaurant, Frank & Freddie's Lunch Wagon, Jaffe's Confectioners, Warners
Shoes	P. Grossman, D. Harris & Son, Ivans
Taxi	Clarence King, Joseph Laspesa, Joseph Santacroce
Tailors	S. Acker, John Karl, Berkowitz, I. Goldstein, Charles Pavelec
Theaters	Glynne's Sag Harbor Theater, The Elite Theater
Variety stores	Greenberg's 5 & 10, E.L. Hansen, Lyon & Sherwood, Ideal Cash Store
Windows and shades	G.H. Halsey

PART I CHAPTER 3

POSTMASTERS

Henry Packer Dering, 1794–1822
Henry Thomas Dering, 1822–29
Samuel Phillips, 1829–41
John Sherry Sr., 1841–44
Peletiah Fordham, 1844
Ezra L.H. Gardiner, 1844–47
Nathan Tiffany, 1847–49
Peletiah Fordham, 1849–53
Thomas E. Crowell, 1853–61
Philander R. Jennings, 1861–77

William M. Halsey, 1877–84
Hannibal French, 1884–89
Genevieve French, 1889–95
Fannie Bisgood Reimann, 1895–99
Genevieve French, 1899–1915
William T. Vaughn, 1915–23
George Farley, 1923–32
Alfred M. Butts, 1932–36
Charles F. Schreier, 1936–49

PART III CHAPTER 4

FIRES AND FIREMEN

Serious Fires in the Village

January 1863	William R. Williamson house on Elizabeth Street
October 1865	Dr. Mitchell's unoccupied building on West Water Street near the Gas Works
March 1867	Daniel McLane house at Legonee Brook
November 1868	J.W. Ripley's barn, corner of Main and Washington
August 1869	The Gas Works on West Water Street
January 1872	Barn and livery stables of John DeCastro on Division Street
November 1873	Dodson's Ice House on Church Street
1873	Six buildings on the west side of business district on lower Main Street: The two-story building occupied by Nickerson & Vail, a three-story building occupied by the Post Office and John Stakelam, a three-story building owned by Mr. Rogers, a two-story building occupied by H.M. Williamson's boot and shoe store, a three-story building occupied by H.M. Gillette, Mrs. E.C. Rogers, and Hedges & DeCastro, and a two-story building occupied by Charles Hedges Jr.'s paint shop
June 1874	Building and storehouse of M.H. Gregory on the east side of Wharf Street
February 1875	John King's new restaurant and George B. Brown's store occupied by Charles C. Bush's stationery shop
November 1875	Charles Archibald's barn adjoining Otter Pond

APPENDIX. SAG HARBOR NAMES

March 1877	William Fordred's house on Green Street
October 1877	Rebecca Glover's house on Main Street
March 1879	Robert G. Cooper's shoemaker shop on Madison Street
September 1879	George Jupiter's house occupied by Peter Johnson at Eastville
October 1879	The Montauk Steam Cotton Mills
October 1880	Thomas Sherman's house on Union Street
March 1881	Catherine Silvia's house on Sag Harbor Turnpike
July 1881	Nine buildings on the west side of Main Street: Elisha King's store, W.L. Cook's Stationery Store, James W. Edwards's Clothing Store, A.D. Ludlow's Bottling Establishment, Harris' Confectionery, Miss Miller's Fancy Goods, G.A. Babcock's Cigar Shop, Phebe Fordham's Confectionery, Miss Hennigar's Millinery Shop
August 1881	The East End Pottery Company
September 1882	The Oakland Works
April 1882	Charles N. Hildreth's Ice House on Suffolk Street
May 1886	The Hedges House, Mott's Saloon, and C.S. Hedges paint shop
January 1887	"Shanty Row," lower Main Street, and the fish market of J.M. Hildreth
January 1895	Merrill's building next to the Union School, I. Abraham's Shoe Shop, and Carl Schropp's Barber Shop
October 1895	Walter Cunningham's barn on upper Suffolk Street
March 1897	Samuel Miller's house on Montauk Avenue
September 1899	Horatio Roger's barn, Max Schwartz' barn, the mill of East Hampton Lumber & Coal Company and Charles H. Payne's carpenter shop
January 1904	Aaron Jaffee's tenement house
February 1904	Frederick K. Field's house occupied by George Champlin on Montauk Avenue
May 1904	The store and tenement on the east side of Main Street occupied by the Bullock family and R.E. Richards' plumbing shop
December 1904	Thomas Ward's house on upper Madison Street
May 1905	The corner of Main and Washington Streets, owned by Robert M. Hildreth and George Kiernan, Ballan & Company and Mrs. Rebecca Eisenberg's. Also, Henry Bramble's house on Glover Street
November 1905	Pardon T. Tabor's house on corner of Division and Rector Streets
February 1906	Vacant tenement of George Kiernan's on Bridge Street
January 1907	Hick Connor's house on Suffolk Street
May 1907	Jerry Butler's house at Eastville
January 1908	Charles Fordham's blacksmith shop, Max Grossman's pool room on west side of lower Main Street
May 1908	William McErlean's house on Glover Street
April 1909	Josiah Hasbrook's house on Liberty Street
March 1911	The Sag Harbor Electric Light & Power Company
March 1911	Alden Douglas' boarding house and livery stable on Meadow Street
June 1912	Mrs. Julia P. French's barn on Jefferson Street
April 1913	Kiernan's Power House of the Electric Light and Power Company
February 1916	Seven stores in downtown Sag Harbor

PART I CHAPTER 6

SAG HARBOR FIRE DEPARTMENT CHIEFS

Noah Washburn, 1840 and 1844–46
John Dayton, 1841–43
William P. Post, 1846–47
Benjamin Huntting, 1848–52 and 1877–79

Shamgar H. Slate, 1853
Abel C. Buckley, 1854–55
Lafayette Douglas, 1856
Edward B. Merrall, 1857–58

APPENDIX. SAG HARBOR NAMES

Charles B. Arnold, 1862-63
Clothier H. Vaughn, 1864 and 82
Thomas Lister, 1865-67
Stephen B. French, 1868
Reuben E. Edwards, 1870
Elijah Cullum, 1874 and 1884
Seymour L. Tooker, 1881 and 1892
A.D. Ludlow, 1885
Charles Zimmerman, 1886
James H. Brown, 1887
A.L. Pierson, 1887
William Bassenden, 1889
J. William Beebee, 1889 and 1910 (one month)
Edward Pender, 1890-91
Thomas Glenn, 1893
E.A. Carpenter, 1894

William Blaiklock, 1895-96
William G. Howard, 1897-1905
Augustus Kiernan, 1906-09
Joseph Finckenauer, 1910-14
Walter Thuerer, 1915-20
Roy Dippel, 1921-22
L.N. Vaughn 2nd, 1923-24
Raymond Heinrichs, 1925
William Kiselyak, 1926
William Chance, 1927
David King, 1928-29
Elmer Butcher, 1930-32
Stephen Battle, 1933-35
William Ross, 1935-36
Wellman Pulver, 1936-39
Robert Olejnik, 1939-40

PART IV   CHAPTER 6

VETERANS AND CASUALTIES OF THE GREAT WARS

The Civil War

Aldershaw, Thomas	Co. H, 16th Connecticut Regt
*Armstrong, Robert	Co. K, 127th Regt
Atkins, William A.	Co. H, 139th Regt
*Babcock, Gilbert	Co. H, 81st Regt
Babcock, Lodowick	
Babson, David	U.S. Navy
Babson, J.B.	Drafted
Babson, L.D.	Drafted
Bachelor, Joseph S.	
Baker, Charles M.	Drafted
Baker, David J.	U.S. Navy
Baker, Henry L.	U.S. Navy
Bassett, Albert G.	
Bates, Alfred	
Beckwith, Charles	
Beckwith, Thomas	Co. H, 81st Regt
Behrens, Augustus	17th New York Infantry
Bennett, Andrew J.	Co. K, 127th Regt
Bennett, James M.	U.S. Navy
Bennett, William W.	Co. H, 81st Regt
Berdan, Charles	Co. K, 13th New York Volunteers
Bill, Edwin	Co. K, 127th Regt (Lawrence Cadets)
Bill, Robert	11th Cavalry
Bishop, Charles H.	
Boan, John J.	U.S. Navy
Boan, Joseph S.	Co. K, 127th Regt
*Bogue, Andrew	Co. H, 81st Regt
Boyenton, John W.	Co. H, 81st Regt

*These men lost their lives in action or died as a result of their wounds. For details, see App. p. 367

APPENDIX. SAG HARBOR NAMES

Brennan, George	Co. H, 81st Regt
Brewer, Nathan	
Brewer, Thomas	U.S. Navy
Brown, David E.	Co. K, 127th Regt
Brown, Sidney Z.	Drafted
Brown, Silas E.	Co. K, 127th Regt
Bruen, George	Co. H, 81st Regt
Brunemann, Joseph	Drafted
*Burke, John Wallace	Co. H, 81st Regt
Bunnell, James E.	U.S. Navy
Burkhardt, Martin	32 New York Battery
Bushnell, Charles	U.S. Navy
Butler, Samuel C.	Co. G, 29th Regt
Carley, Thomas	Drafted
Carpenter, Benjamin C.	Drafted
Carroll, John	United States Navy
Carroll, Thomas	
Casey, John	Drafted
Cass, Albert	Co. K, 5th New Hampshire Regt
Chamberlain, Laurenton	Co. F, Marine Regt
Chichester, Thomas E.	Co. K, 47th New York Volunteers
*Chester, William H.	U.S. Navy
Coates, Charles	75th New York Regt
Coles, Jeremiah E.	U.S. Navy
Colvin, Samuel P.	Co. K, 127th Regt
*Conklin, Henry T.	Co. H, 81st Regt
Conklin, John A.	Co. K, 127th Regt
*Conkling, William	48th New York Regt
Conner, Hickford	U.S. Navy
Cook, Charles P.	Co. K, 127th Regt
Cook, Edward D.	Co. H, 81st Regt
Cooper, Edward M.	U.S. Navy
Cooper, James H.	Co. H, 81st Regt
Cooper, W.B.	Co. K, 13th New York Infantry
Corcoran, James	
*Corey, Joseph	Co. K, 127th Regt
Corwin, John L.	
*Crowell, Benjamin H.	Co. E, 11th Cavalry
Crowell, Stephen H.	Co. K, 127th Regt
Cuffee, James L.	U.S. Navy
Cuffee, Warren N.	
Cuffee, William H.	U.S. Navy
Cullum, Richard	
DeBevoise, Abraham	Co. K, 127th Regt
Decker, C.H.	Drafted
Derby, Austin	Drafted
Depp, Charles W.	Co. G, 29th Regt
Drake, Stephen	U.S. Navy
Dunham, Dwight F.	Co. K, 127th Regt
Dutcher, Samuel B.	Co. H, 81st Regt

APPENDIX. SAG HARBOR NAMES

Earle, George	3rd Regt, New York Volunteers
Earle, Joseph	
Early, Charles	U.S. Navy
Early, James	Drafted
Early, Thomas	Drafted
Edwards, Benjamin W.	Co. H, 81st Regt
Edwards, Charles N.	Co. K, 127th Regt
Edwards, Elbert	Co. H, 81st Regt
Edwards, Eli	U.S. Navy
*Edwards, Henry L.	2nd New York Cavalry
Edwards, Lewis	48th New York Regt
Edwards, Marcus	U.S. Navy
*Edwards, Orlando	Co. K, 127th Regt
Edwards, Roger	48th New York Regt. First to enlist from Sag Harbor and served throughout the war.
Edwards, Stephen H.	Drafted
Eldredge, George A.	
Ellsworth, Jesse	Co. H, 81st Regt
Ellsworth, Robert	Co. H, 81st Regt
Farley, James	Co. K, 127th Regt
Feeley, Michael	Drafted
Fields, James	U.S. Navy
Filer, Charles	1st Artillery
Finckenauer, Edward	Co. H, 33rd Connecticut Volunteers
Flim, Patrick	Co. H, 81st Regt
Folger, Thomas	Drafted
Fordham, Charles	Co. H, 81st Regt (musician)
Fordham, Elbert	3rd Massachusetts Cavalry
Fordham, Nathan C.	2nd Massachusetts Cavalry
*Fordred, Drayson	Co. H, 81st Regt
*Fordred, William	Co. H, 81st Regt
Fosbert, Albert	
Foster, William B.	U.S. Navy
Francis, R.A.	
French, Abel Smith	Drafted
French, Peter	Co. H, 81st Regt (Major)
Gaffga, Peter	165th Regt
Garaghan, Henry T.	48th New York Regt (Captain)
Garrettson, Rutland M.	Drafted
Gilbride, Andrew	U.S. Navy
Gilmore, Robert J.	Co. K, 127th Regt
Gleason, G. Howard	Drafted
Greene, Henry	Co. H, 16th Connecticut Volunteers
Gregory, John H.	Co. E, 11th Cavalry
Hall, William H.	Co. K, 127th Regt
Halsey, Dennis	Co. E, 11th Cavalry
Halsey, Erskine M.	Drafted
Halsey, Henry M.	Drafted
*Halsey, Jesse C.	Co. H, 81st Regt
Halsey, William M.	Co. K, 127th Regt
Hand, Samuel	Co. K, 127th Regt

APPENDIX. SAG HARBOR NAMES

Hand, Shamgar S.	U.S. Navy
Handy, Aaron	Co. K, 127th Regt
Harris, Charles C.	Co. K, 127th Regt
Harris, Edward	Drafted
Harris, James C.	
*Harris, William P.	Co. K, 127th Regt
Haurand, Bernard J.	12th New York Cavalry
Havens, Austin	Co. K, 127th Regt
Havens, Charles	Co. K, 127th Regt
Havens, Henry H.	U.S. Navy
Havens, Joseph A.	U.S. Navy
Havens, Ripley	Co. K, 127th Regt
Hayes, William	U.S. Navy
Hedges, George B.	Union Guards
*Hedges, Jeremiah L.	U.S. Navy
*Hedges, Lyman	Co. K, 127th Regt
Hedges, Robert	Drafted
Hennigar, Charles	Co. H, 139th Regt
Hildreth, Isaac N.	Co. K, 127th Regt
Hill, Edward G.	Union Guards
Holton, William	U.S. Navy
Homan, Gilbert	
Hope, Benjamin K.	Drafted
*Howell, Henry B.	U.S. Navy
Howell, James R.	Co. K, 127th Regt
Howell, John H.	2nd Cavalry
*Howell, William G.	5th Regt
Howland, Edson (Addison)	Co. H, 81st Regt
Hull, Albert P.	
Humphries, Arthur	Co. K, 127th Regt
Hunt, Edgar Z.	2nd Illinois Cavalry
*Huntting, Henry H.	4th Illinois Cavalry
Jackson, D.E.	Drafted
Jagger, William S.	Co. K, 127th Regt
Jerino, Emanuel	U.S. Navy
Jessup, Charles	48th Regt
*Jessup, Edward A.	48th Regt
Jessup, Samuel	Co. K, 127th Regt
Johnson, Rufus	Co. H, 81st Regt
Johnson, Thomas	90th Pennsylvania Regt
Jupiter, George W.	Drafted
Kelly, Edward	U.S. Navy
Kelsey, William	15th New Jersey Regt
Ketcham, Henry	81st Regt
King, George C.	
King, Harvey B.	Co. K, 127th Regt
King, Parker P.	Co. K, 127th Regt
*Knapp, George	Co. H, 81st Regt
Langford, Thornton	
Lawrence, William H. Jr.	Co. K, 127th Regt

Lee, George E.	Co. H, 16th Connecticut Volunteers
Leek, John D.	Co. D, 10th Regt
Leek, Philip A.	Drafted
Leek, Samuel L.	Drafted
*Loper, Charles L.	
*Loper, Henry J.	Co. H, 81st Regt
Loper, George	U.S. Navy
Loper, J.A.	Drafted
Loper, Thomas	Co. H, 81st Regt
Lovejoy, John F.	Co. H, 81st Regt
Lowen, William	U.S. Navy
Ludlow, Charles	U.S. Navy
Ludlow, Silas	
Marshall, Jefferson A.	13th New Jersey Regt
McCabe, James	Drafted
McDonald, William J.	Co. E, 28th Regt
McFarland, George	Drafted
McFarland, James	2nd New York Regt
*McMahon, John	Co. K, 127th Regt
McQuaid, Robert	
*Meigs, Edgar C.	Co. K, 127th Regt
Merchant, Charles	Co. H, 81st Regt
Meyer, John W.	11th New York Cavalry
Middleton, Charles	
Miller, A.H.	Co. K, 127th Regt
Miller, D. A.	Union Guards
Miller, Eleazer	Marine Artillery
Miller, George	48th Regt
*Montcalm, John A.	Co. K, 127th Regt
Mooney, Francis J.	Co. K, 127th Regt
Mooney, John F.	Co. K, 127th Regt
Morgan, Henry	Co. K, 127th Regt
Morran, Thomas	Co. K, 127th Regt
Morris, George C.	Co. H, 16th Regt, Connecticut
*Mulford, William R.	23rd Illinois Volunteers
Murphy, Michael J.	Drafted
Neal, James P.	Union Guards
Nicoll, Edward T.	Co. K, 127th Regt
Nicoll, Sylvester	U.S. Navy
Oldershaw, Absalom E.	Co. B, 1st Marine Artillery
Oldershaw, John	U.S. Navy
Overton, Warren G.	Co. H, 127th Regt
Parker, Giles	Co. E, 11th Cavalry
Parker, Henry	
Parks, Charles A.	Captain, 90th Regt
Payne, Benjamin S.	Co. H, 81st Regt
Payne, Charles D.	U.S. Navy
Payne, Charles E.	Co. H, 81st Regt
Payne, Charles Watson	Drafted
Payne, Clarence D.	

APPENDIX. SAG HARBOR NAMES 365

Payne, E.H.	Co. H, 81st Regt
Payne, E.D.	Co. D, 11th Connecticut Infantry
Payne, Huntting M.	Co. E, 11th Cavalry
Payne, Lafayette H.	
Payne, Robert	U.S. Navy
Pedro, Joseph H.	48th Regt
Perkins, George	Co. K, 127th Regt
Pidgeon, George	U.S. Navy
Pidgeon, H.	U.S. Navy
Pidgeon, Stephen B.	Co. K, 127th Regt
*Pidgeon, Alanson	14th Regt, New York State Militia
*Pierson, Charles A.	Drafted
Pierson, Enoch	Co. K, 127th Regt
*Pierson, Nathan H.	Co. H, 81st Regt
Pollard, George H.	Co. h, 81st Regt
Polley, Samuel M.	4th New Jersey Battery, Artillery
Polley, William L.	Co. F, 6th Cavalry
Porter, Henry B.	Light Artillery
Potter, Jonathan	Co. E, 41st New York Infantry
Preston, James K.	Co. 1, 26th Connecticut Regt
Price, James H. Jr.	Co. H, 81st Regt
Prime, Charles	
Prince, Joseph	U.S. Navy
*Reade, Dr. John R.	Co. E, 11th Regt
Reason, Thomas	Co. H, 81st Regt
*Redfield, Charles A.	Co. H, 81st Regt
Redfield, Henry J.	Co. K, 127th Regt
Rieger, Frederick	Drafted
*Reney, John W. Jr.	Co. H, 81st Regt
Reney, William T.	U.S. Navy
Renkens, Adelaide	Nurse; Co. G, 127th Regt
Rhody, Hugh	Co. H, 81st Regt
Richards, Reuben E.	
Ricker, Frederick	176th Regt
Ripley, William P.	Drafted
Roberts, Edward P.	Co. H, 81st Regt
Robinson, Nathan T.	10th Rhode Island Volunteers
Roe, Thomas	Co. K, 127th Regt
Rogers, David J.	
Rogers, James H.	
Ross, Edward	Drafted
Ryder, William H.	Co. B, 133rd Regt, Groton Artillery
Ryland, William	Co. H, 81st Regt
Schaefer, Christy	Co. K, 127th Regt
Schellinger, George R.	Musician, Co. H, 81st Regt
Sears, George H.	Co. K, 127th Regt
Shearwood, Joseph	U.S. Navy
*Shearwood, William H.	U.S. Navy
Sherman, George B.	Co. H, 81st Regt
Sherman, George R.	7th Connecticut Regt (colored troops)

APPENDIX. SAG HARBOR NAMES

Sherry, David S.	
Silviera, William W.	U.S. Navy
*Simons, John	8th Connecticut Regt
Smith, George W.	U.S. Navy
Smith, John C.	Co. H, 81st Regt
Smith, Julius C.	Co. E, 2nd New York Mounted
Snooks, John O.	Co. H, 81st Regt
Snooks, William H.	U.S. Navy
Snow, Elisha	Co. H, 81st Regt
Spencer, Daniel W.	Co. C, 81st Regt
Spencer, John H.	Union Guards
Squires, Charles	
*Squires, Stephen	Co. K, 127th Regt
*Stanbrough, Isaac	U.S. Navy
*Stanbrough, James	Co. E, 11th Cavalry
Stanbrough, Stephen H.	Drafted
Stanton, Joseph B.	Co. H, 81st Regt
Stanton, Oscar F.	Rear Admiral, U.S. Navy
*Stanton, William C.	U.S. Navy
*Strong, Charles H.	U.S. Navy
Strong, Thomas H.	U.S. Navy
Sullivan, John	New Hampshire Volunteers
Sweezey, Richard M.	Co. H, 81st Regt
Sylve, Jospeh	U.S. Navy
Sythes, William	13th New Hampshire Regt
Tabor, James M.	Captain, U.S. Navy
Taft, Horatio	
*Talmadge, Willaim H.	Co. K, 127th Regt
Tasker, Adolphus	48th New York Volunteers
Taylor, Edward C.	Co. H, 81st Regt
Thatford, Henry	Co. K, 6th Connecticut Regt
Thomas, William	12th New York Regt
Tindall, George William	Drafted
Tinker, Charles W.	Co. H, 81st Regt
Tunison, Abraham	Drafted
Vail, Thomas E.	Co. H, 81st Regt
Van Houghton, James A.	8th Pennsylvania Regt
Van Nostrand, S.	Captain, 27th New Jersey Regt
Vaughn, C.H.	Union Guards
Wade, Charles B.	Co. H, 81st Regt
Wade, Jared	Co. H, 81st Regt
Walker, John	Co. H, 81st Regt
Ward, Abraham B.	Drafted
Warner, Alfred	Co. H, 81st Regt
Washburn, Henry Wheaton	U.S. Navy
Webb, Job	Co. K, 127th Regt
Wheeler, E.F.	Co. H, 81st Regt
White, William	Union Guards
Whitney, Charles L.	New York Cavalry
Whitney, Horace H.	17th Connecticut Volunteers

APPENDIX. SAG HARBOR NAMES 367

These men gave their lives during the Civil War (killed in action, dying from wounds, or illnesses contracted in the service):

Armstrong, Robert	Killed in battle at Upton Hill, Virginia, January 9, 1863
Babcock, Gilbert R.	Wounded at the Battle of Fair Oaks, Virginia, May 31, 1862; died in Bellview Hospital, August 5, 1862; age 18
Bogue, Andrew	Died of wounds received March 3, 1867; age 21
Burke, John Wallace	Killed in battle at Gaines Ferry near Cold Harbor, Virginia, June 2, 1864; age 31. "While at the head of his company, gallantly cheering on his men, he was struck by a musket ball in the forehead and fell to the ground dead."
Chester, William H.	Killed on the U.S. Gunboat *Picket* off Washington, N.C., September 6, 1862; age 22
Conklin, Henry T.	Died at Beaufort, North Carolina, October 3, 1864; age 20
Conklin, William	Killed in battle at Frankfort
Corey, Joseph	Died at Morris Island, November 30, 1864; age 27
Crowell, Benjamin E.	Died of wounds received in battle, May 29, 1867; age 32
Edwards, Henry L.	Killed in battle in the Shenandoah Valley, November 22, 1864; age 25
Edwards, Orlando	Died in service December 27, 1863; age 19
Fordred, Drayson	Killed in battle at Gaines Farm, Cold Harbor, Virginia, June 3, 1864; age 26
Fordred, William Jr.	Died of wounds, February 18, 1869; age 25
Halsey, Jesse C.	Died of wounds at Marine Hospital, October 9, 1871; age 26
Harris, William P.	Died of disease at Hilton Head Hospital, August 31, 1864; age 18
Hedges, Jeremiah L.	Killed on the U.S. Gunboat *Picket*, off Washington, N.C., September 6, 1861; age 23
Hedges, Lyman	Killed in battle at Gaines Farm, Cold Harbor, Virginia, November 29, 1864
Homan, Gilbert	Died in service
Howell, Henry B.	Killed on the U.S. Gunboat *Picket*, off Washington, N.C., September 6, 1862; age 22
Howell, William G.	Died in service at Sallsbury Prison
Huntting, Henry H.	Killed in battle near Franklin, Mississippi, February 3, 1865; age 24
Jessup, Edward	Died in service
Knapp, George M.	Killed in battle at Gaines Farm, Cold Harbor, Virginia, October 25, 1864
Loper, Charles L.	Died of wounds at Brooklyn Hospital, February 7, 1863; age 25
Loper, Henry J.	Killed in battle at Gaines Farm, Cold Harbor, Virginia, June 3, 1864; age 31
McMahon, John	Killed in battle at Honey Hill, November 29, 1864
Meigs, Edgar C.	Died of wounds, August 28, 1862
Montcalm, John A.	Died of wounds, January 5, 1866; age 20
Mulford, William R.	Died in Rebel Stockade Prison, Andersonville, Georgia, July 7, 1864; age 32
Pierson, Alanson	Killed in battle at Antietam, Maryland; age 21. "True to his country and his own soul. Served 15 engagements before receiving a wound in his head."
Pierson, Charles A.	Died in service October 17, 1862
Pierson, Nathan H.	Died in Base Hospital of dysentery, August 2, 1864; age 21
Reade, Dr. John R.	Killed in battle at Antietam, Maryland, September 17, 1862

Redfield, Charles A.	Killed in battle at Gaines Farm, Cold Harbor, Virginia, June 3, 1864; age 21
Reney, John W., Jr.	Died of wounds, September 7, 1876
Shearwwod, William H.	Killed on U.S. Gunboat *Picket* in the Burnside Expedition, December 17, 1862; age 17
Simons, John	Killed in battle at Antietam, Maryland
Squires, Stephen	Died at Morris Island of typhoid fever, July 14, 1864; age 27
Stanbrough, Isaac	Killed on the Sloop of War, *Oneida*, June 26, 1862; age 44
Stanbrough, James	Died of wounds at Washington, D.C. Hospital, October 2, 1864; age 49
Stanton, William C.	Died of wounds at Naval Hospital, Key West, Florida, September 2, 1863; age 27
Strong, Charles H.	Died of wounds, April 1876; age 48
Talmadge, William H.	Died of wounds, November 17, 1872; age 32
Williamson, Edwin Jr.	Died in hospital at Alexandria, Virginia, November 29, 1864; age 21
Willis, Charles	Died in service
Worthington, Edwin F.	Killed on Schooner *City Recruit*, March 1862; age 23

PART VI CHAPTER 5
World War I

Alioto, Vincent F.	Fireman 3rd Class, U.S. Naval Patrol Submarine Service
Archibald, Francis Jerome	Carpenter's Mate 1st Class, U.S.N.R.F.
Avery, Charles E.	Chief Gunner's Mate, U.S. Navy
*Baer, Paul H.	Private, 25th Company, Field Artillery
Barclay, George C.	
Barry, Jane W.	Nurse, U.S. Army Hospital Nursing Corps
Bassenden, William A.	Machinist's Mate 1st Class, U.S. Navy Aero Corps
Bassett, Charles Douglas	Private 1st Class, 337th Aero-squadron
Bates, Alfred C. Jr.	Quartermaster, U.S. Army Transport Service
Bates, William Charles	Private, Ordnance Railway Engineer, 2nd Co., 5th Regt
Bath, William Y.	U.S. Army
*Battle, George F.	Private, Co. D, 308th Infantry
*Beckman, Henry F.	Machinist's Mate 2nd Class, U.S. Navy
Bennett, Edward E.	
Berkowitz, John	U.S. Army
Beyer, Frederick George	Surfman, U.S. Coast Guard, Station #68
*Beynon, Charles N.	
Biechele, Harold	
Biechele, Joseph Theodore	Gun Captain, U.S. Navy. *U.S.S. George Washington*
Bill, Floyd	Surfman, U.S. Coast Guard
Bill, Frank W.	306th Infantry, 77th Div., Company A
Birs, Charles	
Blaschaek, Stephen J.	
Bookstaver, George A.	Private 1st Class, Ambulance Corps, 27th Div.
Booth, Norman T.	
Boreham, Clyde W.	U.S.N.R.F.

*These men and women gave their lives. For details, see App. p. 375.

APPENDIX. SAG HARBOR NAMES 369

*Bourguard, Adolph	Pvt. 1st Class, Co. B, 312th Infantry
Bowe, William	
Boyd, William Cooper	Musician 2nd Class, Headquarters Troop, 2nd Regt, Medical Troop Unit, Marines
Braem, Arnold V.	U.S.N.R.F.
Braem, Ernest Henry	Private, 306th Infantry, 77th Div.
Brewer, Charles F.	Private, 306th Infantry, 77th Div.
Brewer, Joseph H.	Private, 75th Co., 6th Regt, U.S. Marines
Brewer, William T.	U.S. Army
Brown, Herbert H.	
Brown, Herman M.	2nd Lieutenant, 62nd Balloon Co., Aero-service
Brown, Lewis N.	Sergeant, Medical Corps, #87 Par., 38 Headquarters
Brownell, Frank B.	Seaman 2nd Class, U.S.N.R.F.
Browngardt, Carl	Private, 507th Infantry, Co. L
Browngardt, Frederick	Private, U.S. Army
Burns, Edward F.	U.S. Army
Burns, James Raymond	Yeoman 1st Class, U.S. Navy. *U.S.S. Lake Champlain*
Burns, Lawrence J.	Seaman 1st Class, U.S. Navy. *U.S.S. Yarnall*
Cady, Lawrence S.	U.S. Navy Mine Laying Force, *U.S.S. Roanoke*
Carberry, Edward H.	U.S. Army
Carman, Garrett B.	Private 1st Class, Telegraph Batt., Signal Service
Carroll, Joseph A.	Private, Ordnance Depart.
Carroll, Kenneth	
Carroll, Thomas B.	Private 155th Depot Brigade, Ordnance Depart.
*Carroll, William J.	Medical Corps, Hospital Service, Marines
Carter, William Arthur	Boatswain's Mate 2nd Class, U.S. Navy, *U.S.S. St. Louis* and *U.S.S. Arizona*
Chandler, Fred Voltaire	Private, U.S. Marines, Co. 332, 9th Batt.
*Chelberg, James Frederick	Corporal, Co. A, 306th Infantry, 77th Div.
Christman, Carl J.	Ensign, U.S.N.R.F.
Christman, Leslie H.	U.S. Navy, 325th F & G Co.
Cilli, Vitali	U.S. Army
Collins, Edmund J.	Private, U.S. Army
Collins, Frank	Co. K, 12 Regt, N.Y.S. Guard
Collins, James M.	U.S. Army
Collins, John	
Connelly, John P.	U.S. Army
Converse, George Raymond	Private, 7th Regt, Field Artillery Battery E
Cook, Chester	
Cook, Francis H.	Seaman Apprentice, Yale Naval Unit
Cook, Henry	Captain, 5th Field Artillery, 1st Div.
Cook, John F.	1st Lieutenant, Machine Gun Batt. Co. A, 27th Div.
Cooper, Edward M.	Private 1st Class, 30th Co., Field Artillery
Corwin, Lewis O.	Private 1st Class, Co. 8, Batt. F, 54th Regt
Crowitz, David	
Crozier, Robert W.	
*Cunningham, Bertrand	Medical Corps
Cunningham, Harold A.	Lieutenant, U.S.N.R.F., Captain of the *U.S.S. George Washington* and the *U.S.S. Leviathan*
DeCastro, Augustus	
DeCastro, Rudolph Howell	Corporal, Medical Corps, Base Hospital, King's County

APPENDIX. SAG HARBOR NAMES

Deneen, John Watts	Seaman 2nd Class, U.S. Navy. *U.S.S. Dakota*, *U.S.S. North Carolina* and *U.S.S. Granite State*
Densing, George Henry	Printer 1st Class, U.S. Navy Submarine Base
DiCiccio, Rizziero	Private 1st Class, Co. E, 302 Regt, 76th Div.
DiGiovanno, Lewis	
DiPasquille, Anthony	
Dipple, Roy P.	Machinist's Mate, U.S. Navy, *U.S.S. Teresa*, *U.S.S. West Bridge*
Distefano, Carmelo	Private, 39 Company, 157th Depot Brigade
Dolphin, John	Private 1st Class, C.A. Supply Co., 58th Regt, 1st Army Artillery Corps
Donovan, William J.	
Dordelman, Raymond P.	Seaman 1st Class, U.S.N.R.F. *U.S.S. Lebanon*
Dorsey, Grace	
Dumont, Joseph F.	2nd Lieutenant, Co. K, 132 Infantry
Dumont, Veronica	
Dunn, Edward P.	Private 1st Class, Headquarters Co., 107th Infantry, 27th Div.
Dutcher, Harry Howard	Private 1st Class, Headquarters Co., 107th Infantry, 27th Div.
Dyer, John	
Edwards, Cornelius	
Edwards, Harold Gleason	1st Lieutenant, Ordnance Depart.
Edwards, Olin M., Jr.	Private, Medical Corps, Base Hospital #37
Edwards, Otis A., Jr.	Sergeant, Tank Corps, 107th Batt., Co. C
Edwards, Russell	
Eisenberg, Frank	408th Tele. Batt., C.E.
Eisenberg, Meyer E.	48th Aero-squadron
Elecker, Paul E.	2nd Lieutenant, U.S. Infantry Cadet Corps
Enginieri, Joseph P.	Musician 1st Class, Headquarters, 58th Regt, 20th Div. Artillery Band
Fanton, Lloyd Reid	2nd Lieutenant, Field Artillery, 57th Battery, U.S. Army
Farley, George H.	Field Clerk, U.S. Army
Feeney, John Lewis	Major, 316th Field Artillery, 81st Div.
Fenelon, Eugene J.	U.S. Army
Fenelon, Lloyd	Radio Operator, U.S.N.R.F.
Folley, Patrick	
Forcucci, Henry M.	Private, Medical Corps, Co. I, Base Hospital
Fordham, Henry Monroe	Private 1st Class, Co. K, 307th Infantry, 77th Div.
Fordham, Marie S.	Nurse, U.S. Hospital
Fournier, Francis	
Fournier, William L.	U.S. Army
Fox, George W.	Machine Gun Brigade, 103 Battalion, 26th Div.
Fox, William John	Carpenter's Mate, U.S. Naval Aviation, *U.S.S. Rochester*
French, Wade	Seaman 1st Class, U.S. Navy Convoy Service, *U.S.S. Cythera* and *U.S.S. Canton*
Garypie, Albert W.	Sergeant, 301st Infantry, Co. E, 4th Div.
Garypie, George A.	Private 1st Class, Co. A, 2nd Batt., Chemical Warfare
Garypie, Peter J.	Private, Signal Corps, Aero Construction, 15th Co., 81st Div..
Gerlach, William Robert	Machinist's Mate 1st Class, U.S. Navy Submarine Service, *U.S.S. Sub L-8*, *U.S.S. Fulton*
Gilbride, James A., Jr.	U.S. Army, Co. C, 114th Infantry
Gilbride, Joseph A.	Private, 114th Infantry, Co. C.
Gilligan, Martin T.	U.S. Army

APPENDIX. SAG HARBOR NAMES

Gleason, George A.	Chief Radio Operator, U.S. Navy Destroyer
Glenn, Edward	Corporal, U.S. Army
Glenn, Thomas	
Goldstein, Abraham	U.S. Army
Goldstein, Jacob	
Graves, George B.	U.S. Navy
Griffin, Joseph	Co. K, 28th Infantry
Grimshaw, Chauncey	
Grossman, David	
Grossman, Jesse	
Guerin, Claude Mortimer	Machinist's Mate 2nd Class, U.S. Navy
Haddaway, Henry	
Haines, George	
Hale, Edwin B.	Private, 308th Infantry, Co. A
Hall, Joseph	
Hall, Kenneth S.	Seaman 1st Class, U.S.N.R.F.
Hallock, Charles Fremont	Private, 311th Infantry, Co. B, 78th Div.
Hansen, Edward J.	
Harden, Joseph	
Harris, Francis E.	Corporal, 102nd Regt, 26th Division
Harris, Gurden S.	Corporal, U.S. Army
Hart, Cyrus T., Sr.	Corporal Battery E, 30th Artillery
Havens, Ernest	Private, 152nd Depot Brigade, Co. 4
Havens, Norman	U.S. Army
Hayes, Harry S.	U.S. Navy
Haynes, George	U.S. Army
Hedges, John Gardner	Sergeant 1st Class, 302nd Infantry, Machine Gun Company
Hellerman, John W.	Corporal, 312th Infantry, Co. M, 78th Div.
Heller, Israel C.	Sergeant, 306th Infantry, Co. C, 77th Div., U.S.N.R.F.
Hesse, Grace	Yeoman, U.S. Navy Torpedo Testing Station
Heinrichs, Cortland A.	Corporal, Co. M . Engineeers, 59th Regt
Heinrichs, Harry Hugo	Chief Machinist's Mate, U.S.N.R.F., *U.S.S. Sampson*
Heinrichs, Raymond E.	Machinist's Mate 2nd Class, U.S. Navy, *U.S.S. President Grant*
Heinrichs, Stanley Edward	Corporal, 305th Infantry, Co. A, 77th Div.
Higgins, Francis J.	U.S. Army
Higgins, George E.	U.S. Engineers
Hildreth, Elmer	U.S. Army
Hildreth, Herbert Moore	Private, Medical Corps, U.S. Base Hospital #37
Hildreth, Nathaniel	U.S.N.R.F.
Hines, Frederick H.	Medical Corps
Hodenpyl, Eugene	2nd Lieutenant, Military Police, Field Artillery
Holden, James C.	U.S. Navy
Hughes, Peter F.	Machinist's Mate, U.S. Naval Aviation
Hughes, Michael J.	Medical Corps, U.S. Army
Hurd, John	
Jacobs, Stanley	
Jaffe, Lionel	Corporal, Aviation 34th Balloon Company
Jaffe, Mortimer	King's County Hospital Unit
Jaffe, Theodore	Private 1st Class, Medical Corps, Base Hospital #37, Ambulance Corps

APPENDIX. SAG HARBOR NAMES

Janesko, William	Private, 705th American Exp. Force
*Jobe, William E., Jr.	Medical Department #37, also Tank Corps
Jose, Frank H.	Wagoner, 6th Engineer Company C, 3rd Div.
Judlewitz, Samuel	
Keating, William	127th Div.
Keenan, William A.	Aviation Corps
Kilgore, Fred D.	Major, 5th Brigade, U.S. Marines
Killoran, Maurice Richard	Mechanic, Base Hospital #37, 27th Div.
King, Edward	
King, Francis E.	Submarine Service, Ship Fitter, U.S. Navy
King, George	
Kiselyak, Charles	U.S. Army
Kiselyak, William	U.S. Army
Klein, Louis	U.S.N.R.F.
Klinger, Albert	Lieutenant, U.S. Navy, Bureau Ordnance, *U.S.S. North Dakota* and *U.S.S. George Washington*
Kondratowitz, John	
Krommuller, Leslie	U.S. Navy
Krupinski, Alexander	
Kuhlwein, Leonard J.	Chief Machinist Mate, U.S. Navy Convoy Duty, *U.S.S. Walker* and *U.S.S. Jason*
Kylczyski, Izador	U.S. Army
Kunigonis, Joseph	U.S. Army
Kunigonis, Martin	U.S. Army
LaGuire, Darahl	U.S. Army
LaGuire, Raymond Foster	Corporal, 613 Motor Transport Co.
Landrock, Paul	U.S. Army
Laskie, Felix	U.S. Army
Lemay, Louis	U.S. Army
Lemay, Raymond	U.S. Army
Levy, George	
Lewis, Harold F.	Sergeant, 52nd Pioneer Infantry, Co. K
Liberti, Samuel	
Liehr, Joseph H.	Wagoner, 106th Regt. Field Artillery, 27th Div., Battery N
Lipomi, Salvatore	Private, 7th Batt., Co. X, Guards
Logan, John A.	205th Infantry, Co. B
Maier, Christian	
Maikszyk, Jozef	U.S. Army
Mason, Harold F.	Sergeant, 122nd Infantry, Co. E., 31st Div.
McCarron, Joseph S.	U.S. Army
McCarthy, Joseph	
McClain, George	
McClain, John A.	Private 1st Class, Medical Corps, Ambulance Service
McClain, William A.	U.S. Army
McCort, James H.	Captain, Medical Corps, Ordnance Dept.
McDonough, Edward	
McCort, Kenneth Paul	Private, 343rd Regt., Field Artillery, Battery B, 90th Div.
McErlean, Lawrence	U.S. Navy
McErlean, Raymond	
McFarland, George Dalton	Corporal, 58th Artillery, Battery C.
McGovern, Edward	U.S. Army

APPENDIX. SAG HARBOR NAMES

McIntosh, Albert
McIntosh, Raymond John — Private, 151st Regt., 42nd Rainbow Div., Field Artillery, "French 75"
McMahon, Raymond — Mechanic, Field Artillery, 7th Regt, Battery E
McNamara, Burton M. — U.S. Army
Metzger, Otto Charles — Private 1st Class, 25th Regt, 2nd Div., Field Artillery, Battery C
Meyer, Theodore R. — M.D. Surgical Assistant, 60th Artillery
Meyerson, Herman — 1st Sergeant, Coast Artillery Corps, 2nd Co.
Meyerson, Oscar A. — Sergeant, 307th Infantry, 77th Div., Co. D
Miller, John B.
Moench, Francis Jacob — 2nd Lieutenant, Infantry Training School, Co. C
Moench, William E. — Y.M.C.A. War Camps
Montgomery, John Allan — Sergeant, 306th Machine Batt., 77th Div.
Morken, Henry F. — U.S. Army
Morouney, Harold — Aviation Corps
Morouney, Michael — 28th Co., 157th Depot Brigade
Morouney, Joseph
Morris, Harold B. — 2nd Lieutenant, 105th Infantry, Co. H.
Morris, John C. — Sergeant, Student Training Corps, Infantry
Moylan, Michael Joseph
Moylan, William Harry — Batt. Sergeant Major, 78th Div. Headquarters
Mulvihill, Daniel F.
Napier, Charles Dwight — M.D. Major, Medical Reserve Corps
Narvotch, S. — U.S. Army
Neilson, Andrew — U.S. Navy
Nolan, Joseph F. — Private, 305th Infantry, 77 Div., Co. M
O'Brien, Joseph P. — Machinist Mate, 1st Class, Naval Air Service
*O'Brien, Michael William — Seaman, U.S. Navy
O'Brien, Thomas Jr.
Olejnik, Francis Hunt — Seaman 1st Class, U.S. Navy
Page, George J. — U.S. Army
Perdue, Harold Bedford — Private 1st Class, 367th Infantry, 92nd Div., Co. E
Perrottet, Joseph C. — Private, Co. G, Development Batt.
Petzoldt, Frederick C. — U.S. Navy
Phillips, Clinton Aldrich — Yeoman 2nd Class, Torpedo Testing, U.S.N.R.F.
Phillips, Francis Barteau — Private 1st Class, Medical Corps, 102nd Ambulance Co., 25th Div.

Pidgeon, Raymond
Pierson, Harold G. — U.S. Army
Pintavalle, Joseph — Cook, U.S. Navy, Submarine Chaser
Porter, Joseph H.
Price, Helen M. — Y.M.C.A.
Pulver, Wellman Hildreth — Yeoman 2nd Class, U.S. Marines, Ship fitter
Pulver, Wilfred Schaefer — Machinist's Mate 2nd Class, U.S. Navy
Quackenbush, James — U.S. Navy
Rackowski, Anthony — U.S. Army
Regan, Michael
Reney, Howell L. — U.S. Navy
Reutershan, Herbert W. — Private, S.A.T.C. Infantry Union College
Reventlow, Malcolm — Seaman 1st Class, U.S. Navy, *U.S.S. George Washington*

APPENDIX. SAG HARBOR NAMES

Ritz, Albert E.	Gunner's Mate, U.S. Navy
Roberts, William	
Rodd, LeRoy	Lieutenant, Navy Bliss Torpedo Station
Rothenberg, Samuel	Private 1st Class, 304th Regt., 77th Div., Field Artillery, Battery E
Ryder, Charles	U.S. Navy
Ryder, Ellsworth L.	5th Cavalry, U.S. Army
Salvador, Frank	Private, Casual Headquarters, Quartermaster, Depot A.P.O. 713
Salvadore, Mastocchia	Private, Medical Corps Field Hospital #34, 7th Div.
Salvadore, Riggio	Private, Medical Depart.
Sawicky, Stanley	Private, U.S. Army
Saybrook, Otto	U.S. Navy
Schaeffer, Frank W.	U.S. Army
Schaeffer, Frederick	U.S. Army
Schlenz, Otto E.	
Schoville, Kenneth M.	Chief Petty Officer, U.S. Navy
Schremick, Louis	U.S. Army
Schreier, Charles	U.S. Navy, *U.S.S. Newport*
Sczubelky, Antone	
Seaman, John Francis	Wagoner, 305th Infantry, 77th Div.
Seaman, Walter	U.S. Navy
Sears, George A.	1st Lieutenant, 2nd Co. 1st Batt., 151st Depot Brigade
Sears, George W.	Boatswain's Mate 1st Class, U.S. Coast Guard Service
Sears, Percy	2nd Lieutenant, U.S. Army
Seely, Albert	Seaman 2nd Class, U.S. Navy
Seely, Frank Edward	Sergeant, 9th Mounted Engineers Headquarters Co.
Sexton, Edward	
Sexton, Thomas J.	U.S. Army
Shaeffer, George A.	Ambulance Service, U.S. Navy, Section 606
Sherman, Kenneth	
Sieber, Arthur	Private, 308th Infantry, 77th Div., Co. G
Silve, Vaughn H.	U.S. Army
Silvey, Joseph H.	
Simms, Chester Hamilton	Wagoner, Coast Artillery, Battery B, 54th Regt.
Slate, Elizabeth H.	Nurse, U.S. Army, Unit 114
Smith, Edward W.	U.S. Army
Smith, Hosea R.	U.S. Navy
Smith, John Pennington	1st Sergeant, 18th Div., 47th Regt, Infantry
Smith, Raleigh W.	U.S. Army
Somers, William Bernard	Machinist Mate 2nd Class, U.S. Navy
Spath, William H.H.	Sergeant, 104th Signal Corps, 29th Div., Co. A
Spodick, Frank	Sergeant, Co. F, 307th Engineers, 82nd Div.
Spodick, Harry	Sergeant, 20th Co., 152nd Depot Brigade.
Spodick, Louis	U.S. Army
Sterling, James Sayre	Quartermaster 2nd Class, U.S. Navy, *U.S.S. Rhode Island, Minnesota, Lake Superior, Louisiana, Dreshterland* and *Baltimore*
Stubbs, Otto	U.S. Army
Sweezy, William B.	Chief Machinist Mate, U.S. Navy
Tabarski, Wladyslaw	Private 1st Class, 308th Infantry, 77th Div., Co. M

APPENDIX. SAG HARBOR NAMES

Thiele, Charles	
Thomasson, LeRoy	U.S. Army
Thompson, Effie D.	Nurse, American Red Cross, U.S. Naval Hospital
Thompson, Harold E.	Private, 392nd Field Signal Batt., Co. C
Trimpin, Chester G.	Corporal, Pennsylvannia National Guard
Trimpin, Joseph	
Traum, William	
Travers, James E.	320 Field Artillery, 82nd Div.
Trommer, Louis	
VanNostrand, Roscoe L.	U.S.N.R.F.
VanNostrand, William H.	U.S. Army
Vermilye, Herbert	Medical Corps
Viscusso, Mariano	
Wagner, Edmund J.	Private, 312th Infantry, 78th Div., Co. M
Wagner, Ferdinand J.	Sergeant, 305th Infantry, 77th Div., Co. B
Wagner, Henry J.	Corporal, 460th Motor Transport Co.
Ward, Charles	U.S. Army
Wells, Charles Eric	Sergeant, Medical Corps Base Hospital #37
Wessell, Albert	Sergeant, Co. K, 9th Infantry
Wessell, Henry	U.S. Navy
White, Thomas W.	U.S. Army
*Wild, Frederick H.	
Wild, J.A.	
Williams, Burton	U.S. Marines
Williams, Edward	Private, 113th Infantry, 104th Signal Corps
Windsor, Clifford	
Woodward, Harry T.	Private, Student Army Training Corps
Woodward, John M.	Private, Student Army Training Corps
Yudelowitz, Julius	U.S. Army

Those who made the supreme sacrifice:

Baer, Paul Howard	Private, 25th Co. Field Artillery; enlisted March 3, 1918; died at Camp Slocum March 19, 1918
Battle, George Francis	Private, Co. D, 308th Infantry; enlisted September 15, 1917; killed in battle October 12, 1918; buried in France
Beckman, Henry Frank	Machinist's Mate 2nd Class, U.S. Navy; enlisted August 22, 1918; died September 28, 1918
Beynon, Charles N.	U.S. Army; died in France, August 1918
Bourguard, Adolph	Private 1st Class, Co. B, 312th Infantry; enlisted 1917, died in hospital in United States, November 6, 1921
Carroll, William J.	Medical Corps Hospital Service; enlisted in 1917; died in France in 1918
Chelberg, James F.	Corporal, Co. A, 306th Infantry; enlisted August 1917; killed at Vesle River, September 6, 1918
Cunningham, Bertrand	Medical Corps
Jobe, William E., Jr.	Medical Depart. #37, also Tank Corps; enlisted June 26, 1917; died at Brooklyn Naval Hospital, October 4, 1918
O'Brien, Michael W.	Seaman, U.S. Navy; enlisted December 19, 1917; died March 24, 1918
Wild, Frederick H.	

BIBLIOGRAPHY AND REFERENCES

Some often repeated references have been shortened: John Jermain Memorial Library, Sag Harbor, N.Y.—JJML; Society for the Preservation of Long Island Antiquities, Setauket, N. Y.—SPLIA.

PART I   THE SETTLEMENT AND EARLY GROWTH OF THE PORT (1707-1820)

CHAPTER 1

Adams, James Truslow. *The History of the Town of Southampton (East of Canoe Place)*. The Hampton Press, Bridgehampton, N.Y., 1918.
Earle, Alice Morse. *Stagecoach and Tavern Days*. Macmillan, New York, 1922.
Hedges, Henry P.. *Early Sag Harbor; and Address Delivered Before the Sag Harbor Historical Society, February 4, 1896*. J.H. Hunt, printer, Sag Harbor, N.Y., 1902.
Highway Report, East Hampton 1901-1925. Town Clerks Office, Book H, 1925.
Journal of the Trustees of the Freeholders and Commonalty of East Hampton Town, 1772-1807. Transcribed by Harry D. Sleight, 1927.
—— Ibid. 1870-1897.
Merrit Student Encyclopedia, Vol. 17. Macmillan Company, New York, 1982.
Minutes of the Board of Trustees of the Freeholders and Commonalty of the Town of Southampton, filed January 20, 1912. W.J. Post, Town Clerk.
Munsell, W.W.. *The History of Suffolk County, New York, with Illustrations, Portraits and Sketches of Prominent Families and Individuals*. W.W. Munsell & Company, New York, 1882.
Records of the Trustees of East Hampton Town, 1826-1845. Transcribed by Harry D. Sleight.
Sleight, Harry D.. *Sag Harbor in Earlier Days*. The Hampton Press, Bridgehampton, N.Y., 1930.
Sleight, Harry D.. *The Sleights of Sag Harbor*. The Hampton Press, Bridgehampton, N.Y., 1929.
Southampton Town Hall Records. Hog Neck Deeds, October 3, 1665.
Southampton Town Records, Vol. VI.
Third Book of Records of the Town of Southampton, Long Island, N.Y. with other Ancient Documents of Historic Value. John H. Hunt, Sag Harbor, N.Y., 1878.
Trustee Records of the Town of Southampton, N.Y., Part I, 1741-1826. Transcribed by Harry D. Sleight, 1931.
The Connecticut Gazette: May 21, 1784.
The Corrector: Sept. 23, 1905; Nov. 13, 1909.
Frothingham's Long Island Herald: May 1791.
The New York Journal: May 28, 1772.
The Sag Harbor Express: Jan. 17, 1861; Sept. 30, 1869; June 3, 1870; Apr. 20, Sept. 14, 1882; Mar. 31, May 19, June 16, 1898; June 9, 1900; Nov. 18, 1905; Nov. 12, 1912; Sept. 11, 1913; June 4, Sept. 10, 17, 1914; July 20, Oct. 12, 1922; June 12, 1979.
East Hampton Church Records: East Hampton Free Library, East Hampton, N.Y.
Map of Sag Harbor, 1859. JJML.
Odds & Ends Scapbook. Typed account. JJML.
The King's Highway. Scrapbook of clippings. JJML.
Toll House Marker. Route 114, Sag Harbor-East Hampton Road.
Toll House Sign. Sag Harbor Whaling and Historical Museum.

CHAPTER 2

Hedges. Early Sag Harbor.
Standard Reference Encyclopedia, vol. 25. Funk & Wagnall, New York, 1959.

BIBLIOGRAPHY AND REFERENCES

Journal of the Trustees of the Freeholders and Commonalty of the Town of East Hampton, 1870-1897. Transcribed by Harry D. Sleight, 1927.
Minutes of the Board of Trustees of the Freeholders of the Commonalty of the Town of East Hampton, Part III.
Trustee Records of the Town of Southampton, New York, Part I, 1741-1826. Transcribed by Harry D. Sleight, 1931.
The East Hampton Town Records, Vol. IV.
The Corrector: May 23, 1844; Mar. 30, Apr. 6, 13, 20, 27, 1861.
Frothingham's Long Island Herald: June 9, 1791.
The Republican Watchman: Apr. 25, 1835.
The Sag Harbor Express: Nov. 14, 1861; Dec. 4, 1862; May 1876; Aug. 24, 1884; July 23, 1891; Sept. 25, 1900; May 13, 1911; Feb. 10, 1928; Nov. 13, 1931; Sept. 30, 1934; Mar. 26, Apr. 16, Dec. 31, 1936; May 31, 1979.
Cook, Luther D.. Address Delivered Before the Sag Harbor Lyceum and Institute, April 19, 1858. Unpublished manuscript. JJML.
Hazard, Russella J.. Sag Harbor's Long Wharf. Unpublished manuscript. JJML, 1957.
Hazard, Russella J.. Typed article on Windmills. JJML.
Marcus, Grania Bolton. The Corwith Mill. Historic American Engineering Record of the National Park Service, July 1978. Unpublished manuscript.

CHAPTER 3

Andrews, Charles M.. *The Custom Service in America*, Vol. 4. Colonial Period of American History. Yale University Press, 1934-38.
Dictionary of American History, Vol. 11. Charles Scribner's, New York, 1940.
Failey, Dean F.. *Long Island Is My Nation; the Decorative Arts and Craftsmen 1640-1830*. SPLIA, 1976.
Munsell. *History of Suffolk County*.
Southampton Town Records, Vol. VII. January 1871.
Trustee Records of the Town of Southampton, New York, 1741-1826, Parts I and II. Transcribed by Harry D. Sleight, 1931.
Charter of By-laws and Ordinances of the Village of Sag Harbor, 1861.
The Sag Harbor Express: June 26, July 17, 1913; Aug. 4, 1921; July 31, 1947; Sept. 9, 1948.
The Suffolk Gazette: Dec. 22, 1807; Jan. 18, 1808; Mar. 31, 1810.
The Long Island Forum: Oct. 1949.
Dering, Henry Thomas. Journal while on Little Gull Island during the building of the wall in 1817. JJML.
Hazard, Russella J.. Henry Packer Dering. A typewritten account. JJML.
Oakland Cemetery Records. JJML.
Book of Clippings: JJML.

CHAPTER 4

Adams. *The History of the Town of Southampton*
Bayles, Richard M.. *Historical and Descriptive Sketches of Suffolk County*. Port Jefferson, N.Y. 1874.
Sleight. *Sag Harbor in Earlier Days*.
Journal of the Trustees of the Freeholders of the Commonalty of the Town of East Hampton, New York, 1870-1897. Transcribed by Harry D. Sleight.
Wilson, Clarence Hall. Sag Harbor Presbyterian Church 1766-1916; an Historical Address delivered on the occasion of the 150th anniversary of its founding, February 24, 1916. John H. Hunt, printer, Sag Harbor, New York.
The Republican Watchman: June 15, 1833.
The Sag Harbor Express: Dec. 8, 1859; July 12, 1866.

BIBLIOGRAPHY AND REFERENCES 379

The Suffolk County Recorder: Dec. 7, 1816; Jan. 18, June 28, 1817.
The Suffolk Gazette: Assorted issues 1804; May 1805; May 11, Feb. 9, 23, Sept. 7, Oct. 12, 1807: Apr. 7, 14, Sept. 29, 1810; Jan. 9, Dec. 1817; Sept. 19, 1829.
Wade, Oliver. Reminiscences of East Water Street. Unpublished account. JJML.
Gardiner, Mary L.. The Old Brown Meeting House. *The Long Island Forum*, March 1978.
Eliab Byram Scrapbook. JJML.
Mashashimuet Park Program.
Clipping: Sag Harbor as a Secret Society Center, September 1907. JJML.

CHAPTER 5

Adams. *History of the Town of Southampton*.
Barber, John W. and Howe, Henry. *Historical Collections of the State of New York*. S. Tuttle, 1842.
Halsey, William Donaldson. *Sketches from Local History*. Yankee Peddler Book Company, Southampton, N.Y., 1966.
Hedges, Henry P.. Sag Harbor in the Revolution, a speech before the Sag Harbor Historical Society, January 18, 1909.
Munsell. *History of Suffolk County*.
Onderdonk, Henry. *Revolutionary Incidents of Suffolk and King's County*. Leavitt, 1849.
Standard Reference Encyclopedia, Vol. 9.
Weeks, Henry Triglar. Sag Harbor's Old Arsenal. *The Long Island Forum*, Feb. 1945.
The Sag Harbor Express: January 26, 1871, December 17, 1875, July 23, 1903.
The San Francisco Bulletin: The Arsenal's Last Days, by Prentice Mulford. February 14, 1875.
The Suffolk Gazette: June 17, 1806; Apr. 7, June 1, 1807; Dec. 22, Jan. 18, 1808; Mar. 31, Apr. 7, Dec. 1, 1810; Sept. 15, 1814.
Hazard, Russella J.. The Powder House, typed article. JJML.
Court Martial Records, War of 1812, commencing May 1, 1814.
Letters of the Dering/Sleight Collection. East Hampton Free Library, East Hampton, N.Y., Apr. 18, Dec. 1, 1811.

CHAPTER 6

Hazard, Russella J.. *History of the Sag Harbor Fire Department*, 1819-1953. Booklet, 1953. JJML.
The Suffolk Gazette: May 1817.

PART II THE GOLDEN ERA OF THE WHALE FISHERY (1820-1850)
CHAPTER 1 & 2

Adams. *History of the Town of Southampton*.
Palmer, William. The Whaling Port of Sag Harbor. University Microfilm International, 1959.
Sleight, Harry D.. *The Whale Fishery on Long Island*. The Hampton Press, Bridgehampton, N.Y., 1931.
The Corrector: Jan. 24, Mar. 7, 1846; July 16, 1847; May 5, 1900.
The New York Sun: Feb. 7, 1897.
The Riverhead News: 1877.
The Sag Harbor Express: July 19, 1860; Mar. 14, 1861.
The San Francisco Bulletin: May 1875.
Assorted issues of the *Suffolk Gazette*, *Corrector*, and *Republican Watchman* on arrivals and departures.
America's First Scientific Whaler, Captain Thomas Roys (Royce), by Frank H. Winter and Frederick P. Schmidt. *Oceans Magazine*, May/June 1975, Vol. 8 No. 3.
Sag Harbor Business Directory of the 1840s. JJML.

380 BIBLIOGRAPHY AND REFERENCES

Oakland Cemetery Records. JJML.
Hazard, Russella J.. Industries related to the whale fishery. Typed account. JJML.
Sleight, Harry D.. *Henry Lee* sailing from Sag Harbor had only one survivor. 1905. JJML.
Sleight, Harry D..A Vessel with many names had most interesting history. Clipping. JJML.
LaGuire, John. The Adventures of John Gann, Jr. A Story of old Sag Harbor's Whaling Days. Unpublished manuscript. Author's collection.
Wade, Oliver. Reminiscences of East Water Street, Sag Harbor. Unpublished manuscript.

CHAPTER 3

The Republican Watchman: Nov. 22, 1845.

PART III INDUSTRIAL GROWTH AND BUSINESS OPPORTUNITIES (1850-1880)

CHAPTER 1

Adams. *History of the Town of Southampton*.
Failey. *Long Island Is My Nation*.
Halsey. *Sketches from Local History*.
Sleight. *The Whale Fishery on Long Island*.
The Eighth Volume of Records of the Town of Southampton 1893-1927, Part II. Sleight, Harry D., 1928.
Southampton Town Trustee Records, 1741-1826 Part II. Transcribed by Harry D. Sleight, 1931.
The Corrector: June 4, 1842; Assorted issues 1892; Dec. 31, 1898; June 15, 1901; June 6, Oct. 3, 1903; Mar. 19, May 21, Sept. 10, Oct. 1, 1910; Nov. 18, 1911.
Frothingham's Long Island Herald: 1897.
The Sag Harbor Express: Oct. 20, Dec. 1, 1859; May 3, July 12, 1860; Assorted issues, June 27, 1861; Assorted issues 1862; Apr. 23, May 7, Sept. 3, 1863; Sept. 28, Nov. 2, 1865; Assorted issues 1866; Apr. 14, 1870; July, Dec. 19, 1872; Jan. 30, 1873; Assorted issues, May 13, June 8, June 15, Aug. 1, 1875; Assorted issues, June 1, 1876; Sept. 13, 1877; Mar. 29, Sept. 23, 1880; Jan. 18, 1881; Sept. 1882; July 3, Aug. 28, 1884; Sept. 23, 1897; Sept. 14, 1905; Aug. 14, 1909; May 24, 1910; Apr. 29, May 1, June 19, 1913; Apr. 6, May 11, Oct. 12, 1916; Aug. 18, 25, Sept. 25, 1931.
Supplement to the *Sag Harbor Express*: Sag Harbor Up-to-Date, 1913.
The Suffolk Gazette: Assorted issues 1824; assorted issues 1849; May 14, 1825.
Hazard, Russella J. Flag on the Mill. Typed account. JJML.
Hazard, Russella J. Typed account on Ephraim Niles Byram and Benjamin Franklin Hope. JJML.
The 100th Anniversary of the Sag Harbor Savings Bank, 1860-1960. Booklet. JJML.
Oakland Cemetery Records. JJML.
Business Directories: 1840s, 1888-89, and 1910-11. JJML.
Books of Clippings. JJML.

CHAPTER 2

The Corrector: Jan. 18, June 1840; Apr. 1, 1843; July 30, Nov. 12, 1845; Apr. 1, 8, July 28, Aug. 1, 1846; Sept. 27, 1851; Nov. 17, 1894; July 27, 1895; Nov. 10, 1900; Sept. 13, 1902.
The East Hampton Star: Oct. 21, 1892.
The Republican Watchman: Assorted issues 1835; Sept. 12, 1840.
The Sag Harbor Express: Nov. 3, 1859; June 28, 1860; June 25, 1863; May 18, June 8, 1865; Aug. 9, 1866, Dec. 19, 1867; Apr. 15, 1875; Jan. 24, 31, Sept. 11, 1884.

CHAPTER 3

The Corrector: May 21, Aug. 6, 1885.
The Sag Harbor Express: July 24, December 8, 15, 1859; Sept. 6, Oct. 1, 1869; May 26, 1900; Oct. 11, 1902; Aug. 8, 1903; Apr., August 14, 1913.

BIBLIOGRAPHY AND REFERENCES 381

CHAPTER 4

The Corrector: Feb. 14, March 24, 1880; Jan. 8, 1881; Sept. 23, 1893; July 6, 1895; Feb. 13, 1904; Feb. 7, 14, 1914; Apr. 29, 1911; Aug. 1, 1912; Mar. 8, 1915; Mar. 8, 1917.
The Sag Harbor Express: Apr. 30, Oct. 29, 1868; Dec. 14, 1916; Oct. 28, 1897; Aug. 18, 1881; Feb. 17, 1916; Assorted issues 1863-1925.
Hazard. The History of the Sag Harbor Fire Department.

PART IV EXPLORING THE SOCIAL SCENE (1820-1880)

CHAPTER 1

Adams. *The History of the Town of Southampton*.
Hazard, Russella J. 150 Years of Newspapers in Sag Harbor, L.I. 1791-1941.
Tooker, William Wallace. *Early Sag Harbor Printers and their Imprints*. JJML.
The Corrector: Feb. 6, June 5, 1909.
The Harbor Pilot: Dec. 6, 1922; Dec. 5, 1923.
The Long Island Herald: May 3, July 1791.
The Rapid Transit: Jan., Feb. 6, 1889.
The Republican Watchman: Mar. 1, 1828.
The Sag Harbor News: Jan. 29, 1909; May 24, 1912.
The Sag Harbor Express: Feb. 2, 1871; Jan. 5, 1922; Jan. 31, 1980.

CHAPTER 2

The Corrector: Sept. 3, 1845; Oct. 13, 16, 1847; Aug. 27, 1874; Nov. 16, 1876; Apr. 7, 1877; Aug. 4, 18, 25, 1883; Mar. 1884; Apr. 7, 1888; Sept. 9, 23, Oct. 21, 1893; June 6, 1896.
The New York Sunday News: Jan. 1968.
The Sag Harbor Express: Jan. 26, Nov. 15, 1860; Mar. 12, 1862; Mar. 12, 1863; Feb. 13, 1864; Oct. 21, Nov. 1869; May 11, 1871; Aug. 27, 1874; Nov. 16, 1876; Oct. 25, 1883; Nov. 2, 1893.
Wade, Oliver. Reminiscences of East Water Street. Unpublished manuscript. JJML.
Sag Harbor School Attendance Records: JJML.
Book of Clippings. JJML.

CHAPTER 3

Adams. *The History of the Town of Southampton*.
Hedges. *Early Sag Harbor*.
Munsell. *The History of Suffolk County*.
Prime, Nathaniel S. *A History of Long Island, New York*. Robert Carter, New York, 1845.
The Records of the Town of Southampton, New York, Part I, 1741-1826. Transcribed by Harry D. Sleight, 1931.
Wilson, Clarence Hall. The Sag Harbor Presbyterian Church 1766-1916; An Historical Address Delivered on the Occasion of the 150th Anniversary of its Founding. Feb. 24, 1916.
The Brooklyn Eagle: Sept. 1, 1900.
The Corrector: Nov. 29, 1845; July 29, 1869; Sept. 24, 1874; Apr. 19, Oct. 3, 1875; Oct. 18, 1877; May 20, 1880; Mar. 6, July 26, Nov. 20, 1884; Mar. 25, 1893; July 14, 1894; May 15, 29, 1897; Sept. 18, Nov. 3, 1900; Apr. 20, May 2, 1901; Jan. 18, July 12, 19, 1902; May 22, Oct. 10, Nov. 14, 1903; Mar. 28, Dec. 12, 1908; May 29, 1909; Feb. 18, 1911; Oct. 31, 1912; Apr. 20, 1922; Feb. 1, Mar. 29, 1923.
The Sag Harbor Express: Aug. 25, Sept. 1, 15, Dec. 8, 15, 1859; Jan. 12, 26, Feb. 9, Aug. 23, 1860; Apr. 10, Sept. 18, 1862; May 7, 14, July 16, 1863; Mar. 17, May 19, July 7, 1864; Jan. 12, May 20, Nov. 15, 1866; Dec. 20, 1867; Jan. 30, 1868; June 25, 1869; Sept. 24, 1870; Mar. 16, 1871; Dec. 15, 1877; July 8, 1880; Jan. 19, Mar. 2, Apr. 6, May 4, 1882; Nov. 15,

1883; Sept. 18, Oct. 9, 1884; Apr. 30, July 30, Aug. 20, Sept. 10, 1885; May 28, Sept. 10, Nov. 19, 1891; Mar. 3, 1892; Sept. 23, Oct. 28, 1893; Sept. 20, Dec. 14, 21, 1899; Mar. 23, Sept. 29, Oct. 21, Nov. 1, 1900; May 25, 1901; Oct. 22, 1903; Apr. 30, Sept. 5, 1908; May 27, 1909; July 23, 1910; Sept. 30, Dec. 21, 1911; Oct. 24, 1912; Mar. 15, Apr. 17, 24, May 8, 15, June 5, Sept. 18, Oct. 2, 1913; Aug. 5, Oct. 28, 1915; Sept. 15, 1916; Sept. 29, 1917; Mar. 31, Apr. 21, 1921; Feb. 8, Mar. 22, 1923; May 10, Aug. 30, 1929; Nov. 21, 1940.
The Suffolk County Recorder: Dec. 7, 1816; Jan. 18, June 28, 1817.
The Suffolk Gazette: May 11, Oct. 12, 1807.
The Centennial Anniversary of the Methodist-Episcopal Church, July 24–31, 1910. Booklet.
The 90th Anniversary of the Methodist-Episcopal Church, July 22, 1900. Booklet.
List of ministers who served in the Methodist-Episcopal Church. Ethel Ruehl.
Palmer, William. The 100th Anniversary of Christ Church, 1945.
Heatley, Rose. The History of North Haven in Celebration of our Country's Bicentennial 1776–1976.
Our Historic Congregation Looks Toward the Future, pamphlet.
Sag Harbor as a Secret Society Center, Sept. 1907. Clipping.
Odds and Ends Folder of Clippings. JJML.
Assorted clippings. JJML.

CHAPTER 4

Adams. *The History of the Town of Southampton*.
Hedges. *Early Sag Harbor*.
The Corrector: Oct. 1847, Mar. 10, 1877; Apr. 2, 1892; Mar. 4, Apr. 22, Dec. 16, 1893; Jan. 27, Oct. 13, 1894; June 27, July 18, 1896; July 9, 30, 1898; Apr. 27, June 29, 1901; Apr. 18, May 2, 16, 23, 1903; Jan. 30, Aug. 6, 1904; Feb. 25, Apr. 1, Sept. 30, Nov. 4, 1905; Mar. 27, Apr. 3, Oct. 9, 1909.
The Republican Watchman: Nov. 11, 1835; Sept. 5, 1840.
The Sag Harbor Express: Aug. 4, 1859; Mar. 25, 1880; July 14, 1881; Feb. 3, Sept. 29, 1887; May 14, 1908; Jan. 15, 1920; June 26, 1921; Apr. 26, May 3, 10, 1923.
Supplement to the *Sag Harbor Express*: Sag Harbor Up-to-Date, 1913
Book of Clippings. JJML.

CHAPTER 5

Sleight. *Sag Harbor in Earlier Days*.
Vail, L.T. The Geneology of Reverend Robert Fordham. Unpublished manuscript. JJML: 1942.
The Corrector: Feb. 24, 1877; June 13, 1891; June 25, 1898.
The Sag Harbor Express: Apr. 26, 1860; July, Nov. 1867; January 1868; Oct. 1876; Apr. 16, July 30, Nov. 12, 1903; Mar. 7, 1908; May 1, 8, June 25, 1924; Mar. 6, 1944; Aug. 21, 1980.
Bailey, Paul. Our Historical Heritage, *The Sunday Review*, Sept. 23, 1962.
The Long Island Forum: June 1949. Prentice Mulford.
Records of the Sag Harbor Brass Band. JJML.
Clipping. *The New York Times*. 1900.
Book of Clippings. JJML.
Cooper Collection: MV-15 (1858) JJML.

CHAPTER 6

Mather, Frederick Gregory. *The Refugees from Long Island to Connecticut*. J.B. Lyon Company, Albany, N.Y., 1913.
McManus, Edgar J.. *A History of Negro Slavery in New York*. Syracuse University Press, New York, 1966.

BIBLIOGRAPHY AND REFERENCES 383

Munsell. *History of Suffolk County.*
Wortis, Helen. Black Inhabitants of Shelter Island. *The Long Island Forum.* Aug. 1973.
The Long Island Herald: Jan. 11, 1796.
The Sag Harbor Express: June 3, 1880; Assorted issues 1861-1865.
The Suffolk County Recorder: Apr. 12, 1817; July 24, 1821.
The Suffolk Gazette: July 1804; May, June 1805.
The Edwin Rose Post, American Legion Book of Civil War Veterans, JJML.

PART V   INDUSTRY, INNOVATION AND EXPANSION (1870-1900)

CHAPTER 1

The Corrector: Assorted issues 1822-1839; June 17, July 8, Feb. 25, Nov. 11, 1893; Apr. 27, May 5, 1895; Oct. 27, 1894; Mar. 14, 21, June 13, 1896; Sept. 9, 1899; Feb. 1, 1902; Sept. 30, 1905; June 13, 1912; June 25, 1898; May 5, 1904.
The Long Island Herald: Assorted issues 1791-1792.
The Sag Harbor Express: May 9, July 4, 1861; June 19, May 1, 1862; June, Oct. Nov. 5, 1874; Aug. 5, 1875; Feb. 24, 1876; June 2, Aug. 18, 1898; Feb. Mar. 1901; Feb. 13, 1911, July 10, 1913; Jan. 22, Mar. 19, 1914; July 15, 1915.
The Palisades News, Manderville, La.: June 19, 1880.
The Suffolk County Recorder: Sept. 11, 22, 1819; July 17, 1824; Mar. 28, 1829.
Handwritten list of several steam-powered ships. JJML.
Clippings, 1898: JJML.
Clipping, 1926. Harry D. Sleight. JJML.
Information: Patricia Donovan, Sag Harbor, N.Y.

CHAPTER 2

Bayles. *Historical and Descriptive Sketches of Suffolk County.*
Journal of the Trustees of the Freeholders and Commonalty of the Town of East Hampton, N.Y. 1870-1897. Transcribed by Harry D. Sleight, 1927.
Munsell. *History of Suffolk County.*
The Corrector: Oct. 23, Dec. 31, 1847; Oct. 30, 1884; Sept. 25, 1909.
The Sag Harbor Express: Dec. 31, 1874; Apr. 1, 1875; Jan. 1861; Apr. 29, 1880; Aug. 26, 1886; Sept. 16, Oct. 23, 1909; Jan. 22, 1910; Mar. 4, 1911; May 11, 1916; Jan. 15, 1920; May 1921; Sept. 24, 1981.

CHAPTER 3

Pelletreau, William S. *A History of Long Island from its Earliest Settlement to the Present Time*, Vol. III. Lewis Publishing Company, New York and Chicago, 1903.
Huden, John C. William Wallace Tooker. *The Long Island Forum.* Aug. 1955.
The Corrector: Dec. 27, 1883; July 10, 1884; Nov. 21, 1908; Feb. 2, 9, 1909; Apr. 12, 1902; Apr. 22, 1905; Jan. 11, 1908; Jan. 9, 1909; Apr. 4, 1896; Feb. 4, Apr. 15, 1911.
The Sag Harbor Express: Nov. 1875; Feb. 8, Mar. 2, Apr. 6, 1876; Aug. 18, Nov. 11, Dec. 1880; Feb. 10, 17, Mar. 10, 17, 24, June 2, 23, July 14, 28, Nov. 17, Dec. 15, 29, 1881; Jan. 1882; Feb. 26, 1885; July 1, 1886; Sept., Oct. 1891; Feb., Nov. 17, 1908; Feb. 11, 1909; May 4, 1916; Aug. 1917; Feb. 19, 1920; Oct. 12, 1922; Mar. 12, 1925; Oct. 21, 1927; Jan. 4, Nov. 1, 1929; July 2, 1936; Apr. 6, 1939.
The Suffolk Gazette: Assorted issues 1806.
East Hampton-Southampton Register, Lawton Register Company, Auburn, Maine. 1910-1911 Watchcase Factory and Alvin Company employees.
Souvenir Book of the Firemen's Tournament, 1896.
Books of clippings: JJML.

BIBLIOGRAPHY AND REFERENCES

CHAPTER 4

The Southampton Town Trustee Records, Part II, 1741-1826.
Weinhardt, Donald H.. *100 Years of Long Island Bottles*, Vol. I. Suffolk County Antique Bottle Association of Long Island, Inc., Bay Shore, N.Y., 1976.
The Corrector: Mar. 5, 12, 19, Apr. 2, 30, May 14, 28, 1892; Feb. 11, June 14, July 21, 1893; July 20, Oct. 12, 1895; Feb. 1, Mar. 28, May 27, 1896; Feb. 25, 1899; Apr. 27, 1901; Sept. 3, 17, 1910; Feb. 25, 1911.
The Sag Harbor Express: Mar. 21, June 20, Aug. 8, Sept. 5, 1889; July 21, 1920; July 8, 1921; July 22, Oct. 28, Nov. 18, 1937.

CHAPTER 5

Cosmas, Graham A. *An Army for Empire*. Univ. of Missouri Press, Columbia, MO., 1971.
The Corrector: Apr. 2, May 14, Sept. 3, 1898.
The Sag Harbor Express: May 5, Aug., Sept. 1, Oct. 13, 1898.
Oakland Cemetery Records: JJML.

PART VI AN AMERICAN BEAUTY IN THE TWENTIETH CENTURY (1900-1940)

CHAPTER 1

Standard Reference Encyclopedia, Vol. 20.
The Corrector: Oct. 8, 1892; Oct. 29, 1904; Mar. 4, 1905; May 1, 1909.
The Sag Harbor Express: Assorted issues 1905; Sept. 3, 1914; Apr. 15, 1915; Sept. 6, Sept. 20, 27, 1917; Feb. 9, 1922; Aug. 2, 1923; Mar. 20, May 15, 1924; Feb. 12, Apr. 9, 1925; Feb. 24, 1927; Oct. 18, 1979.
Book of clippings. JJML.
Typewritten article by Russella Hazard. JJML.

CHAPTER 2

Bayles. *Historical and Descriptive Sketches of Suffolk County*.
The Corrector: June 15, 1833; Nov. 28, 1908; Sept. 18, 1909; Apr. 9, 30, 1910; Aug. 1, 1912; Apr. 3, 1913; Dec. 15, 1920.
The Republican Watchman: Mar. 27, 1827; Jan. 1, 1836.
The Sag Harbor Express: Jan. 17, 1861; Aug. 1875; Dec. 14, 1878; Apr. 10, 24, May 29, June 3, Sept. 11, 1879; Mar. 25, 1880; Sept. 15, 1881; Feb. 14, Mar. 20, 1884; Feb., Apr. 4, July 18, 1907; June 4, Nov. 5, 1908; Apr. 1, 1909; Aug., Oct. 29, Dec. 31, 1910; Aug., Sept. 3, 1911; Aug. 1, Sept. 12, Sept. 28, 1912; Aug. 21, 1913; Sept. 16, 1915; May 22, 1916; Oct. 17, 1918; Dec. 15, 1920; Sept. 15, 1924; July 16, Aug. 6, 1925; Mar. 6, 1931; Dec. 2, 1932; July 5, 1974.
The Suffolk Gazette: Jan. 14, Dec. 22, 1806; Jan. 9, 1809.
Park Director's Report. Mashashimuet Park and Social Center, Sag Harbor, N.Y. June 1911 & June 1913.
Sag Harbor's 250th Anniversary Program. JJML.
Souvenir of Home Coming Week and 25th Anniversary of the Ladies Village Improvement Society, July 2-7, 1912. Published by the LVIS, Anna Mulford, editor.
Sage and Slocum Scrapbook. JJML.
The Piersonian. Pierson High School paper, 1911 & 1913.
Book of Clippings: JJML.

CHAPTER 3

The Encyclopedia Americana. International edition, Vol. 16, Grolier, New York, 1989.
Standard Reference Encyclopedia, Vol. 15.

BIBLIOGRAPHY AND REFERENCES

The Corrector: Apr. 27, Oct. 12, Dec. 14, 1907; May 1, July 31, Nov. 13, Oct. 2, 16, 1909.
The Sag Harbor Express: Feb. 7, 21, Mar. 13, July 10, 1884; Feb. 2, 1888; Dec. 1895; Jan. 16, Dec. 3, 1896; Feb. 4, Apr. 8, June 10, Dec. 16, 1897; Feb. 9, Apr. 13, 1899; Jan. 9, Mar. 6, 1902; Feb. 21, Nov. 19, 1903; Sept. 9, 1911; Sept. 4, 1912; May 8, Aug. 21, Sept. 11, Oct. 9, 16, Nov. 18, 1913; Mar. 15, Apr. 9, June 4, July 9, Assorted issues 1914; Apr. 21, May 6, June 3, June 10, 17, 24, Sept. 16, 1915; June 7, Dec. 20, 1917; May 6, July 1, Oct. 27, 1920; Jan., Aug. 24, Sept. 2, Oct. 5, Dec. 7, 12, 1922; Jan. 18, Nov. 15, 22, Dec. 21, 1923; Jan. 31, Feb. 7, June 12, July 17, Aug. 14, Sept. 4, 1924; Sept. 2, 1927; July 12, Oct. 11, Nov. 15, 1929; Feb. 2, 9, 28, March 21, Apr. 18, 25, May 5, Oct. 10, 1930; Feb. 27, 1931; Nov. 18, 1932; Mar. 3, June 2, 9, 1933; Feb. 15, Mar. 22, 1935; Jan. 17, Feb. 13, Mar. 19, June 11, July 2, 1936; June 10, 1937.
The Agassiy Association Minutes Book. JJML.
The Sag Harbor Lawn Tennis Club Record Book 1891-1893. First Presbyterian Church Historical Committee, Sag Harbor, N.Y.
Semi-Centenary of Wamponamon Lodge. Clipping, 1908.
Sag Harbor as a Secret Society Center. Clipping, 1907.
Book of Clippings: JJML.
Information: Jane Kiernan, Sag Harbor, N.Y.

CHAPTER 4

The Corrector: Mar. 12, Nov. 1, 1892; June 28, 1902; Nov. 14, 1903; Apr. 16, 1904; July 23, 30, Aug. 27, 1910; Apr. 22, 1911.
The Sag Harbor Express: Jan. 3, May 6, June 3, June 17, July 8, 1910; Apr. 4, May 2, June 6, 1912; Jan. 9, Aug. 7, Oct. 9, 1913; Apr. 16, 24, June 11, Nov. 19, 1914; Mar. 4, 1915; Spring 1918; Apr. 4, 1920; Jan. 31, May 8, 22, Aug. 21, 1924; Jan. 16, 1931; Nov. 3, 10, 1933; Jan. 5, July 27, 1934; June 17, July 1, Aug. 12, 26, 1937.
Sag Harbor in the Land of the Sunrise Trail 1707-1927, Sag Harbor Village Trustees Booklet. 1927.
Letter: Raymond L'Ecuyer, August 29, 1971. Kiss Pottery Works.

CHAPTER 5

Gregory, Ross. *The Origins of American Intervention in the First World War*. W.W. Norton, New York, 1971.
Stallings, Lawrence. *The Doughboys: the Story of the AEF, 1917-1918*. Harper & Row, New York, 1963.
Welsh, Douglas. *The U.S. in World War I*. Galahad Books, New York, 1982.
The Corrector: Oct. 24, 31, 1896.
The Sag Harbor Express: Oct. 22, 1896; Dec. 12, 1901; Mar. 6, May 29, 1902.
American Legion Records of Sag Harbor Veterans. JJML.

CHAPTER 6

The Sag Harbor Express: Jan. 8, 15, 1925.
Clipping: Hazard, Russella J. On the Alvin Silver Company. JJML.

EPILOGUE

Clowes, Ernest S. *Hurricane of 1938 on Eastern Long Island*. The Hampton Press, Bridgehampton, N.Y., 1939.
The Sag Harbor Express: Sept. 22, Oct. 13, 1938.

INDEX

(ILLUSTRATIONS FOLLOW PAGE 96)

Academy and Institute, 163-164
Academy of the Sacred Heart of Mary, 167-168: *illus.*
A.M.E. Zion Church, St. David, 182-183; burying ground, 184, 185; ministers of, 340; *illus.*
Agassiy Club, 297
Aldrich, Mr. and Mrs. James Herman, 283, 296: gifts to beautify Sag Harbor, 242: to Christ Church, 187-188; to North Haven Chapel, 191; moves bandstand to park, 208, 276
Alvin Silver Works, 248-249; burns in 1925, 312-313; *illus.*
American Hotel, on site of early tavern, 58, 196; opens in 1877, 196; during dry years, 268, 269
American Revolution, *See* Revolutionary War
Arsenal, 65-68; *illus.*
Atheneum, 205-207, 287; shows movies, 289; World War I victory celebration, 309; *illus.*

Bailey's Cut Tool Co., 254-255
Bandstand, 208
Baptist Church, Bethel, 173-175; pastors of, 338; *illus.*
Battle of Long Island, 59, 311
Bay Street, 12
Betsy Jose's Fort, 199
Black churches, 182-185; *see also* A.M.E. Zion Church
Blacks, in Sag Harbor, 182-185; seamen, 85
Blacksmiths, 124-125, 348, 351, 352, 354
Bliss Torpedo Co., E.W., 266-267; *illus.*
Bloch Hat Pin Factory, 303
Boarding houses, *See* Inns and Hotels
Bomb Lance, whaling harpoon, 96-97
Bottling Works, 253-254; *illus.*
Brass Band, 207-208
Brass foundry, 115
Breakwater, completed in 1908, 263
Brickmaking, 244-246
Bridges to North Haven, 23-26

Brown, George B., businessman and respected citizen, 122-123, 243
Brown & Tiffany's department store, 123
Brunnerman, Father Joseph, first resident priest, 180; founded Catholic school, 166
Buck, William, pharmacist, 133, 250, 274
Building Block Co., 303
Bull's Head Turnpike Co., 16; *illus.*
Bulova Watch Co., 307
Burke, Michael, Burke Street named for, 13; prominent Catholic, 179
Burying Grounds, 193-195; *see also* Cemeteries
Business directories, late 1700s, 350; 1804-1810, 351; 1840s, 351-352; 1888-89, 352-354; 1910-11, 354-357; 1920s, 357-358
Butts, C. W., factory, 306
Byram, Eliab., 60, 117, 205
Byram, Ephraim Niles, clockmaker and astronomer, 115: profile, 117-118; *illus.*
Byram, Ivan C., mason, 56, 182, 195, 252, 256, 287; pres. of Agassiy Club, 297; in World War I, 309

Cadmus, whaleship, 88-89, 106
Camp Upton, 308
Camp Wykoff, 257
Catholic Church, St. Andrew's, 179-182; marble altar, 182; and Temperance club, 193; priests of, 339
Catholic schools, Academy of the Sacred Heart of Mary, 167-168; St. Andrew's, 166-167; *illus.*
Cemeteries, A.M.E. Zion, 184, 185; Jewish, 189; Oakland, 194-195; Old Burying Ground, 193-194
Census records of 1775, 333
Chapels, 172-173, 190-192
Cholera scare in 1866, 136-137
Churches, early, 48-54; A.M.E. Zion, 182-183; Baptist, 173-175; Catholic, 179-182; Episcopal, 185-188; Methodist, 175-179;

INDEX

Pentecostal, 190; Presbyterian (Old Whaler's), 170-172
Cigar factory, 116
Circus, 43
Civil War, 210-216; explosion at waterfront, 214-215; monument, 310-311; relief organizations, 214; veterans and casualties, 360-368; wages of those serving, 211; whaling ships used in, 98, 106-107
Clark, Moses, donates land for Methodist Church, 53; Mason, 55; officer of Moral Society, 56
Cleveland, George H., builder, 56, 240; Bottling Works, 253; Memorial Chapel, 172; Temple Adas Israel, 189; renovates Atheneum, 206
Cloak factory, 305-306
Clockmaking, 115, 117-119
Congdon, Capt. David, introduces gas lights, 138; starts flour mill, 238
Cook, Henry F., in business with Joseph Fahys, 223; controlling interest in Water Works, 256; in Spanish-American War, 257; officer of Historical Society, 295
Cooper, Caleb, Cooper Street named for, 12
Cooper, Edward, profile, 90-91
Cooper, James Fenimore, 85-88; *Sea Lions* describes Sag Harbor, 87-88; begins *Precaution*, 197; *illus.*
Cooperages, 90-91, 348
Corbin, Austin, president Long Island Rail Road, 222
Corey, Braddock, active early resident, profile, 33-34, 44
Cor Maria, Frank Havens summer mansion, 265
Corwin, Burton D., publisher, 160
Corwith, James, miller, 27
Cotton Mill, Steam, 143, 235-238
Court Martial Trials after War of 1812, 72-74
Cream of Tartar Factory, 116
Custom House and collectors, 36-39; moved to present site, 39; located in Arsenal, 67; *illus.*

David Porter, wreck of, 230-232
Department store, 122-124, 355, 357, *illus.*
Dering, Henry Packer, 51, 65, 67, 68, 69, 152; profile, 37-38; collector of Port, 37; first postmaster, 37, 39; school trustee, 45; officer of Moral Society, 56; backs first newspaper, 151; taxed for slave, 217-218; *illus.*

Dering, Henry Thomas, 38, 39
Division Street, 12
Drugstores and pharmacies, early, 132-135

Eaton, William S., engraver and inventor, 301-302
Education, early, 44-48
Eldredge, Stillman, organizes Methodist Church, 53, 54; officer of Moral Society, 56
Eldredge, Thomas, owns Mill Pond, 126
Eldredge's Coffee House, 196
Electricity, introduced in 1902, 140; power house destroyed by fire, 140
Enigma Club, 116; meets in 1869, 297
Episcopal Church, Christ, 185-188; Masons purchase building, 55; purchases Atheneum, 205; rectors of, 340; *illus.*
Episcopal Society, 53

Fahys, Joseph, builds bridge to North Haven, 24; brings Jews to Sag Harbor, 188; owns Atheneum, 206-207; re-forms cotton mill, 238; watchcase factory, 246-250
Fire Department, established, 76-77; growth of, 144-147; list of chiefs, 359-360
Fire Museum, 53
Fires in Sag Harbor, 1817, 75-76; 1845, 109-110, 122, 196, 197; 1877, 141-142, 198; 1925, 312-313; ice house destroyed, 129; power house destroyed, 140; Academy and Institute destroyed, 164; recollections of a fire fighter, 142-143; list of, 358-359
Flouring mill, Budd's, 126; Hampton, 239-240; Maidstone Steam, 238-239
Fordham, Daniel, 59, 284; share in Long Wharf, 20
Fordham, Ephraim, 59; recalls early settlement, 4
Fordham, Hubbard Latham, artist and land owner, profile, 204-205
Fordham, John W., blacksmith, profile, 124-125
Fordham, Nathan, 27, 59, 273; early settler, 4; stagecoach run, 14; taxed for slaves, 217-218; *illus.*
Fordham, Peletiah (Duke), innkeeper, 197; Suffolk Temperance House, 192
Fraternal organizations, 55-56

INDEX

Freeman, William, opens American Hotel in 1877, 196
French, Hannibal and Stephen B., 164, 274; own flour mill, 238; own *Highland Mary,* 97
Frothingham, David, publisher of first newspaper, 151-152

Gardner, Warren S., publisher, 158-159
Gas lights, introduced in 1859, 138-140; *illus.*
Gold Rush, 202; Polly Sweet during, 101-103; whaling ships in, 89
Golf course, 292-293
Great Meadows, early name for Sag Harbor, 3; allotment to 23 people, 5

Havens, Frank C., wealthy summer resident, raises money for breakwater, 264; builds Cor Maria, 265
Havens, Henry B., 60; builds powder house, 67; mason for Atheneum, 205; opens brickyard, 244
Havens Beach, 294
Health care, in early days 132-137
Hedges, Henry P., historian, 4, 20, 23, 59, 184, 274, 295
Hedges, Jesse, schoolmaster, 45; operates early drugstore, 132
Hempstead, David, profile, 183-184
Henry Lee, voyage of, 99-101
Highland Mary, bark, 97-99
Hildreth, John, shoemaker, profile, 121-122
Hildreth, Peter, owner of Peter's Green, 115
Historical Society, 294-297, 311
Hog Neck, *see* North Haven
Hope, Benjamin Franklin, clockmaker, profile, 118-119; grandfather clock at library, 118
Hotels, *see* Inns and hotels
Howell, Stephen, 65; first known brickmaker, 244; officer of Moral Society, 56; owns whaleship, 82
Hughes, Peter, editor and publisher, 160
Hunt, Harry Wentworth, publisher, 155-157
Hunt, John Howard, publisher of *Sag Harbor Express,* 158-159
Hurricane of 1938, 177, 314-315

Ice harvesting, 127-129

Illnesses and remedies, early, 135-136
Indians, land purchased from, 3; guides on stagecoach route, 14; seamen, 85; live by Round Pond, 127; study of, 250; place names, 250-251
Industries, early, 113-129; *see also* Business directories
Infidels, 54
Inns and hotels, 196-200; during dry years, 268-269; list of, 353, 355, 357

Jail, constructed, 36
Jermain, John, 64, 65; Jermain Avenue named for, 13; builds windmill, 27, 273; organizes volunteer military company, 60
Jermain Avenue, 13
Jewish population, 188-190; Association of United Brethren, 188; *see also* Temple Adas Israel and schools, Hebrew
John Jermain Memorial Library, 284-286; financed by Mrs. Russell Sage, 277; *illus.*

Kiss Art Pottery Company, 304-305
Konohassett, whaleship, 88
Ku Klux Klan meeting, 299-300

Ladies Village Improvement Society, 195, 206, 242, 294; organized in 1887, 298
Land titles, origin of, 7
Law enforcement, whipping post, 33; stocks, 34; local ordinances, 35; jail, 36; police, early, 36
L'Hommedieu, Samuel, 59, 65, 76, 192; profile, 114-115; school trustee, 45; officer of Moral Society, 56; owns ropewalk, 114
Libraries, 283-286; first mentioned in 1806, 284; *see also* John Jermain Memorial Library
Literary Society, 56, 174
Long Island, passenger steamer, 232-233
Long Island Rail Road, tracks extended to Sag Harbor, 241; to ice house, 128; controls waterfront, 223; brick depot built, 242-243, *illus.;* lines closed in 1939, 243
Long Pond, 11; source of village water, 255
Long Wharf, original, 20; extended, 21; steamboats dock at, 221-223; owned by LIRR, 223; leased, 263; *illus.*
Ludlow, Isaac, captain of *Oscar,* 93-96

INDEX

Maidstone Pier, built after 1877 fire, 222; takes over mill dock, 239
Mail delivery, by stagecoach, 15; by pony express, 39; by steamer, 130; by railroad, 130; cost of, 40
Main Street, opened about 1775, 11, 12; *illus.*
Mankesack Island, 22-23
Mansion House, built in 1846, 199, 201
Mashashimuet Park, band concerts in, 208; development of, 274-277; *illus.*
Masonic lodges, 55-56; newspaper devoted to, 159; house whaling museum, 297
Meeting House Hill, 4; stocks erected on, 34; British fort on, 58
Memorial Chapel, 172-173
Methodist Church, built in 1811, 53; second in 1836, 175-177; tower clock for, 117; supports Temperance Society, 192; Sunday school recalled, 177-179; hurricane topples steeple, 177; pastors of, 338-339; *illus.*
Mill Pond, *see* Trout Pond
Mitchell, James, builds bridge to North Haven, 24, 27
Montauk Steamboat Co., 222, 229, 233, 257
Montauk Steam Laundry, 255
Monuments, at historic sites, 296; Civil War, 310; World War I, 309-310; broken mast, *illus.*
Moral Society, forerunner of Temperance Society, 56
Movies, made in Sag Harbor, 291-292; Montauk Motion Picture Theater, 287-288; Star Theater, 288-289; George's, 289-290; Elite, 290
Mulford, Prentice, philosopher and writer, profile, 201-203; recalls Suffolk Guard, 61; the Arsenal, 68; cotton mill, 236-237
Music Hall, Huntting's, 203-204

Nassau House, 198
Newspapers, 151-160; list of, 356
North Haven, also known as Hog Neck, 3; purchased from Indians, 3; bridges to, 23-26; ferry service to, 25; census of 1775, 317; chapel, 190-191; *illus.*
Noyac Chapel, 191

Oakland Works, 115-116, *illus.*
Odd Fellows, organized in 1843, 29
Old Barn Meeting House, first church, 48-51

Old Burying Ground, 193-194; prominent early citizens in, 194
Old Stand, 133
Old Whaler's Church, *see* Presbyterian Church
Osborn, Selleck, publisher, 152-153
Oscar, whaleship, mutiny on, 93-96
Otter Pond, 11, 272-273; skating on, 43, 273; purchased by Mrs. Russell Sage, 273

Pacific, bark, 89-90
Payne, Charles Watson III, 238, 254, 274, 295; profile, 245-246
Pentecostal Society, 190
Peter's Green, industries at, 113-115
Pharmacies, *see* Drugstores
Phillips, John B., schooner captain, profile, 227-229; *illus.*
Phillips, Samuel, editor and publisher, 40, 157
Pierson High School, 278-283; financed by Mrs. Russell Sage, 277; *illus.*
Police, early, 36
Port of Sag Harbor, made port of entry, 36; naval blockade of, 58; whaling from, 84-108
Post Office, first established in 1794, 39; located in Arsenal, 67; growth of, 130-131; list of postmasters, 358
Pottery works, 243-244
Presbyterian Church, early, 51-53; *illus.,* becomes Atheneum, 205; Old Whaler's, 170-172; supports Temperance Society, 192; Ku Klux Klan meeting in, 300; ministers of, 338; *illus.*
Prohibition and dry years, 267-271; rum running during, 270-271

Rayon factory, 306-307
Revolutionary War, 57-60; families flee, 20, 59; Meigs' raid on British, 58-59; monument, 311
Roads, early, 11-13; toll, 15-17
Ropewalks, 114, 348
Rose, Abraham, 69; Rose Street named for, 13; moves Beebe windmill, 28
Round Pond, skating on, 43; ice harvesting at, 127-129
Round Table Club, 263, 297
Royce, Thomas W., inventor of whaling harpoon, 96-97
Rum running, 270-271

INDEX

Rysam Street, named for Capt. William J. Rysam, 13

Sage, Ebenezer, druggist, 65, 76, 132
Sage, Mrs. Russell (Margaret), philanthropist, 56, 188; contributes to Noyac Chapel, 191, and railroad depot, 242; buys Otter Pond, 273; develops Mashashimuet Park, 275-277; profile, 277-278; finances Pierson High School, 278-283; buys land for library, 277, 284-285; *illus.*
Sag Harbor Express, published since 1859, 158-159
Sag Harbor Village, founding of, 3-17; made port of entry, 36; streets paved, 251-252; water to homes, 255; beach, 294; description of, 1804, 31-32; 1819, 40-41; 1834, 83-84; 1875, 223-225
St. Andrews Roman Catholic Church, *see* Catholic Church
Saloons, during dry years, 269
Savings Bank, opens in 1860, 129; present bank built, 1911, 129-130; presidents of, 130
Schools, early, 44-48, students of, 334, *illus.;* 19th century, 161-168; Catholic, 166-168; Hebrew, 189-190; Pierson High School, 278-283
Seabury, Samuel, publisher, 154-155
Segregation, in schools, 165-166
Shelter Island, side-wheeler, 229
Sherry, John Sr., builds Oakland Works, 115; owns brass foundry, 115, sugar manufactory, 117, and grocery business, 245
Shinnecock, steamboat, 233; in Spanish-American War, 258
Ships, embargo before War of 1812, 63-64; steamboats bring trade and tourism, 221-234; list of, 348-350; *see also,* Steamboats, Whaling Ships
Shipyards, Benjamin Wade's, 113-114; list of, 348
Silver Works, Alvin, 248-249
Slavery, whaling ships used for, 103-105; Indians in, 216; widely practiced in Sag Harbor, 216-217; abolition in New York, 218
Sleight, Augustus, 53, 56
Sleight, Brinley D., 298; editor, 156-157; on Board of Education, 164
Sleight, Cornelius, 51, 65

Sleight, Harry D., village historian, and editor, 99, 157, 297
Spanish-American War, 257-259
Spooner, Alden, publisher, 60
Stagecoach travel, 14-15
Steamboats, 221-234; dock at Long Wharf, 221-223; open East End to tourism, 222; continue until 1900s, 223; list of, 348-350; *illus.*
Streets, early, 11-13; paving started in 1898, 251-252
Suffolk County Guards, 43, 196; formed in 1806, 60; disbanded in 1846, 61; reminiscences of, 61-63
Sweet, Polly, profile, 101-103
Synagogue, *see* Temple Adas Israel

Tabor, George W., ran stationery shop for 50 years, 120
Tabor, Pardon, 51, 60
Temperance Societies, 192-193; newspaper devoted to, 159; Suffolk Temperance House, 197
Temple Adas Israel, 188-190; *illus.*
Thames, whaleship, 84-85; black and Indian seamen on, 85
Tourist trade, opened by steam ships, 222
Theaters, Atheneum, 205-207; motion picture, 287-290; music hall, 203-204
Thompson, George W., owns Trout Pond, 126
Tinker, Nathan, cabinetmaker, profile, 120-121; builds American Hotel, 196
Toll roads, 15-17
Tooker, William Wallace, 295, 296; studies Indians, 250; pharmacist, 134; profile, 250-251
Torpedoes, tested in harbor, 266-267; *illus.*
Trout Pond, mills at, 125-127
Tunison, Fannie, profile, 208-209
Turkey Hill, 4, 12; fort erected at, 69

Umbrella House, 116, 302; British cannon marks on, 70
Union School, 199, 258; opens in 1871, 66; becomes fire department headquarters, 147
Union School District, 164-165; students and parents in, 1865-1866, 334-338

Wade, Oliver, describes barrelmaking, 91; uncle's early shipyard, 113; schooldays of, 161-163
Wamponamon Lodge, 55, 206, 229
War of 1812, 38, 68-72; embargo before, 63; Arsenal built, 66-67; monument, 311
Washington Street, laid out in 1787, 12
Water Works, 255-256
Weidlog, C., machinist and inventor, 302
West Water Street, laid out in 1795, 12; changes to Bay Street, 12
Whaling, golden years, 1820-1850, 81-92; standstill during embargo, 82; 1847 most productive year, 82; black and Indian seamen, 85; and discovery of gold, 89; dependence on coopers, 91; in Arctic, 96; decline, 105-108; oil used for lamps, 138; industries related to, 348; *see also* Whaling ships

Whaling and Historical Museum, home of Mrs. Russell Sage, 277; *illus.*
Whaling ships, 84-92, 97-101; mutiny on the *Oscar,* 93-96; sold for slave trade, 103-105; in Civil War, 106-107; list of ships and captains, 340-346; men employed on, 346-347
Wharf Company, 19, 20
Wharves, in early days, 18-22
Whipping post, 33
Wickham, Russell, profile, 119-120
Windmills, 26-31, 126; spiderlegged, 115
World War I, 308-309; monument, 309-310; veterans and casualties, 368-375
W. W. Coit, steam paddlewheeler, 222, 225-227

Yacht Club, 263, 293-294
Youngs, Addison, opens American Hotel in 1877, 196

SPONSORS

Allan M. Schneider & Associates, Inc.
American Hotel
Awning Co. of Sag Harbor
Donna Arcana
In memory of Paul Hedges Babcock, Sr.
  from Encie Babcock
Pace Barnes & Tom Harris
In memory of William C. Bates, Jr.
  from Judy Bates
Baron's Cove Resort
Carol Phillips Beirne
Eva L'Ecuyere Bell
Tanya Berezin & Mark Beers Wilson
For my mother Annie Cooper Boyd
  from Nancy Boyd Willey
Bryan Boyhan & Ellen Stahl
Mr. & Mrs. Franklin Branley
David Bray
Richard P. Browngardt
Burke & Sullivan, Attorneys at Law
Mayor & Mrs. George Butts, Jr.
Dr. David Carney & Mrs. Ellen Carney
Ann & Howard Chwatsky
David & Anne Cripps
Diane Cleveland Cunningham
Helena Curtis
In memory of my mother & father,
  Elizabeth & George Cary
  from Jane Zlobec
John J. Dagney
Duncan Darrow
Myrna & Paul Davis
Joyce M. Dawson
Mr. & Mrs. Mario DiMarco
Edgar L. & Helen Doctorow
Susan, Edward, & Edwina Early
Eastville Community Historical Society
Edmund Winfield Gallery
Cortland, Clark, & Erin Edwards
Mr. & Mrs. Olin M. Edwards, III
Jason Epstein
Robert W. Espach, Attorney at Law

Florence Fearrington, Inc.
Fenelon, Crowley & Tutino, CPA, P.C.
Florence & Lou Fink
Descendants of Daniel Fordham
  Elsie F. Silvey & Dolores McNamara
"4 Eyes"– Mindy & Sy Pollack
Friends of John Jermain Memorial Library
Robert & Michelle Gay
Irwin & Marilyn Gittell
In memory of Robert Greenberg
  from Morris & Lore Dickstein
Doris Gronlund
Whitney & Peter Hansen
Harpoon Realty, Ltd.– Scott Weiss
James Porter Harris
Mark & Mary Heming
Velda Johnston Heslop
The Houser Hoglund Family
Jane Howard
Gregory F. Howell
In memory of Amy Ingersoll, librarian and mother
  of Dorothy Zaykowski, from the Board of
  Trustees of John Jermain Memorial Library
In memory of Amy Ingersoll
  from her grandchildren
In memory of Amy & Herbert Ingersoll
  from Joseph Zaykowski, Sr.
George C. & Jane Elizabeth Kiernan
Helen & Joe Labrozzi
Alexandra Leigh-Hunt
Dr. Arnold Levinson & Marilyn Robin
Deborah Ann Light
Alexander MacN. Luke
Mr. & Mrs. William G. Martens
Alice Mayhew & Leonard Mayhew
Richard James McBride, Jr.
Bob & Elinor McDade
In memory of my grandmother, Liza Brown
  McDonough from Dolores Zebrowski
The McEneaney Family
In memory of Ann McGibbon from Felix
  Adelaide de Menil
Holland R. Melson, Jr.

SPONSORS

Dr. & Mrs. Charles R. Monticone
Linda & Robert Morris
In memory of Daniel F. Mulvihill, Jr. from Jane L. Mulvihill
Beverly & Richard Pesano
William & Patricia Denk Powers
Provisions—Linley Pennebaker Whelan & Kate Plumb
Detlef & Anna Pump
Fiona O'Neil Reeves
In memory of Philip Reichers II from Lee Reichers
Mr. & Mrs. Donald E. Reutershan
In memory of Harold F. Robertson from Margaret Robertson
Marilyn Robin & Dr. Arnie Levinson
Romany Kramoris Gallery
The Sag Harbor Express
The Sag Harbor Herald
Sag Harbor Savings Bank, a division of Apple Bank for Savings
Sage Street Antiques
Mr. & Mrs. R. Chris Salb
John Moore Sampson
John & Julienne Scanlon
Chick & B.J. Schreier
Alison & Evan Schwartz
John & Dorothy Sherry

Melisse & Brett Shevack
Jesse S. Siegel
Nancy Martin Simonson, Rlty.
The Russell J. Smyth Family
Mrs. John Steinbeck
In memory of Donald K. Stevenson from Colleen Stevenson
The Stolz Family
In memory of Selma Teich from her friends
Hugh Smith Thompson, IV
Marilyn Bethany Tivnan
In memory of Dorothy W. Townsend from Charles Townsend
Joan & James Tripp
Michelle Urry & Alan Trustman
The Tuller School at Maycroft
Richard & Lois Underhill Vincent
Gen & Tony Walton
Stewart & Jeanne Waring
Jack A. Watson
Dr. Fred Wilson
Lanford Wilson
Helen Winship
Albert & Astrida Woods
William & Rose Young
Julie, Joe, & Heather Zaykowski

BOOK PRODUCTION

Director of Publications	Pace Barnes
Editor	Alison Bond
Copyeditor	Mary Ann Gauger
Indexer	Joan Whitman
Book design	Loring Eutemey
Picture research	Alexandra Eames
Office manager	John Sampson

Typesetting by Olson Typographic, Brewster, N.Y.

Maps by Ciccariello Graphics, Inc., Sag Harbor, N.Y.

Printed by Amereon Ltd., Mattituck, N.Y.